CIVIL WAR
CAVALRY

CIVIL WAR CAVALRY

WAGING MOUNTED WARFARE
IN NINETEENTH-CENTURY AMERICA

EARL J. HESS

Louisiana State University Press

BATON ROUGE

Published by Louisiana State University Press
lsupress.org

Manufactured in the United States of America
First printing

Designer: Kaelin Chappell Broaddus
Typefaces: Miller Text, text; Isherwood WF, Sweet Sans Pro, display
Printer and binder: Sheridan Books, Inc.

Jacket illustration: Cavalry battle at Kelly's Ford, Virginia, March 17, 1863. Cover of *Frank Leslie's Illustrated Newspaper*, April 4, 1863.

Cataloging-in-Publication Data are available from the Library of Congress.

ISBN 978-0-8071-8444-8 (cloth: alk. paper) —
ISBN 978-0-8071-8500-1 (pdf) — ISBN 978-0-8071-8499-8 (epub)

for Pratibha and Julie,
forever

CONTENTS

ACKNOWLEDGMENTS

I wish to thank Ethan S. Rafuse for his helpful comments upon reading this manuscript. Also, Samuel J. Watson provided equally helpful comments when he read it, and my thanks go out to him. Kevin Brock did his usual fine copyediting job, and Rand Dotson strongly supported this project. Finally, my wife Pratibha, as always, provided what I need to live a good life and to be happy. Her support for my work has always sustained me.

CIVIL WAR CAVALRY

INTRODUCTION

The U.S. government had little need for a large, powerful cavalry force to conduct any of its conflicts before the outbreak of the Civil War in 1861. From colonial times to the American frontier of the 1850s, a small, constabulary mounted force was sufficient for its peacetime needs. Even when wars broke out, they demanded little in terms of cavalry. Only a handful of mounted regiments and companies were organized for the American Revolutionary War, the War of 1812, the Seminole Wars, and the Mexican War. This was in stark contrast to the major nations of Europe, which engaged in numerous major conflicts, maintained large standing forces of mounted soldiers, and developed a strong tradition of doctrine, training, logistical support, and horse care for their mounted arms. By the nineteenth century, the heart of the global heritage of mounted warfare had been centered on Europe for some time already, with North America at best a distant cousin of the main stem of cavalry history.

Thus, the Civil War came as a major shock to those men interested in the American military tradition. It demanded far more of the government and of its armed forces than anything previously experienced in North America. But Americans North and South had an advantage in that they could draw on a strong European tradition of mounted warfare. Their doctrine, training, and ideas about logistical support, weapons, and maintenance of an armed force came from the European model and were fully applicable to the American setting. But the question of how large a mounted force to raise, how to organize it, and what to do with it in the field all had to be worked out according to circumstances peculiar to the context of the Civil War itself. As in nearly everything else associated with their intense conflict, Union and Confederate officials took on the challenge of creating a mounted military force of unprecedented size and complexity when compared to the American military tradition. It was by no means unprecedented when compared to the European tradition, but American officials tended to be nearly overwhelmed by the challenge. They had little time to study European precedents or current practices, even though both were readily available in English-language literature. How Northern officials managed to meet the demands of their war effort (including the role of cavalry) played a large part in their winning the Civil War. Conversely, how Confederate officials failed to meet similar demands played a large role in their losing the conflict.

This study deals with the topic of cavalry by surveying many aspects of waging mounted warfare during the Civil War. It is positioned within the larger context of both American and European cavalry history before 1861 and to a degree after 1865 as well. As far as global history is concerned, the Civil War was not a strongly unique event; it shared most of its characteristics with European warfare of the mid-nineteenth century. But as far as American cavalry history is concerned, it was a wholly unique event, the context of which most Northerners and Southerners were aware and to which they paid attention. And within that context, their efforts to create, maintain, and utilize a large mounted force comes across as herculean in nature.

There are many aspects of mounted warfare in the Civil War to consider. They include examining the European and American precedents for cavalry use and investigating how large mounted forces on both sides of the Civil War were organized and trained. This training was done according to an officially adopted cavalry manual, which was drawn from European training precedents. Its most important objective was to immerse the trooper and his horse in the primary tactics, which were the formations and maneuvers used by mounted units on all levels. Another facet for examination is how well troopers and their mounts employed those maneuvers and formations in field operations. Those actions involved the mounted charge, dismounted fighting, and strategic raiding, which were among the most distinctive components of mounted warfare in the Civil War. Supporting cavalry forces with proper weapons, equipment, and horses became a vital aspect of sustaining mounted warfare. Understanding the human component involves exploring the life of the cavalryman; understanding the animal component involves exploring the experience of the cavalry horse. Both were sentient creatures who acted as a combat team to undergird cavalry effectiveness. Utilizing large formations of mounted power at the higher levels of command had a direct influence on effectiveness; whether to disperse regiments for close support of infantry formations or to group them into large division and corps organizations for independent action was a key question for generals. Working toward effectiveness at all organizational levels and in every aspect of cavalry work marked the extent to which mounted officers and government administrators sought professionalism among the horsemen. Finally, considering the trajectory of American and European cavalry history after Appomattox helps place mounted operations in the Civil War in the global military tradition.

The historiography of Civil War cavalry is large; many previous historians and authors have devoted attention to it and have fed the inherent interest readers see in mounted action. There are many histories of individual units, of salient leaders, of weapons and equipment. Probably no other historian has written so much about Civil War cavalry as has Edward G. Longacre, whose many books cover a wide area of the subject, including the mounted arms of the Army of the Potomac and the Army of Northern Virginia as well as biographies of cavalry leaders such as Joseph Wheeler and John Buford. In addition to Longacre's work, that of Eric Wittenberg stands out for its coverage, especially of cavalry operations in the eastern theater. Stephen Starr's three-volume history of Civil War cavalry, now several decades old, is probably the only general history of the topic and covers the story more fully than others.

What interested readers have at their fingertips is a large body of historical studies that range pretty widely across the war, although admittedly much of it tends to focus on the East rather than the West or the Trans-Mississippi. Also, most of it tends to be narrative history that emphasizes battles, campaigns, leaders, and human-interest stories. There is nothing at all wrong with scholarship like this, but it leaves room for studies that identify important characteristics, trends, and trajectories in the story. Studies that stress analysis and evaluation of important points are needed. Much of that is being done in some of Wittenberg's work and that of Dave Powell.

This book, then, is geared toward key aspects of cavalry operations in the Civil War, to briefly identify and discuss them and to attempt an analysis of what made mounted warfare succeed or fail in that conflict. It should be looked upon as an introduction to those aspects of cavalry history rather than the final word, given the size of the mounted forces of both armies and the complicated history of those commands. I have done much of this kind of work for Civil War field artillery and for Civil War infantry in previous books. This study rounds out my foray through the topic of military effectiveness from the ground up in the Civil War, and hopefully all of them will help inspire more work on the broad topic of how military systems work or fail.

There are several themes in the previous studies by Civil War cavalry historians that seem ripe for reevaluation. First and foremost is the idea that the introduction of the rifle musket for general issue among infantrymen altered the nature of Civil War combat, including the role of cavalry. This interpretation of the weapon has held that the longer firing distance (500 yards compared to the older smoothbore's distance of 100 yards) revolutionized the nature of mounted combat by rendering cavalry charges against infantry hopeless. As indicated by my arguments in *The Rifle Musket and Civil War Combat* (2008), I have long rejected that standard interpretation of the weapon's influence on Civil War operations. Mounted charges against well-formed and disciplined infantry had never worked well even during the smoothbore era before the Civil War. The rare examples of it succeeding have tended to overly impress historians, who in turn ignore the very many examples of it failing. The tactical manuals of the Civil War era clearly state the reality—mounted charges should not be attempted against infantry unless the opposing foot soldiers are in a disorganized state.

A corollary to the notion that the rifle musket rendered mounted charges against infantry useless is that its use also led to a shift away from the cavalry closely cooperating with friendly infantry formations and focusing instead on independent action on the strategic level. In other words, the famed cavalry raids of the Civil War, which saw mounted forces sweeping behind enemy lines to hit communications, were the result of the cavalry's loss of tactical effectiveness against enemy infantry. That is not a convincing argument, not only because of the rifle musket's limited effect on Civil War operations generally but also because of a peculiar blindness that most historians seem to have about the pre–Civil War history of American mounted warfare. That heritage demonstrates that no war before 1861 fought by Americans involved anything that could be considered large numbers of mounted soldiers who performed in either role of close infantry support or independent action. In other words, one does not see mounted strategic raids in pre–Civil War conflicts simply because American armies did not have the force or the mindset to conduct them. It makes no sense that a supposed lack of tactical effectiveness would lead officers to strike out on strategic raids; both modes of operation were legitimate uses of mounted power and were not dependent on each other in any way. If commanders had the numbers and the will to conduct them simultaneously, they likely would have done so. The fundamental problem of believing in the rifle musket's revolutionary effect is that it warps everything connected with a study of military operations, blinds the historian to alternate causes that shaped those operations, and ties the historiography into a straitjacket.

Another theme in the literature of cavalry history is the shift from mounted charges before the Civil War to dismounted fighting during it. There is no doubt that the Civil War witnessed much more dismounted cavalry fighting than ever before in American or even in European history, but it is equally true that mounted charges never diminished or disappeared between 1861 and 1865. They happened just as frequently late in the conflict as they did early on, and this had nothing to do with rifle small arms. Mounted attacks had always been largely conducted against other cavalry forces rather than enemy infantry formations, and that remained true in the Civil War. In fact, a wide reading of reports by cavalry officers reveals that the standard tactical formation they employed throughout the war, from beginning to end, was to dismount some units and keep others mounted for mutual support, the mounted units going in to follow up tactical successes gained by those on foot. Civil War cavalry commanders, in other words, saw great utility in practicing both modes of operation to create what they liked to call a versatile, or hybrid, cavalry force that could operate both mounted and dismounted on demand. And they did this from the start of hostilities fully to the end of the conflict. To some degree regiments tended to specialize in either mounted or dismounted action, but all Civil War cavalry, North and South, was fully capable of fighting in both ways. One mode of combat did not replace the other.

A related point is that, for some reason, it has become rather common to use the term "evolution" when referring to the history of Civil War cavalry. Apparently that resulted from an idea that the conflict witnessed extraordinary changes in cavalry operations that led to something one could call "modern" warfare. This idea seems fraught with limitations and weaknesses. It is true that cavalry during the Civil War was in many ways unique compared to the long sweep of American military history (as indicated in the following chapters). But that was mostly because the American cavalry heritage had been so weak and insubstantial before 1861, far more so than that of infantry warfare and artillery usage. In other words, Civil War cavalrymen worked with a nearly clean slate as far as American operational precedents were concerned. Much of what they accomplished during the war has to be considered within that context; Northerners and Southerners were doing a good deal of catching up with historical trends that had long been evident in the European cavalry heritage. For example, dismounted fighting was by no means an American invention, having been a feature of mounted warfare since the dawn of organized military forces. The Romans during their republican period specialized in it. If mounted fighting had been largely absent in American military history, it certainly was not so in world military history. Likewise, as mentioned before, if Civil War cavalrymen could not break well-organized infantry formations, it was not due to the rifle musket but to the inherent differences in how mounted forces and foot formations operated, as had been proven in the long heritage of European warfare.

If Civil War cavalry was evolving toward something, it is difficult to understand what that was, given that many of its characteristic fighting methods had been worked out in Europe or were adjustments to Americans' heritage of cavalry operations. Moreover, there was a diminishing future for mounted warfare during the decades after Appomattox. Cavalry did not quickly go out of favor or relevance in war making—belligerents in both world wars of the twentieth century maintained large formations of mounted troops and used them in military operations. But the nature of mounted power and its organization, training, equipping, and tactical and strategic utilization did not really change that much after 1865 compared to what Americans North and South had done during the Civil War. And those characteristics of Civil War cavalry were not revolutionary changes compared to what had transpired previously in Europe.

Historians rarely get much attention for arguing that their topic was not revolutionary, or decisive, or all important as a turning point in history. But very often that is exactly what is true. I see the history of Civil War cavalry as a continuum of developments in both the American and European heritage of mounted warfare, not as a decisive or revolutionary break in those traditions. Therefore, using the term "evolution" does not seem to fit what happened to cavalry during the conflict.

Another common idea is that to be a good cavalryman, one had to be a good horseman; Southerners were naturally good at riding, goes this idea, and thus dominated their Northern opponents. That, of course, is an intuitive assumption and holds some water, but it has been overemphasized in the cavalry literature. My own research in the personal accounts of both sides convinces me that the Confederates had no monopoly on good horsemanship. Many Union troopers could match them in that regard, and for that matter not all Confederate cavalrymen could handle a horse well. While it seems to make sense that good horsemanship leads to good cavalrymen, is it really a necessity? There is no doubt that an effective trooper had to attain a certain level of horse-handling ability, but he did not have to be a trick circus rider to be a good horse soldier. In fact, what was required of him was to handle his mount in a way so that both man and horse could follow the instructions of the training regimen. What truly made good cavalrymen was an ability to meet the military requirements of horsemanship, and that was drilled into the man and his horse during the long hours of practicing formations and maneuvers. As long as most troopers learned the military requirements of horse handling, one could count on them becoming good members of an effective cavalry force. Trick riding, such as being able to grab a hat from the ground while galloping past it, was good entertainment while lying idle in camp, but it was not a requirement for knowing how to form columns or lines or moving in a left wheel under fire.

Reevaluation of old conclusions, not for the sake of revisionism as an end in itself but for the sake of finding out if they really are valid, is needed. The war was so big, so complex, and contained so many campaigns and battles along with colorful individuals that the narrative approach to its history tends to dominate everything in the literature. That is the major reason this book is not organized chronologically but topically, so that one can grasp the key characteristics of cavalry warfare in nineteenth-century America more readily. If it was organized chronologically, there would be little room for analysis within chapters crowded with narrative detail.

Context also is important. The most satisfying view is the widest one, incorporating the long sweep of history. This perspective strongly tends to position the Civil War as primarily another episode of global military history with a few distinguishing characteristics. In this way it was not much different from other major wars, all of which had fundamental links with previous developments in military history while exhibiting some unusual features of their own growing out of their individual circumstances.

The Civil War was by no means the last hurrah of mounted power in global history; cavalry would play major roles in other European and world conflicts after 1865. But in the American military tradition, the Civil War not only witnessed the last major use of cavalry power on the outcome of the conflict, but it also was the only one, excepting the series of wars with Native Americans from 1865 to 1890. If someone wanted to look at the epitome of mounted warfare in North America and the best example of American cavalry warfare in global history, the Civil War looms as the only candidate. Its cavalry operations came closer to those of major European wars than those of any other war in the Western Hemisphere. Providing a fresh look at how cavalry power was organized, trained, equipped, and utilized in the field brings us closer to a new appreciation and understanding of the Civil War within both the American and the global heritage of armed conflict.

1

THE CAVALRY HERITAGE

O f the three branches of service in the Civil War, the heritage of infantry and cavalry rested deeply in the recesses of global military history. Both arms developed very early in the story of armed conflict. In contrast, the heritage of Civil War field artillery was much shorter, dating primarily from the introduction of gunpowder in the fifteenth century. Most of the key elements of Civil War cavalry were not new to the Civil War period but had been worked out at various times in the past. Union and Confederate horsemen were perched at the far end of a very long heritage and, without being aware of it, were heavily dependent on that legacy for nearly everything that underpinned their military art.

One can boil down the role of mounted power into major categories. All of them appeared at various times and places throughout the long history of mounted soldiering. The societies that produced cavalry forces emphasized some of these categories over others, but all of these tasks had a role to play across the wide breadth of mounted fighting over the ages.

The categories can be understood as dividing into independent action by cavalry forces versus cooperative action with foot men or, later, with artillery. The former imparted an argument for the existence of mounted power in its own right. The latter, often called combined arms operations in the modern era, emphasized the importance of mounted power as an adjunct, or cooperative force, to infantry and artillery.

Independent action included scouting across wide swaths of disputed territory to gather information about enemy troop positions, strength, and intentions. It also included the collection of forage and provisions for itself and for infantry and artillery forces to consume. Many observers have tended to downplay scouting and foraging, important as they were to the overall success of armies, as mundane, lacking in romance or adventure. A bit more adventurous was the tactic of screening friendly troop movements by blocking enemy cavalry from scouting. But another independent action, raiding behind enemy lines, was filled with the stuff that made cavalry action interesting and glorious in the minds of many.

Cooperative action with the other arms also elicited a good deal of interest among romantics and adventurers, but often only because of the mounted charge against enemy infantry, cavalry, or artillery. Mounted troops, however, were capable of playing several roles in battle. They could act on the defensive as well as on the offensive, fighting either on horse or on foot. Whether they were best at shock action (a mounted maneuver) or utilizing firepower (better done on foot) to achieve their tactical goals on the battlefield became a never-ending argument once gunpowder weapons were introduced. But to a degree, that argument had relevance even during the era of the sword and lance. Whether mounted men could break apart well-disciplined and organized formations of foot soldiers remained a matter of universal argument both before and after the introduction of firearms. No one, however, could argue against the idea that, once broken, all enemy troop formations were highly vulnerable to the slashing mounted attack, which followed up a defeated foe to maximize casualties and confusion in the broken ranks. And no one could deny that mounted power was a superb way to pursue a retreating enemy for days after his defeat on the battlefield.

All of these themes in cavalry history can be seen periodically over the sweep of time, although they tended to develop slowly and uncertainly in some eras, faster and more assuredly in others. But the major point is that all of the themes associated with Civil War mounted power had their precedents in the long, international cavalry heritage that started when men began to use horses for warfare and continued up to the eve of Fort Sumter. That heritage began in other countries and in other eras, culminating in the American experience of warfare in the eighteenth and early nineteenth centuries.

Before Firearms

Cavalrymen have operated far longer with edged weapons than with firearms. Effective use of mounted forces in organized warfare appeared in eastern Anatolia and modern northwestern Iran by the early ninth century BCE. The addition of a chariot increased the shock value of cavalry. That value rested on what cavalry historians have termed "the psychological trauma of being ridden at by a mass of heavy animals, rather than the physical impact of colliding bodies or weapons." In short, shock value was as much a matter of morale as of physical combat. Heavy cavalry—mounted warriors using swords or long spears and encased in body armor—appeared by the mid-eighth century BCE. By that time, cavalry commanders had learned that the best mode of operation was to attack rather than act on the defensive, infusing mounted warfare with an aggressive spirit of quick decision and equally quick action.[1]

For the next several hundred years, mounted raids dominated warfare until the rise of the Greek hoplite phalanx provided foot soldiers a method of dealing with cavalry. With this new form of infantry tactics, developed fully by the fifth century BCE, foot soldiers could withstand mounted attacks. Cavalry received second priority among most Greek city-states except where topography provided good pasture lands for horse raising, such as in Thebes, Thessaly, and Macedonia. Because Greek soldiers largely armed themselves, cavalry became the arm of the social and economic elite, while the infantry arm became the preserve of the middle classes. Mounted warriors could protect their own hoplites and try to catch the enemy formation at a disadvantage; otherwise their role in Greek battles tended to be marginal.[2]

Xenophon provided the era's most prominent manual on horse training, entitled *On Horsemanship*, finished about 365 BCE. He provided insights that have stood the test of time, advocating a gentle and patient mode of training. Xenophon advised taking the horse through crowds of citizens until it was acclimated to large groups of people and unexpected noises. By this period, the saddle had been developed among the Scythians, and its use had spread to other cultures, increasing the rider's ability to fight on horseback.[3]

Cavalry became as important as infantry in some eras. The Macedonians under Phillip II developed a large mounted force that his son Alexander the Great used to good effect on the battlefield during his campaigns of conquest in the fourth century BCE. Phillip had created his mounted arm for shock combat by using a wedge formation and long lances. The wedge could be more easily controlled than a line, and the lance could bring down foot soldiers at a distance. Adding a system designed to replenish the force with fresh hoses and manpower, the mounted arm became a key element in the success of young Alexander. Still, his accomplishments greatly depended on his unusual ability. Alexander personally led mounted charges that broke up infantry formations. But his use of cavalry was highly dependent on contingencies and on his ability to see and to take advantage of breaks in the opposing phalanx. It was only rarely that other commanders in other wars could replicate Alexander's mounted successes. Nevertheless, Alexander proved the shock value of cavalry under the right circumstances and demonstrated good combined-arms tactics, closely knitting the action of cavalry and infantry on the battlefield.[4]

The Romans excelled at heavy-infantry combat and relegated cavalry to a marginal role. The mounted arm was primarily composed of elites before the middle of the republican period, after which it consisted mostly of foreigners fighting for the Roman state. It performed reconnaissance, raiding, protection of infantry formations, and occasionally an attack on foot soldiers. The Roman cavalry resorted to dismounted combat more often than any other ancient mounted force and did it effectively.[5]

The relationship between mounted warriors and foot soldiers did not change much during the medieval period. While many historians have argued that the introduction of the stirrup enhanced the ability of armored knights to ride down infantry in shock action, the truth is that shock had always been an option of the cavalry arm. Developed by 300 AD in China, the stirrup came to the West by the seventh century and spread throughout Europe. It certainly steadied the rider by making it easier to stand up and to maintain or regain balance, but one still had to guide the horse mostly by leg pressure and maintain good posture.[6]

Although the information has to be squeezed out of the sources, there is every indication that the major powers of the medieval era fielded significant forces of mounted men for war. The Carolingians early in the period sponsored what can be called a rebirth of cavalry power after its nadir during the later Roman era. They fielded men fully armed with various weapons who fulfilled several traditional roles of cavalrymen, including scouting, harassment, gathering of supplies, and battle. Operations in the medieval period tended to be placed in one of three major options: siege, battle, or *chevauchée*. The last was an armed raid through disputed or enemy-held territory aimed at the destruction of resources to sap the ability and morale of that enemy to resist. Mounted power was useful in all three options. It could gather much needed food and forage while footmen conducted a siege, and it was fully capable of mounted charges in pitched battles. It was an ideal force to conduct a chevauchée as well.[7]

Firearms and Mounted Forces

The introduction of firearms did not fundamentally alter the role of cavalry in warfare. The mounted arm quickly adapted to this new weapon. Pistols were the first firearms to be used by mounted soldiers in the early fifteenth century, and soon carbines (short-barreled small arms) came into use. Edged weapons continued to be important elements in the cavalry arsenal, as mounted warriors juggled several war tools while on the back of a horse. How to use their firearms while mounted became a fundamentally important task. Many forces developed the caracole method, whereby ranks of mounted men advanced, the first rank firing their weapons and retiring to the rear of the column to reload, then the next ranks advanced to do the same. But the basic functions of the mounted arm remained largely the same. Armies of the early modern era further developed distinctions between light cavalry designed for raiding and reconnaissance in contrast to heavy cavalry for shock action on the battlefield. Salient commanders of the era, such as Gustavus Adolphus, experimented with shock action through mounted attack as well as combined-arms work to achieve some level of cooperation with infantry and artillery.[8]

King Louis XIV of France led the way in developing a large and improved mounted force. The age-old argument between thrusting and slashing with swords continued as French cavalry of the era started with a straight-bladed weapon designed for thrusting and switched to a curve-bladed sword designed for slashing. Riders typically carried two pistols each (wheellocks at first before switching to flintlocks), but specialist mounted units were armed with carbines. While some rifle carbines were employed, they never became standard issue because of expense and difficulty of use. The French tended to rely on shock attacks rather than firepower to achieve their tactical goals. Further specialization was introduced by dividing the mounted arm into several categories, the most important of which were dragoons (who fought as mounted infantry) and hussars (light cavalry for scouting and raiding). In terms of organization, French cavalry consisted of regiments, with squadrons comprising two or more companies. In fact, the squadron became the basic unit of movement rather than the regiment or the company. Squadrons marched in columns of twos or fours and fought in three ranks. Cavalry charges were orderly until the last fifty yards, when the gallop was called and a mounted rush toward the enemy began. Louis XIV, horrified at the heavy loss of infantry-men in pitched battles, sought to avoid expensive combat and to focus on mounted raiding. Thus, even though French cavalry was twice as expensive to raise and maintain as infantry, the size of his mounted arm grew from 9–12 percent of the entire army to as much as 33 percent of it. By 1710, French cavalry had grown to 67,334 horsemen and 147 regiments, which was cut in half after the end of Louis XIV's many wars.[9]

The difficulties of supplying remounts for a large cavalry force were demonstrated by Parliamentarian forces during the English Civil Wars (1642–51). The attrition rate for horses ran as high as 63 percent early in the war overall and 78 percent for the dragoons. Officials tried various methods of finding horses: they authorized officers to act as purchasing agents, pressed mounts into service from reluctant owners, levied assessments on civilians to raise cash for purchases, or worked through local civil councils to provide them. But the most effective method was to rely on agents to purchase animals for resale to the army. While this also led to cartels seeking to gain control of the market and set advantageous prices, the system worked well enough to become the main way of supplying remounts during the English Civil Wars.[10]

The introduction of firearms created a perennial debate about whether firepower or shock action was the main weapon of mounted forces. From the fifteenth through the seventeenth centuries, both methods were used without developing a consensus. English drill books of the civil wars period did not recommend crashing mounted formations into each other, and common sense tends to dissuade anyone from thinking that this could be productive. The initial force exerted on two moving bodies that collide is equal, giving neither an advantage over the other. In horse races the impact is devastating, even deadly, on both horses if mounts run into each other. Yet by the eighteenth and nineteenth centuries, the writers of military handbooks often described the mounted charge as the best tactic for cavalry even if it resulted in head-on collisions. These usually were averted by the psychological effect whenever two mounted forces charged toward each other, with one side veering off at the last moment.[11]

European cavalry developed into a more complex, versatile, and sophisticated force during the eighteenth century. Three primary types became available for different purposes. Heavy cavalry, often called cuirassiers because they wore metal breastplates and helmets, delivered shock attacks. Medium cavalry, often called dragoons, fought dismounted. Light cavalry, called hussars and sometimes armed with lances, scouted, skirmished, and raided. This specialization depended on the availability of different types of horses to suit the different functions. The distinction between the three types was never immutable; it altered and blurred over time and varied between different armies. With this high level of specialization and training, it was widely believed that it took up to five years (sometimes the estimate was less) to properly train a cavalryman.[12]

As a result, different types of cutting weapons and equipment appeared at this time. Cuirassiers and dragoons used straight-bladed swords for thrusting, while light cavalry used curved swords for slashing. The cuirass, or breastplate, was believed to be effective against such weapons; the French estimated it saved 1,600 cavalrymen at the Battle of Laffeldt in 1747. But the breastplate added twenty pounds to the weight the man and horse had to carry, was uncomfortable in hot weather, and could injure the trooper if he fell while wearing it. Footwear specialized as well. Heavy boots were preferred for the heavy cavalry because they gave a good deal of protection when horses were tightly formed in ranks, whereas light cavalry preferred lighter boots because they often fought dismounted, requiring greater agility on foot.[13]

Most commentators thought the mounted charge was superior to the firefight and preferred two or three ranks. They advised starting the charge at a walk, progressing to the trot, and then assuming the gallop— an all-out run always was reserved for the last phase of the movement. Regarding hand-to-hand combat, arguments developed over the best method of delivering a blow. Most advocated thrusting because they believed it injured the opponent more seriously than slashing. But others pointed out that slashing was faster and did not require pulling a sword out of a body. Historian Christopher Duffy believes that most wounds inflicted in cavalry fights were "not particularly dangerous cuts to the sword arm." The victor generally was decided not by the losses sustained, but by the collapse of morale. Men in the second and third ranks of mounted formations were more likely to give way and retreat than their comrades in the first rank.[14]

Frederick the Great of Prussia rigorously trained cavalrymen first on foot and then mounted, taught them to control their horses through body movement, adopted a better saddle, and emphasized shock tactics and thrusting. He was able to employ his cavalry in tight cooperation with infantry forces on the battlefield. At times mounted charges against infantry determined the outcome, but that only happened when the Prussian horsemen managed to catch the opponent at a disadvantage.[15]

More elaborate training regimens spread across Europe in the eighteenth century. In England recruits initially were drilled in foot maneuvers before training on horses that had already been broken. The trooper learned how to ride individually and then as part of a larger group. He then trained in weapons handling, especially the saber. The stress was laid on a "downward cut delivered with main force while standing in the stirrups." Six types of offensive cuts were taught, along with eight parries, in addition to a cut-and-guard method for use against infantry. Learning how to manage the horse and the sword constituted the bulk of cavalry training.[16]

The thorny question of how to arrange for cavalry to support infantry on the battlefield became a topic of debate throughout much of the eighteenth century. The chevalier de Folard, a veteran of the War of the Spanish Succession (1701–14), developed a system of tactics that advocated close mixing of the two arms. His mixed order interspersed mounted units among infantry formations and was heavily criticized because it restricted the horsemen's freedom of movement. Marshal Maurice de Saxe was among those who rejected Folard's mixed order and developed his own system of cooperation between the two arms. Saxe advocated massing cavalry for shock action near the infantry but not interspersed among foot formations. He disparaged the need for light cavalry by arguing that only a heavy mounted force for shock attacks and a dragoon force for dismounted fighting were needed.[17]

The most important theorist of the century was the comte de Guibert, whose work formed the basis for the French Revolutionary army tactics of 1791. Those tactics, through various alterations, guided Western armies to the time of the American Civil War. Guibert's *Essai général de tactique* of 1772 warned commanders never to throw away a cavalry attack on an infantry formation that was ready to receive it. The proper role of mounted troops was to protect the flanks of the infantry and to scout, raid, and perform outpost duty. Cavalry was "only the secondary arm in a well-regulated army," as historian Robert S. Quimby describes Guibert's viewpoint.[18]

Guibert saw that the true distinction between infantry and cavalry was the latter's ability to drive home a shock attack. One needed to increase the speed of the mounted assault without leading to disorder. He believed in using edged weapons for thrusting rather than slashing, favored light cavalry even for shock charges, and recognized that pistols and carbines were as necessary as swords. Guibert favored two ranks and small squadrons of eighty men for more flexible maneuvers. He complained of the trend toward elaborate training in horsemanship, arguing that the trooper needed only "the simplest utilitarian training" in how to ride. Guibert favored the line as opposed to the column and advocated intensive training of a combined-arms nature in peacetime. His ideal field army consisted of 36,000 infantry, 9,600 cavalry (19.6 percent of the whole), and 4,400 artillerymen.[19]

Napoleonic Wars

By the 1790s, the French mounted arm consisted of 33,000 troopers compared to 123,000 infantry. At the Battle of Marengo (June 14, 1800), a mounted charge caught an Austrian infantry column off guard and broke it up. Napoleon inherited a good mounted force from the revolutionary army and used it to the full. In general, 10–20 percent of French field armies operating in the heart of the Continent consisted of cavalrymen, compared to 5–15 percent of French forces operating during the Peninsular War (1807–14). The regiment and the squadron were the basic units of maneuver, although French horsemen were often organized into brigades, divisions, and corps. Classifications had altered by this time. Well-armored cuirassiers continued to serve in the role of heavy cavalry, mounting shock charges, but dragoons seldom fought on foot anymore. Instead Napoleon expected them to conduct battlefield charges in addition to serving in the role of light cavalry. More properly designated medium cavalry now, dragoons became versatile horsemen. They supplemented the light cavalry—called hussars, chasseurs-a-cheval, or light dragoons—who were "expected to be extremely flexible" as historian Rory Muir has put it. With a full brigade typically assigned to each Napoleonic division, the primary roles of light cavalry included the traditional outpost duty, patrolling, and skirmishing but now also encompassed charging in battle, covering retreats, pursuing a defeated enemy, and supporting infantry and artillery. Never written in stone previously, the distinctions between categories of cavalry now became more blurred than ever. But in support of his aggressive battlefield tactics, Napoleon also had increased the size of the heavy cavalry force from one to fourteen regiments and strengthened their body armor by 1810.[20]

Cavalrymen were commonly armed with the full array of weapons—carbines, swords, and two pistols—during the Napoleonic era. French horsemen often mixed firefights with sword play. Both thrust and slash continued to be used in this era, with British cavalry preferring the latter and French preferring the former. Napoleon brought back the lance, which at nine feet long and weighing seven pounds had atrophied as a mounted weapon in the decades before the French Revolution. He was impressed by Polish expertise in the use of this weapon and armed six regiments of dragoons with it. This revival lasted for most of the nineteenth century but sparked heated and ongoing debate. The lance could be useful against infantrymen who had broken their formations, and the psychological effect on unbroken infantrymen could have been significant. But the weapon never came into general use again; it was briefly taken up by a handful of regiments in the American Civil War but with no enthusiasm.[21]

All belligerents in the Napoleonic Wars tended to use cavalry in close cooperation with infantry and artillery far more than did American commanders. Horsemen were placed virtually everywhere within and near the infantry formations—on the flanks, in line before foot soldiers, or in columns behind them. Their almost universal presence on the battlefield led opposing infantrymen to form squares for self-protection, something rarely seen during the American Civil War. At times the French were able to use their cavalry to force enemy footmen into squares, which French artillery then pulverized, demonstrating a close cooperation of the combat arms. The Duke of Wellington advised keeping from half to two-thirds of the available cavalry as a tactical reserve, formed in both line and column, no more than 500 yards from the main infantry force "to exploit success, cover the retreat after a failure, or even to convert a failure into a success by attacking the enemy when they are disordered," as Muir has observed.[22]

Cavalrymen of all belligerents during the Napoleonic era were aware that their duties included rather mundane tasks, but they stressed the attack as their true reason for existence. Charging the enemy had to be done with confidence, élan, discipline, and an ability to rally after a mounted charge had spent itself. "Cavalry was a powerful but fragile weapon which needed an extraordinary mixture of caution and daring in its use," writes Muir.[23]

On the defensive most cavalrymen of the era preferred to meet an enemy mounted charge with one of their own, although the French often held firm and used their carbines to stop an advancing mounted force. When opposing cavalry charged each other, typically one side or the other veered off at the last minute. If they did not, melees, or unorganized close-range fighting, often resulted. These fights were free-for-alls in which officers exercised little control but casualties tended to be light. "Most mêlées were very brief," writes Muir, and ended with "a sudden collapse of resolution."[24]

Most Napoleonic era armies maintained large numbers of horsemen. At Austerlitz, a battle that won for Napoleon the War of the Third Coalition in December 1805, the Russians fielded 12,800 cavalry (17.0 percent of the whole) and 62,400 infantry. Napoleon's 75,000 infantry were supported by 30,000 horsemen (28.5 percent of the whole) during the preliminary movements of that campaign in October.[25]

With so many horsemen assembled in ways that were pretty closely integrated into the organization of field armies, it is no wonder that one saw much more use of cavalry power on Napoleonic battlefields than would be true of the American Civil War fifty years later. The horsemen screened friendly infantry-artillery movements, as Joachim Murat's forces did in the operational phase of the massive Ulm Campaign in 1805. They conducted large mounted attacks on enemy infantry in desperate efforts to stabilize a deteriorating tactical situation, as the French cavalry did at Eylau in 1807, suffering heavy losses while stopping a Russian advance. They participated in the pursuit of a beaten foe, usually in cooperation with infantry and artillery, as happened after the French victory of Jena-Auerstadt in 1806 and Wagram in 1809. Pursuit by cavalry alone was as old as the Greek and Roman era, but Napoleon at times conducted pursuit as a combined-arms exercise.[26]

Borodino was one of the better examples of large mounted forces playing a major role in an infantry-artillery battle of the Napoleonic era. The French massed 133,550 men across a relatively small battlefield on September 7, 1812; 65.9 percent were infantry, 22.2 percent were mounted, and 11.9 percent were artillery. Overall troop density amounted to 44,000 men per mile, probably four times heavier than was typical in the American Civil War. On the decisive sector of the field, Napoleon massed 85,000 men along only one and a half miles of terrain. The Russians used 126,000 men at Borodino, with a troop density that averaged 36,000 per mile. Their infantry constituted 69.8 percent of the total force engaged, while cavalry amounted to 19.1 percent and artillery to 11.1 percent.[27]

Despite the crowded nature of this battle, Napoleon effectively used his cavalry on the tactical level. Concentrating his mounted force on the Russian left wing, his initial infantry attack captured Raevsky's Redoubt but lost it to an enemy counterattack. Then a French cavalry assault on the position was repelled, followed by another cavalry attack from a different direction in conjunction with a renewed infantry assault that captured the work. This unusual example of mounted charges contributing to the capture of a field fortification was possible only because the hill was not high or steep and the poorly made parapets had been severely battered by artillery fire all day.[28]

At Waterloo on June 18, 1815, both sides used cavalry forces in shock action against opposing infantry. A daring charge by two brigades of British heavy cavalry, led by the Duke of Uxbridge, stopped an entire French corps that was on the verge of overwhelming the Duke of Wellington's left wing. While unbroken, the French infantry was not prepared to meet the horsemen and were driven away. Later in the day Napoleon massed his own cavalry in an effort to break Wellington's center. The charge, led by Marshal Michel Ney, threw more than 5,000 horsemen against an infantry force of 18,000 men and failed when the British formed squares. These two Waterloo examples show that the possibilities for successful cavalry attacks against infantry were highly dependent on circumstances.[29]

This was true of cavalry versus infantry throughout the Napoleonic era. In fact, successful mounted attacks on foot soldiers were quite rare, which is why the Duke of Uxbridge gained lasting fame for his brilliant charge at Waterloo. British cavalry had always focused on shock action to the neglect of mundane and common duties such as outpost work. Wellington managed to use a small but effective cavalry force during many of his campaigns in the Peninsular War despite the limitations of that force. By 1813, he had three heavy, six medium, and ten light cavalry regiments in his Peninsular force. The French usually had more horsemen on the battlefield in those campaigns, but at the Battle of Salamanca on July 22, 1812, the British held superiority in that arm and used it very effectively. While the French fielded 3,379 cavalrymen (7 percent of their strength), the British had 4,985 (10 percent of their strength). At the decisive moment of that battle, three battalions of troopers attacked at exactly the right time, when the French infantry was shaken by a flanking movement by British foot soldiers. Three French infantry divisions broke apart and fled the field.[30]

The few cavalry victories over infantry to be seen in the Napoleonic era had an oversized influence on subsequent thinking about the mounted arm. For decades to come, advocates of shock action praised the Duke of Uxbridge's attack while ignoring the defeat of the French cavalry assault at Waterloo. They ignored the far more numerous times that cavalry attacks failed or that mounted troops effectively performed mundane but necessary tasks on the battlefield. Although close cooperation with infantry and artillery, along with shock attacks, had been seen for centuries, the Napoleonic Wars were the most visible and most recent historical examples of cavalry action for the generation that fought the American Civil War. But those wars did not necessarily provide the proper lessons for future cavalry doctrine. Napoleon was unusual in his intense efforts to seek decisive roles for his mounted arm in the middle of infantry battles, more often failing in that quest than succeeding—a fact that few observers recognized.

Another salient lesson of the Napoleonic Wars is that it took an enormous amount of money and effort to build and maintain a large cavalry force. The most damaging cost had always been the expense of mounting and remounting the men. The British 14th Light Dragoons used 1,564 horses in five and a half years of service, three to four times more animals than its average troop strength. The horses lasted two to three years before they gave out or were killed or injured in battle. While Rory Muir has called this an "extraordinary" wastage of horses, it actually pales in comparison to the even heavier wastage of mounts during the American Civil War.[31]

Only nations with adequate reserves of horses and with proper systems of acquiring them could sustain large cavalry forces. The Russian Empire had more horses than any other European state, but its peacetime system of procurement was inadequate in war. The army detailed cavalry officers to purchase animals at fairs or stud farms during peacetime, but that leisurely system failed to fulfill requisitions for replacement mounts during Napoleon's invasion in 1812. A more effective method was to rely on provincial administrators to buy them, but once horse prices tripled because of heavy demand, the most effective method was to allow administrators to substitute horses for peasant recruits. Under this system, four mounts could count for one man, which proved to be a major incentive to meet the tsar's demand for horses and the local population's desire to avoid service. After this system was extended to 44 percent of the provinces in the empire, it garnered 37,810 horses compared to only 29,000 horses raised for service in all of France during the early part of 1813.[32]

European Cavalry in the Nineteenth Century

After the fall of Napoleon, Europe enjoyed relative peace until the mid-nineteenth century. Even so the major European powers maintained large and highly professional cavalry forces. When one compares those peacetime mounted establishments with that maintained by the United States during the same period, the backwardness of America stands out. In terms of organization, administration, training, procurement, and re-supply, most Continental powers far outstripped the small, poorly supported American cavalry arm and also surpassed the British mounted force, which in its turn was superior to the American.

Continental armies built masonry stables to shelter their horses during harsh winters, recruited veterinary surgeons to care for them, made a scientific study of how to shoe the mounts, and organized cavalry schools and veterinary schools to train personnel. The Austrians allowed their troopers to own their horses to encourage them to take better care of the mounts, and generally the quality of horses across the European spectrum was very high. Private as well as government breeding farms not only provided mounts but also generally improved the breed of various types of horses in each country. Rigorous training that continued literally for years underpinned the mounted system. All European armies still maintained different types of cavalry, usually equipped with showy uniforms. Of course, one could argue that this was done more to create a glamorous military force for peacetime parades than for efficient service in war. But whatever motivation underlay it, there can be no doubt that the Europeans far surpassed the Americans in creating large, professional mounted forces in the decades prior to the American Civil War.[33]

The work of the Delafield Commission, which was sent by the U.S. government to observe the Crimean War of 1853–56, fully documented the European cavalry arm as its three members surveyed the military establishments of Britain and the Continent. Capt. George B. McClellan of

Cavalry Forces of Selected Countries on the Eve of the American Civil War

Country	Units and Manpower	Square Miles of Territory
Russia	90 regiments, 90,000 men	8,800,000
Prussia	30 regiments, 30,000 men	134,664
Austria	40 regiments, 40,000 men	269,800
France	63 regiments, 63,000 men	551,500
Britain	27 regiments, 27,000 men	93,628
Sardinia	9 regiments, 9,000 men	116,310
Bavaria	11 regiments, 10,280 men	29,292
United States	5 regiments, 4,460 men	2,940,042

SOURCES: McClellan, *European Cavalry*, 205; Roemer, *Cavalry*, 18, 25.

the U.S. Cavalry paid a lot of attention to the Russian, Prussian, Austrian, French, English, and Sardinian mounted arm.[34]

McClellan was most impressed by the Russians, who maintained a force of 90,000 mounted troops to support the largest nation in the world, 8,800,000 square miles of territory. In contrast the U.S. government maintained a mounted force of 4,460 men for a nation that encompassed 2,940,042 square miles. Russian training involved nine months in the School of the Recruit, with the first two months devoted to horse care. Dismounted drill began in the third month, mounted drill the next, and armed and mounted training in the eighth month. Russian horsemen trained with pistols, sabers, rifle carbines, and lances. McClellan considered their cavalry horses the best in Europe. Light-cavalry mounts from the Ukraine cost on average forty-five dollars each, while heavy-cavalry mounts from the provinces of Tamboff and Worogene cost twice that much. Russian quartermasters expected to get eight years of service from each horse in peacetime, and while preferring mares did use stallions and geldings as well. Whereas most European nations treated dragoons as mounted infantry, riding to the scene of action and then fighting on foot, the Russians trained their dragoons in mounted combat as well as dismounted fighting. Cossacks were an unusual element of the tsar's mounted arm. The term generically referred to irregular cavalry that were organized into separate units and stationed around the periphery of the empire. They had a reputation for hardy campaigning and fierce fighting but were relatively less trained and disciplined than line cavalry.

Cossacks performed light duties—scouting, raiding, and harassment of the enemy.[35]

Prussia, sandwiched between powerful nations to its east, west, and south, embraced only 134,664 square miles but maintained a cavalry force of 30,000 men. Its Germanic cousins to the south, the Austrians, controlled a large, ethnically diverse empire that covered 269,800 square miles of southeastern Europe. The Austrian government supported sixteen regiments of heavy cavalry (eight of dragoons and eight of cuirassiers) and twenty-four regiments of light cavalry (twelve of hussars and twelve of lancers) for a total of 40,000 men. The Austrian cavalry regiment's administration rested on the squadron, with two squadrons commanded by a field officer as the tactical unit and having its own veterinary. McClellan considered the Veterinary School at Vienna the best on the Continent. The several veterinarians of each regiment were superintended by a senior veterinarian who also was responsible for overseeing the shoeing of all horses. In contrast the United States had not provided for any qualified veterinarians for its mounted force.[36]

McClellan was impressed by many aspects of the French mounted system. It consisted of 63,000 horsemen covering 551,500 square miles of territory. The Cavalry School at Saumur, established in 1826, was the best in the world. It offered a two-year course of study in an array of skills and subjects taught by officers and noncommissioned officers. The School of Farriers was attached to the Cavalry School. Among other things, it taught students to keep a register of all horses that included a record of each hoof, necessary because each shoe was carefully molded for a particular hoof. The French system of horse care was so sophisticated that the army administered three different rations for its mounts: one for peacetime, another for an "ordinary march," and a third for active campaigning in wartime.[37]

McClellan paid less attention to English and Sardinian cavalry. The United Kingdom encompassed only 93,628 square miles but administered a sprawling global empire. Its cavalry arm consisted of twenty-seven regiments divided into seven categories (three of household cuirassiers, seven of guards heavy dragoons, three of heavy line dragoons, four of light dragoons of the line, five of hussars, four of lancers, and one of mounted rifles). The squadron consisted of two troops, which also were called companies, and all units used two ranks. One veterinarian was assigned to each regiment, in contrast to the Sardinian cavalry, where each regiment had the services of two veterinarians. The Kingdom of Sardinia had expanded to include much of the Italian peninsula by 1861 and thus, at 116,310 square miles of territory, maintained four regiments of heavy cavalry and five regiments of light cavalry.[38]

American Cavalry

This survey of cavalry forces on the most powerful continent of the world highlights the comparative state of American horsemen on the eve of the Civil War. While the United States maintained a mounted force of 4,460 men from a population of 31,443,321 people, the tiny state of Bavaria, with 4,500,000 inhabitants (about the same population size of New York and Wisconsin combined), maintained a mounted force of 10,280 men. Overall, European nations supported a cavalry force at a ratio of one trooper for every seven infantrymen compared to a ratio of one to five in the United States before the Civil War. The American ratio was higher only because of the very small size of the U.S. infantry force, not because of a large mounted arm.[39]

Of course, there were several reasons why the United States lagged so far behind Europe in cavalry power. Congress sought to save every penny on military matters, arguing that the threat of invasion by a European nation was marginal. A small, poorly trained mounted arm seemed sufficient to maintain order on the frontier. This policy worked well enough as long as the peacetime status quo continued, but when the nation was faced with a large and potentially long war within itself, that force structure became pitifully inadequate. Even the large European armies had built-in plans to expand their force structure at the outbreak of hostilities. This enabled them to begin military operations as soon as war was declared. In the United States, however, an effective wartime force had to be improvised from the ground up for months before serious fighting could ensue.

For example, the French planned to increase their 63,000 cavalry by 59 percent to more than 100,000 men on the outbreak of war. In contrast, the U.S. government increased the army's 4,460 mounted men of 1861 to more than 160,000 troopers by January 1865. That was an increase of more than 3,487 percent and was done without the supporting infrastructure that the French had created over decades. It would be unreasonable to expect the Americans to invest as much money and effort in their peacetime army as the Continental powers, but they are open to criticism for not even trying to close the gap a bit.[40]

Another perspective on why the United States lagged so far behind Europe lays in the meager North American cavalry heritage. No nation in the Western Hemisphere had come close to the Europeans in maintaining a large, well-appointed, and well-trained cavalry arm. This part of the world certainly participated in the Western military tradition, but it occupied only a marginal place within it. Even Great Britain, the early colonizer of the lands that became independent in 1783, was on the periphery of that cavalry heritage, although far closer to its center than any state in the New World.

Mounted forces had rarely been mobilized during the colonial period of early American history. During the Revolutionary War, the largest conflict in the American past before 1861, George Washington's Continental Army maintained only four regiments of cavalry, all of them dragoons. The British also transported few mounted troops to the North American theater of war and suffered from a lack of cavalry when engaging American forces. British commanders often failed to follow up tactical victories, had difficulty feeding their horses, and found that heavy vegetation and fences tended to impede mounted action on the battlefield. Much the same could be said of the Americans; both sides found that severe problems involved in fielding large cavalry forces impeded their operations.[41]

After achieving independence, the U.S. government raised mounted forces only when needed and disbanded them as soon as possible. The country began the War of 1812 with one regiment of dragoons and raised a second regiment, but the states mobilized 46,495 mounted militia and volunteer troops for local defense. All of these local units were disbanded at the end of the war, and the regular mounted force was reduced to one regiment of dragoons, which was itself disbanded a year later. Not until 1833 was a permanent mounted establishment created by Congress with the restoration of the one dragoon regiment. A second dragoon regiment was authorized in 1836, and ten years later, with the start of the Mexican War (1846–48), the army raised a third dragoon regiment and the Regiment of Mounted Rifles. State governments also created eleven regiments, seven battalions, and twenty-six companies of volunteer cavalry for the conflict. This was the largest mounted force organized thus far in American history, but all of the volunteer horsemen disbanded when the war ended. In the regular mounted force, one dragoon regiment also was dissolved, leaving two others plus the Regiment of Mounted Rifles on duty.[42]

American commanders in the field pretty consistently used their mounted troops for scouting, harassment of the enemy, and collecting food and forage. Only rarely did cavalry perform conspicuously on the battlefield. A mounted charge by Kentucky volunteers and regular dragoons played a role in Anthony Wayne's victory at the Battle of Fallen Timbers on August 20, 1794. Another unit of Kentucky volunteers also charged on horse at the Battle of the Thames, contributing to William Henry Harrison's victory on October 5, 1813. During the Mexican War, a mounted attack by the 2nd U.S. Dragoons contributed to American success at the Battle of Resaca de la Palma on May 9, 1846.[43] All of these were tactical events that represented combined-arms action in small but significant engagements.

The territory acquired in the Mexican War required the addition of two regular cavalry regiments in 1855, "an unheard-of thing in the history of the United States," as Albert G. Brackett, who became a major in one of those regiments, put it. Brackett admitted that designating the U.S. mounted troops as dragoons, cavalry, and mounted rifles meant little, for they were part of an all-purpose force, each man required to perform any duty of a horse soldier. Their weapons, however, were varied. During the Mexican War and beyond, the dragoons used musketoons, Prussian dragoon sabers, and horse pistols. The Mounted Rifles had Colt Army revolvers and percussion rifles but no sabers. The two cavalry regiments handled sabers, rifle carbines, and Colt Navy revolvers. By 1861, the regular mounted force consisted of the 1st and 2nd Dragoons, the Regiment of Mounted Rifles, and the 1st and 2nd Cavalry, together a total of 4,460 men. "All cavalry must receive the same instruction," wrote Henry W. Halleck in his 1846 treatise on military affairs. "All should be capable in case of need, of performing any of the duties of mounted troops." That was inevitable in a small, poorly funded cavalry establishment. The government erased these distinctions on August 3, 1861, by redesignating all regiments in the regular service as cavalry.[44]

In terms of force structure, the Americans copied European practices but kept their mounted arm at a low level. They also paid attention to some aspects of European doctrine but not others. Napoleon had not invented shock attack or combined arms, but he greatly emphasized both in cavalry doctrine. Baron de Jomini, in his widely known *Art of War*, popularized Napoleonic dictums on the use of mounted troops by stressing "the simultaneous action of the three arms" as part of "the principles of grand tactics." But Jomini was more careful when it came to shock action, warning that cavalry attacks against prepared infantry were rarely successful. He also reminded readers that mounted troops were vital for an array of supporting roles and stated that a field army should consist of one-sixth cavalry. Few changes in equipment followed the Napoleonic era except that, beginning in Russia and Austria in the late 1850s, cuirassiers gave up their steel body armor.[45]

On the eve of the Civil War, the American military system did not devote much attention to the larger issues of mounted warfare. The U.S. Military Academy was largely oriented toward training engineers for public improvements in the country; its curriculum paid some attention to training a fully rounded officer for various duties after graduation but only to a limited extent. Infantry, artillery, and cavalry training was lumped together in the course structure, but engineering, science, and natural philosophy dominated the training, composing 71 percent of the total class hours over the four-year course of study. Cavalry training was introduced late; only in 1839 did Congress approve the expense of keeping horses at West Point to teach cadets how to ride. It was not until 1853 that coursework in cavalry was added to the curriculum. The cadet practiced riding a couple of hours every other day during his second, third, and fourth years and studied cavalry tactics for only two hours every other day for five weeks during his fourth year.[46]

The army had no postgraduate education programs before the Civil War. The Cavalry School of Practice, established at Carlisle Barracks, Pennsylvania, in 1838, was by its name restricted to practical matters rather than theoretical or tactical discussions. It was really little more than a depot for the equipping and training of men and officers in tactical formations and maneuvers of the mounted arm. No wonder that regular cavalry officers of the pre–Civil War era felt a want of theoretical and doctrinal discussion. Richard Taylor recalled in his memoirs that Richard S. Ewell, an 1840 graduate of the academy who spent most of his pre–Civil War career among small units on the frontier, often complained that "he had learned all about commanding fifty United States dragoons, and forgotten everything else."[47]

Whatever there was of an American cavalry doctrine had to be pieced together by different observers who had the time and inclination to think about the theory of mounted warfare. They paid a good deal of attention to shock action but far less to supporting roles. The Americans liked two ranks and were conversant with ways to form mounted troops in columns for marching, maneuvering, and battle. Halleck argued that a mixed formation, with some units in line and others in column, was the best. Echelon formations also were useful to protect the flanks of a mounted formation. Doctrinaires placed emphasis on regimental columns, but if a brigade was involved, the regimental columns could be lined up next to each other so as to act either independently or in concert as needed.[48]

It is not that American commentators ignored combined arms; they discussed it in a positive fashion. Halleck pointed out that cavalry had little chance to act independently against infantry, and therefore, its proper role in battle was to support friendly foot soldiers. "In connection with the other arms, it is indispensable for beginning a battle, for completing a victory, and for reaping its full advantage by pursuing or destroying the beaten fore." That is similar to what Napoleon said, but the Americans never tried to put this idea into practice. They stressed the futility of mounted attacks against prepared infantry, which is probably the main reason combined arms played such a muted role in their doctrine and practice.[49]

Even so, American cavalry developed a strident culture of attack against other mounted troops. As Halleck put it, the most potent weapon of horse soldiers was the tactical assault. They should never stand still to receive a mounted charge but always counter it with a charge of their own. "The soldier gains great *velocity* by the use of the horse in war," he argued, "but in other respects he is the loser."[50]

Yet Halleck also knew that a mounted assault against unprepared infantry offered real chances of success. Whatever the tactical mission, cavalry command required more of the officer than infantry command required of foot leaders. What was needed in the mounted officer was "a bold and active spirit, which shrinks not from responsibility, and is able to avail itself with quickness and decision of every opportunity." A cavalry commander had to have "a courage and vigor of execution which nothing can shake." No wonder that history afforded so few examples of great cavalry commanders on the level of some who had served Napoleon.[51]

The question of weapons tended to interest cavalry commentators on the eve of the Civil War. With the general introduction of the rifle musket to infantry in the 1850s, the possibility for long-distance small-arms fire seemed to portend a dramatic change in tactics. Many commentators assumed that rifle fire could now damage opposing formations up to 500 yards away, compared with the smoothbore musket's distance of about 100 yards. They believed this would render mounted charges against infantry even less likely to succeed, reducing their already low attention to combined arms. For some observers, the lesson seemed to be that cavalry should fight on foot utilizing the best carbines. But when opposed by other mounted troops, old cavalry doctrine still applied. Commentators urged American horsemen to sharpen their swords and keep in mind that "the strength of cavalry is in the 'spurs and sabre.'"[52]

The U.S. Army retained the basics of cavalry organization, administration, theory, and culture, all of which were drawn more from the European heritage than from its own experience. Governments North and South thus were able to organize cavalry forces on the outbreak of the Civil War. But many questions had to be addressed, and the answers depended on circumstances peculiar to this all-American conflict. These included how large a cavalry force was needed, how much support governmental bureaus could offer the mounted arm, and how effective cavalry regiments might become. Decision makers in Washington, DC, and Richmond, Virginia, had to grapple with these and many other cavalry-related issues during the long war to come.

2

ORGANIZING THE CAVALRY

The United States had followed a military policy geared for its limited peacetime needs, with scant attention to what had to be done in case of a major crisis. It paid the natural cost of that policy when the Civil War broke out. The central government was compelled to rely heavily on loyal state governments to raise a military force capable of dealing with the aggressive Confederates, who started the war by firing on Fort Sumter in April 1861. The first few months of the conflict were chaotic administratively, economically, and operationally, but eventually order replaced confusion, something like adequate supply replaced severe shortages, and both sides managed to create viable military machines to pursue their conflicting strategic goals.

When it came to creating a cavalry arm for service North and South were aided a bit by the fact that a handful of prewar mounted militia companies were available. The 1st Troop, Philadelphia City Cavalry had been organized in 1774 and was still in service eighty-seven years later. After the Ancient and Honorable Artillery Company of Boston, it was the oldest military organization in the United States. The eighty-eight members of the troop equipped and mounted themselves. Half a dozen mounted militia companies in the area around Boston contributed men to the 1st Massachusetts Cavalry, which was organized as a volunteer regiment in September 1861. The 7th Pennsylvania Cavalry drew into its ranks men of the Independent Dragoons, a cavalry militia company in the Nittany Valley. In the eastern part of Washington County, the Ringgold Cavalry Company, originally organized in 1847, provided a handful of men to the 22nd Pennsylvania Cavalry.[1]

Several cavalry militia companies were organized in the South. One company came together at Waterloo, Virginia, in June 1859 and, after several months of service as state troops, was folded into the 4th Virginia Cavalry. A company organized in the spring of 1859 at Talladega, Alabama, calling itself the Mountain Rangers, received uniforms and weapons from the state and drilled regularly. Because of delays in being accepted for Confederate service, more than half the men joined infantry units before the company was mustered in as cavalry during July 1861.[2]

It cannot be said that prewar militia units had any real effect on the process of organizing cavalry at the start of the Civil War. There were far too few of them, and their level of expertise in drill, horsemanship, and camp living was generally low because of infrequent and short-term training periods. Both sides had to rely mostly on units created from scratch by state governments.

At least the North had the prewar cavalry arm of the U.S. Army at its disposal, instituting some changes in it soon after the start of the war. The regular cavalry initially consisted of two regiments of dragoons, one regiment of mounted infantry, and two regiments of cavalry, with a third cavalry regiment authorized in May 1861. It had no heavy cavalry, the force that in European armies conducted shock attacks against infantry, but the dragoons were supposed to be a flexible force capable of fighting on foot and on horseback. The American units designated as cavalry were supposedly the North American version of light cavalry, meant to perform outpost duty, reconnaissance, and raiding. But the American practice had long been to blur these distinctions and treat most mounted troops as an all-purpose force. George B. McClellan had criticized American practice in his Delafield Commission report in the late 1850s, which was republished as a series of trade books after the outbreak of the war. A cavalry captain at that time, McClellan had seen truly good dragoons in Europe and urged that the U.S. Army train its dragoons to be effective at both dismounted and mounted combat.[3]

The Civil War led to changes in the regulars. All pretense of specialization evaporated when Congress authorized redesignation of all regular
mounted units as cavalry on August 3, 1861. The 1st Dragoons became
the 1st U.S. Cavalry; the 2nd Dragoons became the 2nd U.S. Cavalry; the
Mounted Rifles became the 3rd U.S. Cavalry; the 1st Cavalry became the
4th U.S. Cavalry; the 2nd Cavalry became the 5th U.S. Cavalry, and the
newly organized regiment became the 6th U.S. Cavalry. Each of these regular units was expected to be able to fulfill all the varied roles of mounted
troops without specialized training, an eminently sensible policy.[4]

The Growth of the Cavalry Arm

There was no question, of course, that the U.S. government would retain,
strengthen, and redesignate its regular cavalry arm for service in the Civil
War. But surprisingly, there was a good deal of indecision about how far
to go in creating a volunteer cavalry force raised by the states for U.S.
service. Efforts to restrict the growth of the volunteer cavalry force came
from the War Department. Among the motives for such caution was the
assumption that the war would be relatively short, and everyone knew
that it took a long time to train good cavalry soldiers. The enormous expense of cavalry, especially the horses, was another impediment. Finally,
given the nature of the Southern countryside, with its terrain cluttered by
heavy forests, it was assumed cavalry would have little room to operate.[5]

Resistance to a large mounted force came from another source, a theoretical balance between the number of infantrymen, artillerymen, and
cavalrymen in an army. Henry W. Halleck had stated that the mounted
force should range from 16 percent to 25 percent of the number of infantry troops, or one mounted man for every six to four foot soldiers. But
Gov. Edwin D. Morgan of New York tried to adhere to a ratio of 9 percent
of the number of infantrymen in authorizing units raised within his state.
This amounted to one mounted man per eleven foot soldiers.[6]

As Morgan's case illustrates, state governors were largely responsible
for deciding how many cavalry regiments to organize until Federal authorities began to put a brake on the process. By August 3, 1861, the central government had accepted 27 regiments and thirty-two independent
companies of volunteer cavalry, amounting to 24,800 troopers. This was

in contrast to 268 regiments and eighteen companies of volunteer infantry with 279,720 men. The ratio was about one mounted man for every eleven infantrymen, much lower than Halleck's preference but exactly at Morgan's ratio.[7]

The volunteer cavalrymen continued to arrive until, by October 1861, Federal authorities began to protest. The War Department told Morgan that it would not accept any more mounted units, a viewpoint supported by McClellan, now a major general, soon after he became the new general in chief in November. Paymaster General Benjamin F. Larned argued that the army already had too many cavalry regiments, noting, "They are vastly more expensive and less serviceable . . . than infantry." Cavalry officers received forty cents per day for the use of their privately owned horses; Larned estimated the government could save $2–$3 million if that provision was dropped. In addition to refusing new units, the government also tried to reduce the number already accepted. McClellan thought the number of mounted regiments should be reduced to no more than fifty by disbanding the least efficient units. "There are a greater or less number of men in each regiment who will never make efficient cavalry soldiers," he asserted.[8]

But it proved to be politically difficult to eliminate any mounted regiments from the number already accepted or even to stop new ones from being organized. By late February 1862, the government had 62 regiments and 45 companies, with 64,133 men all told. New York and Illinois had fielded 10 regiments each, and Pennsylvania contributed 9 regiments; each of the other states had sent far fewer units. In addition to the 62 regiments already accepted, the War Department had authorized an additional dozen that were not yet completed. By June 30, 1862, a total of 75 cavalry regiments and 65 companies, containing 76,844 volunteer troopers, had been accepted. In contrast, 610 regiments and 174 companies containing 531,361 volunteer infantrymen had been mustered in to U.S. service. That amounted to one mounted man for every seven foot soldiers, nearly Halleck's preference and higher than Morgan's ratio.[9]

By November 1862, the number of mounted units had risen to 86 regiments, but the number of mounted companies had contracted to 37, for a slightly reduced total of 74,793 mounted volunteer troops compared to the June 30 tabulation. But the number of infantrymen had risen sharply

Growth of the Union Cavalry Force, 1861–1863

Time Period	Units	Men
April 15, 1861	5 regiments of regulars	4,460
August 3, 1861	27 regiments and 32 companies of volunteers	24,800
February 1862	62 regiments and 45 companies of volunteers	64,133
June 30, 1862	75 regiments and 65 companies of volunteers	76,844
November 1862	86 regiments and 37 companies of volunteers	74,793
November 1863	168 regiments of volunteers and 6 regiments of regulars	134,883

SOURCE: *OR*, ser. 3, 1:913, 2:183–84, 859–60, 3:990–92.

by November, standing at 816 regiments and 7 companies for a total of 680,539 volunteer foot soldiers. That proportion was lower than Halleck's ratio but exactly matched Morgan's.[10]

Relying as it did on the support of state governors and a high level of war enthusiasm among the people, the central government could not afford to apply a strong brake on enlistments. That is why it never strictly enforced its ideas about how many volunteer cavalrymen to accept. And yet when the dust settled, the U.S. government wound up with about one trooper for every eleven infantrymen, lower than military authorities but not political officials recommended.

Regulating Size and Structure of Mounted Units

The central government had more control over the size and structure of cavalry regiments, although state governors at times set their own standards concerning the size of mounted units. For example, Governor Morgan of New York required mounted regiments to have at least eight companies but allowed for expansion to twelve if necessary. Washington authorities managed to impose uniformity in this regard. By September 1862, they required all volunteer cavalry regiments to consist of twelve companies.[11]

The reason for this lies in a basic issue of military organization. European armies had long relied on the battalion system, wherein the regiment was divided into three battalions of four companies each. These battalions were semi-independent organizations capable of acting by themselves, and one usually served as a depot battalion to handle supply tasks and train recruits before sending them to the field. This was true of European infantry as well. But in the United States, the battalion system had never taken root. The regiment or the company had always been the basic unit of administration and field operations for both infantry and cavalry in the United States.

But given the many and varied duties of mounted troops in a large war, the government shifted toward the battalion organization, which, combined with the organization of squadrons, underwrote cavalry operations. Two companies composed a squadron, and two squadrons composed a battalion. Thus, the twelve companies of a cavalry regiment were divided into three battalions for flexible assignment away from each other and from the regimental command structure. In some regiments the companies were divided into battalions in logical ways. For example, in the 1st Massachusetts Cavalry, Companies A, B, C, and D made up the 1st Battalion, and so on in alphabetical order. But in the 3rd Ohio Cavalry, the 1st Battalion consisted of Companies B, H, L, and M during the early part of the war. Later the system was standardized so that the battalions held companies in "regular alphabetical order."[12]

The U.S. government did not fully adopt the battalion system as practiced in Europe. It was done purely for operational purposes in the field, not for support services. None of the mounted battalions in the Union army was stationed on home territory for the purposes of recruiting men and training them for field service.

But the wisdom of mandating a battalion organization for operational purposes was proven in the field. Many regimental commanders had to detach their battalions to a variety of duties, especially if they were part of an occupying force in captured Southern territory. The 1st Massachusetts Cavalry had two battalions operating in Virginia and one in South Carolina and Florida at the start of 1865. Its component units were further dispersed with one squadron each at Twenty-Fourth and Twenty-Fifth

Corps headquarters; one company at Fort Magruder near Williamsburg, Virginia; one company at Harrison's Landing, Virginia; one squadron at Jacksonville, Florida; one at Deveaux Neck, South Carolina; and two companies at headquarters, Army of the James.[13]

Just before the war, regular cavalry regiments assigned a quartermaster, commissary of subsistence, and other staff members to each battalion so that it could sustain itself as a semi-independent organization. At least some volunteer cavalry regiments mimicked this practice. In those units there were not only three majors to command battalions and three support officers to supply them but also a full complement of noncommissioned officers, such as sergeant majors, quartermaster sergeants, and commissary sergeants. By July 1862, the government dropped all these battalion-level support personnel, probably to save money and also with the realization that, in practice, most cavalry battalions tended after all to act together rather than dispersed. This was especially true of the regiments composing brigades, divisions, and corps in major field armies. William F. Scott of the 4th Iowa Cavalry saw the dropping of battalion-level support personnel as an improvement in unit effectiveness. "The companies were brought into direct relations with the regimental officers," he wrote, "the incessant petty difficulties arising from a division of responsibility were greatly diminished, and the field-and-staff was reduced from its unwieldy size to a force comparatively small and quickly felt." This did not mean the army dropped the battalion organization or the three majors per regiment, but each battalion was no longer the self-sufficient entity it had largely been.[14]

A confusion of terms attended some aspects of cavalry organization. The mounted arm shared the terms "regiment," "company," and "battalion" with the infantry but not the term "squadron." McClellan argued that each cavalry company should be designated a squadron "in order to distinguish it from the infantry unit in reports, returns." No one supported him in this recommendation. In fact, Congress officially defined a squadron as consisting of two companies in July 1861; this practice was also followed in the Confederate army.[15]

More vital was the question of whether a cavalry company ought to be called a troop. The Civil War generation preferred the term "company," al-

Organization of a Cavalry Regiment in the "Volunteer Army of the United States under Existing Laws," 1863

Regiment (12 companies/troops in 3 battalions)	Company
1 colonel	1 captain
1 lieutenant colonel	1 first lieutenant
3 majors	1 second lieutenant
1 surgeon	1 first sergeant
2 assistant surgeons	1 quartermaster sergeant
1 regimental adjutant (an "extra lieutenant")	1 commissary sergeant
1 regimental quartermaster (an "extra lieutenant")	5 sergeants
1 regimental commissary (an "extra lieutenant")	8 corporals
1 chaplain	2 trumpeters
1 veterinary surgeon	2 farriers/blacksmiths
1 sergeant major	1 saddler
1 quartermaster sergeant	1 wagoner
1 commissary sergeant	60 (minimum) to 78
2 hospital stewards	(maximum) privates
1 saddler sergeant	
1 chief trumpeter	

SOURCE: Adjutant General's Office, General Orders No. 110, April 29, 1863, *OR*, ser. 3, 3:175.

though some of its members used "troop" instead. Covering both options, a general order issued on April 29, 1863, referred to twelve companies *or* troops in each mounted regiment. Only in 1883 did the army officially designate mounted companies as troops. When James H. Kidd wrote his memoirs sometime after 1908, he used "troop" instead of "company" because by then the U.S. Army was officially using that term.[16]

Recruiting and Organizing

Unlike infantry and artillery units, which typically were recruited in one step followed by muster in to U.S. service, cavalry regiments typically went through a multistage process of mobilization. They often had to draw men from varied places rather than one locality, wait for needed equipment and mounts to arrive, and train in stages depending on what resources were available. With the need to control their horses, there was some truth to the idea that it took years to produce a good mounted warrior, but neither the Union army nor the Confederate army had the luxury of time.

The 5th New York Cavalry began recruiting at Staten Island after July 1861, but its 1st and 2nd Battalions did not receive houses until October. At that point the regiment moved to Baltimore, where the 3rd Battalion finally was mounted and sabers were issued to everyone. The regiment moved to Annapolis by November 25 but did not enter the theater of war until April 1862, finally receiving revolvers and changing their old saddles for newer McClellan saddles. The 5th West Virginia Cavalry demonstrated how far afield some units had to go to find enough recruits for mounted units. Four companies came from Pittsburgh, Pennsylvania; one from Washington County, Pennsylvania; one from Ironton, Ohio; another from Grafton, Virginia; and another from Wheeling, Virginia. They all met at Beverly, Virginia, late in July 1861 to form the 2nd Virginia Infantry, which was later mounted and redesignated the 5th West Virginia Cavalry.[17]

Cavalry units were equipped in stages. Uniforms were issued pretty early, but equipment, weapons, and especially horses and horse equipment took much longer. In the 3rd Ohio Cavalry, clothes came first along with a handful of government-issued horses. Eventually, when all of the troopers finally had horses, some of them did not have bridles. More than two months after recruitment, the regiment received enough horses and saddles but did not receive sabers until another two months later.[18]

The creation of the 6th Ohio Cavalry was delayed by governmental reluctance to accept another mounted unit. Its men refused to convert to infantry, and the question hung fire for weeks. Authorities tried again to persuade the Ohioans to serve on foot in March 1862, but they refused. Finally given authority to mount the regiment on April 21, the men received equipment. After "severe battalion drill" and saber practice for three weeks, the regiment moved to Wheeling, Virginia, where it received some government-issued mounts on May 10; saddles were another week in arriving. Finally, seven months after the start of recruitment, the 6th Ohio began "to appear something like cavalry."[19]

New cavalry units continued to be organized throughout most of the conflict. President Lincoln's call for 300,000 additional volunteers in the summer of 1862 led to several new mounted regiments. Pennsylvania was called on for three of them. While Gov. Andrew Curtin raised each of his infantry regiments from local areas, these three cavalry units recruited across the state. The twelve companies of the 17th Pennsylvania Cavalry, for example, held men from fourteen counties.[20]

William Douglas Hamilton of the 32nd Ohio Infantry became part of the cavalry recruiting in his home state in 1862. Gov. David Tod asked him to raise one of the two mounted regiments requested of Ohio early that fall. Already on recruiting duty for his infantry regiment, Hamilton tried to avoid the assignment. When Tod told him that any men he had already lined up for the 32nd would be glad to join the new cavalry regiment instead, believing that "boys like to ride horseback," Hamilton countered by admitting that he knew little about cavalry. "You know a horse when you see one?" the governor retorted. Hamilton assured him he did, having grown up on a farm. "That is about as much as any of them can say," Tod stated with finality.[21]

This was how Hamilton became a cavalryman. He managed to organize a battalion and drilled it for four months before taking it to Kentucky for several months of field duty. Then, having found enough young men who wanted to ride horses, Tod called him back to organize and drill the other two battalions in Ohio. Hamilton finally was commissioned colonel of the 9th Ohio Cavalry in December 1863, more than a year after he had begun to create the regiment.[22]

The Anderson Troop, which evolved into the 15th Pennsylvania Cavalry, underwent the most difficult process of organization of any mounted unit in the Civil War. It began in June 1862, when Maj. Gen. Don Carlos Buell, commander of the Department of the Ohio, asked Capt. William J. Palmer to convert his company of cavalry into a battalion. Palmer had organized the Anderson Troop the previous October to serve as the escort of Brig. Gen. Robert Anderson in Kentucky, recruiting it from Philadelphia. By the time it was ready for service, Buell had become commander in Kentucky, and the company became his escort. After War Department approval in July, Palmer opened recruiting stations at Philadelphia, Pittsburgh, and elsewhere. He obtained more enlistees than anticipated from more than thirty counties, so he received authorization to organize a regiment instead of a battalion. The new unit assembled at Carlisle, Pennsylvania, and was mustered in on August 22, 1862. All this was done without the original Anderson Troop, which continued to serve in the field as Buell's escort. That unit was supposed to become Company A of the new regiment, but instead it was mustered out on the expiration of its term of service. Although a completely new organization, many people continued to call Palmer's regiment the Anderson Troop.[23]

This regiment's further organization was very troubled. Only a few weeks after assembling, the men were called to the field to deal with the Confederate invasion of Maryland. The Confederates captured Palmer in a skirmish, and the officers left behind had no clue as to his plan for further organizing the regiment or his preferences for officer selection after the unit returned to Carlisle. The regiment suffered for months without firm leadership. Moving to Louisville in November 1862, the men received horses and trained for a month before reporting to Maj. Gen. William S. Rosecrans, who had replaced Buell. When Rosecrans set out from Nashville on December 26 to meet the Confederate army at Murfreesboro, a rebellion broke out in the ranks of what was still called the Anderson Troop. Most of the men refused to go, saying they had enlisted on the understanding that they would serve as a headquarters guard and escort, not as a line regiment. The officers, most of whom had served in the original Anderson Troop, did little to quiet the men. After two days half the troops consented to take the field. After another day more of them fell in, but a hard core amounting to one-third of the regiment preferred to stay at Nashville as the Federals struggled through the deadly Battle of Stones River only thirty miles from their camp.[24]

The two-thirds of the regiment's men who fought at Stones River did well in their first battle and returned to Nashville to rejoin the one-third who had sat out the engagement. Palmer returned from Confederate imprisonment in February 1863, moved the reunited unit to Murfreesboro, and began to whip it into shape as the 15th Pennsylvania Cavalry. He had to add two more companies to comply with War Department orders but simply moved some men from his ten companies to the two new ones in order to do so. Three companies of the regiment were detached to Rosecrans's headquarters, and men from the regiment often acted as couriers for various other headquarters. According to some members, the promise of escort and courier duty had been a powerful incentive for joining Palmer's regiment from the start. Now, after a troubled beginning, they were finally able to fulfill that promise.[25]

No other cavalry regiment had such a tortuous organizational history as the 15th Pennsylvania, which finally lost the name Anderson Troop in 1863. Its primary problems were the loss of an effective commander at a critical time in its organization and the unwillingness of many men to serve where ordered. Much of this could have been avoided by closer attention to the regiment's problems on the part of the governor and better service by the officers left in control of the regiment after Palmer's capture.

The 4th Massachusetts Cavalry came into being in 1864 through a long process too. Its core was the 3rd Battalion, 1st Massachusetts Cavalry, left behind in South Carolina when the 1st's other two battalions were transferred to Virginia in August 1862. The 3rd Battalion technically remained a part of the 1st Regiment until officially separated in August 1863. For a while it was called the Independent Battalion, Massachusetts Cavalry until incorporated into the developing 4th Massachusetts Cavalry in February 1864.[26]

Meanwhile the 1st and 2nd Battalions, 1st Massachusetts Cavalry operated in Virginia and Maryland for a year and a half before Gov. John A. Andrew received authority to raise a replacement third battalion. Unfortunately he insisted on organizing that battalion entirely from scratch, angering the veteran officers of the 1st and 2nd Battalions who had wanted positions in the new organization. As a result the regiment received 400 green recruits led by equally green officers, who outnumbered the veterans in the older eight companies. "This new battalion went all to pieces" during the first fifteen days of the Overland Campaign, and many men were reassigned out of it to the older two battalions as a way of giving them proper training and experience.[27]

Another way in which new mounted units appeared during the war resulted from the desire of some infantrymen to become cavalrymen. The 41st Massachusetts Infantry had been organized from August to October 1862 and was in the Department of the Gulf by December of that year. It participated in the Bayou Teche Campaign during the spring of 1863 before being mounted in May. Initially called mounted rifles, its name was changed to the 3rd Massachusetts Cavalry after three unattached companies of Massachusetts mounted men were added to it in June. Those three unattached companies had been organized in September 1861 and had served as the only cavalry units in Maj. Gen. Benjamin Butler's Department of the Gulf until the fall of 1862.[28]

Another example of an infantry regiment transforming itself into cavalry concerned the 130th New York. Col. Alfred Gibbs, a cavalry officer in the prewar army, accepted command of this foot regiment when it organized in August 1862 but then worked for months to convert it to cavalry service. The War Department authorized the switch in July 1863, and the men exchanged their infantry trousers for reinforced cavalry pants. They also gave up their Enfield rifles for carbines. Initially designated the 19th New York Cavalry, the men wanted a special name, so the regimental quartermaster suggested 1st New York Dragoons. The state's governor approved, and the new designation was announced in October 1863.[29]

In the Confederate army there was so much desire to transform infantry into cavalry that authorities often had to reject such requests. When the Kentucky brigade commanded by Brig. Gen. Joseph H. Lewis in the Army of Tennessee petitioned for conversion to mounted service, Gen. Joseph E. Johnston refused to give up "good infantry" for "bad cavalry." Johnston argued that the Confederate army as a whole possessed more mounted units than was needed. "The difficulty of maintaining cavalry makes it very injudicious to attempt to support more than we absolutely require. We ought rather to increase our infantry at the expense of the cavalry than the reverse. The former is excellent and the latter indifferent of its kind." Nevertheless, after Johnston was relieved of command, Lewis's Brigade was horsed and acted as cavalry.[30]

The strong tendency of Southerners to prefer mounted service was demonstrated by the large number of cavalry regiments fielded by some states. Louisiana organized twenty-eight mounted regiments and battalions throughout the war. The urge to contribute cavalry only increased rather than diminished with the passage of time.[31]

Dispersed Service and Consolidation

Once organized, cavalry regiments in both armies contended with a strong tendency by higher-level commanders to disperse their component parts to far-flung assignments. No regiment was more decisively dispersed than the 3rd Indiana Cavalry, which was split in two from the start of its history. One battalion of six companies went east, while the other four companies stayed in the West. Because this became a permanent condition, regimental members called them the Eastern Battalion and the Western Battalion. But dispersal went deeper than this; while the Eastern Battalion remained intact, the companies of the Western Battalion were separated from nearly the start of their service in the field. Company G was assigned to the headquarters of Brig. Gen. George H. Thomas; Company H to the headquarters of Brig. Gen. Alexander M. McCook; Company I to Louisville, Kentucky; and Company K to Brig. Gen. William Nelson in December 1861. Not until October 1862 were these four companies reunited at Louisville.[32]

In December 1862 two additional companies were organized for the 3rd Indiana. The original companies of the Western Battalion did not reenlist as units and therefore were mustered out in October 1864, leaving the newer Companies L and M to fend for themselves. They did not do too well. Company L was broken up, its men assigned as teamsters or wagon-train guards; the company was never reconstituted. Company M and men from the original Western Battalion who still had time to serve initially were consolidated with the 92nd Illinois, which was serving as a mounted infantry regiment. A few weeks later they were shifted to the 8th Indiana Cavalry for the remainder of the war.[33]

The Eastern Battalion and Western Battalion never served together in the field. Nevertheless, the governor of Indiana and its field officers acted as if the regiment was one unit. When the colonel, who was with the Eastern Battalion, resigned in March 1863, the lieutenant colonel, who also was with the Eastern Battalion, was promoted and replaced him. The lieutenant colonel vacancy was filled by the major, who served in the Western Battalion, even though neither of those officers could hope to exercise their authority over the entire regiment. Individual members of the Eastern and Western Battalions parted company after only a few weeks of training and never saw each other until their veteran reunions after the war.[34]

While no other mounted regiment experienced such a splintering as the 3rd Indiana Cavalry, many were compelled to consolidate their companies. When the 3rd Pennsylvania Cavalry was reduced in numbers by the summer of 1863, "in order to increase its efficiency," regimental leaders reduced the number of squadrons from six to four through consolidation. It also was normal to consolidate squadrons or companies in a regiment that was going out of service by stages, as happened with the 1st Rhode Island Cavalry and the 1st Massachusetts Cavalry.[35]

Personnel

At the peak of its organizational history, a cavalry regiment included surgeons, chaplains, adjutants, quartermasters, commissaries, several different grades of sergeants, hospital stewards, saddlers, trumpeters, farriers (or blacksmiths), teamsters, and eight sergeants and eight corporals per company. For twelve companies, that amounted to more than 1,200 men per regiment. Add to that number sutlers and servants for the officers, and the number could reach 1,300 personnel plus more than 1,200 government horses and up to 90 private horses. Each supply wagon was pulled by six mules, but the number of wagons varied widely over time. A full mounted regiment was a little community of men and animals.[36]

There were a handful of support personnel whose presence in cavalry regiments is sparsely documented. Infantry units routinely detailed men to serve as pioneers to clear areas for camps, improve roads, and dig entrenchments. In the 1st Massachusetts Cavalry, sixteen men were detailed under command of a sergeant in 1863. They were told to "take down fences, build and destroy bridges, erect barricades, and generally do axe-men's work." Some were given shovels, others picks, and the rest axes, and all rode at the head of the regiment. Lt. James Albert Clark led the pioneer detachment of the 17th Pennsylvania Cavalry at Chancellorsville. It consisted of two men detailed from each of the regiment's twelve companies and "equipped mostly with axes; two had picks and two shovels." Lt. Frederick Whittaker of the 6th New York Cavalry stated that it was typical of all mounted regiments to form a pioneer corps, consisting of twenty-four men led by a sergeant, but the fact that so few cavalrymen even mention pioneers makes one wonder how widespread they might have been.[37]

Pioneers undoubtedly were more common among mounted units than were regimental bands. The expense of supplying proper instruments for playing on horseback played a fundamental role in this. The prewar regular army allowed for mounted bands, but their members were distinct from buglers; the latter, called field musicians, blew signals and orders with bugles and were obviously necessary.[38]

Veterinary surgeons represented another group of support personnel for cavalry units. Their services were badly needed, given the huge number of horses assembled and the outbreak of diseases afflicting them. By March 1863, Congress authorized a veterinary surgeon for each cavalry regiment. The Union army established a system of approving appointments the following August that included regimental commanders and a board of their officers and continued up to the secretary of war. But the real problem was how to find qualified professionals to fill those slots. There were very few trained veterinarians in the United States during the Civil War era. Maj. Gen. George Stoneman, who then headed the Cavalry Bureau, lamented that "one great want felt by the cavalry service is the deficiency of veterinary talent in the country, and the impossibility of obtaining what little there is for the compensation now allowed by the Government." This problem was never solved, and most Civil War cavalry regiments had no trained medical staff to take care of the horses, relying instead on folk remedies and self-trained personnel. In this regard American mounted units were very far behind most European mounted forces.[39]

Continued Growth of the Cavalry

Despite initial resistance by the War Department, the U.S. government steadily built up a large cavalry arm to fight the Civil War. As of August 1863, twenty-one cavalry regiments were in the process of organizing for Federal service. The total mounted force already mustered in represented men from thirty-four states and territories, including Confederate states with loyalist populations. From August to November 1863, the government authorized the states to raise an additional twelve cavalry regiments. As of November 1863, the mounted forces numbered 174 cavalry regiments combined in the volunteer and regular service, with a total of 134,883 troopers.[40]

When Governor Andrew of Massachusetts requested authorization to organize more cavalry in February 1864, Secretary of War Edwin M. Stanton told him the army already had "a number far beyond the capacity of the Government to support. Every State is anxious to raise cavalry, because it is easier to raise than infantry, while it is beyond all comparison more expensive to equip and support." Stanton hinted that "a financial catastrophe" might result if the government did not put a brake on this trend.[41]

By July 1864, not only Stanton but also General in Chief Ulysses S. Grant and Chief of Staff Henry W. Halleck agreed that the Union had enough cavalrymen to finish the war. The government had by then created the largest mounted arm ever to be raised in the Western Hemisphere, a force that rivaled the size of the largest cavalry contingents in European history and the largest to be seen in all of American military history. According to one account, the Union army fielded a total of 232 cavalry regiments, 9 battalions, and 122 companies. The Confederate government fielded a total of 127 regiments, 143 battalions, and 101 companies. A grand total of about 500,000 men served in all of these Union and Confederate cavalry units through four years of conflict.[42]

As the initial resistance to cavalry units had largely stemmed from the expense of creating and maintaining them, many observers offered estimates of the exact cost. Benjamin W. Crowninshield of the 1st Massachusetts Cavalry asserted that the expense of initially equipping a regiment of twelve companies amounted to $300,000. In contrast, Francis Colburn Adams of the 1st New York Cavalry estimated that $500,000 to $600,000 would be needed to create and equip a cavalry regiment, with an additional $250,000 to $300,000 to maintain it for one year of service. James A. Congdon of the 12th Pennsylvania Cavalry argued that the government could expect to spend $1,000 a year to maintain every individual cavalryman in service.[43]

Neither Crowninshield, Adams, nor Congdon provided any support for their estimates, but Halleck did when he informed Grant how much money the Federal government had spent on its cavalry force by February 1865. At that time the Union mounted arm had 160,237 men present and absent, with 77,847 serviceable horses and an additional 9,659 unserviceable mounts. The total expense in "horses, pay, forage, rations, clothing, ordnance, equipments, and transportation" for the past twelve months had been $125 million. It was in Halleck's view "certainly a pretty large sum for keeping up our cavalry force for one year." That amounted to about $780 annually to support one cavalryman, a bit less than the estimate by Congdon but still a sizeable sum. Halleck did not provide comparative figures for the maintenance of infantry and artillery, but he considered cavalry to be more expensive than the other two arms.[44]

The Confederate government shifted a good deal of the expense onto the cavalryman by mandating that he provide his own horse. Quite a few Southern officers were willing to go farther than that and pay for some expenses incurred in creating mounted units. Capt. Hamilton Boykin, for example, spent more than $1,200 to equip a company of cavalry called the Boykin Rangers, which later became Company A, 2nd South Carolina Cavalry. He purchased everything from commissary stores to horse shoes, tent poles, saddles, and rifle slings, keeping accounts in hopes of reimbursement by the government. But even this policy of shifting much of the cost onto the shoulders of cavalrymen could go only so far.[45]

The process of organizing a cavalry arm in both armies was not just an event of 1861; it extended well into the last year of the war. There was much more uncertainty about how many troopers were needed for the conflict than existed for infantrymen and artillerymen. The expense of maintaining mounted units worked against enlargement of the force but failed to inhibit it significantly. The Civil War therefore became the biggest cavalry war in American history.

3

BOOKS, DOCTRINE, AND TRAINING

Like the artillery, the cavalry arm required a great deal of specialized training. While peacetime troopers could afford an extended period of drill and practice, the Civil War cavalryman had to learn his trade without the luxury of time. While training could not substitute for experience in developing an effective horse soldier, it prepared him for field experience in fundamental and important ways.

Training for cavalry service was more complicated than for infantry because mounted soldiers had to drill their horses at the same time that they trained themselves. The process began with understanding how to act and move as soldiers and segued into learning the intricate formations and maneuvers associated with command and control on the march and on the battlefield. Formations referred to organizing mounted units into various types of lines and columns, while maneuvers referred to methods of moving from one formation to another or from one spot on the field to another. Both came under the heading of primary tactics, the most fundamental level of tactics in the Civil War. Cavalrymen learned primary tactics on horseback, teaching their mounts the movements in the process, and also had to become familiar with the basics of fighting on foot. Finally, they had to learn how to handle not one but three weapons—saber, pistol, and carbine—while mounted or on foot.

Manuals and Handbooks

Training was based on tactical manuals officially adopted by the army that explained the intricacies of drill. Handbooks were supplemental volumes written by knowledgeable individuals as aids to the aspiring cavalryman, but they were not adopted or endorsed by the army. In the United States a number of handbooks had been published before the army ever adopted a cavalry manual. Col. John Charles Herries's *Instructions for the Use of Yeomanry and Volunteer Corps of Cavalry* was published in London in 1805. Someone abstracted its contents for American use and published this under the title *Abstract of Colonel Herries's Instructions for Volunteer Corps of Cavalry: Adapted to the Use of the Volunteer and Militia Cavalry of the United States* in 1811. Soon after, American colonel William Duane wrote *A Hand Book for Cavalry*, published in Philadelphia in 1814, to compete with Herries's English book. His primary source was the 1804 French cavalry system. Duane pared those tactics down to the minimum for practical purposes and urged troopers to treat their horses with kindness.[1]

These handbooks were not proper manuals. They lacked the authority of a publication that covered all aspects of cavalry training. The first true cavalry manual adopted by the U.S. government was a translation of the French manual sponsored by Secretary of War Joel R. Poinsett. Adopted on February 10, 1841, it had no credited author but became known as the Poinsett manual. Issued in three volumes of 198, 285, and 106 pages respectively, it covered all the basics of mounted service and was especially directed at dragoons, but its instructions were fully applicable to all types of horse soldiers. The Poinsett manual defined many terms associated with cavalry service but lacked advice about how to use the formations and maneuvers. It identified two ranks as the best formation for lines and defined the marching column as consisting of either two or four men abreast. In battle the distance between individual lines within the column formation was important for command and control and for quickly transitioning into line. Close columns, with the least possible distance between lines (twelve yards), were easier to control. Open columns, however, with lines far enough apart to allow them to wheel right or left and deploy into line, facilitated maneuvers.[2]

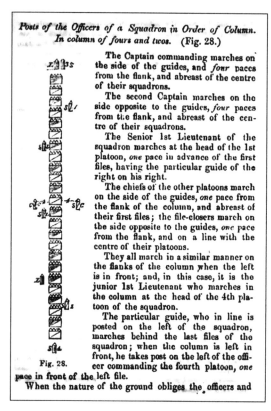

Squadron in Column, Posts of the Officers.
A company of cavalry formed into a column of fours, with the placing of the officers indicated.
Patten, *Cavalry Drill*, 47, fig. 28.

The Poinsett manual defined a wheeling maneuver as "a circular movement executed by a man, or troop, returning to the point of departure." In other words, it was a full wheel of 360 degrees. A half wheel was 180 degrees, with the man or troop winding up facing in the opposite direction from the start. An executed quarter wheel had them facing either to right or left relative to the initial facing. The manual continued in this fashion to "the sixteenth of a wheel," in which the formation faced to right quarter or left quarter of the circle. The oblique march demanded an explanation as well. It allowed the formation to gain ground toward the right or left "without changing the front" and was conducted either by

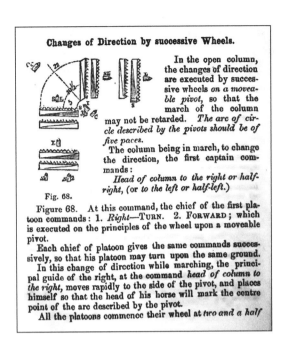

Change of Direction by Successive Wheels.
This diagram illustrates how a column could
change direction ninety degrees to the right by
conducting a quarter wheel on a movable pivot.
Patten, *Cavalry Drill*, 106, fig. 68.

an individual or by a line or column. In both cases the individual or men
in the formation simply faced at an angle in place and moved forward.
To march by the flank involved each man facing right or left and moving
forward to the required spot before stopping and then facing to the front
once more. Poinsett's manual also included instructions for loading and
firing weapons and handling a lance and saber.[3]

The manual sponsored by Poinsett served the cavalry for twenty years.
It was used by all mounted officers when the Civil War broke out and was
held in high esteem by many of them. Albert G. Brackett exaggerated
when writing in 1865 that "almost every cavalry officer of experience" considered it superior to any manual used in the United States at the time.
The contender with Poinsett's manual for preference among American
cavalrymen was written by Col. Philip St. George Cooke, a Virginia-born
army officer. After graduation from the U.S. Military Academy in 1827,

Cooke mostly served in one of the two dragoon regiments, rising in rank from lieutenant to colonel and command of the 2nd Regiment. His family was deeply divided by the war, with a son becoming a Confederate infantry brigade commander and his son-in-law, James E. B. Stuart, becoming the South's most celebrated cavalry leader. Cooke divided his manual into two volumes, with the School of the Trooper, the School of the Platoon, and the School of the Squadron in the first volume of 217 pages. Evolution of a Regiment and Evolution of the Line appeared in the second volume of 96 pages. The War Department officially adopted Cooke's tactics on November 1, 1861.[4]

Cooke created a different tone in his manual compared to that used by the infantry and artillery. The text was written in clear, simple style, covering the basics without too much jargon. Cooke explained the meaning of the terms and organized the content for easier comprehension. This was not merely a translation of a French text but a book made as accessible as possible to an average American.

To be sure, Cooke adhered to a good deal of parade-ground etiquette as was necessary for a manual designed to cover all aspects of military life and likely to be used mostly by a peacetime establishment. He decided to refer to companies as squadrons, a somewhat controversial point, and mandated intervals between them when arrayed in line. Cooke also noted that the senior captain should have his company placed on the right flank of that line, with the second-most-senior captain's company on the far left. The third most senior would be placed fifth from the right, the fourth most senior would be third from the right, and so on in a fully prescribed way. Such an order was true of infantry formations as well and was designed to place the most experienced officers at key points of the regimental line. But Cooke recognized that this carefully worked out scheme was not feasible if the regiment was suddenly called into action.[5]

Cooke divided each company into two, three, or four platoons, depending on its size. For example, if a company comprised eighty or more men, it should be divided into four platoons, each platoon numbered from right to left in the company line. Many of the cavalry maneuvers were based on sets of four men, and to encourage what Cooke called "companionship" among them, he noted that a height roll of the company could be maintained so men of similar height would be grouped together. The tallest were to be placed on the tallest horses and put on the immediate right and left of the center of the company line. The shortest were to be put on the flanks of the line. Cooke believed that placing men according to height would lead to "material assistance in the sets of fours, and to a feeling of responsibility of each to the others in conduct and bravery."[6]

The habitual formation of a regiment of ten companies was a mix of line and column. Four companies formed a line, with intervals between their flanks, while two companies formed in columns of platoons, one to the left rear of the left flank of that line and the other to the right rear of the line. The remaining four companies formed a line of columns of platoons to the rear of the formation. In this way the regimental commander had the option of using either line or column and had both flanks protected.[7]

The men started their training on foot, learning the basic infantry formations and maneuvers to instill a sense of discipline and how to move as a unit. When it came time to train with a horse, they first learned how to mount without a saddle and then how to saddle up their assigned animal. Cooke echoed the lessons taught by a number of authors who wrote treatises on how to deal with horses by urging recruits to handle their animals with care but firmness. "It is of the utmost importance that the horse never be allowed to take the initiative," Cooke wrote. It had to be trained to hold its head up and arch the neck, which the rider accomplished by deft use of the bit and reins. Control was vital to achieving some degree of uniformity in mounted formations and maneuvers. Also, in a melee or close mounted combat, a horse that did not respond readily to bit and reins could become unmanageable. Controlling the mount by the pressure of legs was also important. Another significant aspect of horse training was accustoming the animal to military sounds. Firing a pistol while riding, the playing of military bands, shouting orders, going through the manual of arms, and waving flags near it achieved this goal over time.[8]

"Nothing can be more important to the regularity and order, and often the success, of large bodies of cavalry than uniformity in the gait," asserted Cooke. Therefore, it was necessary for troopers to guide their horses so they would walk at the rate of three and three-fourths of a mile per hour, trot at seven and a half miles an hour, and gallop at ten miles an hour.

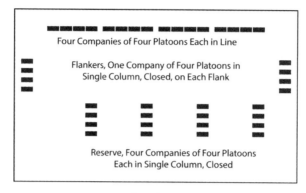

Four Companies of Four Platoons Each in Line

Flankers, One Company of Four Platoons in
Single Column, Closed, on Each Flank

Reserve, Four Companies of Four Platoons
Each in Single Column, Closed

Order of Battle.

This diagram represents a typical mix of line and column in
cavalry tactics of the Civil War. Commanders wanted to utilize
the advantages of both formations. The line served as the basic
formation to confront the enemy, while having reserves to the
rear in column allowed for quicker and easier maneuver to
deal either defensively or offensively with opponents. Flanking
protection also was provided in this basic order of battle.

Cooke, *Cavalry Tactics*, 1:10.

The best way to train for this was to accurately measure a space of half a
mile and practice the horse in walking along it in eight minutes, trotting
in four minutes, and galloping in three minutes.[9]

Formations grouped troopers into tight units for better control by officers. The interval between two mounted men in a rank was designated
as four inches from knee to knee. When in column, two types of formations—open or close—were available depending on the desired distance
between each line within it. For example, a company formed in a column
of platoons would have four lines, each line consisting of one platoon and
arrayed one behind the other in what could be called a single column. In
an open column the distance between each line was large enough so that
the men could deploy into a company line by wheeling to right or left
without hindrance. In a close column the lines within the column were
closed up very tightly to form the most compact column formation possible. In a double column the commander placed two of the four platoon
lines on the right and the other two on the left to double the frontage.[10]

Unlike the man in infantry formations and the cannon and limber in

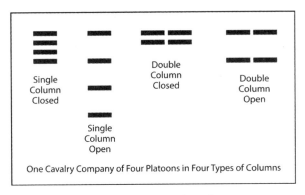

One Cavalry Company of Four Platoons in Four Types of Columns

One Cavalry Company in Column.

This diagram represents a cavalry company of four platoons ployed
in four differing columns. The single column has the company in
four platoon lines stacked one behind the other. In a closed single
column, each of the three following platoon lines are as close to the
one in front as the tactics would allow. In an open single column,
the three following platoon lines are at a distance that would allow
them to wheel to right or left without interfering with the platoon
in their front. Besides the single column, the other common type
was the double column. In this formation the company ployed two
platoons to the right and the other two to the left to double the unit's
frontage and shorten the length of the column, either closed or open.

Cooke, *Cavalry Tactics*, 1:40.

artillery formations, the basic unit in cavalry formations was the horse.
It, of course, was larger than the trooper. Cooke noted that its average
size could be set at one yard wide and three yards long. In other words,
when calculating how much area was needed to form a cavalry regiment,
one had to consider the space taken up by the animal. If, for example,
one mounted unit was to align itself on the formation of another unit, it
should form one horse length to the rear of it.[11]

The formations and maneuvers of cavalry were very similar in general
terms to those of infantry and artillery, except that mounted soldiers usually conducted the maneuvers in groups of fours rather than as platoons
or companies. The infantry manual recognized the concept of fours but
rarely used it, while the concept was irrelevant for artillery maneuvers.
The use of fours facilitated quick maneuvers on horseback.[12]

Like the infantry, cavalry could wheel a line or column either on a fixed or on a movable pivot. The former had one flank pinned to a spot while the rest of the formation moved in a right or left wheel to front a different direction than its original orientation. The latter had the entire formation moving but wheeling at the same time, a much more difficult maneuver with its lack of a pivot point.[13]

Other maneuvers included the direct march, which involved going straight ahead in line or column. The march by a flank meant moving the formation right or left, while the oblique allowed the formation to gain ground to right or left without a change of front. There actually were two ways to conduct an oblique maneuver. One was by the individual oblique march, with each man moving at an angle to right or left while the line or column remained intact. The other was the oblique march by troop, with each subdivision aiming to march at an angle to the right or left.[14]

Communication was accomplished by twenty-six bugle calls, with an additional nine calls for skirmish duty. But officers regularly communicated their orders verbally through a prescribed three-part method. The command of caution was "Attention," which represented "the signal to preserve immobility and to give attention" to the officer. The next part, called the preparatory command, "indicated the movement which is to be executed." Finally, the command of execution, the third part, was the signal to start the movement. "The tone of command should be animated, distinct, and of a loudness proportional to the troop which is commanded," wrote Cooke, and the execution commands "should be prolonged."[15]

By page forty-five of volume one, Cooke had completed his long introduction to cavalry training with many of the basic concepts. He then began the core training with the School of the Trooper, Dismounted, which detailed how to train a man by starting with one trooper at a time up to a squad of eight men drilling together. As with the artillery manual, Cooke cautioned instructors not to touch the trainee except to carefully correct mistakes. This was an effort to avoid physical coercion in the training regimen. Individual, dismounted training also involved saber exercises, drilling with the pistol, inspection of arms, and even target practice. Cooke also included an introduction to dismounted drill for the platoon, squadron, and regiment in this section, substituting "walk" and "trot," two

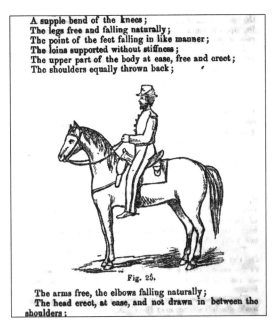

A supple bend of the knees;
The legs free and falling naturally;
The point of the feet falling in like manner;
The loins supported without stiffness;
The upper part of the body at ease, free and erect;
The shoulders equally thrown back;

Fig. 25.

The arms free, the elbows falling naturally;
The head erect, at ease, and not drawn in between the shoulders:

How to Sit a Horse.
The manuals minutely specified the proper way for
a trooper to sit on his horse to achieve what is often
termed a proper "seat" that not only looked martial but
also facilitated the use of the trooper's body for giving
signals to the horse about how and when to move.
Patten, *Cavalry Drill*, 32, fig. 25.

terms connected with mounted movements, for infantry terms such as
"quick time" and "double quick time."[16]

Next Cooke took trainees into the School of the Trooper, Mounted, in
order to make them "skillful in the management of their horses and arms."
Details concerning how to mount; how to hold the body while horsed;
and how to use reins alone, then legs, then reins and legs in unison when
moving the horse to all commands filled this section. Cooke urged the
instructor to have troopers change horses each day so they could become
accustomed to the peculiarities of different mounts.[17]

Graduating to the School of the Platoon, Mounted, trainees drilled
within a formation of twelve to twenty-four men, including two corpo-

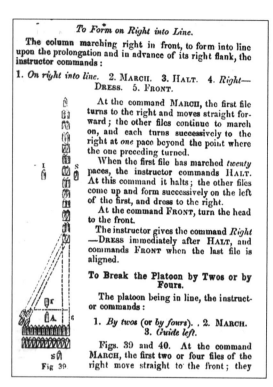

The figure content:

To Form on Right into Line.

The column marching right in front, to form into line upon the prolongation and in advance of its right flank, the instructor commands:

1. *On right into line.* 2. MARCH. 3. HALT. 4. *Right*—DRESS. 5. FRONT.

At the command MARCH, the first file turns to the right and moves straight forward; the other files continue to march on, and each turns successively to the right at *one* pace beyond the point where the one preceding turned.

When the first file has marched *twenty* paces, the instructor commands HALT. At this command it halts; the other files come up and form successively on the left of the first, and dress to the right.

At the command FRONT, turn the head to the front.

The instructor gives the command *Right*—DRESS immediately after HALT, and commands FRONT when the last file is aligned.

To Break the Platoon by Twos or by Fours.

The platoon being in line, the instructor commands:

1. *By twos* (or *by fours*). . 2. MARCH. 3. *Guide left.*

Figs. 39 and 40. At the command MARCH, the first two or four files of the right move straight to the front; they

Fig 39

To Break the Platoon by Twos or by Fours.
This maneuver allowed the platoon to go
from line to column in a particular way.
Patten, *Cavalry Drill*, 61, fig. 39.

rals. Here they learned how to count off fours from right to left while in line and began to work on the complicated process of wheeling, each man looking to right and left to gauge how slow he should go and how to adjust his progress to maintain alignment. More sophisticated and demanding saber practice appeared in this section. Cooke advised the construction of a track ninety yards long and at least thirty yards wide fixed with several posts from which were suspended blocks of wood to simulate an enemy saber, lance, or bayonet. Balls of hay covered by rawhide or canvass simulated the heads of enemy troops for the practice of cutting and slashing.[18]

In the School of the Squadron, Mounted, Cooke described formations and maneuvers that were "the base of the evolutions of the regiment."

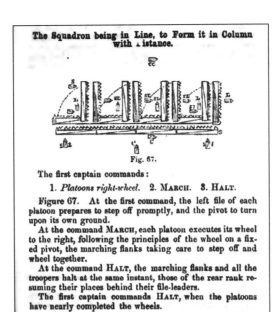

The Squadron being in Line, to Form it in Column with ⊥istance.

Fig. 67.

The first captain commands:

1. *Platoons right-wheel.* 2. MARCH. 3. HALT.

Figure 67. At the first command, the left file of each platoon prepares to step off promptly, and the pivot to turn upon its own ground.

At the command MARCH, each platoon executes its wheel to the right, following the principles of the wheel on a fixed pivot, the marching flanks taking care to step off and wheel together.

At the command HALT, the marching flanks and all the troopers halt at the same instant, those of the rear rank resuming their places behind their file-leaders.

The first captain commands HALT, when the platoons have nearly completed the wheels.

**The Squadron Being in Line to
Form It in Column with Distance.**

This maneuver allowed the cavalry company
to go from line to column by wheeling.

Patten, *Cavalry Drill*, 105, fig. 67.

When a line ployed into a column, either the right or left of that line wound up at the head of the column; as Cooke phrased it, "columns are *right in front* when the subdivisions originally on the right in line are in front; and *left in front* when those of the original left are in front." It was a general rule that when the right was in the lead, then the formation guided on the left as it moved. This meant that as the formation moved forward, all were to incline to the left to keep the formation solid and aligned properly. Otherwise it would loosen with consequent loss of control by the officers. If, however, the left was in the lead, then the formation guided on the right as it moved. Cooke pointed out that if the men understood that this was the default method of moving, there would be few problems. If the commander wanted to change it, he had to issue a command to that effect.[19]

Cooke stressed flexibility. He wanted every platoon to "march or fight,

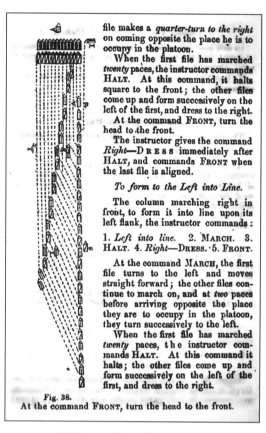

file makes a *quarter-turn to the right* on coming opposite the place he is to occupy in the platoon.

When the first file has marched *twenty* paces, the instructor commands HALT. At this command, it halts square to the front; the other files come up and form successively on the left of the first, and dress to the right.

At the command FRONT, turn the head to the front.

The instructor gives the command *Right*—D R E S S immediately after HALT, and commands FRONT when the last file is aligned.

To form to the Left into Line.

The column marching right in front, to form it into line upon its left flank, the instructor commands:

1. *Left into line.* 2. MARCH. 3. HALT. 4. *Right*—DRESS. 5. FRONT.

At the command MARCH, the first file turns to the left and moves straight forward; the other files continue to march on, and at *two* paces before arriving opposite the place they are to occupy in the platoon, they turn successively to the left.

When the first file has marched *twenty* paces, t h e instructor commands HALT. At this command it halts; the other files come up and form successively on the left of the first, and dress to the right.

Fig. 38.
At the command FRONT, turn the head to the front.

To Form to the Left into Line.
This maneuver allowed the column
of cavalry to deploy into a line.
Patten, *Cavalry Drill,* 60, fig. 38.

equally, whether at the right or the left of any other platoon," and to "be accustomed to feel equally confident in sudden formations in every direction." In fact, there was more flexibility in cavalry formations and maneuvers than in infantry and roughly an equal amount of flexibility in artillery evolutions. The horse infused a great deal of difference in mounted operations; cavalry often found itself engaged in highly mobile movements with a need to quickly change directions and formations. Like all good manual authors, Cooke recognized this and worked it into training with

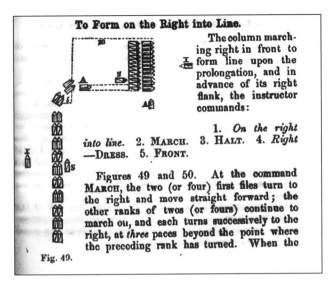

To Form on the Right into Line.

The column marching right in front to form line upon the prolongation, and in advance of its right flank, the instructor commands:

1. *On the right into line.* 2. MARCH. 3. HALT. 4. *Right* —DRESS. 5. FRONT.

Figures 49 and 50. At the command MARCH, the two (or four) first files turn to the right and move straight forward; the other ranks of twos (or fours) continue to march on, and each turns successively to the right, at *three* paces beyond the point where the preceding rank has turned. When the

Fig. 49.

To Form on the Right into Line.
This was how a column could deploy to the
right into line without wheeling.
Patten, *Cavalry Drill*, 67, fig. 49.

use of fours and platoons as subunits of companies in order to ensure maximum flexibility in evolutions.[20]

While in the School of the Squadron, Mounted, Cooke's manual had the men exercise the charge in line, in column, and as skirmishers. The column formation for the charge was open, with substantial distances between individual lines within the column. As skirmishers, the mounted troopers were to disperse "and direct themselves in couples upon the point each wishes to attack" while keeping in sight of their officers. When charging as a unit rather than skirmishers, the formation was to start at a walk, then shift to trot after twenty paces, to gallop after sixty paces, and finally charge at eighty paces. Only at the last were they to point their sabers at the enemy. Cooke told instructors to halt the formation after it had charged no more than sixty paces so as not to overstress the horses in training. He recommended charging as skirmishers if attacking artillery or pursuing a broken enemy, but it was all important, after a frenzied attack, to regroup the survivors for further action.[21]

Cavalry skirmished for the same purpose that infantry did—to prevent the enemy from approaching the main line too closely, to find information about the opposing position, and to contest the enemy advance long enough to allow the main line to prepare. Typically two companies skirmished to cover the regimental front, with four-pace intervals between each man. Cooke advised that the two flank companies of the regimental line be sent out to skirmish, one covering the left wing and the other the right wing. The colonel usually appointed the senior captain of those two companies to command the skirmish line, but he could appoint a field officer to do so.[22]

After explaining the basics of formations and maneuvers in volume one, Cooke moved on to the evolutions of a regiment in volume two. How a regiment formed and maneuvered was much like that of a company, so there was more space now for him to offer recommendations on how to use those formations and maneuvers. In this Cooke differed a good deal from the infantry and artillery manuals, which contained much less of this sort of commentary. For example, he favored the double column over the single column for ease of maneuvering. Cooke also explained a formation typical of cavalry service, which was to form each company in a column and then align each column into "a line of squadron columns," mixing line and column within the regimental formation.[23]

Cooke liked the versatility of echelon formations, which lent themselves "very readily" to attack or defense "in every direction." They also could allow units to maneuver "with great simplicity." This formation protected the flank and could be used to threaten the enemy's flank as well. "Échelons being contiguous and unmasked, they with advantage follow up a successful charge, or cover one which is repulsed. If successful, whilst the rest of the enemy's line is engaged with you, the successful échelon attacks him in flank or rear."[24]

The charge received a good deal of attention in Cooke's commentary. He advised the commander to place no more than one-third of his men in the first line and form his supporting force in squadron columns 300–400 yards to the rear. The reserve should be "in close column" at a similar distance behind the support. He recommended starting the charge "within 200 paces of the enemy at the trot, then galloping with increasing speed, the charge is commanded at 50 or 60 yards." Cooke urged troopers to

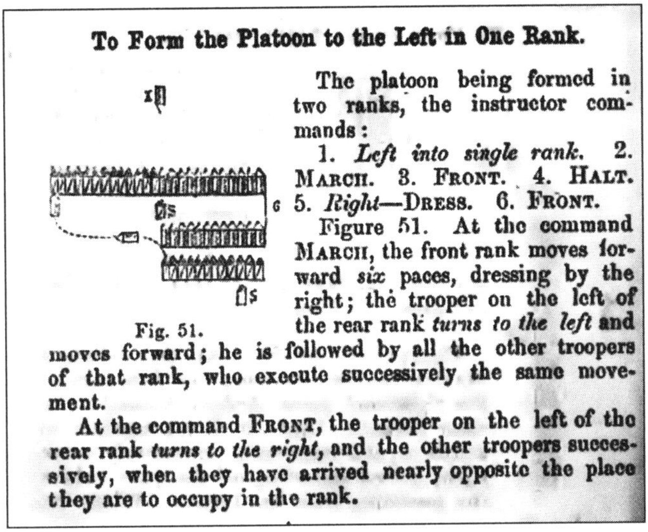

To Form the Platoon to the Left in One Rank.

The platoon being formed in two ranks, the instructor commands:

1. *Left into single rank.* 2. MARCH. 3. FRONT. 4. HALT. 5. *Right*—DRESS. 6. FRONT.

Figure 51. At the command MARCH, the front rank moves forward *six* paces, dressing by the right; the trooper on the left of the rear rank *turns to the left* and moves forward; he is followed by all the other troopers of that rank, who execute successively the same movement.

At the command FRONT, the trooper on the left of the rear rank *turns to the right,* and the other troopers successively, when they have arrived nearly opposite the place they are to occupy in the rank.

To Form the Platoon to the Left in One Rank.

Given the heated arguments over whether one rank or two ranks were better for cavalry lines, tactical manuals provided information about how to form both ways. This diagram shows how one could transform a two-rank formation into a one-rank formation.

Patten, *Cavalry Drill*, 68, fig. 51.

consider the condition of their mounts during a charge. "Crowding and pressure, when the horse is exerting his powers, impedes him, and makes him uncontrollable; every jostle or rub diminishes his strength." Horses should not "arrive exhausted, or even distressed and blown" when contact is made. Charging in skirmish formation eliminated this jostling because of the intervals between each horse. It also had "the advantages of great freedom of motion and will in the troopers; [and] of less loss from fire."[25]

Cooke's manual offered the best cavalry training thus far in America. It was a well-considered guide to the intricacies of mounted formations and maneuvers with recommendations about how to use them. The only controversial aspect was that Cooke mandated a single-rank formation, breaking from the historic tradition of at least two ranks. This hindered the regard accorded the manual from many cavalry officers who favored two ranks during the Civil War.[26]

While Cooke's product remained the officially sanctioned cavalry manual, Civil War officers had a number of handbooks available to supplement it. These were written by other cavalry officers and often were heavily based on Cooke's manual or other handbooks. They often contained the personal opinions of the author.

The major handbooks included Capt. Louis E. Nolan's *Cavalry: Its History and Tactics*, originally published in 1853. Nolan, a captain in the 15th Hussars of the British service, was killed in the famous charge at Balaklava in 1854 during the Crimean War. His book had gone through its third edition by the time of the Civil War. Nolan broke from rigid concepts of formations and maneuvers, arguing that it was useless to worry about whether a formation was right in front or left in front when in column. He asserted one had to make quick decisions and seize the moment. "What is easiest is generally best in the long run," he concluded. Cavalry-on-cavalry fighting was the most difficult because the enemy could quickly take advantage of one mistake. With infantry or artillery, the opponent was relatively slow, so a mistake would be less dangerous. A thirty-five-year-old captain at the time, Nolan believed in the shock value of a mounted column, "but the *burst*, the charge itself, must always be reserved till within 50 yards."[27]

George B. McClellan also was in his mid-thirties when his *Regulations and Instructions for the Field Service of the U.S. Cavalry in Time of War* appeared in print early in 1862. It derived much of its content from the report he had produced as part of the Delafield Commission during the Crimean War, with substantial chunks from the official cavalry manual. McClellan paid less attention to spectacular subjects such as the charge and much more to administration, organization, scouting, and outpost duty. His coverage was comprehensive, much more like a manual than a mere handbook.[28]

English-born Jean Roemer lived a varied life in Europe before coming to the United States. He moved with his family as a child to the German state of Hanover and later to the Netherlands, where he participated with Dutch forces in the Belgian revolt against Dutch rule in 1830–31. Later, Roemer became a cavalry captain in the army of the Netherlands before moving in 1846 to the United States, where he became a professor at the New York Free Academy two years later. Eventually, he wrote eight books, including a history of the English language. Roemer's cavalry book, published in New York in 1863, is filled with comments on mounted operations. For example, he argued strenuously that the widespread adoption of rifle muskets by the 1860s did not relegate cavalry to a marginal role on the battlefield. Roemer pointed out that all major European armies had either maintained or enlarged their mounted force since the introduction of the rifle.[29]

Another handbook by an American, James A. Congdon, was more widely cited than Roemer's. A major of the 12th Pennsylvania Cavalry—he dated the preface April 22, 1864—Congdon based his short text largely on personal experience during the war, filling up the rest of the book with extracts from the cavalry tactics, the articles of war, and the acts of Congress relating to cavalry service. He sought to provide a handy guide for noncommissioned officers and privates about a wide range of duties associated with mounted life in the army, including horse care, daily responsibilities, soldier health, care of arms, and how to conduct oneself in combat.[30]

None of these handbooks published in the North were readily available to Confederate cavalrymen, so a handful of handbooks were published in Southern cities during the war. Col. J. Lucius Davis of the 10th Virginia Cavalry compiled *The Trooper's Manual; or, Tactics for Light Dragoons and Mounted Riflemen*, published in Richmond during the spring of 1861. A graduate of the U.S. Military Academy and prewar regular officer, Davis admitted that his book was "a cheap, plain, brief compendium of Cavalry Tactics" that he "abridged and arranged" from other sources.[31]

Among the books mined by Davis for his short compendium was that by Dabney Herndon Maury, a Virginia-born graduate of the U.S. Military Academy experienced in combat during the Mexican War and an officer in the Regiment of Mounted Rifles during the 1850s. Maury wrote *Skirmish Drill for Mounted Troops*, originally published in 1859, which the War Department adopted as a supplementary manual to the *Cavalry Tactics* of 1841, although only for the Mounted Rifles. In adopting the book, Secretary of War John B. Floyd specified that the one-rank formation, as recommended by Maury, be used in service against Native American forces, while the two-rank formation remain general policy for all other mounted operations.[32]

George Washington Patten, born in Rhode Island and a graduate of the U.S. Military Academy, had seen service during the Seminole Wars and in Mexico before writing *Cavalry Drill and Sabre Exercise,* which was published in Richmond in 1862. He pitched it to "the tyro in military knowledge" so "the intelligent private" could "fully understand the various movements in which he takes a part." Patten offered clear and explicit information, such as when noting that the distance between two ranks in a line was only two feet when closed and six yards when open. He described the two types of oblique maneuvers as one "by an individual movement of each man" and the other as "the movement, at the same time, of each of the sub-divisions of a troop in line." Patten explained how to go from two ranks to one and how to form columns of one, twos, and fours. To keep the regiment aligned during a direct movement forward, each trooper should "feel lightly the boot of the man on the side of the guide, and march at an equal gait" with him. If they pushed too much toward the end of the regimental line, the last man was instructed to extend his arm forward to indicate that everyone should ease off until he lowered his arm again.[33]

The Confederate government never officially adopted a tactics manual, but Joseph Wheeler wrote perhaps the closest thing to it. Georgia born and a graduate of the U.S. Military Academy in 1859, he served in the Regiment of Mounted Rifles on the frontier before the outbreak of war led him into Confederate service and successive command of a cavalry brigade, division, and corps. Wheeler's *Revised System of Cavalry Tactics for the Use of the Cavalry and Mounted Infantry* was a mix of tactics manual and handbook. Out of 432 pages, at least 220 of them were taken in a body from Cooke's manual, with attribution to the original author. But there are at least seven other sections that seem to be Wheeler's original writing, covering skirmish drill for mounted troops and including discussions of reconnaissance, cavalry organization, picket duty, and bugle signals. Wheeler included excerpts from Polybius about Roman cavalry and brought in examples of mounted operations from Napoleonic battles. He strongly advocated the use of one rank rather than two.[34]

All of these books, North and South, were theoretically to inform and instruct cavalrymen, although not all of those men could find copies. Lt. William W. Blackford commanded a Virginia militia company called the

Washington Mounted Rifles in 1859. He could not find a cavalry tactics book, so read the infantry tactics compiled by William J. Hardee in 1855. After studying it "intently," he drilled his mounted troops through the winter of 1860–61. The company became part of the 1st Virginia Cavalry after the secession of the state.[35]

Cavalry Doctrine

The tactical manuals and handbooks were especially strong in detailing the formations and maneuvers of horse service from the individual trooper to the regimental level, and that regimental level could easily be transposed onto brigade- and division-level formations and maneuvers. There was a good amount of advice sprinkled among these manuals and handbooks as well, although that did not amount to a comprehensive doctrine for cavalry operations. In fact, this was the only area in which the instructional material was weak. There was, in short, no real cavalry "doctrine," if one defines that term as a well-rounded theoretical discussion officially sanctioned by the War Department of either side.

But that does not mean that the Civil War soldier lacked advice about how cavalry should behave in the field. A number of commentators offered their opinions, and there was general consensus on at least one key element of cavalry operations—the need to keep the arm highly mobile and highly aggressive in the field. Ironically, while this was vitally important, it was by no means all that cavalry should have been doing. Mounted troops had more roles to play in operations than infantrymen, but the doctrine, such as it was, failed to focus on many of them. For example, the mounted arm's role as the eyes and ears of the army was arguably its most important responsibility, and yet commentators tended to ignore it. Outpost and picket duty simply was not glamorous, and commentators took it for granted rather than discuss it in detail.

Joseph Hooker provided a good reason why the doctrinaires should have paid more attention to outpost and picket work. The general lamented the fact that he could gain little information about the enemy due to Confederate screening of their position in mid-June 1863. "You may depend upon it," he told President Lincoln, "we can never discover the whereabouts of the enemy, to divine his intentions, so long as he fills the country with a cloud of cavalry. We must break through that and find him."[36]

While largely ignoring outpost and picket duty, the doctrinaires paid only slightly more attention to how cavalry should closely support infantry on the battlefield. This also was a relatively mundane task that seemed to offer little hope of decisive effect on the course of events. "The cavalry should be distributed in echelon on the wings and at the centre, on favorable ground," noted the *Revised United States Army Regulations* of 1861 (with amendments and changes of 1863). What it should do after that, whether and when to attack or defend, was left up to circumstances and individual choice.[37]

But when it came to independent operations, breaking cavalry's tether to infantry, commentators crafted a vibrant and appealing if unofficial doctrine for the mounted arm. "The success of cavalry manoeuvers depends on the rapidity, steadiness, and boldness with which they are executed," wrote Wheeler. "Cavalry cannot, like infantry, rely upon fire-arms as a potent support; neither can it stand firmly and defend a position, against an aggressor." Its only strength lay in its horses, trained to act in unison at the control of equally trained riders. In short, the main strength of the mounted arm was mobility, which lent itself to shock action. "Cavalry has therefore but one system of attack and defence, which consists in throwing itself rapidly upon the enemy."[38]

Attitude, in other words, was the key. For commentators, the mounted charge was the ultimate experience of cavalry warfare, amounting to a cult within the cavalry subculture of Civil War America. "The charge is the decisive action of cavalry," asserted Cooke. "Its opportunities pass in moments. Its successful commander must have a *cavalry eye* and rapid decision." He urged mounted commanders to attack at the drop of a hat and "with the greatest velocity and regularity possible; in speed and order there must be a mutual sacrifice," but the commander should try to "attain the maximum of each." In other words, a quick and determined but disorderly attack would have better chances of success than a delayed but orderly charge. Writers also urged commanders, after breaking the first enemy line, to seek the second line and force the defeated fragments of the first into it "until they are thoroughly disorganized." But as Cooke noted, commanders should always reform their formation after every success so as to maintain control over the flow of events to follow.[39]

Doctrinaires sought to instill a determined spirit into officers and enlisted men alike. "Cavalry should never surrender," declared Cooke. "If overpowered or surrounded it can cut its way [out] by charging at full speed, in close column." This was not just an American conceit. Louis E. Nolan used similar language when he penned his handbook. "Cavalry never surrenders, under any circumstances, in the open field, but must always attempt to cut its way through, or, by scattering, elude pursuit." This spirit of defiance, mobility, and aggression was shared by all well-developed cavalry forces globally. It derived from the mounted nature of cavalry service and underwrote the distinctive pride of the mounted arm.[40]

Union and Confederate cavalrymen accepted this as a doctrine of mounted service. They looked on outpost and picket duty as chores, enjoyed long raids into contested territory, and thrilled at the prospect of mounted charges against enemy cavalry. Officers agreed that making snap decisions (and hopefully the right ones too) was important. They also believed that attacking rather than retreating or standing on the defensive was the correct course of action.

Training

Cavalrymen agreed that their training was more comprehensive, demanding, and longer lasting than that in the infantry and artillery. Foot soldiers largely concentrated on mastering the formations and maneuvers associated with infantry operations and spent little time on how to use their weapons. Artillerists devoted most of their training to managing their crew-served weapons and secondarily learned the limited formations and maneuvers associated with their arm. But cavalrymen learned the full range of foot drill, the various mounted formations and maneuvers, how to manage and care for their horses, and how to use not one but three weapons while on foot and on horseback.[41]

The training proceeded in stages that were mandated in part by the manual but often because horses were issued weeks or even months after the regiment assembled. Until receiving mounts, the men learned foot drill and saber use. McClellan noted that training in infantry formations and maneuvers should proceed only insofar as it instilled a sense of discipline, carriage, and control in the recruits. In other words, it was something like a basic training in how to act like a soldier. The other advantage, and it was a major one, was that extensive foot drilling enabled the cavalryman to fight dismounted when called on to do so.[42]

How much the experience of serving in prewar mounted militia units prepared officers and men for their intensive training in national service was an open question. William Douglas Hamilton, colonel of the 9th Ohio Cavalry, had two militia officers in his regiment and noted that what they had learned before Fort Sumter "was of no value in our war." On the other hand, Alfred N. Duffié, who had served as a noncommissioned officer in the French dragoons and hussars during the 1850s, acted as "the best regimental cavalry drill-master" when he commanded the 1st Rhode Island Cavalry.[43]

Regimental commanders were responsible for the instruction of their units. Col. Owen P. Ransom of the 1st Ohio Cavalry, a prewar regular, required all officers to acquire a copy of the manual and attend officer school. Company commanders were required to establish schools for their noncommissioned officers. Lt. William H. Harrison recalled that the 2nd U.S. Cavalry officer school involved an effective way to demonstrate primary tactics. "We had blocks representing the different units of formation, officers, file closer, platoons, squadrons and regiments" to graphically show what the manual described. Capt. Luman Harris Tenney of the 2nd Ohio Cavalry felt embarrassed by officer school. He made "several ignorant blunders" and found it vexing "to make mistakes. I wish I knew more. I am so ignorant on all subjects." But Tenney really enjoyed the discussions that flowed from class participation.[44]

Cavalrymen entered a new and distinctive phase of their training when they received their horses. In the 1st Maine Cavalry, most of the mounts had never been ridden and most of the recruits had never sat on a horse. This led to a wild time. "There was kicking and rearing," wrote Edward P. Tobie, "and running and jumping, and lying down and falling down, on the part of the horses, and swearing and yelling, and getting thrown and being kicked, and getting hurt and sore in various ways, by the men." Even after the initial barrier between man and mount was broken, the recruits continued to struggle with their new mode of mobility. "There was crowding in the ranks, and getting out of place and striving to get back into place, and pushing forward and hanging back, and going backwards and sideways, and all ways but the right way."[45]

If time allowed, the best way to accustom horses to military service was by stages. In the 15th New York Cavalry, which organized in the summer of 1863, the process began with bareback riding "for several days." Then a blanket was added, to be followed by the saddle, which caused "the agony" endured by the horse to increase. After a few days of getting adjusted to the saddle, stirrups were added. It was a long process and trying for the men as well as for the horses.[46]

Acclimating horses to military sounds was next. Mock battles involving artillery fire or shooting carbines and pistols near them was the typical way to do this necessary task. "I never thought that horses would learn so fast," commented John H. Black as he praised the smooth process of sound acclimation in the 12th Pennsylvania Cavalry. "I delight in drilling with horses and would not on any condition be in an Infantry regiment." The 5th Iowa Cavalry took this a step further and practiced charging toward friendly infantry and artillery while the defenders were firing blank cartridges. Infantry also advanced toward stationary cavalry formations "with muskets & fixed bayonets."[47]

The next stage of horse training involved practicing jumps over obstacles. Officers found "low fences and narrow ravines and gutters" for the recruits, who urged their often reluctant mounts to jump over them. In the 1st Massachusetts Cavalry, the horses tended to be shy about jumping over ditches and often balked, sometimes causing their riders to fall, but they had little hesitation about jumping over piles of timber.[48]

The process of training with horses was a two-way street. Not only did the horses have to adjust to having humans on their backs and then to become familiar with sounds and obstacles, but many of the recruits also had to learn how to work with a horse from scratch. Even farm boys who had grown up with horses had to learn from the start how to mount them the military way. Most of these men "thought that to mount a horse was to climb on its back in any manner that suited their notion," wrote Chaplain James R. Bowen of the 1st New York Dragoons. But the army taught them that "there was a right way and a wrong way of doing" it. The manual also instructed recruits about the proper way to apply bridle and saddles and to pack belongings on their horses. Recruits learned not to use both hands to guide the horse, as was typical of farmers, but to use only the left hand so the right could be free to use weapons. The army also frowned on guiding by the voice. The men were not to say "Get up" or cluck at the horse but to only use the bit, spur, and knee pressure. If anyone forgot themselves and did any of these forbidden methods, Col. Alfred Gibbs shamed them by yelling, "'Here, you old market woman, stop that.'" Anyone who let their elbows fly about while trotting were called pump-handle lubbers, and those who tried to ride a horse as if they were a circus performer landed up for the night in the regimental guardhouse.[49]

Once all the basics of riding and horse control were mastered, recruits drilled from small mounted units of fours and platoons of eight men to "marching and wheeling in sections of twenty-four or in company front." Training became more difficult as it progressed to larger units. Keeping proper intervals between individuals became more important as well. If in wheeling the end of the moving line failed to keep proper pace and interval, it often caused jamming in the middle of the line, and men "would get the legs almost crushed off them between the horses."[50]

In fact, accidents and injuries were a common adjunct of mounted training. "There was some wild riding," recalled the historian of the 3rd Ohio Cavalry. "One horse was killed, one man's leg broken, one officer's horse bolted with him and ran wildly all the way back to camp." A man of the 6th New York Cavalry was so injured when his horse threw him that he never fully recovered throughout his three years of service.[51]

Despite the relative danger, troopers had to persist in mounted drilling. Cavalry doctrine urged each man to "consider his horse as part of himself, and the perfect management of the horse cannot be learned either in schools, or in a few weeks of practice," according to Henry L. Scott in his *Military Dictionary*. If a cavalryman did not persist in daily riding, "both horse and man [would] return to their natural state, and such mounted men cease to be efficient."[52]

Cooke urged a hefty dose of target practice in firearms for cavalry training, providing detailed instructions on how to set up targets. In neither infantry nor artillery instruction was target practice so stressed or so minutely detailed. While artillerists engaged in substantial practice firing during their training period, infantry did very little of it. Col. T. Lyle Dickey organized a target shooting competition in his 4th Illinois Cavalry. The men painted a man-sized board to resemble an enemy and placed it 200 yards away. Thirty troopers of each battalion were selected to compete, and officers chose the method of firing. The contestants of the 1st Battalion entirely missed the board when they fired by volley, and only seven men of the 2nd Battalion hit it. The 3rd Battalion won, although only eleven of the thirty contestants hit the target.[53]

Everyone found that learning how to use a saber was the most difficult part of weapons training. In some regiments it was even looked upon as ridiculous and unnecessary. The 1st Maine Cavalry initially had no sabers, so the men used wooden lathes. "The exercise was looked upon very generally as a farce, was laughed at by outsiders, and was discontinued after a very short time." Col. Washington L. Elliott arranged for a German fencing master named Graupner to teach his 2nd Iowa Cavalry use of the saber. Officers paid him $5 each and enlisted men were charged $2.50. Apparently, the Iowans got their money's worth, for the regimental historian concluded that Graupner "was a master of the science, and under his instructions the majority of the regiment acquired a good degree of efficiency in the use of the saber."[54]

The saber exercise involved mastering the art of hitting an enemy all around the periphery of the man on the defensive. It included thrusts or cuts to right, left, front, and rear. The word "cut" referred to swinging the saber onto the target from above, while the "thrust," also called "point," involved stabbing the target. The third category was "parry," a defensive posture to fend off blows from an enemy. "Moulinet" was a circular motion of the sword meant to prevent an opponent from reaching you with his own cut or thrust. The saber exercise always began on foot, but the real test came when mounted, for that was how such hand-to-hand combat took place.[55]

"How my wrist ached when I came in after two hours' saber exercise!" wrote Stanton P. Allen of the 1st Massachusetts Cavalry. The right and left moulinet "was what took the tuck out of me." Twenty-five years later Allen still dreamed of it. "I go through the 'right and left moulinet' and

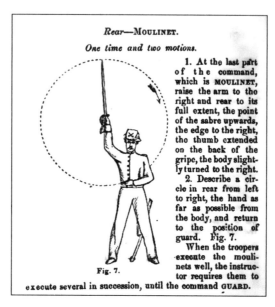

Rear—MOULINET.

One time and two motions.

1. At the last part of the command, which is MOULINET, raise the arm to the right and rear to its full extent, the point of the sabre upwards, the edge to the right, the thumb extended on the back of the gripe, the body slightly turned to the right.
2. Describe a circle in rear from left to right, the hand as far as possible from the body, and return to the position of guard. Fig. 7.
When the troopers execute the moulinets well, the instructor requires them to execute several in succession, until the command GUARD.

Fig. 7.

Rear Moulinet.
The moulinet, a circular movement of the saber, was a
defensive move to ward off the blows of an opponent.
It could be deployed to the rear, side, or front.
Patten, *Cavalry Drill*, 18, fig. 7.

'cut and parry' movements in my sleep. And the old pain in the wrist and shoulder is there too."[56]

Some came to believe that the saber was the key weapon of mounted service and that training in it was crucial for effectiveness. But others criticized saber training, especially when the regimental commander did not believe in the weapon. Frederick Whittaker of the 6th New York Cavalry was among the critics. Historian Stephen Z. Starr noted that a survey of more than seventy Union cavalry unit histories revealed that almost all referred to saber drill. Starr concluded that it reflected an assumption that the saber would be the major weapon of mounted service.[57]

Weapons training often culminated in sham battles, probably more often than in the infantry and artillery. Extensive mock engagements, for example, took place at Benton Barracks just south of St. Louis in the fall of 1861. They began with contests between a cavalry regiment and an infantry regiment and continued daily as the artillery joined in. Sham

Left—Cut.
One time and three motions.

Fig. 17.   Fig. 16.

1. At the last part of the command, which is CUT, turn the head to the left, raise the sabre, the arm extended to the right, the hand in quarte, and as high as the head, the point higher than the hand. Fig. 16.
2. Cut diagonally to the left.
3. Return to the position of guard.

Left Cut.
An offensive move, the left cut was an effort to disable an opponent on the left.
Patten, *Cavalry Drill*, 22, figs. 16, 17.

In quarte—PARRY.
One time and two motions.

1. At the last part of the command, which is PARRY, turn the hand and carry it quickly to the front and left, the nails upward, the edge to the left, the point inclined to the front, as high as the eyes, and in the direction of the left shoulder; the thumb extended on the back of the gripe, and resting against the guard. (Fig. 20.)
2. Return to the position of guard.

Fig. 20.

For the head—PARRY.
One time and two motions.

1. At the last part of the command, which is PARRY, raise the sabre quickly above the head, the arm nearly extended, the edge upward, the point to the left, and about *six* inches higher than the hand. Fig. 21.
2. Return to the position of guard.

Against infantry right—PARRY.
One time and three motions.

1. At the last part of the command, which is PARRY, turn the head to the right, throwing back the right shoulder, raise the sabre, the arm extended to the right and rear, the point upward, the hand in tierce, the thumb extended .

Fig. 21.

2

In-Quarte Parry and For-the-Head Parry.
The parry was a defensive move and could be adapted to protect any part of the trooper's body.
Patten, *Cavalry Drill*, 25, figs. 20, 21.

battles and large-scale movements by mounted regiments were exciting affairs, invoking the real sensory experiences of an engagement.[58]

When John H. Black joined the 12th Pennsylvania Cavalry, he was told it would take three months to train raw recruits for mounted service. That estimate was not far from the truth. On completing its organization, the 2nd Iowa Cavalry shifted from Davenport to Benton Barracks to begin its training on December 17, 1861. After two months of intense work, it left for field service on February 17, 1862. But other units spent much more than two months learning how to soldier on horseback.[59]

Training took place much the same in the Confederate cavalry as in the Federal service. At the start of his handbook, J. Lucius Davis states, "all American Cavalry should be well trained on foot in the Light Infantry exercises" and should prepare to use its weapons "mostly on foot." That was an extreme view of dismounted combat; few cavalrymen North or South would have agreed that the majority of their fighting should be on foot. But Confederate horsemen theoretically embarked on a fairly well-rounded training regimen to incorporate all types of combat into their repertoire.[60]

But just how far the Southern cavalry went to fulfill a thorough training regimen is open to question. Maj. Gen. Stephen D. Lee, who commanded the mounted force in the Department of Mississippi and Eastern Louisiana early in 1864, was highly critical. He found it very difficult to instill a sense of order and discipline in his mounted units because of what he viewed as the slipshod and unsystematic way in which they had been trained. On the other end of the spectrum, Chaplain Robert Franklin Bunting thought the men of the 8th Texas Cavalry "perform[ed] in a very scientific manner" at their foot drill, skirmish drill, and review.[61]

The handbooks, however, tried to instill a proper sense of what was to be imparted to Southern recruits. Davis warned that experienced horsemen might become impatient at the step-by-step nature of instruction in how to lead, saddle, mount, and control a horse, but it was important to do these things intelligently rather than intuitively. The most vital point was that the horse should be guided by legs and arms, leaving the hands free to handle weapons.[62]

As in the Union mounted arm, the quality of Confederate officers was an important factor in unit effectiveness. The 1st North Carolina Cavalry experienced "severe drill & discipline" under Col. Robert Ransom, a graduate of the U.S. Military Academy, from June until October 1861. But the 2nd North Carolina Cavalry "did not have the same thorough military training" because its first commander, Col. Samuel B. Spruill, was a political appointee without army experience. "This made a great difference," wrote William P. Roberts, who commanded the 2nd late in the war. "I addressed myself to discipline" in the winter of 1864–65, he reported, "and there was drill and dismounted dress parade every day."[63]

Many Confederate cavalrymen trained in carbine, pistol, and saber use. In the 1st Mississippi Cavalry, this was done both on foot and mounted. In the 8th Confederate Cavalry, which was organized after the Battle of Shiloh by consolidating six Alabama and four Mississippi companies, training was just as intense late in the war as early in its service. "We drill almost incessantly under" Wheeler's guidance, wrote Capt. George Knox Miller in April 1864. Wheeler had the men practice against dummies made of old clothes stuffed with straw and positioned in a line 100 yards long like infantrymen. Sixty yards behind this line were Confederate dismounted cavalrymen with blank cartridges in their carbines. A mounted line charged and overran the dummies, after which the dismounted men fired a volley at the horsemen and retreated. It was "dangerous and fatiguing" for the mounted men, and "several were unhorsed and seriously bruised."[64]

Wheeler also stressed saber exercise in his handbook. He advised starting with the moulinet as a way to limber up the arms and wrists. "Skill and suppleness" rather than brute force were the keys to effective saber work. Wheeler also cautioned the trooper not to hit his horse with the weapon when going through the exercise while mounted. He advocated the use of thrusts rather than cuts: "They require less force, and their result is more prompt, sure, and decisive. They should be directed quickly *home* to the body of the adversary, the sabre being held with the full grasp, the thumb pressing against the guard in the direction of the blade."[65]

While infantry and artillery also underwent some degree of refresher training, it was more persistent in the cavalry arm. Brig. Gen. Samuel W. Ferguson's Brigade underwent intensive drill during March 1864 by concentrating on the basics. It consisted mostly of "the movements by fours and the formation of lines of Battle in the different directions at the several gaits and the movements in line." This was the kind of drill that green troopers underwent, even though Ferguson's men had seen service since early in the war.[66]

North and South shared much in the cavalry-training experience. One of the basic aspects was the fact that good training instilled a sense of discipline and self-control that proved vital to survival on the battlefield. When Stonewall Jackson's attack on the Eleventh Corps at Chancellorsville engulfed the 17th Pennsylvania Cavalry, Col. Josiah H. Kellogg averted panic by drilling the men within sight and sound of the battle. "He wheeled us by squadron, first to the right, next to the left, advancing then by regimental front," recalled Adj. James Albert Clark. "These swift evolutions so occupied the minds of the men that they had no time to think of aught else."[67]

If anyone wondered why it was necessary to spend several months breaking in green recruits to mounted service, they only had to ponder the experience of the 17th Pennsylvania Cavalry at Chancellorsville. A knee-jerk response to an order from a trusted officer returned a gaggle of confused men into an effective military unit. Just as importantly, the horses had to be trained in their unrequested duties. Man and animal were a military team, and both had to be willing to obey when called on. Proper training based on precepts laid down in the manuals and handbooks, which in turn were based on centuries of deep experience in Europe, was the foundation of cavalry effectiveness.

4

FORMATIONS AND MANEUVERS

Civil War cavalry leaders had a fulsome body of literature about the complicated system of formations and maneuvers and utilized it in a vigorous training regimen. How well did troopers North and South fulfill the directives contained in those manuals and handbooks while operating in the field? Did they improvise formations and maneuvers to suit particular needs or alter the prescribed tactics because they thought the books were wrong? Was there a distinctive American way to conduct mounted tactics, or did Civil War cavalrymen adhere to the European model contained in their literature? All these questions point to an evaluation of mounted effectiveness.

The most basic level of tactics, that of formations and maneuvers, can also be termed primary tactics. This level deals with the way in which cavalry units were formed in static positions and in which they were moved from one spot to another in order to change formations or to place the unit in a different position. After that, the level of secondary tactics dealt with how those formations and maneuvers were utilized for larger goals on the battlefield, whether to attack or defend, for example, or how to follow up an advantage. In other words, primary tactics provided order to a mass of mounted men, while secondary tactics provided ways to use that ordered mass to achieve tactical goals in combat.

One Rank or Two?

In the area of primary tactics, the only controversial point for cavalry-men was the nagging question of how many ranks should constitute a mounted line. At the time of the Civil War, one versus two ranks was a raging debate in Europe and the United States, and it had been going on for decades. William Duane had advocated two ranks in his book published in 1814 while noting that three ranks had become unpopular in Europe by that time. In his book on cavalry, Louis E. Nolan included a letter on this issue written by Arthur Wellesley, the Duke of Wellington, in 1833. The duke did not believe that two ranks provided more mobility and was certain the second rank could not aid the first rank when contact was made. Those horsemen would become involved in the defeat of the first rank rather than help it achieve success. Nolan included the opinions of lesser lights in the British Army. "In one rank all movements are made with greater precision and more rapidity than in two," according to Maj. Gen. Anthony Bacon, a veteran of Waterloo.[1]

Nolan himself did not agree, preferring two ranks. When the *United Service Gazette* advocated one rank, which was called the "Rank Entire System," in its issue of March 12, 1852, Nolan mounted a strong criticism in his cavalry handbook, which was published the next year. He preferred the use of small squadrons in two ranks for greater flexibility and argued that countries that experimented with one rank had given it up and reverted to two ranks. George B. McClellan noted in his Delafield Commission work that Prussia used two ranks, although he did not consistently report on what other European armies were doing in that regard.[2]

In the United States there was deep division among cavalry commentators on this issue. McClellan endorsed the one-rank system "as covering the greatest extent of ground, admitting the most rapid movements, and bringing every man to bear to the greatest advantage." Henry L. Scott, in his *Military Dictionary*, preferred two ranks, at least for training purposes, as did Dennis Hart Mahan, the well-known professor at the U.S. Military Academy. When Lt. Dabney Herndon Maury prepared a tactics manual for the Regiment of Mounted Rifles, which was approved in the spring of 1859, he based it on the one-rank system. Secretary of War John B. Floyd mandated that one rank would be used by the Mounted

Kilpatrick at Waynesboro, Georgia.
This cavalry engagement took place at Waynesboro on December 4, 1864,
near the end of Sherman's March to the Sea. The illustration shows
a mounted attack by Brig. Gen. Judson Kilpatrick's command
in line, one rank. *Harpers Weekly,* January 14, 1865, 24.

Rifles when operating against Native Americans but two ranks would be
used "for the present in garrison service."[3]

Philip St. George Cooke, author of the official cavalry manual, was
convinced that the one-rank system was the correct choice. The tipping
point for him was the experience of a British legion operating in the Liberal Wars, also known as the Portuguese Civil War, of 1828–34. The legion
experimented with the one-rank formation and found it useful. That example removed Cooke's initial resistance to the concept. He concluded
that forming in a single rank "greatly simplified all cavalry movements;
a great recommendation," especially when considering that the United
States would need to train green recruits in the event of a major war.
Cooke also sensed that one rank was growing in favor among European
commentators, although most of the Continental armies had not yet adopted it. He also knew that over the long span of time, European armies
had gone from as many as six ranks down to two currently, and that trend
was likely to continue until only one rank became the norm.[4]

But Cooke anticipated a bit too much. During the Civil War, both Union and Confederate cavalry forces remained deeply divided on the utility of one or two ranks without resolving the question. This represented the only divided opinion on a significant aspect of primary tactics in any of the three branches of service during the war. Some units used one and others two ranks, with no consensus as to which was better.

The fact that the official manual switched from the 1841 book (which mandated two ranks) to Cooke's manual (which mandated one rank) on November 1, 1861, seven months after the outbreak of war, created some degree of confusion. All Union cavalrymen who joined before November 1861 began their war service using the older tactics of 1841 and either liked it or found it wanting. Edward Tobie reported that the 1st Maine Cavalry "made slow progress" in training with two ranks, but when Cooke's manual became official, the men "advanced rapidly" in one rank. In fact, Tobie credited the one-rank tactics for his regiment's success during the war because of "the facility with which a regiment can be handled and can change its position under them." But he also noted that the 1st Maine Cavalry was in a minority. Most other regiments trained in two ranks and liked it. There was, he thought, a "prejudice" against the single-rank system, and he probably was correct. In fact, Benjamin W. Crowninshield of the 1st Massachusetts Cavalry thought Tobie's regiment was the only one in the Army of the Potomac that favored one rank.[5]

Regiments entering service after the adoption of Cooke's manual started their training with the single rank. But in many units a switch back to two ranks was mandated by commanders on the regimental level and above. The 11th Pennsylvania Cavalry began drilling in two ranks during the fall of 1861 but converted to one rank with the adoption of Cooke's manual by January 1862. Yet by that spring, an order was issued to revert to the two-rank system. In contrast, the 6th Michigan Cavalry had started its service using Cooke's tactics in September 1862 but switched to the 1841 manual with its two ranks in the winter of 1863–64. "The utility of the change was, to say the least, an open question, and it necessitated many weeks of hard and unremitting toil," recalled Maj. James H. Kidd. But he thought the switch had an overall positive effect because the regiment had just absorbed more than 200 recruits who needed intense training.[6]

While Union cavalry in the Army of the Potomac strongly favored two ranks, mounted regiments in the West were much more open to one rank. The 4th Iowa Cavalry started with the 1841 manual but switched to Cooke's during the winter of 1861–62. "It was a great change, but it was popular because the Cooke methods were more simple and easy, and appeared to be more effective." The 3rd Ohio Cavalry began its service in 1861 with two-rank drill, which the men found "a cumbersome and unwieldy affair." Switching to single rank in 1863 "simplified matters" a great deal.[7]

One can find examples of the use of both systems on the battlefield throughout the war. The 9th New York Cavalry, for instance, formed in one rank at Second Bull Run to cover the fall back of Union infantry on August 30, 1862. Col. Alfred Duffié used one rank during operations in the Shenandoah Valley in June 1864, and the Michigan brigade did the same when fighting on foot at Cold Harbor.[8]

Overall, however, advocates of two ranks can be said to have won a slight victory by war's end. They had ruled in the East throughout the conflict and by early 1865 had implanted the system onto the biggest, most important cavalry concentration in the West. Brig. Gen. James Harrison Wilson had headed the Cavalry Bureau for a time early in 1864 until taking command of the Third Division of the Cavalry Corps, Army of the Potomac. Here he was immersed in the two-rank system and brought it west when appointed to command the cavalry of William T. Sherman's Military Division of the Mississippi in October 1864. Wilson did not impose the two-rank system on the western cavalry until January 1865 while intensely training his command at Gravelly Springs, Alabama, in preparation for a massive raid into the Deep South.[9]

For the western troopers, switching from one to two ranks was a jolt. There was "some dissatisfaction in our division," wrote a captain of the 4th Iowa Cavalry. That division was commanded by Brig. Gen. Emory Upton, who shortly after the war authored tactical manuals that promoted the single-rank formation not only in the cavalry but also in the infantry. William Forse Scott of the 4th Iowa Cavalry pointed out that the one-rank and two-rank systems were not compatible. "The differences in detail are so great that a knowledge of the one system is not of much value in a study of the other." Thus, the troopers spent a great deal of time retraining from February 19 to March 14, 1865.[10]

Scott believed that Wilson's motivation was the belief that the coming campaign would take place in heavily "wooded and hilly country," so spreading a regiment out in a single rank would create very long lines difficult to control. He also noted that Wilson required two-rank formations only in mounted operations; dismounted combat could be conducted in single ranks, and most of the actual work during the campaign happened to take place on foot. So the men, despite their hard retraining early in the year, were often able to employ their preferred one-rank formation.[11]

Wilson's men at Gravelly Springs came to terms with this late-war change in tactics, but other troopers had more trouble with it. "The order is not kindly received by our officers," wrote Capt. Francis T. Moore of the 2nd Illinois Cavalry, "as we have worked in both styles of drill, and for convenience and quick work prefer the single-rank formation."[12]

When troopers fought in one rank on foot by themselves, all went well. But a single rank did not promote close cooperation with infantrymen because foot soldiers had no training in one-rank formations. The 5th Massachusetts Cavalry preceded Brig. Gen. Edward W. Hinks's Third Division, Eighteenth Corps during an advance in Virginia in June 1864. Moving forward on foot and in one rank, the troopers had difficulty forming because the regiment had "drilled only in Cooke's single rank cavalry formation, which entirely unfitted it to act as infantry in line." In contrast, the 123rd Illinois, organized and trained as infantry, switched to mounted infantry service in 1863. The men became confident fighting in one rank when they realized their Spencer repeating carbines' increased rate of fire negated the need for additional fire support from a second rank.[13]

While two ranks tended to rule in the Union cavalry, one rank found more favor than two in the Confederate service. J. Lucius Davis asserted that single-rank formations and maneuvers were superior for all cavalry work in North America. But he admitted that double ranks were useful "for reviews, parades, and manoeuvres in contracted limits." To cover the question, he provided information about both systems in his 1861 handbook. Evidence that single ranks were used comes from Harry Gilmor's experience. When ordered to take temporary command of the 18th Virginia Cavalry, he formed the regiment in one rank for a mounted attack.[14]

But Joseph Wheeler became the most prominent advocate of single ranks. Frustrated by the "antiquated two-rank formations," as W. O.

Dodson put it in a book about the general, Wheeler compiled his own handbook of cavalry operations, which was published in 1863. The most important point in it was to promote the one-rank formation as easier to manage and quicker to re-form. Wheeler used the book as the basic tactics manual in his command.[15]

The Civil War took place during an interesting phase of discussion in both Europe and America about the number of ranks appropriate for cavalry operations. That debate had been going on for at least thirty years and represented the end of a long period in which the depth of mounted formations had reduced from several ranks down to two. The question of whether that process should continue until only one rank was left was settled soon after Appomattox. When Upton authored his infantry manual, which was adopted by the War Department in 1874, he provided instruction on the use of either one or two ranks for foot soldiers. Yet in his book on cavalry tactics, which also was adopted that year, Upton promoted single-rank formations. The Civil War thus became the last hurrah of double-rank champions.[16]

Formations in the Field

Official reports and personal accounts testify to the widespread use of lines and columns in operations throughout the war. Those formations had a geometric appearance when diagramed on paper, which is why some mounted units employed wooden blocks as teaching tools. Franklin Benjamin Hough, an inspector for the U.S. Sanitary Commission, witnessed such a learning session that involved a dozen wooden blocks colored black and white. Mounted company commanders were ordered by their major to construct various formations using those blocks on a table to demonstrate how well they understood them. Training such as this allowed units, when forming up for action, to obey the instructions in the manuals strictly, preserving intervals and mixing lines and columns. Commanders often reported placing flankers, formed in lines, on both sides of a formation for all-round defense.[17]

While lines were simple and consistent formations, columns were far more varied. Brigades formed in columns of regiments, regiments formed in columns of battalions, battalions formed in columns of squad-

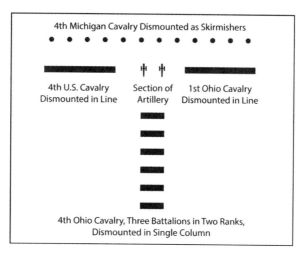

Mix of Line and Column.

Another example of a typical mix of line and column, this time with
dismounted troopers, depicts skirmishers out in front and a section of
artillery planted in the middle of the position. This sketch represents
the array of Col. Robert H. G. Minty's First Brigade of Brig. Gen.
Kenner Garrard's Second Cavalry Division in the action at Nash's
Farm on August 19, 1864, during Brig. Gen. Judson Kilpatrick's
raid on Confederate railroads late in the Atlanta Campaign.
OR, 38(2):824.

rons (each squadron consisting of two companies), squadrons formed in
columns of companies, and companies formed in columns of platoons.

There are references to columns of half platoons, of eights, of fours,
and even of twos. While these very narrow formations were often used
for marching, they also were handy on the battlefield for moving troops
from one cluttered spot of terrain to another and often were used for
fighting as well. McClellan recognized the validity of moving mounted
units by file (a column of one) or by any number above that if needed.[18]

Cavalry more often used narrow columns both for marching and fighting than did infantry. While foot soldiers typically formed double columns
(half the regiment on the right and the other half on the left, with a close
interval between), cavalry more rarely employed this formation. Col. Russell A. Alger, for example, formed the 5th Michigan Cavalry in double column at Gettysburg "closed in mass," then the troops dismounted to await

Column of Fours in Motion.

To move along a roadway in a column of fours was typical of Civil War cavalry. In this view a column marches past a loop-holed stockade work built to defend the nearby railroad and telegraph line in mountainous territory.

Frank Leslie's Scenes and Portraits, 379.

Six Companies of the 4th U.S. Cavalry,
Line of Company Columns, at Stones River.

Capt. Elmer Otis formed his command in this way at the start of fighting on December 31, 1862. He explained the formation and why he adopted it in his official report: "Each company was in column of fours, led by the company commanders; the companies on a line parallel to each other, company distance apart according to the following diagram, leading the center myself. This was owing to the wooded country and fences that were obstructions to the ordinary line of battle." *OR,* 20(1):649.

developments. One rarely sees any other reference to double columns in cavalry reports, and it seems never to have been used to attack.[19]

Alger closed his double column at Gettysburg in mass, forming the tightest column possible for better control of the men. But closed columns seem to have been pretty rare in the mounted arm. The reason was, as McClellan pointed out, enough distance had to be maintained between the subdivisions of a column to allow them to wheel by fours into line at a moment's notice. That was impossible to do in a closed column. Commanders frequently reported wheeling from column into line by fours and had to maintain proper distance between subdivisions to do so.[20]

When several columns, no matter what their size, were organized as a larger unit on the battlefield, the formation became broader. There are many references to these larger formations in battle reports, indicating the widespread application of columns to fighting on horseback. When Brig. Gen. Hugh Judson Kilpatrick's Third Cavalry Division broke out of a dangerous situation at the Battle of Nash's Farm on August 20, 1864, he arrayed the men in a linear formation consisting of columns of brigades with 100-yard intervals between the columns. Two of the five brigades with Kilpatrick, which were detached from Brig. Gen. Kenner Garrard's Second Cavalry Division to accompany the raiders, were led by Col. Robert H. G. Minty. He formed his own First Brigade "in line of regimental columns of fours" while directing Col. Eli Long to form the Second Brigade "in brigade column with regimental front" to the rear of the First Brigade. In other words, while Minty's brigade was arrayed on a broad front of regimental columns, Long's was packed in a narrow brigade column, with each of his regiments stacked one behind the other in regimental columns.[21]

It was easier to organize these larger formations on relatively open ground, and the lower Shenandoah Valley provided such a venue. At both Third Winchester and Cedar Creek in 1864, Federal mounted brigades formed columns of regiments for movement across largely uncluttered battlefields. Brig. Gen. George A. Custer found the sight to be particularly impressive at Third Winchester. Mounted bands played national tunes, and the sun reflected on "one moving mass of glittering sabers. This, combined with the various and bright-colored banners and battle flags, intermingled here and there with the plain blue uniforms of the

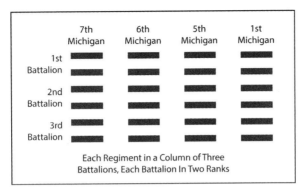

	7th Michigan	6th Michigan	5th Michigan	1st Michigan
1st Battalion				
2nd Battalion				
3rd Battalion				

Each Regiment in a Column of Three
Battalions, Each Battalion In Two Ranks

A Brigade Line of Battalion Columns.
This illustrates a brigade formed in a line of battalion, or
regimental, columns, a typical arrangement during the
Civil War. Col. James H. Kidd's First Brigade of Brig. Gen.
Wesley Merritt's First Division assumed this formation
at the Battle of Cedar Creek on October 19, 1864.
Kidd, *Riding with Custer*, 422.

troops, furnished one of the most inspiring as well as imposing scenes of
martial grandeur ever witnessed upon a battle-field."[22]

Lines of columns were formed on nearly all levels of cavalry organization. They tended to be open columns to make it easy for the troopers to
go from column to line. One sees references to lines of regimental, battalion, squadron, and company columns, especially during the last year of
the war, when the Union mounted arm reached the zenith of its combat
effectiveness. There was no difference in this regard between the volunteer cavalry and the regular regiments; both operated the same way.[23]

With experience, mounted regiments could go from one type of column to another or into line when confronted with tactical challenges. At
Brandy Station in 1863, the 1st Maine Cavalry advanced four miles along
a road in a column of fours and then stopped in the woods to dismount
and rest horses. On remounting, the troopers moved "at full speed" into
a clearing, "at the same time changing from column of fours to column
of squadrons and drawing sabers." In a fight at Gallatin, Tennessee, on
August 21, 1862, the 5th Kentucky Cavalry (U.S.) approached the Confederates in a column of fours until only forty yards away, when it wheeled
into line to open fire. McClellan had stated that all deployments should

be conducted at the gallop; the 5th Kentucky must have done so, for the men were able to open fire before the Confederates started to fire back. Wheeling by fours from a column formation either to form a line or to temporarily avoid some obstacle was common practice. The 2nd Ohio Cavalry did this to navigate tangled woods. All of this demanded a clear mind on the part of commanders, dexterity on the part of troopers who knew the formations and maneuvers, and a discipline that could only come from thorough training.[24]

Doctrine urged the mixing of lines and columns in any given mounted formation, and there is ample proof that this was done. Lines were good for confronting the enemy, and columns allowed a commander to take advantage of any success. Brevet Brig. Gen. Edward F. Winslow was convinced that this mix of formations "materially increased" the success of his brigade during Wilson's Raid through Alabama and Georgia in 1865. Typically commanders everywhere placed their columned troops to the rear of their lined troops, but they could also place them in the center, with lines to the right and left flanks. This became a bit easier in regiments where companies tended to specialize in weapons use. Several units had designated saber companies and rifle companies; Maj. Datus E. Coon fought the rifle companies of his 2nd Iowa Cavalry in line and on foot while keeping his saber companies mounted in column and ready for a charge. Many other commanders mixed mounted and dismounted subunits along with mixing line and column in their tactical formations for any given engagement.[25]

Union cavalry commanders commonly employed the echelon formation, whether it was for a division, brigade, or regimental front. They did this for defense and attack alike. At Third Winchester the 9th New York Cavalry conducted a left half wheel, "bringing the regiment in echelon by squadrons, the most effective formation for a cavalry charge," wrote Newel Cheney. It then struck the Confederates in succession by squadrons and drove them from the field. Echelon formations were favored far more in the mounted arm than in the infantry service. Artillery employed them at a frequency somewhere between the other two arms.[26]

In the Confederate cavalry one sees a similar adherence to the type of formations explained by tactical manuals and handbooks as in the Union army. Columns of fours, columns of squadrons, and columns of

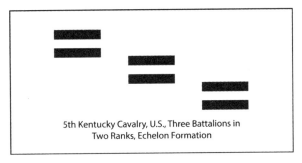

5th Kentucky Cavalry, U.S., Three Battalions in
Two Ranks, Echelon Formation

Fifth Kentucky in Echelon Formation.
A cavalry regiment, when formed in echelon, provided its
own flank protection, at least to a degree, and increased
the maneuverability of the unit. The 5th Kentucky Cavalry
(U.S.) assumed this formation near Griswoldville, Georgia,
on November 22, 1864, during the March to the Sea.
OR, 44:382.

battalions appear in Confederate reports and personal accounts. Moving
from one formation to another was usually done at a gallop. When using
carbines in battle, commanders changed from column formation to line,
but charging was typically done in columns. Wheeler admonished his
readers not to attack in close column, however, advising either half or
full distance between subunits "so as to have plenty of space to wheel."
But many officers ignored this advice. There are several references to the
use of closed columns for a cavalry charge. The Confederates employed
flankers to protect their formations and mixed mounted and dismounted
units in the same formation.[27]

Commanders could more easily maneuver a mounted column on the
attack than they could a line. This was in direct contrast with the infantry,
which typically attacked in line rather than column. When advancing in
column, the worst problem infantry encountered was that any obstruction
to the formation, such as an outburst of heavy enemy fire, stopped the
head of the column, causing the rest of it to bunch up and disintegrate.
Cavalrymen could avoid that by quick use of their horses. For example,
Lt. Col. Frederick W. Benteen organized a cavalry brigade in a column of
regiments with the 10th Missouri Cavalry in the lead at the Battle of Mine
Creek on October 25, 1864. In a spirited attack, the Missouri regiment
slowed down when receiving first fire. To avoid entangling his regiment,

Maj. Abial R. Pierce ordered the 4th Iowa Cavalry, the second unit in the column, to move to the right out of formation and advance on its own. The regiment did so, even though three companies on its left wing rode through the stalled Missourians in their front. The Iowans broke the Confederate line, demonstrating the high level of dexterity possible in a mounted column on the move. There simply is no similar example of any element in an infantry column moving with such speed and decision to avoid collapsing a column formation.[28]

Mounted columns also had another advantage over mounted lines on the battlefield. If friendly forces in the first line broke apart because of an enemy attack, the retreating men often disrupted the secondary line behind them. This happened to Lt. Col. Matthew H. Starr's 6th Illinois Cavalry in a fight during the Meridian Expedition of 1864, "scattering one battalion of my regiment." It had also happened to Maj. Robert Klein's 3rd Battalion, 3rd Indiana Cavalry at Stones River. Klein noted sarcastically of the other unit's hasty retreat, "this movement, had it been in the opposite direction, would have been a most gallant charge."[29]

Maneuvers in the Field

Maneuvers took units from one formation to another, and the cavalry conducted them quickly, at a gallop, when near the enemy. Because of their nature, maneuvers were more difficult to conduct than making formations; the unit was in a state of flux that demanded more discipline and attention to detail. The cavalry regiment that could maneuver well possessed a qualitative edge over a less-well-trained enemy.

How frequently the bugle signaled commands to maneuver is difficult to determine. Very few references are made to bugle signals in the heat of combat. Eli Long, according to Capt. W. L. Curry of the 1st Ohio Cavalry, stated that he "maneuvered his brigade by bugle commands or signals as he had never seen done before or since in a battle." The rarity of bugle signals as noted here might have been something characteristic of the western Federal cavalry, or it may have been more universal across theaters and with the Southern cavalry as well.[30]

One universal characteristic of cavalry maneuvers, however, was that everything was done on the basis of fours. All mounted soldiers counted fours before doing anything. Samuel B. Barron of the 3rd Texas Cavalry described how this was done just before the Battle of Wilson's Creek in 1861. He rode along the line "requiring each man to call out his number, counting, one, two, three, four; one, two, three, four, until the left was reached. This gave every man his place for the day, and every man was required to keep his place. If ordered to march by twos, the horses were wheeled to the right, number 2 forming on the right of number 1; if order was for fours, numbers 3 and 4 moved rapidly up on the right of numbers 1 and 2, and so on."[31]

But what if troopers lost their place in the line for some reason? In the 1st New York (Lincoln) Cavalry, the men had counted off early on the morning of September 5, 1864, but during subsequent moves had largely forgotten their numbers. When Maj. Timothy Quinn ordered "By fours, to the right about," confusion ensued. "As you were," Quinn then ordered and told them to count again. The men did so as bullets fell over and then executed the order. "All this took less than a minute," asserted William H. Beach. After counting off, each trooper of the 9th Kansas Cavalry was warned not only to remember his number but also "not to swap places" with anyone.[32]

Many times cavalry units maneuvered in larger segments than by fours. It was not uncommon when going from one formation to another or moving from one spot to another to do so "by divisions," which referred to the next subdivision of the unit. If in a regiment, that would be the battalion; if in a battalion, that would be the squadron; and so on down the organizational chart. But company commanders, it seems, typically moved by fours rather than by platoons.[33]

Commanders could maneuver their units in sections especially when covering a withdrawal. Sgt. William Gardiner of the 1st Rhode Island Cavalry recalled "executing a brilliant manoeuvre in retiring by battalions" at Second Bull Run "by which a force was continually facing the enemy in regular line of battle *at a halt*. This movement of retiring was made at a *slow walk*" and under heavy artillery fire. In referring to Lt. Col. Matthew Van Buskirk of the 92nd Illinois Mounted Infantry, Col. Smith D. Atkins wrote that he was "skillfully revolving his companies around one another" while covering a fall back.[34]

In another example of maneuver by divisions, Luther S. Trowbridge recalled a fight his 10th Michigan Cavalrymen engaged in during the McCook-Stoneman Raid. "Falling back by alternate squadrons, constantly presenting an unbroken front to the enemy; wheeling out of column into line, and steadily delivering their vollies [*sic*] from their Spencer carbines until they could see another squadron ready to receive the shock of the enemy; then wheeling into column and falling back to a new position."[35]

The complicated maneuver by successive subunits of a larger formation was executed with aplomb by well-trained units. The same was true of conducting oblique maneuvers, which involved moving the formation partially to right or left without changing the direction it fronted. McClellan mandated that the individual oblique should be used "as much as possible" as the least disruptive way to conduct such a maneuver. Reports and personal accounts never mention whether an oblique movement was done by individuals or by units, but they often were conducted. When Brig. Gen. Wesley Merritt ordered Brig. Gen. Thomas C. Devin to advance two of his regiments to attack Confederate infantry that had just emerged from a patch of woods at Third Winchester, Devin directed his regimental commanders to do so "by changing front obliquely to the left, the evolution being splendidly executed by both regiments at the gallop."[36]

Cavalry units could wheel to change the direction of their front, although Confederates sometimes had a quaint way of referring to this maneuver. Capt. George Knox Miller of the 8th Confederate Cavalry mixed up maneuvers when he wrote that his division commander ordered "a left oblique wheel." And George W. Beale of the 9th Virginia Cavalry recalled that his commander set a left wheel in motion by telling the men to "be slow on the left and fast on the right." But the majority of Confederate officers knew and used the proper commands to initiate a wheel. "The movement was well and steadily executed," reported Paul B. Means of the 5th North Carolina Cavalry of a wheel conducted during a fight in early April 1865.[37]

Very often wheeling was conducted by fours in both armies by simply adding the phrase "by fours" to the command. The 3rd Virginia Cavalry conducted this maneuver twice to bypass a line of Federal cavalry and enter Mt. Jackson in November 1864. Union troopers employed the wheel by fours on many occasions. Wheeling was rarely conducted by smaller segments, although Lt. Daniel H. L. Gleason of the 1st Massachusetts Cavalry

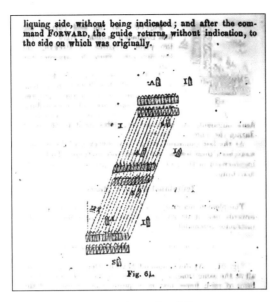

Moving by the Right Oblique.
This maneuver brought a line of cavalry
forward, sliding to the right in the process
while keeping its alignment intact.
Patten, *Cavalry Drill*, 86, fig. 61.

ordered it to be done by threes in order to ploy from line to column and charge along a road that he felt was too narrow for a column of fours.[38]

Choosing the right combination of maneuvers to deal with a tactical situation reflected good training. Capt. George N. Bliss always remembered how Colonel Duffié used five different maneuvers to reposition the 1st Rhode Island Cavalry to support a battery when the enemy suddenly threatened the guns at the Battle of Cedar Mountain in 1862. The regiment ended up in a dip of ground where it was largely shielded from fire but was able to protect the battery at the same time. The movements "showed good military judgement upon the part of our Colonel," Bliss wrote.[39]

Most cavalry units learned their trade thoroughly on the drill ground and honed their ability to utilize that training through hard experience on the battle ground. This applied to Confederate as well as Federal cavalry. In peacetime it might have taken years to form a good cavalry soldier,

but they should not be repeated too frequently at the *gallop*, in order not to fatigue the horses.

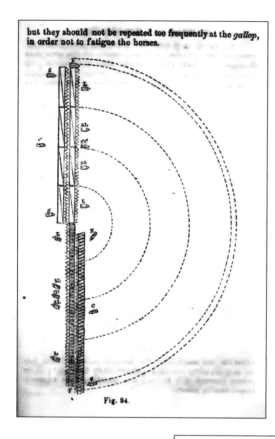

Fig. 84.

Half Wheel.

A half wheel took a line of cavalry around to face to the rear relative to its original facing. A full wheel brought it back exactly where it started with the original facing.

Patten, *Cavalry Drill*, 137, fig. 84.

To Wheel on a Movable Pivot.

This quarter wheel to the right was conducted with a movable pivot on the right as opposed to a fixed pivot, wherein the right flank of the line remained rooted to one spot.

Patten, *Cavalry Drill*, 138, fig. 85.

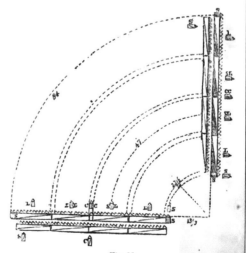

To Wheel on a Moveable Pivot.

In the wheels on a moveable pivot, the pivot should describe *an arc of circle of twenty paces*, at the same time slackening the gait; the marching flank increases its gait. The sixth file of the second platoon, which is the middle of the radius of the wheel, preserves the gait at which the

Fig. 85.

squadron was marching. The troopers placed between this file and their pivot diminish proportionally their gait; those placed between this file and the marching flank augment proportionally theirs.

but neither belligerent in the Civil War could afford that much time. It was highly possible to form a good mounted soldier in months rather than years.

Moreover, the use of formations and maneuvers in the field reflected strict adherence to the tactical manuals. There is no reason to believe that either Union or Confederate officers changed those primary tactics in any significant way; they used them faithfully in actual combat, testifying to the value of the manuals and the tactical system so thoroughly explained in them. This was the most important legacy of Civil War cavalry: it had hundreds of years of hard experience primarily in Europe to bank on, and the U.S. Army had the good sense to take that legacy seriously by copying the tactical system it inherited.

5

MOUNTED OPERATIONS

The manuals and handbooks offered a detailed understanding of the formations and maneuvers involved in the primary tactics of cavalry, but they offered little advice about how to use them on the battlefield. The drill ground did not provide insight into whether to attack an enemy or defend against him, how to choose the best position, or when it was wise to break off an engagement. Civil War armies did not have schools to teach such things to officers. Much depended on whether the individual studied the great campaigns of the past or gave thought to how best he could meet and defeat his opponent. Experience proved to be the best teacher, yet that involved a steep learning curve with varying results. But because it proved to be a long, arduous conflict, the Civil War provided many opportunities for mounted commanders to learn their bloody trade.

Secondary tactics—using the formations and maneuvers to fight the enemy on the battlefield—varied more widely for the cavalry than for the infantry or artillery because of the multiple tasks demanded of mounted units. They skirmished, fought against infantry, fought against opposing cavalry, dealt with opposing artillery, raided behind enemy lines, and performed a huge amount of picket and outpost duty. Mounted units often dismounted to fight on foot, something that was done more commonly in the Civil War than probably any previous conflict in history. To a limited degree both sides put infantry units on horseback to increase their mounted force, but that did not change anything because even regularly organized cavalry regiments often fought on foot. Throughout all this, the charge remained the ultimate experience for most mounted soldiers in their distinctive type of warfare.

Skirmishing

As Philip St. George Cooke put it in his tactical manual, the purpose of skirmishing was "to cover movements and evolutions, to gain time, to watch the movements of the enemy, to keep him in check, to prevent his approaching so close to the main body as to annoy the line of march, and to weaken and harass him by their fire, to prepare the way for the charge on infantry, by renderng them unsteady, or drawing their fire." Arrayed in dispersed order whether on horse or on foot, the skirmisher relied to a greater extent on his own resources than did the man in line of battle or in column. He was "much thrown upon his own intelligence and resources; as much coolness and watchfulness is required of him; and he should especially guard against exciting his horse." Skirmishers had to be aware of the terrain, taking advantage of cover. Their role was vital to the operations of the main force.[1]

Cooke asserted that the proper skirmish force was a platoon for each company, representing the rule of thumb that the next lowest subdivision of any given unit should be sent to the skirmish line for the whole. For example, Col. Oscar H. La Grange deployed one regiment to cover the front of his brigade in a fight during October 1863 in Tennessee. He dismounted four companies of that regiment to skirmish while keeping a mounted company on each flank of the skirmish line and holding the regiment's other six companies mounted as a skirmish reserve. There was no fixed distance for the skirmishers to be placed ahead of the main body. At the Battle of Kelly's Ford in 1863, J. Irvin Gregg put his skirmish line 300 yards in front, a distance that was about as close to average in the Civil War as one could get.[2]

Whether to skirmish on horse or on foot became a question difficult to answer. Maj. Gen. James E. B. Stuart issued general orders at the end of July 1863 requiring subordinates to deploy skirmishers in all instances either mounted or dismounted, depending on the nature of the terrain.

Mounted Skirmish Line.
Cavalry could skirmish mounted or dismounted. This illustration shows what
a mounted skirmish line might look like in open country, the close order
replaced by sizable intervals between each trooper-horse combination.
Frank Leslie's Scenes and Portraits, 482.

Both modes of skirmishing were common throughout both armies. Of
course, mounted skirmishing exposed horses to enemy fire if there was no
cover nearby, as happened with the 6th Ohio Cavalry near Middleburg,
Virginia, in June 1863. As Wells A. Bushnell advanced in the skirmish line
over open country, bullets "struck the ground all around me kicking up
a little puff of dust, the horse next to me on the right was shot dead, and
another near me was wounded."[3]

Dismounted skirmishing worked just as well as skirmishing on horseback. Colonel La Grange advanced four companies of the 1st Wisconsin Cavalry as dismounted skirmishers against mounted Confederate
horsemen during the Wheeler-Roddey Raid of October 1863. "Taking
advantage of the ground and moving rapidly from cover to cover," his men
drove the enemy for two miles. They had a noticeable advantage over the
Confederates. "Being dismounted, our men were able to fire with much

greater rapidity and precision than the enemy, who were exposed by remaining on horseback, and fired high above our heads."[4]

In fact, Maj. Louis H. Carpenter of the 5th U.S. Cavalry thought skirmishing was best performed dismounted. "In less than half a minute a troop could dismount and deploy as skirmishers. Sometimes the line would be reinforced to about one man to the yard, but never heavier, and this answered all purposes." Despite its appearance, a dismounted skirmish line was surprisingly strong and resilient, "flexible, bending, but rarely breaking, keeping up its continuity, and showing a wonderful power of resistance." Carpenter also felt that dismounted skirmishing allowed a man to develop soldierly qualities. He became "accustomed to losing the touch of his comrade, became more self-reliant and dependent on his own resources, taking advantage of all the cover and shelter possible, and more difficult to be persuaded that he was whipped."[5]

Cavalry and Infantry

It was uncommon for cavalry to closely support infantry on the battlefield during the Civil War. The difficulties were akin to mixing oil and water because the main advantage of the mounted arm, its horse-based mobility, was neutralized by being tied to the movements of foot formations. On the tactical offensive, cavalry units may have been able to deliver a mounted charge that could take advantage of dislocation and confusion in enemy ranks. But on the defensive, cavalry soldiers were reduced to a level even lower than foot soldiers because they were armed with short-barreled carbines, which usually were no match for infantry small arms. No wonder that cavalry-infantry cooperation often did not work very well.

Heavily vegetated battlefields also contributed to the lack of success in this aspect of combined-arms operations in the Civil War. The 8th Texas Cavalry often dismounted in its efforts to cooperate with infantry on the far left of the Confederate line at Shiloh because of terrain obstacles. When wooded country prevented Federal cavalry from taking part in the main fighting at the Battle of Corinth in 1862, it found a role in dismounted skirmishing and patrolling the streets of the town. Unwilling infantry officers sometimes spoiled interbranch cooperation. Col.

Edward M. McCook's division covered numerous roads during the late May phase of the Atlanta Campaign, but he could not count on help from nearby infantry. Brig. Gen. John H. King sent word that the cavalry "could expect no infantry re-enforcements in any emergency." McCook reported this remark sarcastically to superior headquarters. "Privately this thing of covering the flank of the infantry seems to be a one-sided affair; if they are attacked I am to pitch in, while if I am attacked by a superior force I can expect no assistance."[6]

The results of cavalry-infantry cooperation on the battlefield were decidedly mixed. Much depended on the circumstances to be found in any given fight. At Gaines's Mill in 1862, those circumstances spelled disaster. Capt. Charles J. Whiting placed his five companies of the 5th U.S. Cavalry twenty rods to the rear of several Union batteries as support. None other than Philip St. George Cooke, now a brigadier general, told Whiting to wait until he saw the Confederate infantry appear over the crest of the rise in front and then "charge at once, without any further orders, to enable the artillery to bring off the guns."[7]

In a few minutes the troopers could see Rebel bayonets appear above the crest. Then Whiting gave the order to "'Trot! March!'" and, as William H. Hitchcock recalled, "as soon as we were fully under way he shouted, 'Charge!'" The five companies cheered as they swept forward in column of squadrons, "but our formation was almost instantly broken" not by Confederate fire, but by the Federal guns directly in their front. The column had to break to right and left. In fact, as he was passing one piece, Hitchcock noticed a gunner about to pull the lanyard and yelled for his comrades to veer to the right. He "felt the shock of the" discharge and then they closed back toward the left.[8]

The troopers soon encountered the advancing infantry. The Rebels had broken the Union infantry line and were closing in on the artillery when the Federal horsemen tried to stop them. The foot formation was somewhat scattered, but "the cry was heard, Cavalry! Cavalry!," recalled C. F. James of the 8th Virginia Infantry. "There was no panic and no sign of wavering. The foremost boys simply stopped and waited for those behind to close up and fall into a sort of line." The Confederates opened fire when the 5th U.S. Cavalry was but seventy yards away. This abruptly ended the mounted charge. Hitchcock's horse panicked at the sight of a line of infantrymen presenting bayonets. It "reared upright . . . and ran away partly to our rear, perfectly uncontrollable." He had great difficulty regaining control of the steed. Of the 250 troopers who made the attack, only 100 were available for duty the next day.[9]

The attack by the 5th U.S. Cavalry at Gaines's Mill is probably the most famous mounted charge against infantry in the Civil War, but it has too often been cited by historians as proof that the rifle musket rendered such action futile as a rule.[10] That is not the lesson to be learned from Whiting's charge. The Confederates did not open fire until the horsemen were 70 yards away, well within the lethal distance of fire by smoothbore muskets rather than the maximum distance of 500 yards theoretically afforded by the rifle musket. Even if the Confederates had been fully armed with smoothbores, they could have devastated the mounted formation at that distance, for it is a mistake to assume that the smoothbore musket was an ineffectual weapon. Typically cavalry had an advantage when striking infantrymen who were not ready to receive them, but in this case the foot soldiers quickly closed ranks in time to deliver short-distance fire and stop the mounted charge. The age-old rule that a cavalry attack had little chance if the opposing infantry was ready to receive it still held true.

There were other failed cavalry charges against infantry in the Civil War. At Cedar Mountain four companies of the 1st Pennsylvania Cavalry tried to save Federal guns by attacking over open ground. Their charge failed with heavy losses: out of 164 men, only 71 were left for duty after the battle. Soon afterward at Second Bull Run, the 1st Pennsylvania managed to place itself near the flank of a Confederate infantry column as the Rebels were advancing. The regiment tried to distract the enemy. It "rode along the flank . . . and expended nearly all of its carbine ammunition. . . . They paid no more attention to us, however, than if we were so many gnats flying in the air." This incident begs the question as to how effective carbine fire could be as a rule.[11]

There were very few examples of a mounted charge directed at infantry forces in the western theater, but one stands out. At the onset of Brig. Gen. Nathan Bedford Forrest's raid into West Tennessee, he met Federal infantry at Salem on December 19, 1862. Forrest sent a column of cavalry along a road to attack the Federals. For the first 100 yards, the Confederates advanced cautiously, then sped up to a brisk trot before starting to charge at a point 150 yards from the waiting foot soldiers. Cheering wildly as they rode, Forrest's men were stunned by the first well-directed volley, fired at a distance of only 30 yards according to one report. A number of horses fell in the road, obstructing the way for all behind them, as half a dozen riderless mounts continued running right through the Union infantry line. "The enemy's cavalry farther to the rear still rode forward and got jammed up with those in front," wrote Col. Adolph Engelmann of the 43rd Illinois. The infantrymen poured in another volley, after which horses and men "could be seen rushing in headlong flight across the fields."[12]

In short, mounted charges against infantry generally failed, but cavalry had better chances of dealing with enemy foot soldiers when the horsemen dismounted to fight. At the Battle of Pickett's Mill during the Atlanta Campaign on May 27, 1864, dismounted Confederate troopers held the right end of a hastily assembled infantry line. Although the skirmishing swayed back and forth, the horsemen protected that end of the line as Union infantry columns slammed into Rebel infantry units to the cavalry's left. At the Battle of Burgess's Mill on October 27, 1864, during the Petersburg Campaign, Lt. Col. John K. Robison's 16th Pennsylvania Cavalry dismounted "and aligned, joining the infantry left" to protect the flank. Ten minutes later it helped repel a Confederate foot attack.[13]

But two factors seriously limited dismounted cavalrymen's ability to handle enemy infantry: they had only rudimentary training in the primary tactics of infantry forces, and carbines were generally no match for rifle muskets. Colonel La Grange watched as Confederate infantry advanced in column over the bodies of fallen Rebel cavalrymen toward his position during the battle at Dandridge in East Tennessee on January 17, 1864. "Disregarding our fire, which fell steadily among them," the Rebel foot soldiers calmly began to deploy only thirty yards from the Union position in preparation for an attack. "Without waiting so hopeless a contest as must have taken place between dismounted cavalrymen and a superior force of trained infantry," he retired.[14]

All examples of cavalry supporting infantry, infantry supporting cavalry, and mounted forces contesting with enemy foot soldiers fall under the general heading of combined-arms operations. The concept existed in the Civil War even if the modern phrase describing it was foreign to its commanders. The era was not conducive to effective combined-arms operations except when it came to infantry and artillery cooperation, which was tight and effective. But when it came to cavalry and infantry coordination, the mix was unpredictable at best. It tended to be more effective when cavalry descended to the level of infantry by dismounting and fighting on foot, but even then horse soldiers were at a disadvantage due to their training and arms.

Yet Civil War commanders recognized different levels of combined-arms cooperation. The more basic level consisted of tight relationships such as cavalry units mixing with infantry units. But a more detached mode of combined arms separated cavalry formations from infantry formations while placing them in close proximity to each other. In this way the mounted force operated as a self-contained formation to utilize its inherent advantages and training while remaining in supporting distance of the foot formations. Such a situation took place at Gettysburg when Union cavalry forces formed to the right and left of the army's infantry line and engaged in battles with Confederate cavalry. Those engagements were set-piece cavalry-versus-cavalry fights, with supporting artillery on each side, but they were conducted within the zone of the infantry combat at Gettysburg. William Brooke-Rawle of the 3rd Pennsylvania Cavalry marveled at this circumstance. "This was one of the few battles of the war in which the three arms of the service fought in combination and at the same time, each within supporting distance and within sight of the other, and each in its proper sphere."[15]

Rawle's reference to a "proper sphere" strikes a chord in the discussion of combined-arms operations during the Civil War. For the mounted arm, separating itself into wholly mounted formations on the flanks of great armies to protect the infantry was its proper sphere. But it is a bit astonishing that this happened in only a minority of Civil War battles rather than in the majority of them. Using mounted forces in this way was far more common in European military history than in that of North America.

Mounted Infantry

Putting infantrymen on horseback in order to move them quickly to then fight on foot was different than training cavalrymen to fight dismounted.

The trooper could fight either on foot or on horse, but the mounted infantryman supposedly was only trained for foot combat. The other key difference was that the mounted infantryman supposedly was armed with an infantry weapon that could outclass the cavalry carbine on the battlefield. Yet these clear distinctions rapidly evaporated during the Civil War. Mounted infantry units tended to act like other cavalry regiments, while cavalry regiments continued to frequently dismount and fight on foot.

While mounting infantrymen seemed to be a good idea, Civil War commanders were not the originators of this concept. It dates back at least to early seventeenth-century Europe, but the distinction between mounted infantrymen and genuine cavalrymen became blurry.[16]

Before the Civil War, only one regiment of mounted infantry was part of the U.S. mounted forces, and it was officially redesignated as cavalry soon after the start of the war. But several volunteer infantry regiments were converted into mounted infantry during the conflict. On the Union side a brigade led by Col. John T. Wilder, consisting of five regiments, was horsed in the spring of 1863 and remained mounted to the end of the war. It soon was incorporated into the cavalry force of the Department of the Cumberland and acted like any other cavalry unit. A handful of other infantry regiments also converted to mounted infantry, including the 4th Kentucky and the 9th Illinois. On the Confederate side Brig. Gen. Joseph H. Lewis's Kentucky brigade of five regiments was mounted in the latter part of the war. Still, the number of mounted infantry units remained comparatively small, with probably no more than about 30 out of about 2,500 infantry regiments combined on both sides converting to mounted duty. One reason for this limited application was resistance from on high. The War Department allowed it only in a few cases because, as Maj. Gen. Henry W. Halleck put it, "mounted infantry are neither good infantry nor good cavalry."[17]

Cavalry and Artillery

Interbranch cooperation included adding artillery units to cavalry formations, although the mix was somewhat difficult. Artillery moved more slowly than cavalry, and it needed time to select good positions and fire for a while before it could have an effect on the course of events. Given the highly fluid nature of cavalry operations, the artillery often had little opportunity to practice its craft. This is why the big guns rarely made much of a difference in cavalry battles.

Batteries converted from infantry support to cavalry support with very little alteration in their equipment. None of them downgraded to lighter pieces, and as a result 12-pounder Napoleons, 10-pounder Parrotts, and 3-Inch Ordnance Rifles rather than 6-pounders supported mounted units in the field. Cavalry batteries lightened their load a bit by dropping one of the three ammunition boxes on their caissons. Artillery officers also had to adjust to the task of fighting alongside cavalry. The commander of the 6th New York Battery officially thanked Brig. Gen. William W. Averell for helping him with advice in his first battle supporting cavalry at Kelly's Ford on March 17, 1863.[18]

In the East, Federal authorities preferred to use regular artillery units to support cavalry. By August 1863, all of the batteries assigned to cavalry in the Army of the Potomac were regular army units except for the 6th New York Battery. In fact, of the fifty-six batteries in the five U.S. artillery regiments assigned to field duty, twenty-two were dedicated to cavalry units. In the West only a handful of volunteer batteries supported cavalry formations. They included the Chicago Board of Trade Battery, the 18th Indiana Battery, the 25th Ohio Battery, and the 10th Wisconsin Battery. On the Confederate side the Army of Northern Virginia fielded a sizeable artillery force with its cavalry. One battery was assigned to each of four brigades, with another held as a reserve, by November 1862.[19]

On the battlefield cavalry units frequently supported batteries by forming in small columns on the flank of the gun formation. Sometimes they remained mounted and at other times formed on foot, with skirmishers advanced. But the support cavalry offered did not always help the guns. Capt. John C. Tidball of Battery A, 2nd U.S. Artillery argued that carbines were no match for opposing infantry weapons. "As soon as the enemy opens fire the cavalry find themselves of no service [so] naturally and very properly retire." Unfortunately for their sake, artillerymen assigned to cavalry units could never be sure their mounted comrades would protect them on the battlefield.[20]

Whether the artillery could support mounted operations, much depended on circumstances. Very often the fluid nature of cavalry battles nullified artillery effectiveness, but in at least one case it did not. Capt. Eli Lilly's 18th Indiana Battery was just coming onto the battlefield at Fair Garden in East Tennessee on January 27, 1864, when he saw that the 4th Indiana Cavalry was formed in column of fours on the road to his left "ready to charge with the saber." He quickly positioned his pieces at a gallop 500 yards from a Confederate battery and opened fire just when the Indiana troopers started their advance. He first fired "across their front until they reached the main road" and then turned his fire to the right so as not to hurt his comrades. Lilly then advanced one piece at a gallop, supported by the 1st East Tennessee Cavalry (U.S.), to further support the 4th Indiana in a successful attack.[21]

In a few battles one sees effective combinations of artillery and cavalry to repel enemy mounted attacks. For example, canister fire and a countercharge by the 6th Missouri Cavalry (U.S.) blunted such an assault during an engagement of the Red River Campaign in 1864, even though the Confederate horsemen were only twenty yards away.[22]

Artillerymen who cooperated with cavalry learned they had a good chance to survive if the enemy overran their position in a mounted charge. This happened to a Confederate battery at Brandy Station. The Federals rode through the left section of the battery when the 6th Pennsylvania Cavalry and 6th U.S. Cavalry attacked. "Not a man from the battery left his pieces," recalled Robert J. Trout, "but gun detachments, due to their discipline, sprang between the wheels—horse holders and drivers between their horses—and thus escaped injury." This was possible only because the attacker was mounted and focused on moving on to other targets.[23]

Although it is counterintuitive to place artillery on skirmish lines, exposed to the give and take of operations, this happened often during the Civil War. William N. McDonald believed that Rebel artillery got into the habit of supporting cavalry on the skirmish line beginning in May 1864 and extending through to the end of the war. On the Union side this had been taking place as early as the spring of 1863. There seems to be no example of a battery commander losing his guns on the skirmish line.[24]

Yet it cannot be said that artillery played a decisive role in promoting cavalry operations on a consistent basis. Cavalry actually needed artillery less than artillery needed cavalry. Wherever the guns deployed, they absolutely required support from friendly troops. Artillery simply could not survive on the battlefield alone, whether it accompanied infantry or cavalry. The guns sometimes represented a burden rather than an asset for fast-moving mounted formations without offering cavalry a guaranteed advantage over the enemy in battle.

The Legion

A handful of people in Civil War America believed in the legion concept, which combined infantry, artillery, and cavalry in one small unit roughly the size of an infantry regiment. A small combined-arms unit theoretically could bring to bear on the battlefield all the advantages of the three separate arms. One could envision it moving about on contested fields as a self-contained unit, able to deal with any threat.

There were solid precedents for the legion concept in pre–Civil War American history. During the Revolutionary War, British officials recruited American Loyalists to form the British Legion, which consisted of about 200 infantry and 250 mounted men but no artillery. Under Banastre Tarleton, it became infamous for aggressive, often brutal, action on and off the battlefield. Several years after gaining independence, the U.S. government organized its entire central army as the Legion of the United States, with four sublegions each consisting of infantry, artillery, and cavalry. This organization lasted from 1792 to 1796, when the legion concept was abandoned in favor of regimental organizations and the separation of the three arms.[25]

But the limited experiment with the legion concept in the Civil War did not work. The addition of the cavalry was the only unique factor because artillery batteries were uniformly attached to infantry brigades in both armies from the start of the war. The Confederate army included at least fifteen legions, all of which joined infantry and cavalry but only a few added artillery to the team. For example, Cobb's Georgia Legion included seven infantry companies, four cavalry companies, and one battery, while the Holcombe Legion of South Carolina consisted initially of eight, later ten, infantry companies and four cavalry companies but no artillery. Seven other Confederate units were legions in name only, having adopted the term to designate a regiment. In the Union army, at least fourteen units also were legions in name only, but the Purnell Legion of Maryland was a true legion with nine infantry companies, two cavalry companies, and two batteries. Literally all of these true legions were broken up within a few months of organization, their artillery and cavalry units separated from the infantry companies.[26]

When the 36th Illinois organized in 1861, its officers sought to add a legion flavor to the regiment by incorporating two cavalry companies. This mounted force continued to be part of the regiment for nearly a year before it was separated from the infantry. This became necessary, according to regimental historians Lyman G. Bennett and William M. Haigh, because of "the radical difference in the nature of the duties required of the two arms of the service, and from their widely divergent fields of action."[27]

No one expressed the futility of mixing cavalry with infantry or artillery into the same unit more forcefully than William T. Sherman. He dealt with this issue in June 1864 when a subordinate, Brig. Gen. Alvin P. Hovey, insisted on creating a division-size legion for himself. Hovey had been allowed by the president to recruit five infantry and five cavalry regiments during the early months of 1864. The infantry units became the basis for a small division he commanded in the Twenty-Third Corps of Sherman's army group, but Hovey wanted the five cavalry regiments added to his command as well. The first problem he encountered was that the government had difficulty finding horses for the men, so Sherman insisted they take the field as foot soldiers to guard his supply lines in Kentucky. The second problem was that Sherman adamantly refused to sanction the creation of a legion of any size. "I cannot put cavalry and infantry into the same division," he told Maj. Gen. John M. Schofield, Hovey's corps commander. "It never was done and never can be done, even if Mr. Lincoln promised it. Divisions must be a unit, and five regiments of infantry and five regiments of cavalry will no more make a unit in a good whole than oil and water will commingle."[28]

This strong resistance to the legion concept was based on sound ideas. The legions never proved to be any more effective than separate infantry, artillery, or cavalry units; in fact, they proved less effective because the mounted components were either too closely tied to the other two branches to be able to fulfill their proper role or they were detached so much to perform that proper role that it made no sense to keep them within the legion organization. Cavalry was the odd man out in the triad of military forces that fought the Civil War on land and needed to be on its own.

Picket and Outpost Duty

Civil War cavalry fulfilled a vital role as "the eyes and ears of the army," which meant guarding friendly forces from surprise and gathering information about the enemy. It was the prime information-gathering element of Civil War armies. With its horses, cavalry also was the most convenient element to send out on picket duty. As a result troopers spent far more time on lonely vigil along the picket line and in isolated outposts guarding other troops than they spent on the battlefield.[29]

The formation of an advanced guard for the larger field force was complex. Dennis Hart Mahan, professor at the U.S. Military Academy, authored one of the few treatises on the subject, which was published in 1847. He divided the advanced guard into four parts, starting with the grand guard, consisting of clusters of men placed on the major roads leading to the friendly encampment. The commanders of these grand guards established outposts farther toward the enemy; from those outposts, sentinels or videttes advanced to form the first warning line of men placed with large intervals between them. Mahan recommended that the outposts be placed 1,500 yards apart and the line of sentinels or videttes 600–800 paces in advance of the outposts. The fourth component consisted of pickets placed along the lines of approach between the grand guards and the main force whose task was to slow down an enemy advance. These pickets also could be arranged as a line across the countryside. He recommended regular patrols to keep these detached segments in contact with each other.[30]

Mahan's theoretical discussion of outpost duty was based on research in the rich body of American and European military literature available to him at the academy library, but it did not fully represent what cavalrymen actually did during the Civil War. Lt. James Albert Clark, adjutant of the 17th Pennsylvania Cavalry, described the typical process of posting

Mounted Videttes.

Videttes were placed at the advanced posting of a covering force to
give the first warning of enemy approach. This illustration shows
mounted videttes deployed along a roadway; they are lancers,
as distinguished by the unusual weapon they carry.

Frank Leslie's Scenes and Portraits, 359.

advanced guards. When he had been chief duty sergeant of the regiment, Clark was given twelve men, placing them eight miles from camp and establishing communication with the other two outposts to his right and left. He and the noncommissioned officers in charge of the other outposts arranged to conduct regular patrols "right and left, at agreed upon hours, and agreed upon points for meeting. These agreements were made afresh every day" to confuse the enemy. Fulfilling this plan was especially important during the night. Clark changed the relief every two hours and made sure his men did as they were told. Confederate patrols hit his area twice during the ten days his dozen men were on duty.[31]

Civil War cavalrymen often established long picket lines that stretched across the country in addition to posts along avenues of approach to the friendly encampment. Sometimes they also advanced yet another line of sentinels, calling them videttes, farther out from the picket line. This most distant line had fewer men placed at greater intervals than the picket line and provided the earliest warning of danger. Cavalry also established grand guards, more often referring to them as picket reserves, to back up both the picket and vidette lines. All of this only generally followed the outlines described by Mahan, with much variation on the details and even the terminology.

When the 1st Ohio Cavalry was stationed at Calhoun, Tennessee, in December 1863, one-third of its 250 men "were on patrol or picket duty all the time," recalled company commander John P. Rae. Whether the men enjoyed it depended entirely on their preferences. The historian of the 11th Pennsylvania Cavalry noted that picket work "was considered a favored duty because it relieved men from the drudgery of camp life." They had more opportunity to forage for provisions in the countryside as well. But boredom was the price, "spiced by an occasional dash," as Wells A. Bushnell put it.[32]

Capt. Charles Francis Adams Jr. enjoyed picket work. It was "very pleasant, this getting away from camps, brigades and infantry, away from orders, details and fatigue duty, out to the front with no army near, the enemy before you and all quiet along your line." The 1st Massachusetts Cavalry rotated men for three-day shifts on the picket line every nine days, and that was enough for Adams. "By the third day I generally feel as if I had been in the anxious seat long enough."[33]

Cavalrymen not only picketed their own camps but often protected those of other units. That was not exactly fair; infantrymen were fully capable of picketing their own camps. "During the whole expedition my command was employed in picketing for the infantry, artillery, and train, in front, flanks, and rear, in addition to its regular patrolling and picket duty," complained Brig. Gen. Benjamin H. Grierson during the Tupelo Campaign in July 1864. Capt. George C. Eckert was careful to point out how much picket duty his 2nd Pennsylvania Cavalry performed during the month of August 1864. It amounted to fourteen days, interspersed with three days of fighting and traveling a total of 200 miles. In other words, the regiment performed picket duty half the month while fighting only one-tenth of it.[34]

Some units excelled at picket duty, while others did not. Lt. Frederick Whittaker of the 6th New York Cavalry thought "there was much slackness on both sides in the matter of picket duty." The tendency was to place too few men and establish the picket line too close to camp, which led to many unnecessary surprises that could have been avoided if twice the number of men had been established at least a mile from camp. The shortage of manpower and the need to preserve the strength of their horses meant that patrolling was not as vigorous as it should have been. Whittaker recommended that all picket reserves should be placed on roads, the most likely avenue of approach by the enemy, and that these roads should be barricaded. A line of sentries should be established only 100 yards from camp as a last alarm. The manual stipulated that pickets should remain mounted, but that wore out the horses as well as the men.[35]

Long picket lines required the most arduous service to maintain. Following the Union occupation of a zone along portions of the North Carolina coast near New Bern in early 1862, Rebel cavalrymen created long picket lines to protect their own occupation zones to the west. "This was the severest service the regiment saw in its history," recalled William A. Graham of the 2nd North Carolina Cavalry. The picket line was established twenty-five miles from the nearest concentration of infantry and only a quarter to half a mile from the Union pickets. For ten days at a time, the troops stood guard in all weather, keeping their horses saddled half the time, which often led to sore backs, and skirmishing with the Federals now and then.[36]

In the West Joseph Wheeler maintained a long picket line with two brigades just before the Battle of Stones River. This was a continuous position stretching many miles to cover the approaches to Murfreesboro, Tennessee, from the northwest and located about ten miles from the state capital. It consisted of a picket line in front and a broken line of picket posts and grand guards placed on the roads from 300 to 1,000 yards to the rear of the picket line.[37]

In fact, Wheeler devoted a good deal of space in his cavalry handbook to picketing. He advised subordinates to use from one-third to one-half their manpower, establishing picket posts on the major roads in the area and spreading other posts to right and left of the road. Then they were to advance a line of videttes 400–500 yards toward the enemy in an "outer chain." The officers had to send out patrols to right and left to contact similar patrols from other posts and send forward patrols to maintain contact with the vidette line. This had to be done all through the night, especially from 3 a.m. until dawn. Wheeler urged his officers to send still more patrols forward from the vidette line at least two miles toward the enemy. All pickets and videttes were to keep their horses saddled at all times. At the grand guard stations, only one-third of the men could feed and water their mounts at any time, but even then they could not remove the saddle. Wheeler also advised the videttes, who were the most isolated members of the picket force, to take position at the base of slopes during the night for better concealment. If pressed by the enemy, everyone was to fall back slowly if they could not restrain their opponent. In a circular issued by his headquarters in April 1864, Wheeler further stipulated that pickets should protect themselves by felling trees across roads.[38]

Confederate cavalrymen complained of long and arduous service on the picket line more often than Federal troopers. "Cavalry service is a hard duty, always on the out Post duty," wrote James Michael Barr of the 5th South Carolina Cavalry. According to some Confederates, this eventually helped their comrades become better cavalrymen. John S. Mosby was convinced that "the discipline and experience of a life on the outpost soon converted the Confederate volunteers into veterans."[39]

Scouting

Cavalry units often provided scouts to gather information for the army. Mosby, who resigned as adjutant of the 1st Virginia Cavalry to become a scout attached to General Stuart's headquarters, defined this service. "A scout is not a spy who goes in disguise," he wrote after the war, "but a soldier in arms and uniform who reconnoitres either inside or outside an enemy's lines."[40]

Good scouts became a fruitful source of intelligence. They supplemented information gathered by cavalry patrols. Infantry units also provided scouts, but cavalry, given its assignments in no-man's-land, tended to provide more of them. Cavalry scouts already were mounted and usually were familiar with the area.

One can understand the process of detailing scouts by looking at how it was done in the 5th West Virginia Cavalry, which began as the 2nd Virginia Infantry (U.S.) before converting to mounted service. C. W. D. Smitley of Company B led a group of scouts from the regiment. It included at least two other men and a soldier drawn from the 55th Ohio plus five civilians. After the regiment became part of a brigade commanded by General Averell, the brigade leader reorganized the scouting. He retained Smitley as the leader but formed a new group by detailing eight other men from the 5th West Virginia plus two from the 3rd Virginia Infantry (U.S.) and some from the 10th Virginia Infantry (U.S.), the 1st Virginia Cavalry (U.S.), and the 14th Pennsylvania Cavalry. Averell, in short, got rid of the civilians and increased the proportion of brigade scouts from loyalist regiments. Probably he felt they could be more effective, given their upbringing in western Virginia.[41]

Wheeler was careful to organize his scouting resources. In July 1864 the general mandated that all scouts should be organized into one unit under the direct control of each division commander. But there were times when Wheeler could not offer much help to his scouts if he sent them on dangerous missions. J. R. Rion recalled that the general sent him with messages to two cavalry detachments near Murfreesboro and Smyrna, Tennessee, in October 1863. "I asked you when I left you how I would get back to you," Rion wrote to Wheeler thirty-five years later. "You said you did not know, that if I got back, it was all right and if I never got back, it would be all right, but not to be captured and I never forgot it." Rion delivered the message to one detachment but not the other. "I made every effort possible to get back to you," he stated, but he had to stay "in the mountains and hills till the war ended."[42]

As with everything else, much depended on the quality of the men. Maj. John T. Wright of the 8th Confederate Cavalry "never could learn tactics and could not move his Regt. from 'lines' to the front, flank, or rear by a proper order," remembered Capt. George Knox Miller. But Wright was "a fearless daredevil sort of man and a good woodsman," so he often was sent out to scout.[43]

Like picketing and outpost duty, scouting took place in the nebulous zone separating friendly from hostile forces. All three were demanding duties that tended to devolve on cavalry forces, although foot soldiers found themselves doing each often enough. Scouting was the most difficult of these tasks and demanded the right kind of personality, while picket and outpost duty could be performed by all mounted soldiers.

Mobility

Cavalry forces were the most highly mobile element of Civil War armies. The horse was their key asset, allowing them to move much faster than foot soldiers and faster than artillery that was slowed down by guns and caissons. While infantry and artillery did well to march twenty miles in one day, cavalry could move thirty miles on a regular basis and often exceeded that when pressed. Moving cavalry units required preparing man and horse for the march, establishing a system for riding along roads, paying attention to march discipline, and devising methods for bivouacking during the night, for marching in darkness when necessary, and for crossing streams. Cavalrymen endured much more time on horseback moving from one place to another than they spent under fire.

For every move, horses were checked to see if shoes needed to be replaced, feed was readied, and riding equipment was placed in order. The soldier had to prepare for his own needs too, which meant cooking rations and receiving an issue of ammunition. Each man also received two spare horseshoes for use during the march. With these preparations completed, the cavalryman was ready to go at short notice. The 92nd Illinois Mounted Infantry needed only three minutes to saddle horses. Members of the 8th New York Cavalry needed only five minutes to go from an exhausted state of resting during a hard march to being ready to mount.[44]

Even though highly mobile, cavalry formations used wheeled transportation to carry supplies, forage, personal baggage, and ordnance, quartermaster, and medical stores. How much transportation was necessary varied from command to command. Samuel W. Ferguson allowed his Confederate brigade a substantial amount in March 1864. He included one wagon for every regimental headquarters, one to be shared by all company officers, one baggage wagon for every twenty-one men, and one forage wagon for every eighty horses. The general also permitted one tent for each regimental headquarters. Many times mounted men carried their forage on the horses to spare wagons, as wheeled vehicles slowed down a mounted column. Henry Norton of the 8th New York Cavalry described how it was done: "We would take our surcingle and halter and tie them around a bundle of hay and then put it on our horses."[45]

Maintaining march discipline reduced straggling and kept the men under control. George McClellan stated that the normal rate of march was about three miles per hour, which amounted to seventeen miles per day but could go as high as thirty miles if needed. "Small detachments of cavalry may make marches of 40, 50, or even 70 miles; but this refers only to exceptional cases." In contrast, Henry W. Halleck believed that "an ordinary day's march for cavalry" was about thirty miles a day and up to fifty miles if a forced march. The men could move at a moderate trot, according to McClellan, but should stop for ten or fifteen minutes every hour and reduce the horse's pace down to a walk "for some distance before each halt."[46]

The need to maintain control of the men was illustrated by Maj. Gen. Stephen D. Lee's marching orders in Mississippi during September 1863. He adopted a much earlier order issued by Maj. Gen. Earl Van Dorn and mandated that anyone galloping their horse during a march without orders would be dismounted and forced to walk to the next camp. Lee and Van Dorn wanted each brigade to maintain a distance of one mile from each other but only 150 yards between each regiment in a brigade. "Regiments will however be well closed up and in good order." Division leaders would tell brigade commanders when to water horses or communicate that order through bugle calls. The columns would halt for fifteen minutes every two to three hours to allow the men to dismount and adjust their saddles. The order prohibited firing of weapons and taking private property without authority, and guards would trail each regiment to collect stragglers. If a man had to fall out "for necessary purposes," he had to report to the commander of the guards for permission.[47]

In general, McClellan's prescriptions and the order issued by Lee reflected the reality of mounted movements in the Civil War. Captain Adams noted that the 1st Massachusetts Cavalry typically marched in columns of fours and averaged three miles an hour, although it rarely halted for rest. The 2nd Massachusetts Cavalry stopped every four and a half hours "to rest the horses a few minutes, and adjust the saddles to prevent galling." If circumstances permitted, a mounted column could take a two-hour break to feed its horses before moving on. It was inevitable that some mounts would need reshoeing on the march, so the 1st Rhode Island Cavalry placed a blacksmith at the rear of its column. If a man needed help, he dropped out of the ranks and went to him, taking but a few minutes to fix the problem, and then rejoined the column.[48]

This described a cavalry column on the move in relatively safe areas, but if it advanced within close proximity of the enemy, additional safe-guards were needed. On the Confederate side John N. Opie of the 6th Virginia Cavalry described the standard formation. A mounted man rode half a mile ahead of the column, and an advance guard of two companies rode halfway between him and the column. When reaching a road junc-tion or a patch of woods, the advance guard posted a picket to prevent a surprise attack. Once the column had passed, these pickets joined the rear guard of the column, which rode a quarter mile behind the main body.[49]

Similar arrangements were followed by Federal mounted units. In the 1st Massachusetts Cavalry, the advance guard consisted of a platoon com-manded by a lieutenant or a sergeant. One to three of its men rode ahead of the guard 100 yards, carbines ready for use. If they saw the enemy, they stopped and waited for the rest of the guard and the lieutenant to catch up. Service in the advance guard called "for lots of backbone," wrote Stanton P. Allen, especially in wooded country. The rear guard worked to corral stragglers and guard the wagons; it often had to drop well behind the column to keep the train moving. The 1st Massachusetts Cavalry also deployed flankers to ride on both sides of the regimental column. Each man rode behind his comrade to the front and kept in sight of him. The front and rear of these two lines of flankers bent inward to keep relatively close to the head and rear of the column, forming something like a half circle. "The flankers must ride on through jungles and swamps," wrote Allen, "up hill and down dale, through briars and brambles, making their way through almost impenetrable labyrinths; scratched and bruised and bleeding on they go."[50]

Maintaining this level of march discipline was strenuous, nerve-racking, but necessary when within easy reach of the enemy. Even more stressful was marching in the dark. On a night scout Captain Adams could not see over three feet ahead of his horse. He had to rely on the jingle of riding equipment coming from the man in front to guide his movement and 'blindly followed" the sound, "relying on my horse not to fall and to keep the road." Norton guided himself by the sparks that occasionally flashed in the dark when the hooves of other horses struck the crushed stones on a macadamized turnpike the 8th New York Cavalry was riding along. At times he realized he was twenty yards behind and closed the gap so quickly as to crowd the men in front, which led to "some tall swearing."[51]

The pace of marching varied widely due to circumstances but typically was at a trot. The 2nd Ohio Cavalry moved mostly at this pace for twenty miles one day. But if there was a need for speedier arrival at a given point, faster paces were necessary and available. The 2nd North Carolina Cavalry galloped for more than a mile to reach the fighting at Brandy Station. Individual horses varied in their level of stamina; only 60 of 250 mounts in the 4th Pennsylvania Cavalry kept up the gallop intermittently used during a twelve-mile march from Fayetteville to Marion, Pennsylvania, during the Gettysburg Campaign.[52]

The need for speed often ran against the limitations of horseflesh. Fast paces could be expected only for short distances. When Col. Robert H. G. Minty received an order to gallop his brigade to secure a bridge over the Etowah River as Sherman's army group approached the span, he did so and took control of the crossing. But his command paid a heavy price for it. "This five mile gallop rendered about 300 horses totally unserviceable," Minty reported.[53]

Short spurts of heavy riding were bad enough, but worse was to continue it for hours at a time. Rapid riding over long distances characterized many marches by cavalry forces during the Civil War. The 1st Maine Cavalry rode 80 miles in thirty hours during an expedition in Virginia during July 1862. Brig. Gen. August V. Kautz claimed his command rode 30–40 miles a day for six days during a raid south of Richmond in May 1864. One finds it hard to believe that the 6th Pennsylvania Cavalry rode over 60 miles in fourteen hours, but that is what Sgt. Thomas W. Smith claimed. But Sheridan's report that his cavalry moved on average 18 miles each day, with "the longest march being 30 miles," during his first raid in the spring campaign of 1864 is fully believable. Maj. Gen. Sterling Price's campaign in Missouri during the fall of that same year witnessed Brig. Gen. John B. Sanborn's brigade moving 62 miles on October 27 and then an additional 104 miles in thirty-six hours. The Stoneman Raid into western North Carolina early in 1865 lasted twenty days, during which Federal cavalry moved a total of 870 miles, 43.5 miles on average per day.[54]

Short rations and bad weather made long marches worse. Winter temperatures had frozen the dirt roads of West Tennessee when General Forrest raided the area in December 1862, and his men found little forage. "Our horses were half dead with starvation and exposure," wrote Dan W. Beard of the 2nd Kentucky Cavalry (CS). Chasing Confederates during the Wheeler-Roddey Raid in south central Tennessee during October 1863, Robert B. Mitchell regularly "threw out all weak and lame horses" so he could maintain a fast pace. The animals were not unsaddled for days at a time, and his men moved as much as fifty-seven miles in one twenty-four-hour period.[55]

When making leisurely marches, cavalrymen could enjoy the ride and feel as if their choice of branches in the army had been a good one. But when circumstances required hard riding for long distances, the demands were extraordinary. The most vulnerable element of a mounted column on a hard march was the horse, the very element that gave it mobility. Heavy movement probably accounted for as many horse casualties as hostile action on the battlefield during the Civil War.

Stream Crossings

Another major feature of long-distance marches was the need to cross numerous streams, ranging from sloughs and bayous to creeks and rivers. Most of them were without bridges, forcing mounted columns to improvise methods of dealing with them. Wading, or fording, was the fastest and easiest way, with soldiers often noting how far up their horse the water level rose as they rode through. The deeper the water, the more the rider got wet. While crossing the swollen Potomac River on the retreat from Gettysburg, Robert T. Hubard Jr. was soaked up to "eight inches above the knees," he recalled. Officers ordered their men to shift cartridge boxes and cap boxes to prevent them from getting wet during crossings or gave the command "Legs up" to save them the trouble of dealing with soaked trousers. During a night crossing of Stones River, Confederate troopers could not even see the water but felt its chilling effect as it rose halfway up their horses' side. Sub-zero temperatures prevailed when men of the 1st Maryland Cavalry (U.S.) swam their horses through Goose Creek near Harpers Ferry, Virginia, on New Year's Day, 1864. "Their heavy boots had gotten full of water which had frozen," recalled C. Armour Newcomer, "and their boots were cut from their feet."[56]

In water too deep to ford, the horse became the mode of crossing streams. McClellan had noted that the Austrian cavalry taught recruits to hold the mane and look at the opposite bank, not at the water, so they would not become giddy. If a man fell off, he was told to continue holding on to the mane or the horse's tail and let the mount take him out of danger. It all depended on the ability of the horse to swim strongly enough, but Civil War cavalrymen could not always count on their steed. "Had great difficulty in making the horses swim," noted Lt. Col. Robert A. Alston when his 9th Tennessee Cavalry (CS) tried to cross the Cumberland River during Morgan's Raid in July 1863. Troopers of the 14th Illinois Cavalry found that their horses were willing to swim, but the current of Green River in Kentucky was swift when the regiment crossed, and some horses could not deal with it. "They would go down, strike bottom, and again came to the surface, plunging fearfully," wrote Capt. Henry C. Connelly.[57]

When confronted with rain-swollen Cotton Indian Creek in the Kilpatrick Raid during the Atlanta Campaign, the 1st Ohio Cavalry stretched a picket rope across the watercourse. "It was no doubt the first attempt of some of the horses to swim," thought W. L. Curry, and their uncertain efforts caused some riders to lose their seat. They "were saved only by the ropes." Even so, "a number of soldiers were drowned." Forty or fifty horses and some mules also were lost.[58]

It usually was safer to separate the men from their horses when crossing a difficult stream. This involved moving the troopers and their saddles and equipment on small boats while leading the swimming horses by the reins. When the 7th Tennessee Cavalry (CS) tried to cross the Tennessee River, they used a number of small dugouts twenty feet long. Only three men and their equipment could fit into each, with two men rowing and one holding the reins of their three horses. John Milton Hubbard had to pull tight on the reins of his own horse to keep its nose above water. Most of Forrest's men separated from their horses to cross the Tennessee River at the start and end of their raid into West Tennessee in December 1862.

On the way west they pushed their horses over the river bluff, which was ten feet higher than the water level. The horses were naturally confused by this behavior and swam in circles in the water until most of them saw campfires on an island more than halfway across the stream and swam for that beacon. But others exhausted themselves in trying to climb back up the nearly vertical bluff, and several died in the attempt.[59]

It was faster to ride the horses across a shallow part of the stream, but the current became a major factor in that method. Chaplain Charles A. Humphreys of the 2nd Massachusetts Cavalry noted that when crossing a ford of the North Anna River, the current was just strong enough to drift horse and man a bit downstream, which influenced the rest of the column behind them. As a result, when his regiment came to the bank, it missed the ford altogether and hit deep water. Some riders lost their seat as their horses floundered, and Humphreys was knocked into the river when his colonel fell off his own mount. The chaplain was bruised by plunging horses and nearly drowned during this confused crossing.[60]

The 2nd Ohio Cavalry had learned how to cross difficult streams while serving in the West early in the war and brought those skills to the Virginia theater. On the march to the Battle of Waynesboro early in 1865, Sheridan's cavalry crossed the swollen Shenandoah River. The regiment formed three men abreast who acted as a unit, supporting each other in battling the current. The trio angled upstream as soon as they hit water's edge, and when their horses' hooves left the bottom at deep water, they let their mounts swim as they steered them straight for the other bank. The current took the trio some distance downstream but in a managed way. The only difficulty was that the horses tended to kick and jump when their feet hit solid bottom again, so the troopers had to be ready to handle this jostling.[61]

Every stream crossing involved some degree of risk, and many resulted in some loss of man and mount. This happened because many troopers and horses lacked the skill to swim well or were timid about surmounting water obstacles. Even when using boats, accidents happened. When a flatboat capsized while crossing the Obion River in western Tennessee, the 19th Pennsylvania Cavalry lost seven horses. Later that day the regiment lost an additional twenty-three mounts while riding through a swamp. In fact, a surprising number of horses died in crossing swamps during the war, even though the water level was shallow compared to streams. The mucky bottom became a deathtrap for some mounts, whose thrashing and struggling only served to engulf them deeper.[62]

A Confederate mounted column under the command of Brig. Gen. William E. Jones raided into western Virginia in April 1863 but had to cross the swollen South Branch of the Potomac River. Some men in the brigade refused to swim their horses across, fearing the worst, and the fate of a handful of troopers proved that there was reason for caution. The 6th Virginia Cavalry, for example, lost three horses and one man. "When a horse lost its footing," recalled John N. Opie, "he rolled over and over in the current, like a barrel, until, finally, he disappeared in the raging torrent below. Two of the men who lost their horses seized the tails of other horses, and were thus dragged across. The man who was drowned caused his own death and that of his horse by swinging to the bridle rein; and thus the two rolled down the current together."[63]

Stream crossings became far more deadly when the enemy contested them. At times the defender planted impediments such as wire under the shallow water to trip up horses. But if the way was not impeded by obstacles and the horse was fearless, the cavalryman could cross a defended stream. "She had a mind of her own," wrote Jacob B. Cooke of his horse, "and that mind was always to be in the front." Cooke's mount got him across a heavily defended stream during the Battle of Kelly's Ford.[64]

Brig. Gen. Rufus Barringer's Confederate brigade pushed across Chamberlain Run during the latter stages of the Petersburg Campaign on March 31, 1865. Not only the main streambed but also the bottomlands were flooded for seventy-five yards on both sides. There was only one place for horses to cross, so he dismounted the 1st North Carolina Cavalry into line on the left to advance and draw Union fire. Then Barringer charged the 2nd North Carolina Cavalry mounted in a close column of eights across the ford, with the 5th North Carolina Cavalry dismounted as a reserve. The attack succeeded, even though the water was up to a dismounted man's armpits. Barringer lost more than 110 men "killed, drowned & wounded."[65]

The military role of cavalry ranged across a wide spectrum, from skirmishing to picket and outpost duty, supporting friendly infantry and artillery, and fighting hostile infantry and artillery. Mounted troops contributed their fair share of combat to Civil War operations. Off the battlefield, cavalry enjoyed an unparalleled mobility and generally fulfilled the potential of that mobility, although the price to be paid was high in terms of worn-out animals and exhausted men.

The key to combined-arms effectiveness was that each arm had a distinctive capability that, when combined with the other arms, made for an effective whole. Although some Civil War field commanders tried to achieve true combined-arms effectiveness, it cannot be said that any of them succeeded very well. The main reason for this limited success was the difficulty of matching the highly mobile nature of mounted warfare with the comparatively slow nature of infantry and artillery operations. Only rarely throughout history had commanders managed to do so effectively, among them Alexander the Great and Napoleon. But they were exceptions to the rule, and Civil War commanders fit far more comfortably within that rule than with the exceptions.

6

MOUNTED CHARGES AND PERSONAL COMBAT

For most cavalrymen in blue or gray, the ultimate experience of their war service was participating in a mounted charge on the enemy. Among all the varied duties expected of horse soldiers, this was the one that stamped them as true cavalry warriors. They shared this attitude with millions of horse soldiers before them because the mounted charge was as old as cavalry itself. The speed, the wild enthusiasm, the shock effect, and the prospects of a quick and decisive victory combined to make it the epitome of cavalry's potential. The mounted charge was a very public event, in contrast to isolated duty on the picket line; it was a showcase for the skills, discipline, and emotions of a horse soldier and symbolized the essence of mounted warfare.

This emphasis on the mounted charge led to another development distinctive to mounted warfare. Cavalrymen engaged in personal combat far more often than did infantrymen and artillerymen. The charge deliberately brought mounted soldiers into close contact with their opponents, encouraging hand-to-hand combat in the form of melees (unorganized group fighting at arm's length) and hot pursuits on horseback (wherein men were close enough while riding in the same direction to fight each other on the move). While it is true that not every mounted attack resulted in close fighting, enough of them did so to propel the cavalryman many times into such close quarters that he could reach his enemy with an edged weapon.

The Mounted Charge

For at least two hundred years, the charge had been an orderly, controlled event that took into consideration the capabilities and limitations of the horses. Cooke's drill manual stipulated that the charge should begin with a walk, then shift to a trot after 20 paces, to a gallop after 60 paces, and an all-out run at 80 paces. According to Henry W. Halleck, a horse could move 110–120 yards per minute while at a walk; 220–240 yards at a trot; and 330–360 yards at a gallop. In the last phase, after the gallop, horsemen gave their mounts full rein and pointed their sabers toward the enemy. Prussian doctrine differed from the American, with walking and trotting for the first 500 paces, galloping for the next 200 paces, and charging for the last 100 paces.[1]

Civil War cavalry commanders gave instructions about the form and pace of a mounted attack in varied ways. "When you charge," yelled Col. Alfred N. Duffié to the 1st Rhode Island Cavalry at Kelly's Ford in 1863, "you don't gallop, when you charge, you walk, you trot, you touch your next man's stirrup, you keep closed up in line; you don't shoot until you see the whites of their eyes, then you give 'em hell." Philip Sheridan's instructions to George Custer at Yellow Tavern in 1864 were more succinct. "I ordered Custer to charge, first on a walk, then on a trot, and when he got near enough for the horses to hold out, to go for those guns on a run. He did it beautifully."[2]

Three things were associated with a mounted charge in the minds of cavalrymen. First, it highlighted the use of the saber, the distinctive weapon of mounted warriors. Second, there was no excuse for a cavalry unit to surrender even if encircled by the enemy. The mounted charge could and often did save a formation from the indignity and risk associated with giving up on the battlefield; one could always try to cut his way out of any encirclement. And third, if a careful commander wanted to hedge his bets, he retained a reserve, "without which cavalry almost never can charge without great risk," as Edward L. Bouvé of the 4th Massachusetts Cavalry noted. Of course, maintaining a reserve was impossible if the command was surrounded and meant to break free by charging.[3]

While there was general agreement among cavalryman about how and when to conduct a mounted charge, and firm agreement that it was a central part of their existence, everyone had their own way of expressing this doctrine. Maj. Gen. James E. B. Stuart enunciated his version of it in general orders. "An attack of cavalry should be sudden, bold, and vigorous; to falter is to fail," he wrote soon after the Battle of Gettysburg. "The cavalry which arrives noiselessly but steadily near the enemy, and then, with one loud yell, leaps upon him without a note of warning, and giving him no time to form or consider anything but the immediate means of flight, pushing him vigorously every step with all the confidence of victory achieved, is true cavalry; while a body of men equally brave and patriotic, who halt at every picket and reconnoiter until the precious surprise is over, is not cavalry." Stuart wanted his men to maximize the impulsive nature of the mounted charge by starting to gallop when only fifty yards from the target. "Too much importance cannot be given to the shock of the charge, the furious impact of horse against horse, for in that will consist the success of the charge."[4]

Stuart heavily emphasized the emotional aspect of the mounted charge, an interest shared by many cavalrymen. Respected officers who made a big show of leading an attack created lasting impressions. Jacob B. Cooke of the 1st Rhode Island Cavalry remembered the sight of Maj. Gen. Philip Kearny at the Battle of Chantilly, "dashing across the field, his horse flecked with foam, the bridle reins in his teeth" because Kearney had lost his left arm during the Mexican War. The general held his saber "high in [the] air, the very incarnation of the spirit of war."[5]

The sight of drawn sabers was as inspiring as the flashy actions of officers. Many cavalrymen recalled the impressive sight of massed steel blades pointed in the same direction, especially if the sunlight glinted off the polished metal. Even without drawn sabers, the impression given by a large mass of cavalry moving at speed was more potent than a similar mass of foot soldiers moving slowly forward. "There was a seething mass of men and horses rushing on like an avalanche," reported Isaac Gause of the 2nd Ohio Cavalry, "that must sweep everything in front of it. The bravest men cannot withstand it." The emotional aspects of the mounted charge were so compelling that many men yearned to experience it. "I want a chance to make one saber charge," Maj. Peter Weber confided to James H. Kidd, both of the 6th Michigan Cavalry. He had that chance during the fight at Falling Waters on July 14, 1863. Weber led a successful charge on retreating Confederates and was killed in the process.[6]

The often fatal allure of the cavalry charge did not diminish its attraction, and it often succeeded, as had Weber's attack at Falling Waters. Custer ordered a mounted assault by the 1st Michigan Cavalry at Cold Harbor on the last day of May 1864. "This charge produced the desired effect. The enemy, without waiting to receive it, threw down their arms and fled." Confederate George W. Hunt informed his friend that an attack by two mounted brigades on a Union wagon train in East Tennessee worked in a similar way. "This terrible yelling and rapid movement demoralized" the Federal cavalrymen who escorted the train, and they fled.[7]

Even when a mounted attack failed to deflate the opponent, it often could succeed in its objective through sheer weight of rapidly moving numbers. A classic example of a cavalry charge used to escape a trap took place in the Kilpatrick Raid during the Atlanta Campaign. Nearly cut off by the enemy during the fighting at Nash's Farm on August 20, 1864, the Federals mounted a spirited assault. Samuel B. Barron of the 3rd Texas Cavalry was on the receiving end of it. "As they came on us at a sweeping gallop, with their bright sabers glittering, it was a grand display." Ross's Texas Brigade was the target, and it "was there and then literally run over" by the Federals. The physical damage to the Confederates was not overwhelming, perhaps eighty-five men missing, at least two killed, and several wounded. In addition, "a number of the men were pretty badly hacked with sabers." Kilpatrick's troopers broke cleanly out of the trap and escaped. "To say that we were crest fallen and heartily ashamed of being run over is to put it mildly," admitted Barron.[8]

To achieve results like this, most cavalrymen were convinced that a mounted charge had to be made with suddenness, and that meant the commander had to make a quick decision. "In a fight of cavalry against cavalry the advantage is with the party that moves first," concluded William H. Beach of the 1st New York (Lincoln) Cavalry. Capt. W. L. Curry of the 1st Ohio Cavalry agreed that "the commander must not halt or hesitate in an emergency, but must act immediately."[9]

It is possible the Confederates adhered to this rule more faithfully than did the Federals. Turner Ashby, according to an admiring writer, tried "always to meet the enemy with bold and determined charges, and when they were defeated to press them with the utmost vigor." John S. Mosby had a rule "not to stand still and receive a charge, but always to act on the offensive." Mosby aimed a gendered insult at the mounted warrior who failed to seize every opportunity to attack: "The cavalry officer is like a woman who deliberates—he's lost." Or one had to get "the 'bulge on 'em,'" as W. H. Cheek of the 1st North Carolina Cavalry recalled.[10]

But what the most fervent supporters of this aggressive doctrine rarely admitted was that it could just as easily place a mounted command in grave danger. Attacking quickly without knowing what lay ahead was risky in the extreme, and it sometimes resulted in failed assaults or outright disaster. Two companies of the 8th Indiana Cavalry led the van of a large Union column during the McCook-Stoneman Raid of the Atlanta Campaign. "Fired on at almost every turn of the road, they charged repeatedly through the darkness without knowing or caring whether their foe numbered 1 man or 1,000." That was a highly commendable spirit, but it did not always work out. While these two companies managed to enter Newnan, Georgia, they were driven out again by superior numbers. Other small units found themselves in a hornets' nest of trouble because they attacked, suffered high casualties, and wrecked their organization.[11]

Despite these less than successful outcomes, everyone continued to argue that an aggressive attitude was the best for cavalry operations. "The men learned from such examples of prompt action that in cavalry fighting the chances were vastly in favor of the body that 'got on the move' first," argued Beach, "and that they could shoot before them more accurately than they could shoot behind them. They were successful or unfortunate, as they attacked quickly or waited to be attacked." Brig. Gen. Emory Upton was convinced that the small number of casualties in his division during Wilson's Raid would have been much larger if not for the aggressive spirit that animated the men. "Whether mounted or dismounted, but one spirit prevailed, and that was to run over the enemy wherever found or whatever might be his numbers." In this he was supported by the existing doctrine. Dennis Hart Mahan, professor at the U.S. Military Academy, wrote that any "body of cavalry which waits to receive a charge of cavalry . . . must either retire or be destroyed."[12]

Cavalry-versus-cavalry action tended to be mostly a contest of nerves.

Members of the 1st Rhode Island Cavalry watched intently as a Confederate mounted charge neared their position at Kelly's Ford. Some of them shouted to encourage the enemy to close in for a fight, while one or two others fired their carbines without orders. Colonel Duffié put a stop to the firing and ordered his men to draw their sabers. "A line of cold steel flashed in the waning sunlight," recalled Rhode Islander Cooke as the Confederates shifted from a gallop to a charge. But Duffié waited until the enemy was very close before he gave the order to charge, a move that broke up the Confederate formation and led to the enemy scattering in retreat.[13]

"The intention of the cavalry charge is to produce shock by the momentum of the bodies of horses running at full speed," commented John B. Turchin, a Russian-born Union infantry general. "The charging squadron is nothing else but a living ram to batter down or scatter the enemy's infantry or cavalry, hence the full speed of horses is the main factor of its success."[14]

Men who witnessed the physical collision of two mounted columns testified to the fact that the battering ram concept came true on a number of battlefields. Capt. William E. Miller of the 3rd Pennsylvania Cavalry wrote of "a crash like the falling of timber" that arose from such a crunch at Gettysburg. "So sudden and violent was the collision, that many of the horses turned over end over end and crushed their riders beneath them." In a fight during Stoneman's Raid in the Chancellorsville Campaign, Capt. James E. Harrison of the 5th U.S. Cavalry charged a larger mounted column that immediately countercharged, with both columns colliding. "The shock of the charge *was so great that my foremost horses were completely knocked over*," reported Harrison. Harry Gilmor recalled a similar result as his command was hit by a Federal mounted charge. "When the two forces met the shock was tremendous, and several men and horses rolled on the ground."[15]

Success or Failure

Many cavalrymen insisted that most of the mounted charges they participated in were successful, and the key was demonstrating superior determination to make it succeed. Whether or not this was true is difficult to say, for there are many examples of unsuccessful mounted attacks. One thing seemed consistent: if one side stood still and received the shock, they usually were defeated. At Yellow Tavern the successful charge that captured a Confederate battery and mortally wounded General Stuart was aided by the fact that the Confederates were "simple enough to receive the charge in a stationary position," as Sheridan put it.[16]

There were a number of factors that contributed to the failure of a mounted charge during the Civil War. Knowing the predilection of cavalry commanders to instantly attack the moment an enemy appeared, crafty officers used small decoy forces to lure them into an ambush. In fact, even without a decoy or ambush, a small attacking force could easily run into a larger enemy force during an impromptu charge, as happened with Francis Washburn and part of the 4th Massachusetts Cavalry at the Battle of High Bridge during the Appomattox Campaign. Numerous terrain obstacles impeded the momentum of a charge, including fences, ditches, and streams with steep banks. Thick brush and dense timber offered equally difficult obstacles. At times straggling soldiers or overly excited and riderless horses got in the way.[17]

Ultimately, horses were the key to a mounted charge. They often were called on to do more than was possible under difficult circumstances. Their limitations determined how far a cavalry regiment could surmount landscape problems. The 6th U.S. Cavalry attacked at Upperville on June 21, 1863, across "heavy and marshy ground, intersected by a most difficult ditch and terminating in a hill of plowed ground," according to Capt. George C. Cram. This so exhausted the mounts that "it was impossible to bring or keep them for such a distance at a charging pace."[18]

While horse fatigue was a major factor in mounted charges, the most prominent terrain obstacle were the fences that tended to appear in many places on Civil War battlefields. In most cases the horsemen could not simply jump over them, especially when packed in tight column formations. If there was time, skirmishers could open gaps in rail fences. This type of fence was the easiest to disrupt because the sections were loosely joined at an angle. Isaac Norval Baker of the 18th Virginia Cavalry described how this was done. "Two men going to the corner of a worm fence and one man throwing one rail one way and the other man throwing the other rail the other way and in this way, two panels will look like rails stacked." A more stout type of fence consisting of posts and rails was built in a straight line, with the ends of rails mortised into heavy posts. Still, some cavalrymen tackled them successfully. Col. Thomas T. Munford dismounted half of his 2nd Virginia Cavalry to tear down one such fence while under artillery and small-arms fire at Gettysburg.[19]

Rarely did cavalrymen try to jump over fences during a charge. Col. Robert H. G. Minty's men confronted a rail fence while charging with Kilpatrick at Nash's Farm, and the leading horses leaped over it, the legs of some knocking the top rails off. "Gaps were soon made, through which the columns poured," Minty noted. But this was impossible with stout post-and-rail fences and those made of stone. While conducting a countercharge at Gettysburg, the 7th Michigan Cavalry ran up against a fence it could not handle. Either made of stone with a superstructure of rails or a post-and-rail fence (both were described), it stopped the Federals and caused them to bunch up within close distance of Confederates on the opposite side. "To have stopped and dismounted and tear it down in the face of so strong a force would have been impossible," recalled Col. Russell A. Alger.[20]

There were times when terrain obstacles led a commander to decide against an attack. Quickly judging whether fences, ditches, uneven ground, or trees posed more of a hazard than the enemy, he declined to seize the fleeting moment for offensive action. But more often than not, commanders grabbed that moment even when they knew the terrain posed many problems for their men—they either overcame those obstacles or failed in the attempt to bring shock to the enemy. Everyone drew the line, however, when it came to charging in darkness unless it was done by small units and along routes where the roadway itself could serve as a guide for forward movement.[21]

Merely uncomfortable situations did not deter the cavalryman. The Battle of Waynesboro in the Shenandoah Valley took place in wretched weather on March 2, 1865. When the 22nd New York Cavalry participated in a mounted charge along a dirt road at full gallop, "the mud and water flying in every direction," everyone became splattered with the muck. Men and horses were "soaked bodily in the soft mire of the road."[22]

Relying on cold steel, imbued with the spirit of aggression, and willing to risk bad weather, terrain impediments, upended horses, and hand-to-hand fighting, Civil War cavalrymen deserved a good deal of respect. They were proud of their ability to risk danger and bring mounted combat to an eye-ball level. Capt. Joseph G. Vale of the 7th Pennsylvania Cavalry proudly reported that Colonel Minty's brigade conducted five successful saber charges against Confederate infantry and four successful ones against artillery. It also accomplished more than a hundred successful saber charges against Confederate cavalry. The brigade made twenty-five dismounted charges, in three of which it captured fortified positions.[23]

The Proper Weapon

No matter what their opinion about the tactical usefulness of the mounted charge, everyone agreed that the saber was the only weapon to employ while moving swiftly toward the enemy. It had emotionally charged symbolism as well as utility in mounted hand-to-hand combat that neither the pistol nor the carbine possessed. Cold steel became a metaphor for determination and a symbol of mounted effectiveness.

Many officers encouraged their units to use only cold steel. "Keep to your sabres, men!" they shouted before and during the charge in an effort to prevent the troopers from using firearms. At least one regimental commander even threatened his men if they disobeyed his order to "use sabres alone" by yelling, "I will cut down the first man who fires a shot."[24]

In some cavalry regiments the weapons were divided among companies, creating a tactical specialization. The 2nd Iowa Cavalry's 3rd Battalion possessed sabers and carbines and "did most of the charging," wrote Lyman B. Pierce. The 1st and 2nd Battalions used Colt's revolving rifles and "receive and repulse more of the charges of the enemy than do the saber companies." In short, the saber units specialized in mounted charges, while the rifle companies concentrated on dismounted fighting.[25]

Some Federal veterans asserted that the Confederates never adopted the saber as a favored weapon even in charging and close fighting, but a survey of reports and accounts fails to support that view. Some Confederate horsemen preferred handguns, but others relied heavily on sabers. On one extreme Mosby was so dedicated to pistol work that he completely discounted the value of the edged weapon. He not only had "great faith in the efficacy of a charge" but also firmly believed in "the superiority of the revolver over the sabre." Describing a close fight with the Federals, Mosby wrote: "The remorseless revolver was doing its work of death in their ranks, while their swords were as harmless as the wooden sword of harlequin. Unlike my adversaries, I was not trammeled with tradition that required me to use an obsolete weapon."[26]

When men tried to use firearms in a mounted charge or a melee, they found it difficult. "A soldier should have three hands" to fire a gun while mounted, thought William McGee of the 15th Pennsylvania Cavalry: "one to manage his horse and the other two to fire and load his carbine." But it was possible to fire a pistol with one hand while holding the reins and a saber in the other, as did 2nd U.S. Cavalry troopers at Brandy Station. Most Union and Confederate horsemen used only one weapon at a time. They recognized that, despite Mosby's extreme view, most horse soldiers believed that "for close work the sabre, freely used, surpasses" the pistol and the carbine.[27]

Saber Work

The strong belief in charging at the enemy propelled cavalrymen into hand-to-hand combat very often. Close fighting within arm's length of the enemy was a consequence of charging a determined foe. While bayonet attacks by infantry units were fairly common, they rarely resulted in hand-to-hand fighting. The defending side more often than not pulled away before close contact ensued. Most infantrymen served through the entire war without ever engaging in hand-to-hand combat.[28]

Cavalrymen were aware that their doctrine of spirited charges resulted in eyeball confrontations with the enemy. "Our custom implied close contact, hand to hand," wrote Henry Murray Calvert of the 11th New York Cavalry, "and some men of the regiment had been horribly disfigured, some indeed had been killed outright by saber cuts." Numerous stationery producers printed letterhead illustrations that depicted hand-to-hand fighting on horseback, and *Frank Leslie's Illustrated Newspaper* also publicized images of saber duels by mounted opponents.[29]

Many cavalry commanders reported that their men excelled at sabering the enemy during a mounted attack and referred to the blows suffered by their own troops as proof of their courage. "The charge was spiritedly made and sabers freely used, as the heads of my men will attest," reported Lt. Col. Addison W. Preston of the 1st Vermont Cavalry. Maj. Abial R. Pierce of the 4th Iowa Cavalry personally cut eight Confederates "from their horses with my own saber" during a mounted attack at the Battle of Mine Creek on October 25, 1864.[30]

When two men hacked away at each other with sabers, it was natural to assume the result would be bloody. But it is surprising how many saber duels resulted in little injury. When John N. Opie of the 6th Virginia Cavalry chased a Federal horseman in a skirmish, he struck him two or three times "over the back, without making any impression." Then Opie "turned my sabre in my hand to give him the tierce point. The fellow was bending over on his horse's neck, and I lunged at his back with all my strength. My sabre point entered under his clothes and ripped them up his back, and, I suppose, scratched him a little." At that point the Federal surrendered. In a heavy skirmish near Waynesboro, Georgia, during Sherman's March to the Sea, Confederate officer Felix H. Robertson led a charge against members of Kilpatrick's cavalry division. Robertson used his saber on fleeing Union horsemen, but that weapon had lost its cutting edge from rattling in his metal scabbard. "I found it impossible to force the point through the Yankee jackets." The Federals also were riding in the same direction as Robertson, which made it more difficult to come to grips with a target. He then tried to lunge the point at the exposed necks of the Federals and "succeeded very well," he explained, "in doing some execution. As soon as I would finish disposing, with my sabre, of one man, I would spur my horse forward and reach another." Robertson eventually was shot in the elbow and disabled for further action that day.[31]

Robertson did not report how seriously he injured the men whose necks he hit, but many who engaged in hand-to-hand combat suffered only minor cuts. Col. Frank A. Montgomery of the 1st Mississippi Cavalry struggled to injure Lt. Col. Quincy McNeil of the 2nd Illinois Cavalry during Earl Van Dorn's raid against Holly Springs, Mississippi, on December 20, 1862, but McNeil suffered only a nearly severed finger as a result. Capt. Benjamin F. Medina of the 5th Virginia Cavalry almost had his nose severed during a close-range saber duel.[32]

Capt. George N. Bliss of Company C, 1st Rhode Island Cavalry provided one of the most detailed narratives of personal combat to emerge

George N. Bliss.
Captain of Company C, 1st Rhode Island Cavalry, Bliss here
wears the sword that would become the center of his remarkable
story of charging through the 4th Virginia Cavalry. Photograph
by Manchester Brothers of Providence, Rhode Island.
LC-DIG-ppmsca-71011, Library of Congress.

from the Civil War. He was in charge of the provost guard when Confederate horsemen forced in Col. Charles Russell Lowell's brigade outposts near Waynesboro in the Shenandoah Valley on September 28, 1864. Lowell wanted him to push back, and Bliss commandeered a squadron of the 3rd New Jersey Cavalry, leading it in a mounted charge with sabers in the air. Along the way Bliss and two Jersey troopers rode far ahead of the rest; before he realized it, Bliss was riding in the middle of a group of retreating Confederates, with half a dozen of the enemy behind him, three to his left, and one to his right. He continued to ride forward and soon put fifty Rebels behind him while swinging his saber freely to right and left. Bliss knew he struck half a dozen blows and remembered that two Confederates dodged his weapon by moving their heads at the last minute. He later found out that two of the four men he wounded were Lt. William A. Moss and Hugh S. Hamilton of the 4th Virginia Cavalry.[33]

When Bliss saw a side road to the left, he rode through the Confederates and onto it, gaining about twenty yards ahead of half a dozen Rebels who pursued him. One of them shot his horse, and the animal fell, dismounting Bliss. As the captain was rising from the ground, two Confederates rode up and hacked at him with saber and carbine. Bliss was able to parry the carbine blow but was cut on the forehead by the saber. Answering a call to surrender, he decided to give up but was not yet out of danger. Just after the captain surrendered his weapons, a lone Confederate rode up and thrust his saber into Bliss's back. The blow forced him two steps forward. Later Bliss figured out that he could have been skewered by this blow except that his assailant, "in his ignorance of the proper use of the weapon . . . had failed to make the half turn of wrist necessary to give the sabre smooth entrance between the ribs." Nevertheless, the tip of the saber had injured his lung. Yet another Confederate raised his carbine to shoot, and Bliss saved himself by calling loudly for protection as a Freemason. That brought Capt. Henry C. Lane, acting adjutant of the 4th Virginia Cavalry, to his rescue. Bliss found out later that his horse had only been stunned, not killed, and was appropriated by someone in the Rebel regiment.[34]

Bliss endured several months of awful conditions in Confederate prisons before returning to his own army. He survived the war and had the interesting experience of corresponding with the men he had injured in his fight on September 28. "I engaged you with the sabre, and was at once put on the defensive by your superior swordsmanship," wrote William A. Moss in 1884, "which kept me active to prevent a thrust from you." At that point, he reported, one of the two Federals who accompanied Bliss shot Moss with a handgun, and the Confederate could not control his horse.

Before Moss could disengage, however, Bliss struck him with his saber "on the back of the head; I tried to draw my pistol, but having my sabre knot over my wrist and being disabled in the bridle hand, I could not do so." As Moss watched, the captain rode on and hit two more Confederates.[35]

Robert L. Baber was another man Bliss wounded that day. "I received three sabre wounds on my head," he wrote in 1902. Baber was tickled at that late year to learn the identity of "the man who gave me such an awful drubbing." But the wounds were not disabling; they led to a welcome sick furlough of six weeks for Baber. That same year Thomas N. Garnett also wrote to Bliss to tell him of the saber cut on the head the captain had given him that long-ago day. Bliss had given him "a right cut and passed on." Garnett pursued him into the side road and shot the captain's horse.[36]

The saber that Bliss wielded so adroitly on September 28 had a subsequent history. The captain gave it as a token of surrender to Thad Sheppard, who in turn gave it to Garnett. But the latter was unable to keep it when the war ended. On his way home after Appomattox, Garnett reached Lynchburg, where other ex-Confederates warned him to get rid of all weapons so the Federals would not suspect him of being one of Mosby's men. So Garnett hid the saber under a rail fence ten miles from his home. Nine years later the landowner, B. F. Sheppard (no relation to Thad Sheppard), moved that fence and found the weapon, keeping it as a relic of the war and using it to kill rodents in his barn. Bliss became interested in finding out where his trusty saber had landed up and placed a notice in the *Richmond Dispatch* that brought out the information. Garnett saw the notice and talked to Sheppard, who told him he wanted five dollars for the saber if Garnett intended to send it back to Bliss. If the Confederate veteran wanted to keep it himself, Sheppard was willing to give it up free. Garnett paid the man and sent the weapon to Bliss, who was utterly delighted to receive it. The saber still had a prominent dent one-third of the way down from the hilt caused by Bliss parrying the blow of the carbine as he struggled to rise from his stunned horse. It reached Bliss in time for him to exhibit it at a reunion of the 1st Rhode Island Cavalry veterans on August 9, 1902. Hamilton, one of the men Bliss had wounded on September 28, attended that reunion.[37]

This intriguing story of the sword, its wielder, and its victims came full circle thirty-eight years after the fighting that had taken place on September 28, 1864. Bliss had not planned to ride virtually alone into a mass of retreating Confederates, but once there he reacted in true cavalry fashion. Instead of retreating he continued to put on a bold front and rode along, using his skill at mounted combat to stay alive. As he injured one Confederate after another, the remaining Rebels around him became very angry. "Kill that d—— Yankee!" they yelled. Not until they disabled his horse was Bliss doomed to failure. Their efforts to harm him even when he was down and struggling to disentangle himself from his fallen horse had arisen from the emotions engendered by the fight, and Bliss barely survived the cruel blow from behind delivered by an anonymous Rebel.[38]

But with the passage of time, everyone involved in this little drama saw it in a different light. It is interesting that the majority of them did survive it; there is no evidence that anyone died as a result of Bliss's exploit, and most of his victims lived well long after the war. Everyone who witnessed the episode marveled over it. "Although the daring ride of yours was at our expense," wrote Hamilton in 1903, "we have never owed you any grudge for it, but have often made mention of it as showing what was possible for a determined man to accomplish who was well mounted and knew the use of the sabre."[39]

Hamilton was right. Bliss's adept swordsmanship kept him alive, and it had been based on the saber training he received. Moreover, the lack of skill at swordsmanship displayed by the man who stabbed him in the back also saved his life. Bliss's exploit encapsulated much of what was possible and impossible in the use of the saber in close, personal combat during the Civil War.

Melees and Chases

When many opposing cavalrymen came close enough to use their sabers, melees often ensued. Defined as a frenzied and unorganized hand-to-hand fight, they occurred more often in the mounted service than in foot or artillery warfare. They could be dangerous but were exciting affairs. "For a few moments the air was bright with the flashing of sabres," re-

Sixth U.S. Cavalry, Mounted Melee at Slatersville, Virginia, on May 9, 1862.
This distinctive form of frenzied, disorganized, hand-to-hand combat,
called a melee, resulted from the aggressive,
go-ahead spirit of nineteenth-century cavalry doctrine.
Frank Leslie's Illustrated Newspaper, June 7, 1862, 153.

called Edward L. Bouvé of the battle at High Bridge during the Appomattox Campaign. The air also was "shattered by the explosion of carbine and pistol, while screams of rage mingled with the cries of the wounded and all the hideous sounds of a savage hand-to-hand fight." One could easily be "swept along with the current" and become isolated among a crowd that mingled friend and foe. At Gettysburg three or four Federals, however, managed to work shoulder to shoulder through such a tangled mass to escape one crowded fight, while others undoubtedly were engulfed by the melee. There are reports of horses falling and bringing down other mounts with their riders in these packed, chaotic masses. If men had no sabers, they used pistols, often clubbing their opponents with the barrels or using their hands to pull them out of the saddle.[40]

A melee was a stationary fight, but a moving battle occurred more often. They resulted from hot chases, as one mounted force decided it was better to escape than to fight and was closely pursued. These running fights often resulted in a mixing of individual horsemen and resultant hand-to-hand combat. The participants cut and thrust with their sabers, fired pistols at short distance, and clubbed each other with weapons. They also used their fists at times while riding at high speed.

Many veterans believed that the saber was the most effective weapon in a chase. Capt. Amasa E. Matthews "never worked harder" in his life than when trying to keep his men from "using their pistols, shooting themselves, and breaking up the ranks," during a chase. "I thought we were doing the best, so long as the saber points kept them running." The length of these hot pursuits varied widely. Some lasted only 300 yards, while others went "three miles at full speed." A handful of reports indicate the chase could extend for even ten or twelve miles. But George A. Custer insisted that at the battle of Tom's Brook, the most "complete and decisive overthrow of the enemy cavalry" during the war, his pursuit "was kept up vigorously for nearly twenty miles, and only relinquished then from the complete exhaustion of our horses and the dispersion of our panic-stricken enemies." It was not unusual for pursuers to ride past enemy horsemen who were in the rear of the retreating column in their eagerness to catch up with the van. Riderless horses often continued to run after the trooper fell off, and if a mount stumbled and fell, its unlucky rider could easily be trampled by other horses.[41]

The Consequences of Personal Combat

Close-range personal combat that arose from melees and hot pursuits rarely resulted in large numbers of casualties, and those that occurred tended to be only lightly wounded men. Sgt. William B. Baker of the 1st Maine Cavalry recorded several running fights in June 1863 in which men received slight cuts from sabers. Simeon A. Holden got "a sabre thrust in the right side, he says he run his sabre through the rebel who inflicted his wound." Capt. Andrew B. Spurling was hit three times with a saber, the last cutting the knuckle of his forefinger on the right hand pretty badly; he received sick leave to recuperate.[42]

No one boasted more of his prowess in personal combat than Harry Gilmor, a Maryland Confederate cavalry officer. His memoirs are littered with detailed descriptions of how he bested Union opponents, sometimes with mortal results but more often with slight wounds. In one melee he fired several times at a Federal officer, and no matter how close they were, "great was my astonishment that he did not fall." With empty pistols, both men drew their sabers and closed in. "As I ranged up alongside I made a right cut, which he defended by a *tierce* parry; but, before he could recover, I made a *moulinet,* which carried the sabre out of his hand, and, as I raised mine to cut him down, he threw up his hand and surrendered." In another incident Gilmor chased a Federal on horseback and managed to get alongside him. "I made a tierce point at his neck, but the blade went clear through his hat, and with such a weight on the point I could not make a cut; his skull was saved." That Federal escaped, and Gilmor had to break off pursuit.[43]

Gilmor enjoyed the challenge of hand-to-hand fighting. Once when he rode toward a Union officer, the Federal encouraged him to come on and fight. "This promised good sport. I closed with him, making a powerful front cut, which he parried, and at the same instant made a right cut at my neck. By bringing my sabre down in time, my side caught the blow. Now I had the advantage. Quick as a flash I cut him across the cheek, inflicting a large gash." Gilmor than took his opponent prisoner.[44]

Many Confederate cavalrymen preferred to use handguns rather than sabers in melees and running chases. Dunbar Affleck told his parents of confronting two Federals, "one of them, I am certain that I killed, shooting him in the back . . . about ten steps from him, the other I shot in the body somewhere, with my pistol, he fell off his horse, but [I] did not stop to see whether he was dead or not." In the East John Gill of the 1st Maryland Cavalry (CS) tried to use his saber in a melee with the 6th Michigan Cavalry but failed. It was "a poor specimen of Confederate iron. I made a right cut which missed him, and which nearly unhorsed me. Scarcely recovering my seat, I saw an officer coming straight at me at the tierce-point." Gill then drew his pistol, leveling it at close range, and compelled the officer to surrender.[45]

Effective use of any weapon was the key to surviving a melee or hot chase. Capt. Thomas H. Malone saw "a red-headed blacksmith, farrier for

Fight for the Guidon.

No other branch of the army witnessed as much personal, hand-to-hand combat as did the cavalry. This illustration vividly shows one trooper thrusting his saber into the throat of an opponent. It exemplifies the feelings of some cavalrymen like Harry Gilmor, who enjoyed besting their opponents in personal fights like this, regardless of how much injury or death it caused.

Frank Leslie's Illustrated Newspaper, January 31, 1863, 301.

the regiment," swing his rifle at a Union trooper and hit him "immediately under his chin, breaking his neck, I have no doubt, for he seemed to fly from his saddle." Then a Federal rode near Malone "and was in the act of giving me as he passed a right rear cut with his sabre, but before he could strike I thrust my pistol against his side, just under his uplifted right arm, and fired." His assailant fell off his horse. In yet another confrontation, Malone exchanged pistol shots with a Union officer at twenty paces. The officer's bullet sliced through the brim of Malone's hat, but the Rebel's round made the dust fly from the breast of the Federal's coat, mortally wounding him.[46]

Even fists could be a useful weapon at close quarters. Lt. Daniel H. L. Gleason of the 1st Massachusetts Cavalry was chased by some Confederates while on picket duty. One caught up even with him and presented his pistol, but Gleason grabbed his head and held it across his own chest, using his right fist to beat the Rebel. The Confederate could only strike blindly with his handgun, but he managed to cut Gleason near both eyes. When the pair came to a muddy spot in the road, both horses jumped over but not at the same time. As a result both men fell off. Gleason's horse continued to ride away, but the Confederate horse remained, allowing the Rebel to remount and escape before the lieutenant could regain his feet and stab him with his sword. In a twist of irony, this same Confederate horseman was captured later in the day, and Gleason happened to come across him—"his eyes and face were black and blue, and he looked as if he had been through a powder-mill explosion." The man turned out to be a second lieutenant with the 6th Virginia Cavalry. He and Gleason chatted for a moment. "We both laughed when we compared our emotions and impulses" in their personal fight.[47]

While many cavalrymen were able to view hand-to-hand combat as something to laugh about, personal fights often resulted in elevated levels of rage that in turn led to unnecessary brutality. Henry C. Meyer, a clerk on the division staff of Brig. Gen. David M. Gregg, watched at the battle of Brandy Station as a Confederate sabered a Federal cavalryman twice, even though the blue-clad trooper offered to surrender. In a skirmish near Dalton, Georgia, Lt. Osborn D. Thompson of Company H, 8th Confederate Cavalry was pinned to the ground when his horse was shot and fell. Thompson was "wounded and helpless," in the words of George Knox Miller, yet an enraged Union officer rode up and assailed him, "rising in his stirrups" every time he struck at Thompson with his saber and literally split the Rebel's head open.[48]

Hand-to-hand combat with sabers could result in fearsome and sometimes deadly injuries. Henry Calvert of the 11th New York Cavalry never forgot his first sight of men who had been disfigured by saber strokes and retained a horror of it for the rest of his life. "I had seen a handsome man changed into a hideous one by a slash right across his face, rendering him perfectly unrecognizable by his nearest friend. I had seen an officer picked up from the Second Bull Run battlefield with no less than thirteen saber cuts on his face and various parts of his body, not one of them mortal but which combined to make him helpless and of frightful appearance."[49]

Neither in the infantry nor the artillery did a doctrine develop that matched the cavalryman's ideas about the value of a charge on the battlefield. That cavalry doctrine also resulted in far more personal combat than occurred in either of the other arms. Although they did not admit it, troopers may have taken solace in their aggressive dogma because they were aware that relatively few men fell in melees and hot chases, even though injuries inflicted by sabers could be gruesome.

There was a strange element of sport in mounted personal combat. Many troopers seemed to enjoy the excitement and the challenges, while the rest at least endured them without complaint. Typically little was accomplished by melees and mounted chases except in a microenvironment on the battlefield. Very small units and the men in them were affected, but little else changed whether one side bested the other. It is astonishing how personal the Civil War so often became for the typical cavalryman of that conflict.

7

DISMOUNTED FIGHTING

The practice of dismounting cavalrymen to fight on foot was not an innovation of the Civil War but extended far into the global cavalry heritage. While dismounted fighting occurred sporadically in many other time periods, Roman cavalry of the republican era specialized in it much as Civil War cavalry did in the 1860s. Dismounting cavalrymen for foot combat added a good deal of flexibility to the mounted arm, gave commanders more tactical choices, and increased the effectiveness of horse soldiers. It also reinforced the practice of crossing artificial boundaries that defined specialization in the armed forces. On one level it seemed counterintuitive to deny the cavalryman his horse. But on another level it made sense to train him so he could be proficient at both mounted and dismounted fighting.

Given that mounted combat was more complex than fighting on foot, the well-trained cavalryman was the most versatile soldier of the Civil War. It was easier for him to learn how to fight on foot than it would have been for an infantryman to learn how to fight on horseback. That was the difference between a cavalry unit and a unit of mounted infantry—the former started as horse soldiers, while the latter did not.

Through experience, most Civil War cavalrymen quickly learned how to dismount for action. "In two minutes from the word, 'prepare to fight on foot,' a line of three-fourths of the men is formed, who go to the front at a run," recalled Lt. Frederick Whittaker. "The rapidity exhibited in going into action by dismounted cavalry is marvelous, and the simplicity and adaptability of the system admirable."[1]

All commanders mixed dismounted fighting with mounted action in much the same way they mixed columns and lines in their tactical thinking. They always considered the dismounted unit of a mixed formation to be the primary force, whether it was a line of skirmishers or a full battle line, and the mounted element to be the reserve. The mounted element also was usually held in column formation and often screened the flanks of the dismounted line. There could be rare occasions when every unit in a mixed formation dismounted for close combat with the opponent. At other times dismounted units regained their horses to conduct a saber charge after fighting for some time on foot. But usually the mixed formation was held constant for the duration of an engagement, utilizing horsed and unhorsed units in close cooperation.[2]

The fundamental reason for mixing mounted and dismounted units was to use their individual strengths in combination with each other. Dismounted cavalrymen added stability to the defense and a slow punching power to the attack. Mounted formations could take advantage of success achieved by the foot formations and utilize its mobile punching power to break up enemy units and chase a retreating foe. "I was unable to reap the fruits of the victory gained by my dismounted men," lamented Brig. Gen. Kenner Garrard of a fight at Stone Mountain during the Atlanta Campaign. In this case the terrain was "so unfavorable" for mounted formations, another reason why Civil War commanders so often dismounted their troopers.[3]

Weapons Use

Dismounting horse soldiers greatly intensified a specialization in weapons use. Sabers were of no account to a man fighting on foot. Whenever the order to dismount was given, troopers knew that, "in the opinion of the commanding officer, it was an occasion demanding the most effective execution in the use of the carbine or musket." While most cavalrymen carried short-barreled carbines, which were not suitable for long-distance firing, a number of Confederates were armed with long-barreled weapons mostly because there were no carbines available. In the 2nd North

Carolina Cavalry, the commander detailed those men with small arms capable of long-distance firing to form his skirmish line at the Battle of Brandy Station.[4]

As time wore on, there was a tendency for units to specialize in the use of weapons. Some companies within a regiment gave up sabers and relied only on carbines or muskets, while the others retained their sabers. The saber companies often protected the flanks of the companies using firearms. At times entire regiments or even brigades specialized in weapons use. The cavalry commanded by Maj. Gen. Lunsford L. Lomax in the Shenandoah Valley during the fall of 1864 was "armed entirely with rifles and [had] no sabers, and the consequence is that they cannot fight on horseback," reported Lt. Gen. Jubal Early. "In this open country they cannot successfully fight on foot against large bodies of cavalry."[5]

James H. Kidd spelled out how specialization worked in George Custer's brigade. The 1st Michigan Cavalry "had been designated as distinctively a saber regiment." In contrast, the 5th Michigan Cavalry and the 6th Michigan Cavalry relied on Spencer repeaters, while the 7th Michigan Cavalry and 1st Vermont Cavalry also specialized in saber work. Sometimes the entire brigade fought on foot and at other times charged mounted, but the latter tactic occurred less often than dismounted fighting during the last year of the conflict. The brigade mostly fought on foot in the cluttered landscape of the Overland Campaign but mostly fought mounted in the open country of the lower Shenandoah Valley. Kidd considered the saber-wielding 1st Michigan Cavalry the premier unit in Custer's brigade, with the 7th Michigan Cavalry as its understudy; both relied on sabers. The 5th and 6th Michigan Cavalry worked especially well together because both relied on rifles.[6]

Specialization based on weapons use occurred in Civil War field artillery as well. During the early part of the conflict, all batteries North and South fielded a mix of guns and howitzers and of rifle and smoothbore pieces, which added flexibility to the battery's delivery of fire. But by the latter part of the war, the trend was strongly toward making batteries all smoothbore or all rifles.[7]

Only limited specialization of weapons use occurred in the infantry. Early in the conflict, the prewar practice of arming two companies of an infantry regiment with rifle muskets to serve as skirmishers, while the other eight companies were given smoothbore muskets, continued for a short time within the volunteer units. But very soon the majority of all volunteer regiments wanted rifles, and that specialization vanished. When repeating rifles began to appear, some regiments used them for skirmishing and became relied on for that duty, but this trend never reached the proportion of weapons specialization in the artillery or cavalry.[8]

Tactics

Commanders of mounted formations fully recognized the value of dismounted fighting. It was the most effective way they could deal with enemy infantry, even though their men were armed with short-barreled carbines that were no match for the rifle musket. In many engagements, cavalry officers dismounted whole brigades to meet enemy foot soldiers. Brig. Gen. David M. Gregg placed two brigades of his division on foot and moved them about the battlefield of Burgess's Mill during the Petersburg Campaign. In other words, he fully used them as infantry. "All of my fighting had to be on foot," declared Brig. Gen. John Buford of his division's work near Boonsborough, Maryland, on July 8, 1863. His men fought dismounted for twelve hours that day and drove the Confederates four miles. Brig. Gen. Thomas C. Devin proudly reported his brigade's success in a fight at Deep Bottom on July 28, 1864: "This short but brilliant engagement . . . established the fact that our cavalry can dismount and with their carbines successfully repulse their own front of veteran infantry."[9]

Even though cavalry doctrine strongly emphasized a quick decision to conduct a mounted charge, some unit commanders rejected that idea. When unexpectedly faced with a mounted attack, one squadron of the 3rd Pennsylvania Cavalry dismounted and stopped the charge with firepower alone in a skirmish near Williamsburg, Virginia, in May 1862. Most effective were commanders who were willing to switch from fighting on foot to regaining their horses and vice versa. "We were in the muss as deep as any until the infantry came up," wrote Theodore H. Weed of the 10th New York Cavalry about fighting near Cold Harbor in July 1864. "Then we mounted our horses and off to find another row and so we go from one place to another."[10]

There were some technical advantages to fighting on foot. One was the ability "to fire with much greater rapidity and precision." If the opposing formation was mounted, other advantages accrued to the dismounted horseman. The enemy troops not only were higher and thus more exposed to fire but also tended to return fire too high to do much damage to the men on foot. There are examples of dismounted horsemen driving enemy units by advancing on foot and firing pistols rather than carbines. A dismounted cavalryman also could use his horse as a shield. Rather than allow every fourth man to take his own and three other horses to the rear, troopers hid behind their mounts and fired over them. This did not happen often for obvious reasons, the chief one being the horse was the cavalryman's most important asset. But it did happen on rare occasions when the men needed some degree of protection to save themselves.[11]

Environmental factors affected dismounted fighting. Dense woods not only compelled troopers to fight on foot but also posed a serious obstacle to the dismounted formation. "For fifty yards at times my feet did not touch the ground," recalled Confederate George W. Beale of the fighting at Reams Station on August 25, 1864. "We had to walk over felled trees or crouch down to get through them."[12]

Dismounted formations sometimes mimicked infantry formations. Troopers formed on foot into lines, sometimes adopting two ranks like the infantry and at other times only one rank to be true to their mounted training. They also formed dismounted columns of fours but used these as maneuver formations rather than fighting formations. Cavalry commanders never formed their dismounted men into columns to attack the enemy, as the infantry sometimes chose to do.[13]

Led Horses

Tactical manuals and handbooks described the process of dismounting to fight on foot, which meant getting off the horse in a prescribed, military way. But those books did not describe how to handle loose horses while their riders were busy fighting on foot. The biggest problem here was keeping the mounts where they were readily available when needed but far enough from the shooting so as not to endanger them. This meant detailing some men to control the horses and often assigning an officer or a noncommissioned officer to superintend all of a regiment's led horses, even though this decreased the number of guns on the battle line.

The process of dismounting was similar for all mounted regiments. In the 28th Mississippi Cavalry, recalled Harry S. Dixon, it began with the order "by fours left wheel; right dress; dismount to fight; number four hold horses!" In the 6th New York Cavalry, the numbers 1, 2, and 3 men strapped their sabers on the saddle, since that weapon was worse than useless for dismounted fighting, then handed their bridles to number 4. In all mounted units, "the position of number four became very popular" as a result. At times the lucky man's joy led him to shout "Bully" rather than four when counting off for the purpose of dismounted fighting. Nathan Bedford Forrest happened to hear one of his men shout like this as he rode along the line and decided to teach him a lesson, ordering that "two, three, and bully will advance, No. 1 may hold the horses."[14]

If they had time the three men going into battle entrusted their few belongings to the fourth man. "Look out for my grain" or "take care of my haversack" were some such requests. In addition to sabers the three men attached anything that they did not want to lose to their saddles, taking along extra cartridges and canteens. "Everything of value was left with the led horses," recalled Edward P. Tobie of the 1st Maine Cavalry.[15]

Dismounting a regiment for combat took away one-fourth of the available manpower from the fight. "So many men are required to take care of the horses," reported Brig. Gen. August V. Kautz of action at Petersburg on June 15, 1864, that "our line was really weaker than the enemy's in men." Some commanders looked for ways to minimize this loss. Lt. Col. Jonathan Biggs of the 123rd Illinois Mounted Infantry instructed one man to lead eight rather than four horses at the attack on Selma, Alabama, during Wilson's Raid. Five months before, Col. Israel Garrard told Maj. Daniel A. Carpenter of the 2nd East Tennessee Mounted Infantry to tie up his horses in the rear instead of holding them so as to "put as many men in the fight as I could" during an engagement near Rogersville, Tennessee.[16]

The other major problem of dismounted fighting was maneuvering the led horses close to the fighting line for fast remounting. But how far should they go from the fighting to be safe and yet accessible? For Col.

Russell A. Alger of the 5th Michigan Cavalry, the ideal distance was 500 yards. Terrain features could be used to help in this way. At Gettysburg the led horses of the 3rd Pennsylvania Cavalry were hidden in a depression with higher ground in front of them, "which in some measure protected them from the enemy's fire." It was more difficult to find a safe place from artillery projectiles. In many cases the mounts became "restive and mixed up" when rounds fell near or among them and became difficult to control. In other cases it was a simple matter of moving the led horses from one field to another to avoid fire. Much depended on the individual circumstances of every engagement. Because of that, many regimental commanders assigned a high-ranking subordinate to control the horse holders and the mounts. In addition, some appointed an enlisted man to take charge of all led horses for each company.[17]

Typically a cavalryman carried extra rounds in his saddlebags or improvised some other storage on his mount. During a heavy dismounted engagement, he either had to go back to the led horses or send word for the horse holders to bring forward more ammunition. This provided another reason for the holders to remain as close as possible to the fighting.[18]

In some ways the led horses became a liability. Enemy forces often targeted them either with artillery fire or with efforts to capture them. To a significant degree commanders had to maneuver their dismounted formations with the need to protect the led horses in mind. "Nothing is so demoralizing to a cavalryman, fighting dismounted, as to find his horse in danger of capture," wrote Albert B. Capron. Confederate dismounted cavalryman saw their led horses being moved to the rear during a fight near La Fayette, Georgia, in June 1864 and "became greatly confused." They broke ranks to retrieve them, not knowing that it was a planned move. But seeing this, brigade commander Col. James J. Neely ordered the horses moved back to reassure them. During a battle at Dandridge, Tennessee, a "desperate hand-to-hand fighting took place for the possession of the horses" after Confederate troopers bypassed the Union formation and tried to capture them. In another engagement Union brigade commander Horace Capron reported that the Rebels not only gained possession of his men's led horses but also employed them to charge the rear of his command as he retreated during a fight that occurred in the McCook-Stoneman Raid of the Atlanta Campaign.[19]

Many cavalrymen deplored the duty of tending three mounts in addition to their own. It was a thankless job, even though it took them out of immediate danger. Charles Crosland of the cavalry attached to Hampton's Legion wound up taking care of led mounts for three to four days and found it an enormous burden. "I was worried greatly with my horses, keeping them fed and watered and keeping the blankets under saddles, which was a job, with no rider they were always working out; then keeping luggage on saddles, running night and day hither and thither with them to be in reach of men if needed and out of reach of the enemy." It was a happy day when his comrades returned and took charge of their own mounts.[20]

Regaining their horses was a relief for most cavalrymen who fought on foot. But sometimes that did not happen cleanly. When the 1st Maryland Cavalry (U.S.) was ordered to remount after fighting on foot at Appomattox on the morning of April 9, 1865, the horses "were found to have been moved without authority," reported Col. Andrew W. Evans. "They were only discovered after much search, scattered over the fields south of the road and some were even taken several miles distant." In short, control of the mounts had completely dissolved. On other occasions cavalry officers found that their led horses were still in a group and still controlled by the holders, although not as close as they had expected them to be. Led mounts of the 2nd Arizona Cavalry were one and a half miles behind the regiment when they were needed during a fight in the Red River Campaign. Many troopers of the 9th Kentucky Cavalry (CS) had to flee on foot because their horses were too far to the rear for a fast retreat during a skirmish in south central Tennessee during March 1863.[21]

Obviously there were problems inherent in dismounting cavalrymen for action. Their equipment, including boots and spurs, were not made for walking. If they dismounted while still some distance from the enemy, the troopers were forced to move on foot to make contact. Brig. Gen. James R. Chalmers's Division maneuvered for two miles before reaching the field of battle at Tupelo, Mississippi, which "proved very exhausting to men unaccustomed to marching on foot." The 8th Confederate Cavalry considered half a mile too long to move dismounted. Some units had less experience at dismounted fighting than others. General Kautz noted that his cavalry division was at a disadvantage when retiring from a small engagement at Petersburg on October 7, 1864. "Unused to foot service the dismounted men fell back in some confusion, and it was impossible to rally them."[22]

A corollary to this theme was the difficulty encountered by cavalrymen who could not obtain a remount for some time. These unfortunates typically were assigned to foot service for guarding wagon trains and were compelled to march like infantrymen for weeks at a time. With cavalry boots and feet unused to punishing walks along bad roads, they suffered a good deal. Moreover, they no longer could use horses to carry their belongings and did not have knapsacks, which were issued only to infantrymen.[23]

Many cavalrymen complained about dismounting so often to fight. When the 2nd Alabama Cavalry was sent to the Army of Tennessee during the Atlanta Campaign, it had had little prior experience on the battlefield. "When we came up here and were told we would have to fight in the breastworks we thought it awful," wrote Harden Perkins Cochrane to his cousin. "The idea of a Cavalryman dismounting, sending his horse a half mile off and he going into the trenches like an ordinary Webbfoot!" In fact, both Union and Confederate cavalrymen performed duty in the earthworks a great deal during the Atlanta Campaign. Brig. Gen. Kenner Garrard's cavalry division relieved Maj. Gen. John M. Schofield's Twenty-Third Corps in the works from August 1 to August 15, skirmishing and picketing in addition to filling the trenches with a battle line.[24]

The cavalryman suffered another disadvantage when ordered to hold earthworks. He had no available entrenching tools with which to build, maintain, or improve the works. Infantrymen did not carry entrenching tools either, but they could get them from a quartermaster on a temporary basis when needed. Cavalry quartermasters did not stock such tools because no one anticipated they would be needed by the mounted service. "We sometimes had a few axes," recalled Col. Thomas T. Munford, "but in the four years of war I never saw a cavalryman with a spade or anything better than a shingle pulled from the roof of some house near by with which to throw up breastworks."[25]

Another element of dismounted service involved its cost. Battle casualties tended to be less heavy for mounted warfare than for foot service. The primary reason was the horse, which gave the trooper a wonderful chance to escape danger. Even melees and hot pursuits rarely resulted in heavy losses for either side. But take their horses away, and cavalrymen became more exposed to heavy casualties. "The greatest loss that the Regiment sustained was when the men were dismounted to fight as infantry," wrote George B. Guild of the 4th Tennessee Cavalry (CS).[26]

Despite the problems and limitations, dismounting troopers for foot combat was widespread in both the Union and Confederate armies. Col. John R. Chambliss Jr. thought Federal horsemen in Virginia increasingly relied on dismounted action by 1864 because they were armed with good carbines. Operating on foot "has become very popular, and comprises the best share of their fighting," the Rebel officer wrote. As Confederate brigadier general Rufus Barringer put it, "the sabre grew into less and less favor" while "the revolver on horse and the rifle on foot" became more popular.[27]

After the war a handful of Confederate veterans claimed that their comrades were the first to employ dismounted fighting. Some gave the credit to Wade Hampton in the East, while others insisted that Forrest, John Hunt Morgan, and Joseph Wheeler were the ones to start this trend. At least one Union veteran argued that the eastern Confederates were the first and his comrades in the Virginia theater had to follow suit. No one offered convincing proof for any of their claims.[28]

Judging from reports and personal accounts, it is clear that no individual deserved credit for initiating dismounted combat. It was a tactic that developed naturally among regimental and brigade officers in a grassroots sort of way and expressed the commonality of their cavalry experience. No matter where or when it began in the Civil War, dismounted cavalry fighting was hundreds of years old by 1861. American horsemen did not originate it even if they can be said to have practiced it more intensely than any cavalry force in world history.

Some markers chart the rise of dismounted fighting in the Civil War. By 1863, Brig. Gen. Wesley Merritt reported that the troopers of his brigade, "from long and constant practice, are becoming perfect in the art of foot-fighting and skirmishing." Dismounted combat increased dramatically with the start of the Overland Campaign the next year, even though mounted charges also continued to be employed. In the West there was no such period in which dismounted fighting suddenly rose to prominence.

Union and Confederate horsemen west of the Appalachian Highlands had always mixed mounted and dismounted combat in equal proportion during their operations.[29]

When they evaluated the usefulness of dismounted fighting, Civil War troopers split on the results. Many never liked it, believing that a true cavalryman needed to be on his horse. "It is very much against the spirit and training of a cavalryman to dismount and fight at necessarily great odds with infantry solidly massed against him," wrote Chaplain Charles A. Humphreys of the 2nd Massachusetts Cavalry. "Not only is there the disadvantage of the unaccustomed position and movement, but also the *greater* disadvantage of the short range of his carbine as compared with the muskets of the infantry." While the horseman could admit that fighting on foot was necessary, he retained a natural right to protest against "being transformed into an infantry soldier," asserted Chaplain Samuel L. Gracey. Others referred to mounted combat as "the legitimate way" for cavalry to operate. John Bell Hood, a firm believer in aggressive combat morale, argued in his memoirs that making a cavalryman fight both mounted and dismounted robbed him of expertise in either mode. Soldiering on foot ruined his ability to conduct a mounted charge. "He who fights alternately mounted and dismounted, can never become an excellent soldier of either infantry or cavalry proper."[30]

But the majority of men North and South praised the ability of their comrades to fight on foot, saw great utility in the tactic, and were proud of their ability to serve in a hybrid style of mounted warfare. It taught the men to fight with versatility and resourcefulness. "The most effective cavalry we now have are those armed with the revolving rifle, and dismount when going into action," wrote Brig. Gen. James W. Denver in December 1862.[31]

Even though "fighting on foot is not half as romantic as dashing upon the enemy mounted on a spirited charger," as Stanton P. Allen argued, this hybrid form of mounted warfare was strong and enduring throughout the Civil War.[32] Most commanders used dismounted fighting to deal with terrain unsuitable for mounted operations, with enemy infantry forces, and with the lack of sabers in their command. It was far better to rely on cavalry, which had some exposure to infantry drill, to transition into foot service than to rely on mounted infantry, which had no drill in cavalry tactics, to transition into mounted warfare. In fact, hybrid cavalry largely neutralized the importance of mounted infantry.

Frederick Whittaker of the 6th New York Cavalry admitted that dismounted fighting as an "idea is an old one. But the extent to which it was carried was purely an American innovation." He only complained that the world had not fully recognized Civil War cavalrymen for this innovation in the years after the conflict. "European cavalry officers and the world at large have no conception of the extent to which dismounted fighting was used in the American civil war and the perfection attained in it by our men after very little practice."[33]

8

RAIDING

R aiding behind enemy lines was a unique capability of the mounted arm. Moving swiftly through dangerous territory and hitting enemy facilities, usually railroads and towns, cavalry formations accomplished a task the infantry and artillery were incapable of performing. Whether the risks and the wear and tear on horseflesh and manpower justified the usual results of these raids became a matter of controversy. But regardless of what anyone thought about them, raids were widely popular with cavalrymen.

A few Civil War horsemen recognized that their comrades had not originated the concept of raiding. It was quite old in cavalry heritage. But even these knowledgeable men believed that the Civil War emphasized raiding more than any conflict in global history. Many more definable raids took place, involving longer distances under more daring circumstances than to be seen in other wars. It became a matter of national pride to argue along this line.[1]

Civil War cavalrymen also spelled out exactly what constituted a raid. "It was the custom," wrote Adj. Charles D. Mitchell of the 7th Ohio Cavalry, "to call all independent distance movements by cavalry, when not supported by infantry, *raids*, because in the earlier stages of the war cavalry was attached to infantry commands as eyes and ears, and not as brains nor muscle."[2] Horsemen tended to define even short movements as raids as long as they were conducted independently of infantry formations and aimed at meeting or evading the enemy while hitting important resources. Long movements greatly increased the problems and more severely tested the stamina, resolve, and luck of mounted formations. They tended to draw the lion's share of attention, while shorter movements remained obscure unless they resulted in heavy fighting or destruction of enemy resources.

The Experience of Raiding

Before setting out, cavalrymen specially prepared for raids. They streamlined their baggage carried on horseback to the minimum. In Joseph Wheeler's command, that meant no more than one blanket and one oilcloth per man. Officers closely examined wagons, limber boxes, and caissons for private property and destroyed anything above the minimum. James E. B. Stuart instructed his subordinates to collect fresh horses from Unionists along the way, put a man in charge of three of them, and keep these led horses in the center of each brigade column for safekeeping.[3]

Stuart's order related to the biggest problem of long-distance raids, losing horses to enemy action, exhaustion, poor feed, and disease along the way. Every commander devised methods of dealing with this issue. It was common for men to walk their mounts as much as possible, only rarely running them for short distances. "It refreshes horses greatly to take off their saddles and let them roll," recalled Edward Wall of the 3rd New York Cavalry. "They seem invigorated by it."[4]

Riding practices to save horse flesh were possible only during certain phases of a raid when the enemy was far away, but rapid and unrelenting movement took place during other phases. These were the times when raiding exacted a heavy price on the raider. The first to suffer were the mounts, and pursuing troops witnessed the result. "A great many horses were abandoned by the enemy," wrote Alfred Pleasanton while chasing Sterling Price in 1864. His men kept the better ones, but most wound up in the hands of local civilians to be nursed back to condition. During other raids, dead horses rather than live ones littered the trail, and on occasion it was obvious that steaks were carved from some of the carcasses for famished men to eat. Of thirty-three horses belonging to Company D, 1st Maine Cavalry in the Kilpatrick-Dahlgren Raid, only six came back to Union lines. During Sheridan's first raid as commander of cavalry for the Army of the Potomac, his men left behind an average of four dead mounts per mile.[5]

"All expeditions to the rear of an enemy are attended with great difficulties," wrote Wheeler. Long raids prevented the men from carrying food for all their needs, forcing them to live off the countryside. While chasing Wheeler during October 1863, John T. Wilder's brigade marched 404 miles. But the extra riding to look for forage and food every evening added an estimated 100 miles to the total.[6]

What to do with the sick and wounded troopers along the way of a long raiding movement became a painful problem. If they were able to ride, they had a chance of making it to safe territory. If not, they were left behind, with hopes that the enemy or local civilians would take care of them. Only the worst cases were left behind. Badly wounded and in the enemy's country, the emotional stress of being abandoned is difficult to imagine.[7]

Fatigue in all its forms, for man and horse, was the chief characteristic of raids. "Many horses give out, and the riders throw away everything in order to keep up," wrote Adj. Charles D. Mitchell. "Some fall asleep and drop from their horses to the ground without waking, and cry as children cry when disturbed. The continuous march in the saddle has caused feet and ankles to swell, and many cut their boots from their feet, because they are too tight to be removed otherwise."[8]

Troopers taking part in a little-known raid from Memphis into Arkansas during January 1865 became terribly exhausted and had to hold on to "the horses' mane and the cantle of the saddle, lest we should fall when our feet hit the ground," wrote Henry Murray Calvert of the 11th New York Cavalry. He also saw some men "who were lusty and strong cry on that raid from sheer physical suffering." George Dallas Mosgrove of the 4th Kentucky Cavalry (CS) described his extreme fatigue on one raid. "I became so desperate as to seriously think of withdrawing from the column to lie down by the road-side." But he tried to continue by resorting "to all manner of expedients to keep awake." Once when the column halted for a short rest, Mosgrove woke up in fifteen minutes with the idea that the column had continued moving. "I wandered about in search of my horse," stumbling into the wagon train that carried the wounded before realizing that everyone was still resting.[9]

Images of mounted columns sweeping boldly down on enemy lines of communication, evading opposing troopers, and returning to home territory to reap their laurels filled the imagination of aspiring cavalrymen. But the reality of raiding was so different as to compel questions about the cost. There was a very high price to be paid for every venture, a price exacted on horse supply, troop strength, physical and mental exhaustion, and waste of expensive mounted power. The real question, often avoided by cavalry commanders, was whether the unpredictable results of a raid justified the very predictable cost to their forces.

Raids That Were Worth the Cost

What follows is a survey of eight mounted raids that took place during the Civil War. Half of them could be considered worth the cost compared to the results, but the other half resulted in such a high price as to nullify their usefulness. In fact, some raids in this latter category were unmitigated disasters that no amount of destruction inflicted on the enemy could justify. This is not an exhaustive survey of strategic raids during the war but a mix of large and small operations that cover the geographic extent of the conflict. While each operation had its own characteristics that led to problems as well as advantages, they also shared many attributes. Chief among those common elements was the fact that isolated but mobile forces entered disputed territory with their wits, endurance, and fighting ability as their chief assets.

GRIERSON'S RAID

Col. Benjamin H. Grierson conducted a famous raid from West Tennessee through central Mississippi, ending at Baton Rouge, Louisiana, in the early spring of 1863. He traveled across three states primarily to distract the enemy as Maj. Gen. Ulysses S. Grant reached a critical stage in his efforts to move the Army of the Tennessee down the Louisiana side of the Mississippi River to bypass the Rebel fortress of Vicksburg. In that basic mission Grierson succeeded admirably. He also handled his brigade with skill and foresight, providing a model raid that was closely tied to larger operational and strategic objectives of the Union army.

The Union column started from La Grange, Tennessee, on April 17, 1863, with 1,700 men. Over the course of the next sixteen days, Grierson moved more than 600 miles and engaged in four battles with several Confederate columns sent out to intercept him. But the colonel managed to outmarch, outfight, and avoid his enemy, losing only 24 men (5 of whom were left sick along the way). His troopers destroyed 60 miles of railroad and telegraph lines, captured and destroyed more than 3,000 small arms, nabbed 1,000 horses and mules, and took over 500 prisoners, who they paroled and left behind. A key element in his success was authorization from his superiors to exercise choice in how he reached Union lines. If Grierson deemed it too difficult to return to La Grange, he could continue south to Union-held Baton Rouge. He kept his options open until the midpoint of the raid before deciding to continue south, baffling his pursuers. When the Confederates realized his true course, they continued to pursue, but Grierson enjoyed a one- or two-day advantage on them that proved decisive in his safe arrival at Baton Rouge.[10]

Grierson devoted much energy to deceiving the enemy. He sent small detachments to different places along the route, giving the impression his main body was moving in a false direction. Soon after starting the ride, he sent part of his brigade back to La Grange, choosing the poorer horses and weaker men for this move. Grierson continued to push his main column south, obliterating its tracks as it moved, efforts that distracted the Confederates into believing the entire force had ridden north. This gave him a small but important edge. Grierson used J. H. Colton's pocket map of Mississippi as a navigational aid; it was small but "very correct," he recalled.[11]

A corps of scouts supplemented the map's information. Grierson tasked Col. Edward Prince to find the "most venturesome and daring" men of the 7th Illinois Cavalry for this service. Quartermaster Sgt. Richard W. Surby led this group of ten men. Operating singly or in pairs, they hovered about the van and flanks of the moving column, rode as much as twenty-five miles to gather information, located sources of food and forage, found replacement horses, and noted the road system and streams to be crossed. The scouts dressed in whatever civilian clothes they could find and carried concealed weapons as they operated singly or in pairs. It soon became apparent that a handful had volunteered for scouting in order to plunder civilians, so Surby replaced them with more reliable men. His scouts obtained information by pretending to be Confederate soldiers and gaining the confidence of citizens. In fact, civilians often mistook many of Grierson's men for Confederates because their blue uniforms were caked with dust or mud.[12]

Grierson's success was based on deception, good use of his ten scouts, and placing himself in the enemy's shoes to guess what they expected him to do. Once he satisfied himself of this latter point, the colonel "did not do what was expected of me." The Federals neutralized much civilian resistance by restraining themselves. On entering Louisville, Mississippi, residents were terrified that their homes would be burned, but Grierson controlled his men and treated the citizens well.[13]

Yet this strategy of deception collapsed near the end of the raid. The Confederates grew better at predicting both Grierson's target and his line of march and tried to converge several columns to intercept him. "The enemy were now on our track in earnest," he reported. Through captured couriers, Grierson learned from the dispatches they carried what his opponents were doing and barely kept ahead of them to reach safety in Baton Rouge on May 2, his tired men riding the last seventy-six miles in twenty-eight hours.[14]

Grierson's Raid was successful not because of the destruction it inflicted, but for the distraction it created. The ride was masterfully planned and executed. Adept use of his resources, playing tricks on Confederate perception, and having maximum choice in where he could go were the keys to its success. Grant's move south along the Louisiana bottomlands would certainly have succeeded without this cavalry raid, but the troopers helped ensure it did.

JONES-IMBODEN RAID

From the famous Grierson Raid to the hardly known Jones-Imboden Raid, one goes from one successful expedition to another. Brig. Gen. William E. Jones led his mounted brigade from Rockingham County in the Shenandoah Valley to hit the Baltimore and Ohio Railroad west of Cumberland, Maryland, from April 21 to May 20, 1863. The success of this effort rested heavily on the fact that Federal forces in the area were scattered, small, and with few mounted resources. Jones largely operated alone, although he cooperated with another column under Brig. Gen. John D. Imboden for part of the raid. Jones left behind his unfit men and horses before starting and set out through a mountainous "rough and sterile country."[15]

The Confederates encountered little resistance along the way. When Jones's men neared Bridgeport, five miles east of Clarksburg in the soon-to-be state of West Virginia, they captured forty-seven Federals and burned a railroad bridge, running a captured train off the flaming trestle. The raiders burned three bridges, each sixty feet long, and a tunnel near Cairo. But the most spectacular destruction took place at the Burning Springs oilfield, also known as Oil Town, in Wirt County on May 9. The facilities were owned by Southern men who had fled and were now operated by Northerners. The crude product was shipped down the Little Kanawha River to a refinery at Parkersburg and marketed in the North as illuminating oil and as machinery lubricants. Jones's men destroyed all the oil they could find as well as tanks, barrels, pumping engines, engine houses, and wagons. "In a word," reported the general, "everything used for raising, holding, or sending it off was burned. The smoke is very dense and jet black. The boats, filled with oil in bulk, burst with a report almost equaling artillery, and spread the burning fluid over the river. . . . By dark the oil from the tanks on the burning creek had reached the river, and the whole stream became a sheet of fire." The Confederates destroyed an estimated 150,000 barrels of oil that day. By 1864 oil prices, which were $8 a barrel, the destruction amounted to at least $1.2 million. It was about a year before the fields could be put back into operation.[16]

Although encountering light resistance, the stress of rapid marching and the labor of destruction wore on the Confederates. "A good many of our men were . . . deterred by faint-heartedness or weak horses," reported Lt. Col. Thomas Marshall of the 7th Virginia Cavalry. He lost fifty of them to the wear and tear of the expedition. To replace horses that gave out along the way, the Confederates either purchased or impressed new mounts.[17]

Jones could easily declare that his expedition had paid dividends worth the cost. His command captured nearly 700 Federal soldiers, two trains, and one artillery piece. It burned sixteen railroad bridges and destroyed a tunnel and the extensive oil facilities at Burning Springs. Jones brought back 1,000 head of cattle and 1,200 horses. He lost only ten men killed, forty-two wounded, and fifteen missing.[18]

The primary reason for Jones's success was that the Federals were not prepared to deal with him. Their scant manpower was isolated in occupation posts and could not easily be gathered into a mobile column to intercept him. The level of destruction, especially to the Baltimore and Ohio Railroad and to Burning Springs, was significant but not crippling. The railroad was terribly exposed to Confederate raids throughout the war and constantly suffered similar levels of destruction. Its corporate leadership was staunchly Unionist, however, and repaired breaks at the company's expense. Jones did not shut down the Baltimore and Ohio Railroad for long. Although one of the more successful raids on the operational level, it had no significant effect on the strategic level.

ROUSSEAU'S RAID

Another successful raid on the tactical level was conducted by Maj. Gen. Lovell H. Rousseau, commander of the District of Tennessee, with headquarters at Nashville. It was an effort to support Maj. Gen. William T. Sherman's drive toward Atlanta in the summer of 1864. In this case Sherman himself ordered the movement and recommended that Rousseau use 2,500 troopers supported by pack mules rather than wagons and no more than two artillery pieces. His command would have to forage for its sustenance. After assembling this force at Decatur, Alabama, Sherman wanted Rousseau to move at a slow and quiet pace as far as the Coosa River and then make speed until reaching the West Point and Montgomery Railroad, one of the three rail lines feeding the Confederate Army of Tennessee by way of Atlanta, between Opelika and Chehaw Station, Alabama. "Avoid all fighting possible," he told Rousseau while impressing on him that his troopers were to work night and day on destroying the track as thoroughly as possible, twisting and not just bending the rails. The column should join Sherman's army group somewhere near Marietta, Georgia, or if necessary head for Union-occupied Rome, Georgia, or Pensacola, Florida.[19]

Rousseau followed his instructions to the letter. He carefully selected his regiments, taking horses from other units for all unmounted men, and assembled the force into two brigades. Leaving Decatur on July 10, the men crossed the Coosa River on the evening of the thirteenth. Here Rousseau inspected his command and sent 300 weak horses and "ineffective men" back to Tennessee. He encountered resistance south of the Coosa but brushed it aside, reaching the railroad near Lochapoka by sunset of July 17. Only small detachments of Confederates were near enough to bother his men as they tore up miles of track. Half of the men destroyed the railroad, while the rest guarded their work and controlled led horses.[20]

The construction design of the West Point and Montgomery Railroad "greatly facilitated" its destruction. It had been built "on the old plan with wooden stringers, six by eight inches and probably fifteen feet long, mortised into the ties and held in place by wooden wedges; and on these stringers, iron straps one inch by two and a half inches were spiked." Using fence rails as levers, the men raised fifty to a hundred feet of track at a time, disassembled it, and piled the pine ties and stringers for burning. The heat warped the iron rails that were laid on top of the piles so they could be twisted or bent.[21]

Rousseau divided his force into three groups and positioned them at separate places along the track to work toward each other. For a total of thirty-six hours, they tore up the railroad, taking only short breaks, until the command had destroyed about thirty miles of track. Rousseau called a halt to the destruction at 10 a.m. of July 19, when the Federals were near Opelika, and later that day headed northeast. He left early enough to avoid significant Confederate forces racing toward the railroad and was not bothered at all on his ride to Marietta, reaching Sherman on July 22.[22]

On the tactical level Rousseau's Raid was a surprisingly easy and clean success because the Confederates were taken completely by surprise. They had no clue that a railroad 200 miles from Union-occupied territory was vulnerable. Rousseau did not try to accomplish more than was prudent and thus avoided trouble while getting back to friendly territory. But the raid had no appreciable effect on the Atlanta Campaign. Despite their meager resources, the Confederates repaired the thirty-mile break within a relatively short time.

A number of cavalry commanders on both sides learned how to deal with the tactical challenges of a mounted raid and conducted them with skill and success. But it is important to raise our sights above the tactical level and consider what if any effect even a successful raid had on the larger course of the war. This has always been the crux of the question concerning the value of mounted raids. Most contemporaries and latter-day historians have been fixated on the tactical success without considering whether it translated into something that could influence the strategic level of war. Forrest, Morgan, and Stuart succeeded in most (but by no means all) of the many raids they conducted, but the Confederates still lost the Civil War. Their opponents were hurt by their exploits but absorbed the loss and recovered quickly. One might say that these three cavalry commanders handed their friends a good deal of morale-boosting raids, but that uplift lasted only until the next Confederate defeat.

VAN DORN–FORREST RAID, DECEMBER 1862

One of the few cavalry raids that had a clear effect on the operational level was the coordinated strikes conducted by Maj. Gen. Earl Van Dorn and Brig. Gen. Nathan Bedford Forrest in December 1862. Hitting the logistical support of Grant's forces as they drove south into northern Mississippi, the Federals were caught unprepared and suffered enormous losses of material, depots, railroad tracks, and especially bridges. While Van Dorn hit the Union depot at Holly Springs, Mississippi, Forrest struck at Union rail lines in West Tennessee and actually inflicted more damage on Grant's supply line than did Van Dorn. The combined results of these two expeditions led Grant to call off the possibility of a continued advance overland south toward Vicksburg, his ultimate target, and concentrate on using the Mississippi River as his supply line.

Van Dorn started out from Granada, Mississippi, on December 16 with 3,500 troopers and largely evaded detection as he moved toward Holly Springs. When he attacked the Federals there, it came as a complete surprise, largely because the commander of the garrison was utterly unprepared. His subordinates had no warning but tried to resist, resulting in a brief but losing battle on the morning of December 20. For the rest of that day, the Confederates destroyed everything possible. Van Dorn estimated the destruction amounted to $1.5 million worth of Federal property, although Union authorities later evaluated the dollar amount much lower.

After that, Van Dorn continued moving north along the Mississippi Central Railroad but was unable to inflict much damage. He attacked a small Union garrison at Davis's Mills, where the line crossed the Wolf River, but was decisively repulsed. Soon after that failure, he turned south and, evading Union columns, returned to Granada on December 28.[23]

Forrest mounted a longer, more difficult, and more destructive raid. Starting from Columbia, Tennessee, with 2,000 troopers on December 11, he crossed the Tennessee River near Clifton December 13–15 and met the first resistance near Lexington, Tennessee, on December 18. The Confederates overwhelmed the small Union force there and moved on to Jackson, where a large Federal garrison defended the town. A serious mounted charge by the raiders was repelled by Union infantry fire, which led Forrest to bypass the place and strike at several small towns along the Mobile and Ohio Railroad between Jackson, Tennessee, and Columbus, Kentucky, to the north. Many of them fell to his forces because he brought a sizeable number of Confederates against small, static garrisons, keeping one or two days ahead of the cavalry and infantry that Grant organized to give chase. The Rebels had just enough time to inflict considerable destruction. Long trestles spanning the bottomlands of the South Fork and North Fork of the Obion River, which burned from December 24 to December 26, especially hurt Union logistical support for Grant's army. When Forrest judged he had reaped all the benefits possible, he turned his command back toward the Tennessee River and was nearly trapped. One Union column blocked his retreat in a fierce battle at Parker's Crossroads on December 31 as another column attacked the rear of the Confederate force. Only through hard fighting and fast riding did Forrest extricate his men from disaster, losing almost a quarter of them as casualties.[24]

The combined effects of Van Dorn's and Forrest's raids played a major role in altering Grant's operational plan for his first strike against Vicksburg. But it has to be pointed out that Grant had never relied exclusively on an overland march along the Mississippi Central Railroad to carry his attack on the river city. Part of his force, under Maj. Gen. William T. Sherman, was about to leave Memphis for a river-born approach to Vicksburg when Van Dorn struck Holly Springs. Grant's plan was to continue edging his way south along the railroad with only the possibility of going all the way to the target. In fact, General in Chief Henry W. Halleck had all along told him not to rely on the railroad but to put all his resources on the river route; the Confederate raids merely convinced him that Halleck had been right. The river-born supply line was the key to Grant's capture of Vicksburg six months later. So, while the Van Dorn–Forrest Raid certainly was a success on the tactical level and affected the operational level too, it did not alter the eventual strategic result, which was the fall of Vicksburg.

Raids That Were Not Worth the Cost

For every raid that could be said to have been worth the cost, there was at least one other that clearly was not. For the most part, individual factors affected which ones would be successful and which would result disastrously, but there were common factors that linked the good raids compared to the bad ones. The chief factors tended to lie within the realm of resources available to the defender to counter raids on their lines of communication, the most common target of all raiding forces, and whether the personnel in charge of those resources had the ability to use them to intercept and stop the raiders.

STREIGHT'S RAID

One of the sorriest expeditions of the war took place in northern Alabama and northern Georgia in the spring of 1863. Col. Abel D. Streight was ordered to mount a raid on the Western and Atlantic Railroad, the supply line of the Army of Tennessee. Under pressure from Washington to pay the Confederates back for the raiding they had done and short of cavalry forces, Maj. Gen. William S. Rosecrans gave Streight a provisional brigade of infantry units and ordered him to Nashville on April 7, 1863. There he found enough mules for about half of his 1,700 troops and was told to mount the rest by scouring the countryside along the way. Assembling men and mounts at Fort Henry by April 12, Streight was astonished to find that the mules were "poor, wild, and unbroken colts," many of them only two years old and others with "horse distemper." In fact, about fifty of them were "too near dead to travel."[25]

Despite this obvious weakness, Streight's command moved by river steamer to Eastport, Mississippi, on the Tennessee River. The men left that port on April 21 and marched eastward, joining a column of 8,000 infantrymen under Brig. Gen. Grenville M. Dodge. The joint force moved to Tuscumbia by April 24, Streight's men collecting mounts along the way, and Dodge gave him 200 additional mules and some wagons as well. At Tuscumbia, Streight weeded out the unfit to pare his force down to 1,500 men. Of that number 150 had no mounts and another 150 had mules so weak they could not carry a man. The two Union forces parted company at Tuscumbia, as Dodge moved to distract Forrest's pursuing forces while Streight moved east, collecting more horses and mules until he found enough for all his men.[26]

The expedition had a fair chance of success if Dodge could keep Forrest off Streight's trail for a few days. Unfortunately for the Federals, that did not occur. Once he realized what was happening, Forrest broke away from Dodge and raced after the raiders. From that point on, the Confederates had all the advantages. First contact was made on April 30, and from then the campaign developed into a running fight toward Rome, Georgia. The mules gave out rapidly; most of those taken from the countryside were not shod, and even if properly prepared, mules could not compete with horses in a running contest. Streight's column decreased in size until the Confederates surrounded the survivors on May 3 short of Rome, where the Federals surrendered.[27]

Streight's superiors recognized that the odds were stacked against him. In filing his report, the colonel identified the mules as his chief problem. If he had even 800 good horses to mount half of the command, he would have had a fighting chance. Moreover, Streight believed that if Dodge could have held Forrest's attention for one more day, it would have given him an important advantage. His subordinates also cited a two-day delay at Eastport and another two-day delay at Tuscumbia as contributing to the disastrous result of the expedition.[28]

Another point not cited by the participants was the forlorn hope that putting infantrymen on mounts of any kind without training in mounted warfare might work, especially against experienced enemy troopers. Even the best cavalry in Rosecrans's army would have found it difficult to penetrate enemy territory in the face of Forrest's command, and Dodge could not hold Rebel troopers in place with his foot soldiers. The invading force was far too small, too poorly suited for the job, and improperly supported to have much chance of success. The entire Federal column was killed,

wounded, or captured before it even came close to the Western and Atlantic Railroad.

The most disastrous Confederate raid of the war was the work of Brig.
Gen. John Hunt Morgan in the summer of 1863. He commanded 2,460
troopers at the start and had authority only to raid within Tennessee and
Kentucky. But Morgan disobeyed his orders and crossed the Ohio River to
ransack northern territory. He began this operation at Sparta, Tennessee,
and rode by way of Tebbs Bend, a crossing of the Green River in Kentucky,
where he was repelled by a small force of Federal infantry on July 4. The
Confederates then bypassed the bend and crossed the Ohio River near
Brandenburg, Kentucky, on July 8. Creating great disruption of civilian
life, the Rebel column defeated a force of militiamen at Corydon, Indiana,
on July 9 and laid tribute on the town in lieu of destroying it. From the
beginning, Federal cavalry pursued the raiders, and Union commanders
also arranged for other forces to converge toward their likely route. These
columns began to catch up with the Confederates. Morgan entered Ohio
on July 13, skirted Cincinnati, but was decisively rebuffed with the loss of
many men captured when he tried to cross the Ohio River back into Kentucky at Buffington Island on July 19. Now desperate, he continued riding
northeast in hopes of finding an alternate crossing until his remaining
men were surrounded and gave up near Salineville, Ohio, on July 26. It
had been a long journey of more than 1,000 miles and one of the hardest
rides of any cavalry raid during the war.[29]

Pursuing Federals managed to keep up a grueling pace. They typically
rode twenty-three out of twenty-four hours and made sixteen consecutive
all-night marches. Morgan's men picked up the best horses along the way,
leaving the Federals poor mounts. Capt. Theodore F. Allen of the 7th Ohio
Cavalry called them "soft, grass-fed, big-bellied animals that gave out after making only a few miles at the rapid pace set by the seasoned cavalry
horses." Allen praised the army's veteran mounts. They were "hard as nails
and tough as leather" and "knew how to strike the pace of the column
and keep it at an even gait day and night." The stress on men was great
as well. Isaac Gause of the 2nd Ohio Cavalry was almost continuously in

the saddle for twenty-seven days and nights, traveling on average fifty-five miles a day.[30]

Was Morgan's Raid worth it? The answer can only be a decided no. Capt. Henry C. Connelly of the 14th Illinois Cavalry put it well. "This raid was a disastrous failure on Morgan's part; the damage he did to the country through which he passed was only temporary. He sacrificed a splendid body of soldiers without securing an equivalent. His reckless daring and his disobedience of orders gave him some fame, but this was purchased at a fearful sacrifice, and he never regained the confidence of his superiors in the southern army." Morgan literally destroyed his command in a raid that served the Confederacy no real purpose.[31]

WILSON-KAUTZ RAID

On the Federal side two big and almost equally disastrous raids as that conducted by Morgan took place in Virginia and Georgia during the summer of 1864. The first was led by Brig. Gen. James H. Wilson in conjunction with Brig. Gen. August V. Kautz, representing a joint venture by the Third Division, Cavalry Corps, Army of the Potomac and four regiments of Kautz's division, Army of the James. Those 5,500 troopers set out from Petersburg to raid the South Side Railroad and the Richmond and Danville Railroad on June 22, 1864. They hit the South Side track not far west of Petersburg and destroyed it for more than twenty miles between Sutherland Station and Blacks and Whites. Then the troops ranged along the intersecting Richmond and Danville Railroad, which ran from northeast to southwest to connect the Confederate capital with North Carolina. The Federals stopped at the crossing of the Staunton River near Wylliesburg, Virginia, where a small but well-fortified Rebel force barely managed to prevent the Unionists from torching the railroad bridge. To this point the destruction of the track had been facilitated by poor construction. Like the West Point and Montgomery Railroad in Alabama, the Danville line was an old-fashioned construction, with iron straps laid on wooden stringers. It was easily taken apart and burned, and the thin iron straps were heated and twisted out of shape.[32]

So far the Federals largely had a free hand in the raid. But the work of destruction was exhausting. Lt. Col. George A. Purington of the 2nd

Ohio Cavalry reported that the temperature rose to 105°F in the shade by midafternoon of June 26. In places there was a shortage of fence rails and other combustible material near the track, and men had to search for something with which to start fires. After marching day and night to reach the railroad, riding fifty miles in nearly twenty hours, working with blazing fires in a hot sun was a severe trial. Purington believed that "many of the men have not and never will recover from" the experience.[33]

But the worst was yet to come. Even as Kautz attempted to reach the bridge over the Staunton River on June 25, Confederate cavalry were pressing the Federal rear areas. Wilson decided to make his way back to Petersburg. Three Confederate cavalry divisions and one infantry division nearly surrounded the Federals on June 29. Only through desperate fighting and hard riding were they able to extricate themselves but had to abandon virtually all transportation and many artillery pieces. In fact, Purington said that Wilson told him "to rely upon my own judgment and get out the best way I could." Fifteen minutes longer, the lieutenant colonel thought, and the entire Union force would have been compelled to surrender. The raiders trickled back in groups beginning July 1 and for several days afterward. Wilson reported 900 casualties during the expedition and the loss of sixteen cannon plus thirty wagons and ambulances. The trip encompassed a ride of 335 miles; Wilson claimed to have destroyed sixty miles of track and to have fought four battles along the way.[34]

Horses wore out on the Wilson-Kautz Raid at an alarming rate. When abandoned, they were shot to prevent the Confederates from using them, and when necessary horse equipment also was destroyed. Sgt. Roger Hannaford of Company M, 2nd Ohio Cavalry estimated that one horse was abandoned every quarter mile of the route and believed that half of these mounts could have been rehabilitated. It often took four or five rounds to kill one animal, and Hannaford got the impression that some members of the rear guard actually enjoyed it, for they would seek out any horses that had hidden away in a fence corner and kill it. Most troopers were able to keep moving only because the Federals had managed to find some remounts along the way.[35]

Evaluating the results and the costs of the Wilson-Kautz Raid, most Federal survivors did not want to repeat the experience. Surgeon E. W. H.

Beck of the 3rd Indiana Cavalry believed the losses were far too high. "I would not go on annother [*sic*] such a raid for 2000 dollars—cash & pray we may not be sent again," he told his wife. Three railroads (the South Side, Richmond and Danville, and Weldon) were damaged, but not so much as to shut them down for very long. Grant received reports from refugees that the Weldon Railroad was repaired and twenty-five miles of the Danville line had yet to be rebuilt by July 14. The raid had been timed to coincide with the Second Union Offensive at Petersburg, a move west along the fortified lines, but that move resulted in a blunt repulse on June 22–23.[36]

Once again the element of surprise allowed the raiding party to hit lines of communications in the early part of a sortie behind enemy lines. But the Federals were stymied by a small garrison behind well-placed earthworks to protect a major bridge over the Staunton River. More importantly, the Confederates organized a large-scale force of cavalry and infantry to intercept the raiders and nearly inflicted a catastrophic defeat. No one could afford to trade significant amounts of manpower and horse flesh for only temporary disruption of the enemy's lines of communications.

MCCOOK-STONEMAN RAID

A similar scenario developed during the McCook-Stoneman Raid, organized by Sherman in late July 1864 as he launched a major shift of his infantry around the periphery of Atlanta. The big difference between this and the Wilson-Kautz Raid was that McCook and Stoneman failed to inflict any appreciable damage on the railroads feeding the Confederates in Atlanta. Converging Rebel columns also came far closer to destroying their commands. This expedition became one of the best examples of a mounted raid that did not pay.

Sherman launched a major attack on the Macon and Western Railroad that led into Atlanta from the south with most of his available cavalry force. It moved in two columns that planned to unite south of Atlanta. Maj. Gen. George Stoneman led 2,104 troopers to bypass the city on the east, while Brig. Gen. Edward M. McCook led 1,700 west of Atlanta on July 27. Both columns inflicted damage but were never able to form a junction. Worse, they fell prey to converging mounted columns directed by Wheeler. Stoneman managed to reach a point within twelve miles of Macon and then tore apart five miles of the Central Railroad east of the city on July 30. North of the town, McCook reached the Macon and Western Railroad at Lovejoy's Station and destroyed tracks, buildings, government cotton, and telegraph lines.[37]

After the initial phase of destruction, Stoneman received word that Confederate cavalry was headed for his location, so he began his return to Union lines. Unfortunately he chose to go back by the same route he had taken. The Federals ran into Confederate cavalry near Sunshine Church on July 31, and a heavy battle ensued. Stoneman personally led a rearguard action that allowed two-thirds to three-fourths of his men to escape before he surrendered. The escapees found it difficult to make their way to friendly territory, harassed by the Rebels along the way. They straggled into Union lines during the early days of August. Of the original 2,104 men, only 839 made it back. The rest, 60 percent of the total, were counted as casualties: 58 percent of the casualties were missing and presumed captured.[38]

McCook's fate was only slightly better. His command hit the Atlanta and West Point Railroad coming in from the west (which joined the Macon and Western at East Point six miles south of Atlanta) on July 29. His men then rode to the Macon and Western at Lovejoy's Station for more destruction. Just as with Stoneman, troubles began with the homeward journey. McCook decided to return by way of Newnan; his men tore up more track at that town but encountered heavy opposition to the north near Brown's Mill on July 30. A fierce battle erupted, and only a mounted charge allowed most of the Federals to break out of encirclement, 1,200 escaping and making it back to Sherman. McCook proclaimed the raid "a brilliant success" because his losses, about 500 men, were not too severe for the damage inflicted.[39]

But Sherman did not consider it a success. He had counted on the cavalry to close the rail lines for an extended period as an adjunct to his infantry operations, but the troopers failed. The Confederates had ample cavalry resources that they could shift to intercept the raiders. There were only a limited number of routes the Federals could take back home, and the Confederates could cover those routes more effectively than the Unionists could find and use them.

When the defenders had shorter lines of march, operated in known territory, and converged mounted columns, they had many opportunities to protect their lines of communications. Small raiding forces could destroy only limited amounts of resources in the short space of time made available to them, which typically led to railroad shutdowns of only a few days to a few weeks. The defender usually was able to deal with that readily enough. It was only when the raiding force was big enough to seize and hold the lines for a long period of time that disrupting lines of communications became significant. Moreover, the high level of mobility of mounted commands instilled a get-up-and-go attitude that was not conducive to the careful work of burning ties, twisting rails, filling in cuts, chopping down telegraph poles, and hiding the telegraph wire in places like swamps.

"Normal" Cavalry Raiding

While striking at enemy lines of communications topped the list of objectives for mounted raids, many excursions into disputed territory had less ambitious goals. These were typically small expeditions that had little to do with the operational or strategic levels. They could be designed to keep the enemy occupied, to search for him in disputed territory, or to gather resources of food, forage, and animals. After the Federals fully adopted a policy of enlisting Black men into the army, they also sought to free as many slaves as possible from local plantations. This type of operation took place in regions that had become backwaters of the war and usually did not result in much fighting.

The 2nd Iowa Cavalry made many such raids while occupying north Mississippi during and after the campaign against Vicksburg. Large areas of this region were not controlled by either side. The regiment participated in a move from La Grange, Tennessee, toward Senatobia, Mississippi, beginning on May 11, 1863, while Grant was marching toward Vicksburg. The Federals were in search of the main Confederate force in the area, Brig. Gen. James R. Chalmers's mounted brigade. They never made contact with it but did capture sixty stray Rebels and take in 600 horses and mules and 400 refugee slaves in an operation that covered 180 miles in five days.[40]

A month later, while Grant was besieging Vicksburg, the 2nd Iowa

Cavalry participated in another expedition to find Chalmers, this time from La Grange toward Panola, Mississippi. Two cavalry brigades left on June 16 and reached Panola three days later, but Chalmers refused contact. The Confederates sent a detachment to the east bank of the Mississippi River to fire on Union steamboats supplying Grant's army, and in the process one woman and two children were killed. In retaliation the 2nd Iowa Cavalry burned the area where this took place, destroying buildings, provisions, and cotton, estimated by Southern newspapers at $15 million worth of material. The Iowans returned to La Grange by June 24 with 1,000 horses and mules and nearly as many Black refugees.[41]

Considering their limited objectives and light cost, raids such as these were well worth the effort. Denying the Confederates the use of horses and mules and freeing slaves who also were widely used by the enemy were goals that promoted the Union war effort at little cost in manpower and horses.

Evaluating the Raid

When most participants of the Civil War thought of cavalry raids, they imagined the large expedition that struck into dangerous territory to achieve some decisive result. Those were the controversial raids, the ones with limited chances of success and great potential for disaster. Not surprisingly, opinions differed widely as to whether they were worth the high cost.

Many men believed these raids were not only worth the cost but also that they were exactly what the mounted arm was created to do. "The cavalryman is always in his element when on [a] raid, teeming with dash and adventure," asserted Lt. William L. Curry of the 1st Ohio Cavalry. These expeditions served to "raise the morale of the cavalry arm," increasing "the endurance, and intelligence of the soldier." Noble D. Preston of the 10th New York Cavalry called the raid "a cavalryman's delight," for it excused him "from the strict enforcement of the rules of discipline as applied to camp life." He recalled that many cheered when they realized that the mounted column was heading toward disputed territory. "If you would please an old cavalryman give him a raid," declared Capt. Smith H. Hastings of the 5th Michigan Cavalry.[42]

Confederate success at conducting raids early in the war led many Federals to apply pressure for similar efforts. Proposals for mounting 20,000 infantrymen were bandied about with little regard to the financial burden of fielding such a force. But even small parties of mounted men seemed capable of disrupting Rebel lines of communications. "Every cavalry expedition of any force on either side, so far as my memory serves, has been in a great degree, successful," wrote Quartermaster General Montgomery C. Meigs.[43]

Maj. Gen. Philip Sheridan had a vested interest in promoting the utility of raids after finishing his first expedition with the Cavalry Corps, Army of the Potomac. He argued that the losses were not so heavy as to nullify his accomplishments. Sheridan reported that seven out of eight horses returned after the raid, losing 400 horses along the way and having to turn over only 341 animals as "unfit to make the return trip." His loss in manpower from May 9 to May 25 amounted to 46 killed, 210 wounded and evacuated with the column, and 40 too badly wounded to be taken along; 54 more men were captured. His troopers had won a major battle at Yellow Tavern in which Major General Stuart, commander of the Army of Northern Virginia's cavalry, was mortally wounded, and then had ridden south to threaten Richmond.[44]

But many other observers concluded that cavalry raids were wastes of time and resources. These naysayers tended to be infantrymen rather than cavalrymen, but they often were highly placed authorities. Many were responsible for deciding whether to launch such expeditions.

"I have lost faith in cavalry raids," admitted Sherman after the Atlanta Campaign. Other Federals came to similar conclusions by the latter part of the war. The fascination with mounted raids had largely been sparked by Stuart's famous ride around the Army of the Potomac June 12–15, 1862, which resulted in little real damage to the Federals but a lot of publicity for Stuart. "It was something new," recalled Col. Charles Wainwright, artillery chief of the First Corps. The proliferation of mounted raids on both sides, however, exposed their limitations. "These raids have never amounted to anything on either side beyond a scare, and proving that once in within the enemy's line a good body of cavalry can travel either country with perfect freedom for a long time." Even the scare factor decreased with repetition until such raids produced "very little harm."[45]

Maj. Gen. Jacob D. Cox evaluated the value of mounted raids in his memoirs. These operations became fashionable, "an amusement that was very costly to both sides." It diverted cavalry officers from "the comparatively obscure but useful work of learning the detailed positions and movements of the opposing army by incessant outpost and patrol work." Writing of the raids conducted during the Atlanta Campaign, Cox concluded that "the game was never worth the candle. Men and horses were used up, wholesale, without doing any permanent damage to the enemy."[46]

On the Confederate side the most vocal critic of mounted raids was Gen. Braxton Bragg, longtime commander of the Army of Tennessee before becoming military adviser to Confederate president Jefferson Davis. Bragg had effectively used his cavalry arm for raiding Union wagon trains during the Stones River Campaign. But long-distance raids deep into Union-controlled territory were another matter. He had every reason to be incensed with Morgan for his foolish ride to Indiana and Ohio, directly violating Bragg's order and wasting his entire brigade. Morgan and a few of his men escaped Union confinement and returned to duty, but that general's star was clouded thereafter. He mounted a raid into Kentucky in the spring of 1864 that few paid attention to, including Bragg. "The accounts received so far do not indicate any satisfactory result of the movement into Kentucky by General Morgan. Should he ever return with his command it will as usual be disorganized and unfit for service until again armed, equipped, and disciplined. The large number of prisoners we always lose by these raiding expeditions has been the source of great evil."[47]

The steady decline of Confederate cavalry and the increasing effectiveness of Union defensive measures to protect railroads greatly reduced the effectiveness of Rebel raids The Federals also developed by 1864 a capability unprecedented in global military history to rapidly repair breaks in their rail lines. Lt. Col. David C. Kelly of the 26th Tennessee Cavalry Battalion put it well when he reported that "the enemy could repair more rapidly than we could destroy." After the war John Bell Hood also admitted that the Federal use of massive blockhouses to protect railroad bridges was almost impossible to overcome. "The cavalry could do nothing with them," he said.[48]

The Atlanta Campaign demonstrated the rise of railroad protection by the Federals. Sherman relied on 375 miles of rail line, protected by block-houses at key bridges, supplemented by extra supplies at major depots, and strengthened by 2,000 construction workers ready to repair breaks. The Confederates mounted a major effort based on the assumption that Sherman could be turned back if they shut down the railroad for one month, "which I think we can do," wrote J. M. Smith of the 8th Texas Cavalry. Wheeler's troopers tore up 25 miles of the East Tennessee and Georgia Railroad in August 1864, but it was "speedily repaired" by construction crews. His command then rode across Tennessee and hit the line between Nashville and Decatur in early September. A short while later Forrest also hit the Nashville–Decatur route and inflicted more damage. The two raids tore up 30 miles of track and destroyed several huge bridges. Federal crews restored the line between Nashville and Columbia, Tennessee, "at once," but the line was a secondary route of supplies and could easily be ignored until a more opportune time to finish the rest. That delay played to Federal advantage. When Hood invaded Tennessee in November and December 1864, he was desperate to restore the line between Nashville and Decatur, which Forrest had recently destroyed, to supply his starving army. But the Confederates had no resources with which to do this. After Hood's retreat from Tennessee, Federal construction crews finished repairing the entire route within two months.[49]

Even with a far more limited repair capacity, the Confederates worked to restore rail lines broken by Federal raiders. After the war ex-Confederate authorities told Wilson that it took them nine weeks to repair the damage inflicted on the South Side Railroad during his raid with Kautz in June 1864. Grierson's raid on the Mobile and Ohio Railroad in mid-December 1864 put that line out of operation only until January 6, 1865. That included restoring ten miles of track and 20,000 feet of bridges and trestles. While in both examples the Federals could have rebuilt much sooner, it is surprising that the Confederates managed to restore the damage so quickly.[50]

Therefore, a number of observers pondered the worth of mounted raids with skepticism. Chaplain Robert Franklin Bunting of the 8th Texas Cavalry noted that Wheeler's raid of Union wagon-train routes leading to Chattanooga in October 1863 "doubtless did the enemy much damage," but he wondered at the damage to the Confederate cause. By rampant foraging, Wheeler's men alienated many Tennessee civilians, and his command lost at least 1,000 troops out of a force Bunting believed amounted to 8,000 men. The raid hurt the Federals but failed to force them to evacuate the beleaguered town.[51]

The overwhelming majority of mounted raids had little effect on the war except on the most local, regional, or tactical level. Only rarely did a raid affect the operational level. They produced a lot of temporary excitement and disruption that settled down once the raid had ended. A strong argument could be made that the mounted forces would better have been employed in close cooperation with large infantry-based field armies in a working relationship of combined arms. But Americans had precious little experience with infantry-cavalry cooperation before 1861 and only furtively experimented now and then with it during the war. Besides, the lure of a mounted raid was strong, almost irresistible, for the mounted warrior.

9

WEAPONS AND EQUIPMENT

avalry was armed quite differently than the other two branches in the Civil War. While infantrymen used one shoulder arm and artillerymen worked with crew-served cannon, the fully armed cavalryman managed three weapons; a short-barreled carbine, which either was breech-loading or a magazine-fed repeater, supplemented a pistol and a saber. Each was suited to a particular circumstance. The carbine was best for open spaces, although its potential for distance firing was limited. The pistol was suited for short-distance fighting, and the saber could be used only in hand-to-hand combat.[1]

Mounted regiments commonly specialized in weapons use, with some concentrating on sabers and others on carbines. Even within a few regiments, selected companies likewise specialized. This developed as commanders recognized that certain weapons were more useful for certain types of tactical action. Sabers became the weapon of choice for mounted charges, carbines for holding a line on foot or for skirmishing, and pistols for melees.

The Civil War represented a significant step forward in terms of arming the mounted force. In comparison, U.S. dragoons of the Mexican War used musketoons (a short-barreled smoothbore weapon), horse pistols (which Civil War cavalrymen abhorred), and sabers based on a Prussian pattern that were heavy and unwieldy. American mounted riflemen were armed with

Cpl. Elias Warner, Company K, 3rd New York Cavalry.
Warner shows the three weapons most Union cavalrymen used
in the Civil War—a carbine (his is an 1852 Slant Breech Sharps),
a pistol, and a saber. Warner was twenty-two years old when
he enlisted on October 17, 1861, as a private. He reenlisted
on December 16, 1863, and was transferred to the 1st New
York Mounted Rifles just before muster out on July 21, 1865.
Regimental rosters also spell his last name as "Warnear."
LC-DIG-ppmsca-31688, Library of Congress.

percussion rifles and Colt Army revolvers but no sabers, while cavalrymen used rifle carbines, Colt Navy revolvers, and sabers in the Mexican War.[2]

But with the huge expansion of the mounted arm during the early phase of the Civil War, neither government could afford to be choosy about weapons. Many arms had to be purchased in Europe. To at least a limited degree, Confederate cavalry recruits supplied their own weapons. When the call went out for men to make up the 8th Texas Cavalry, it included a notice that the recruits should bring their own arms with them, which primarily meant double-barreled shotguns and revolvers.[3]

The multilevel way of arming Union and Confederate cavalry led to a bizarre variety of weapons in those early months of the war. When Lt. William A. Graham Jr. placed his Company K, 2nd North Carolina Cavalry on picket duty in the spring of 1862, he recorded what types of weapons the thirty-five men possessed. Two had Sharps carbines, six were armed with Hall carbines, five had Colt revolvers, four had Mississippi rifles, and a dozen used double-barreled shotguns. The remaining six had nothing but "pairs of old one-barrel 'horse pistols.'" While Graham's company possessed an unusual variety of guns, most Confederate mounted units were far from uniformly armed in this early time period.[4]

As the war lengthened, efforts were made to streamline weapons across the board. In the Confederate cavalry this process took much longer than in the Union mounted arm. As late as March 1864, Ferguson's Cavalry Brigade in Mississippi was weeding out inferior weapons with an order to turn in all guns except those authorized for each regiment. The 2nd Alabama Cavalry was allowed Enfield rifles, artillery carbines, and Springfield muskets. The 50th Alabama Cavalry was authorized to keep Austrian rifles, while Col. Horace H. Miller's Mississippi regiment gave up literally all of its weapons. The brigade ordnance officer appraised and paid for all private arms.[5]

But not all Civil War cavalry units created a uniformity of weapons. Much planned mixing of arms occurred, which was more prevalent in the Union force. This added enormous flexibility in tactics and probably excited the interest of many cavalrymen who prided themselves on effective use of weapons.[6]

Sabers

Sabers were the most unique weapon of the cavalryman; no one else was issued an edged weapon. In the infantry, artillery, and cavalry, officers were expected to purchase their own swords, which were of a different pattern for the first two branches than the cavalry saber. Unlike the officer's sword, the cavalry saber was meant to be used in deadly work.

Before the Civil War, American cavalrymen employed a heavy dragoon saber of the Prussian pattern, like those used in the Mexican War. A common variant of this type was made by the Ames Manufacturing Company of Chicopee, Massachusetts, beginning in 1833. It was thirty-nine inches long, the blade accounting for almost thirty-four inches of that length. Another common type was the Heavy Cavalry Saber, Model 1840, which was more than forty-one inches long with a blade less than one yard in length. "Both were ponderous weapons," declares historian Stephen Z. Starr, "slightly curved, tapered to a point, and made with a 'false' or rounded cutting edge."[7]

During the period 1860 to 1862, the army introduced the Light Cavalry Saber, Model 1860, to replace the old dragoon weapon. It was thirty-five inches long with a blade of thirty inches that was one inch wide at the hilt. This improved weapon was "much shorter, lighter, and more manageable" than the older sabers, but with "much greater curvature of the blade, it was less well adapted to delivering a thrust than the nearly straight and longer dragoon saber." The Federal government invested a great deal in cavalry sabers. In 1864 alone it issued 90,000 of them to its 160,000 cavalrymen.[8]

The lighter saber was universally welcomed by cavalrymen, who gave up the older dragoon saber. Members of the 10th New York Cavalry called the Prussian type "D —— D old cheese knives." The 1st Massachusetts Cavalry began its service with the Ames variant of the Prussian model and replaced it with "a lighter weapon, of English make" in 1863. The 4th Iowa Cavalry entered service with the dragoon saber until substituting the lighter cavalry model in the winter of 1864–65.[9]

In the Confederate army saber armament ran the gamut of types. The government found only 1,215 sabers in the U.S. arsenals seized at the start of the war and never made or purchased enough to fully arm its mounted force. Shortages led to great variety and generally low quality. Rebel horsemen had "sabres of all sorts," recalled Benjamin W. Crowninshield of the 1st Massachusetts Cavalry, "usually English make, but sometimes . . . a heavy Austrian cavalry sabre." The 4th Kentucky Cavalry (CS) used a heavy English saber that was "exceedingly wearisome, especially to the right hand and arm," during drill. "The boys became so disgusted that they ever afterward rebelled against carrying any such weapon," wrote George Dallas Mosgrove. His comrades "generally managed to 'lose' them."[10]

Such poor-quality sabers were available in the South that homemade versions cropped up. Federal troops found one at a Rebel camp near Cross Hollow, Arkansas, in October 1862. As Vincent B. Osborne of the 2nd Kansas Cavalry described it, the weapon had been "made out of an old mill saw the blade was about three feet in length ground sharp on both edges wooden gripe [*sic*] with a single piece of steel for a guard."[11]

Carrying the saber became something of a problem. The metal scabbard created what Crowninshield called "ceaseless noise." The men learned to fasten the scabbard directly to the side of the saddle "nearly parallel to the horse's body." They could readily draw the weapon when mounted, and the saber was properly stowed when they dismounted. Another problem concerned the saber's edge, which became dull from rattling about in the metal scabbard, which also promoted rust. Many Civil War cavalrymen thought that a scabbard made of leather or wood was the answer, but that probably would not have worked. When he was in Europe before the war, McClellan learned from the Austrians that wooden scabbards easily became dented or broken. Only metal scabbards were used during the Civil War.[12]

An important aspect of saber use centered on whether the cutting edge should be sharp or dull. Civil War horsemen had differing views, and the question was never settled. According to McClellan, Europeans believed in a sharp blade. Austrian horsemen ground their sabers every two or three weeks, assuming that "a dull sabre is entirely useless." They tended to use it for slashing rather than thrusting.[13]

While Continental armies believed in sharpened sabers, those in Great Britain and the United States generally did not. At most these cavalrymen only partially sharpened them. Henry Murray Calvert of the 11th New York Cavalry heard of a man who received thirteen cuts at the Second Battle of Bull Run without suffering death because of partially sharpened enemy blades. Lt. Joseph N. Flint of the 1st New York Dragoons believed it was an "unwritten military code" that cavalrymen were not to sharpen their sabers "more than ten inches from the point," while Lt. James Albert Clark of the 17th Pennsylvania Cavalry reported that the allowance was eighteen inches. The reason for leaving much of the blade dull apparently was an assumption that the saber would be used for thrusting rather than slashing. At least during the training phase, there was a good reason to keep the entire edge dull. Sharpened sabers were dangerous to use in exercises, especially when mounted, as not only the cavalrymen but their horses could be injured by mishandling the weapon.[14]

While many cavalrymen believed in dull sabers, others wanted to sharpen their weapons. "The sabre is *supposed* to be sharp," asserted Crowninshield. Lt. Frederick Whittaker of the 6th New York Cavalry was so intent on keeping his saber sharp that he was willing to invest an hour in grinding it. Ames Manufacturing produced dull sabers, forcing Whittaker to do the hard work. Enlisted men from many regiments wrote of having to sharpen their blades before a campaign, always knowing that such an order portended action in the field.[15]

Whether dull or sharp, was the saber a useful weapon? The Confederates generally seem to have liked it less than the Federals. Capt. William Brooke-Rawle of the 3rd Pennsylvania Cavalry asserted that it was "never a favorite weapon" with his opponents, and John S. Mosby declared that he "had no faith in the sabre as a weapon."[16]

Wiley N. Nash, a member of Harvey's Scouts, discussed this topic at length. His unit had been created for work behind Union lines, and its members preferred firearms. They complained that sabers made too much "unnecessary noise when traveling in the night & when silence was essential." It also weighed too much and was "greatly in the way when the men dismounted to fight, and made a soldier less active in every respect." Nash and his comrades preferred to use a Spencer repeater, when they could take them from Federal troopers, plus two pistols each.[17]

Like any weapon, the saber was liked by some and hated by others. It also was one that required a certain type of terrain for its full use. Cavalrymen North and South noted that saber work was not possible in wooded country. "The sabre is just as much out of date for cavalry in a country like ours as the short sword of the Roman soldier is for infantry," stated James H. Wilson after the war. "It is in the way and is of no value whatever in a fight, as compared with repeating rifles, carbines, and pistols." That edged weapons were useless in dismounted fighting was an undisputed fact among Union and Confederate cavalrymen.[18]

Whether the saber became a useful or worthless item in the cavalry arsenal depended much on the individual. Many soldiers became adept at using it, and others never acquired enough familiarity to use it effectively. Albert Robinson Greene of the 9th Kansas Cavalry was one of the latter. "I never have liked the sabre particularly," he wrote after the war. It was "an unhandy thing" to carry on foot or on horse. During saber drills, he could make a right cut and a left cut well enough but failed to deliver the rear and front moulinet without endangering his horse, his gear, or himself; he tore into his rolled up overcoat and nicked his mount's hind quarters. "I watched the officers do it, and they told us to do exactly as they did. They could make that old cheese knife spin like a circular saw all around them, but it was no go with me."[19]

Moses Harris of the 1st U.S. Cavalry argued that most volunteer horsemen had confidence in the saber "as soon as some training and experience in its use had rendered its grasp familiar." He felt that it usually was effective in battle, "and its successful use brought into existence a moral force which became an important factor in cavalry efficiency." He may have been right, but no amount of experience could make good saber men of troopers like Albert Greene.[20]

For most volunteers, becoming saber adept required a lot of work to learn the complicated technique of cuts, parries, and moulinets. But imparting the proper spirit was equally important. The men had to believe in the weapon until they were "at home with the saber," wrote Henry Norton.[21]

William E. Meyer of the 1st Rhode Island Cavalry required some experience to learn how to manage his saber and pistol in the heat of battle. The edged weapon had a leather strap, one end attached to the saber and the other end wrapped around his wrist. He could therefore drop the saber without losing it and whip out the revolver, which he kept in his boot leg. This worked only if the man purchased and wore the right kind of boot because the government did not issue footwear suited for carrying revolvers. "My friends in Newport paid five dollars in postage to get my boots to the front to me," he wrote after the war.[22]

The Confederates never equaled their opponents in the issue of good sabers, the relentless drilling in their use, or the fervent belief that they were the heart and soul of cavalry work. Many Rebels disdained sabers as useless, placing their reliance on handguns. "How far can you kill a man with those things?" recalled J. K. P. Blackburn of the 8th Texas Cavalry. But Confederate president Jefferson Davis deplored this attitude. He wanted to find ways to manufacture edged weapons for the mounted arm. In fact, he preferred that Confederate cavalrymen not be issued firearms at all. "He tho't that if our cavalry were to depend on the sabre alone that they would then come to close quarters, & run off their antagonists," reported Josiah Gorgas, chief of ordnance.[23]

The rise to greatness of the Union cavalry by the last year of the war was built on a number of material factors. These included sheer numbers of men and horses, the widespread issue of the latest firearms, and the creation of larger units commanded by aggressive leaders as well as shifting the focus of cavalry work from cooperation with infantry to independent action against the enemy. But an equally important factor was morale, the building of self-confidence that led to unit pride. It is highly possible that the Union cavalry surpassed its opponents in spirit as well as in weaponry, organization, resupply of material, and aggressive operational theory. The saber became the symbol of superiority because if a mounted warrior mastered its use, he mastered the most difficult weapon in his arsenal and knew he had the mettle to stand up to anything the enemy offered him.

Most of the references to effective saber work come from Union reports and personal accounts, not Confederate sources. On many battlefields Federal soldiers reported that most of the Rebel losses were dispatched by edged weapons. "Nearly all the wounds were inflicted with the saber," wrote Col. Oscar H. La Grange of the 37 Confederates killed and wounded by his 1st Wisconsin Cavalry in a skirmish in East Tennessee. Fifty-eight of the 109 Confederates captured by the 7th Pennsylvania Cavalry in one fight had been wounded by sabers. The litter of injured Rebels along the trail of a running fight by the 5th Iowa Cavalry included men "with ears and noses off, cut in the shoulder, run through and through," recalled J. S. Lemmon. He also saw one Confederate "with his head split open."[24]

These sources remind us that saber work, when well executed, produced horrifying injuries. For some cavalrymen not yet experienced enough to realize this, the sight of a light saber wound became a badge of military honor. Capt. Charles Francis Adams Jr., whose company of the 1st Massachusetts Cavalry had not yet been engaged in heavy fighting, referred to one of his fellow officers as receiving "a handsome sabre cut" and giving the enemy "quite a collection of lovely gashes." If he had seen men with skulls split open, Adams would not have viewed saber injuries in such a sophomoric way. The weapon instilled a strong sense of spirit in its users, but it was also a deadly weapon in the right circumstances.[25]

Cavalrymen learned how to use the saber, employed it without stint on the battlefield, and noted but refused to become unnerved by the results on enemy bodies. Most Union horsemen recalled with fondness this edged weapon that so distinctly marked their branch of the service. "It was a beautiful sight to see the glittering sabres swing together, and hear the swish of the twirling blades," recalled Crowninshield of saber drill. Many were equally impressed by its utility on the battlefield. "Give them your hardware, boys!" yelled Capt. John Hammond of Company H, 5th New York Cavalry when going into a fight. Chauncey S. Norton noted that "some of the trusty old sabres were brought home by the men as relics" after the war ended. These troopers began as young, green recruits new to saber work, had grown to appreciate and rely on the weapon, and then kept it as a companion of their life. They had spent the greater part of their existence living with the saber.[26]

Pistols

While Federal cavalrymen emphasized sabers more than did their counterparts, Confederate horsemen emphasized pistols more than did Union troopers. In contrast to sabers, which had changed little over the centuries, modern handguns with revolving magazines were widely available only for about thirty years before the Civil War.

From the start of the war, Confederate cavalry units received pistols but were not consistently issued sabers or carbines. Sometimes state governments rather than the central government issued pistols, and at other times men brought their privately owned shotguns. Often the handguns were old models, relics of the past like the "flint pistols" given Company I, 3rd Virginia Cavalry in June 1861. Horse pistols, a cumbersome old model, also appeared quite often in the hands of early war Confederates.

But some units had good weapons from the start. The Mountain Rangers, which became a company of the 8th Confederate Cavalry, used a combination of Colt Navy revolvers and pistols manufactured by British gun-maker Robert Adams, which were in some ways better than Samuel Colt's American products. Officers and noncommissioned officers carried two handguns each, and privates had one, all provided by the state of Alabama. In fact, Adams's establishment, the London Armoury Company, sold thousands of revolvers to the Confederate government, but they were not of his own pattern. His cousin, James Kerr, had developed a five-shot pistol made by Adams's company that became a favorite of many Confederate units.[27]

Revolvers of all types tend to dominate the reports and personal accounts emerging from Confederate cavalry units. Perhaps no other regiment favored revolvers more than the 8th Texas Cavalry. At the start the men supplied their own pistols, and when someone was killed or wounded his friends used his weapon. The Texans also captured revolvers from the Federals "so that after a few months most, if not all, had two weapons of this kind, and some even tried to carry three or four."[28]

Dunbar Affleck fairly represented the regiment's association with pistols. He purchased one just before the Stones River Campaign but soon after traded it for "a brass mounted" revolver costing eighty dollars. In the Battle of Stones River, he captured a Federal revolver that he later sold for sixty dollars and intended to continue trading until he obtained two revolvers of the same make. The desire for pistols was so great in the 8th Texas Cavalry that Affleck's brass-mounted gun was stolen by March 1863. At the same time rumor had it that a man in Texas was making six-shooters and selling them for sixty dollars each. Affleck urged his father to purchase two for him because the current price in Tennessee was much higher. But by September 1864, Affleck's only pistol was a weak, ineffective device that "shoots with such little force and the ball is so small, that it would hardly kill a man if it hit him, unless it was in a vital place."[29]

Early in the war, when the 8th Texas Cavalry was well armed, Brig. Gen. John A. Wharton thought it was "better prepared to meet the enemy cavalry than other regiments in the brigade." The reason was its handguns. "The proper weapon for cavalry had proven to be the revolver," he reported.[30]

Pvt. William Anthony Holland,
Company K, 10th Virginia Cavalry.
Confederate cavalrymen typically did not have the full complement
of carbine, saber, and pistol that Union troopers used. Holland
displays only a Colt Army Model 1860 revolver and a Bowie knife.
LC-DIG-ppmsca-32769, Library of Congress.

Most commentators thought that Confederate cavalrymen excelled at the use of the pistol. There are reports of Rebels repulsing a Union mounted charge with revolvers alone and at close distance. Confederate troopers found ways to handle the weapon in conjunction with controlling the horse by holding the reins in their teeth or by simply dropping the reins and managing their mounts with their knees.[31]

While the Federal cavalry never came to rely on pistols, there is much information about revolver use in Union reports and personal accounts. Federal cavalrymen mentioned a variety of handguns and commented on their value. The Lefaucheux Model 1858 had been developed for the French navy but was not issued by the French army except in a very limited way. Cavalry units that participated in the French intervention in Mexico carried it. This single-action (it had to be cocked at every use) firearm was not a favorite among Unionists. August Bondi of the 5th Kansas Cavalry characterized these weapons as "worthless, would not carry a ball over fifteen steps." The Pettengill, a .44-caliber double-action weapon manufactured by Rogers and Spencer of Willowville, New York, saw wider service in the war. The Federal government purchased 2,000 of them in the fall of 1862 and issued them to at least seven cavalry regiments. It presented a unique appearance because there was no external hammer. Much more widely issued was the Starr revolver, a product of the Starr Arms Company. It was a double-action weapon when the war began, but the Federal government preferred a single-action variant, which the company provided to the tune of 25,000 pistols. The Starr did not receive high marks from William Forse Scott of the 4th Iowa Cavalry. "Its shot was very uncertain, its machinery often failed to work, and it had a vicious tendency to go off at a wrong moment." The firearm held five rounds and used a paper cartridge with percussion cap but was "of a bad pattern and poorly made."[32]

Only a portion of the 4th Iowa Cavalry received Starr revolvers at the regiment's organization, but all of the men received horse pistols. Scott described these as smoothbore muzzleloaders that had been used in the Mexican War—probably the Harpers Ferry Model 1805. Manufactured by the U.S. arsenal at that Virginia location, the Model 1805 was the standard horse pistol of the U.S. Army before an improvement appeared in the Harpers Ferry Model 1855. This later version also was stored in a saddle holster and featured a ramrod mounted on a swivel, but it had rifling. The horse pistol had a longer barrel than a regular pistol and could take a detachable stock for steadier firing. Scott considered it "far more easily managed" and more effective than the Starr revolver. The 4th Iowa Cavalry used them until replaced by Colt revolvers in 1863.[33]

But Scott was in a minority when evaluating the horse pistol. "They were good kickers," recalled Byron Phelps of the 3rd Illinois Cavalry, and very loud. In the 3rd Indiana Cavalry, this weapon seemed to kick "about as hard as it would shoot" and was very "hard on trigger." For most cavalrymen burdened with this relic, the horse pistol was "huge and unwieldy," not suited for mounted warfare.[34]

Mounted Union Trooper with Revolver.
This Federal cavalryman holds his pistol at the ready. His saber is sheathed
at his side, but there is no sight of a carbine. His accoutrements and the
accoutrements and harness of his rough-and-ready horse are also evident.
LC-DIG-ppmsca-37512, Library of Congress.

The most common pistol of the Civil War was the Colt Army Model
1860. Manufactured by Colt's Manufacturing Company, 129,730 were sold
to the U.S. government during the war. It was a .44-caliber cap-and-ball
weapon, single shot with six rounds in the revolving magazine, and accurate from seventy-five to a hundred yards. Crowninshield called it "an
excellent weapon" on foot as well as on horseback. His comrades kept
it in a case hung on their belts or "inside the right boot leg." Frederick
Whittaker liked the Colt revolver best because of its accuracy. It was very
effective in melees and "as a defensive arm for patrols and couriers."[35]

There are many examples of Federal cavalrymen using revolvers to
good effect on the battlefield. Handgun firing alone checked some Confederate advances, while in other cases it was a combination of pistol
and carbine fire. In melees Whittaker advocated the use of a cord a yard
long, one end attached to the revolver and the other to the person, so the
horseman could drop the weapon and use his saber as needed.[36]

Both the Union and Confederate mounted arms utilized revolvers, but the weapon was considered more important among Southern horsemen. In general Confederates made better use of the handgun, tended to rely on it, and excelled the Federals in its employment. At times that made a difference in who won and who lost an engagement.

Carbines

While the Federals had better sabers, and the Southerners excelled in the use of revolvers, the Unionists exceeded their opponents in the quality and use of carbines. Federal supremacy in this area was most notable during the last year of the war, when Union small arms dominated the Rebels on many battlefields. The Richmond government's inability to purchase or make enough good carbines was as important as the shortage of replacement horses in the decline of Confederate cavalry.

Shoulder-fired small arms for cavalry service fell into three categories. The musketoon, a shorter-barreled version of an infantry musket, was a single-shot muzzle-loading weapon. This had been the mainstay of cavalry shoulder arms for decades before the war. The second category was the carbine; in the Civil War this was typically a breechloader that had a shorter barrel than the infantry firearm. They had been around for some time but were not yet generally issued in the mounted arm. Most makes of carbines were still single-shot weapons but easier and faster to load than musketoons. Finally, the third category was the repeater, a carbine with a magazine capable of firing several rounds before reloading. Musketoons appeared early in the war on both sides before they were replaced by carbines. Repeaters were rare in the Confederacy but became fairly widespread in the Union cavalry by the last year of the conflict. But for the majority of horsemen in blue or gray, some kind of breech-loading single-shot firearm was the norm in shoulder-fired weapons.

The musketoon was essentially an infantry weapon with a shortened barrel. In the United States the common model was the Springfield 1847, a smoothbore muzzleloader that had been issued to dragoons. The British Enfield Company made a musketoon version of its infantry small arm in 1861 with a twenty-four-inch barrel for artillery and cavalry use. It was a rifle muzzleloader. No Civil War cavalryman praised his musketoon, always identifying them as a stopgap measure until carbines became available.[37]

The primary problem was that any muzzleloader proved to be inconvenient for use on a horse. The shorter barrel lessened this problem but did not eliminate it. In this regard Confederate horsemen were in complete agreement with their opponents. Nevertheless, many Rebel cavalry units made do with musketoons or long-barrel muzzleloaders because there were no alternatives. Some men in the 6th South Carolina Cavalry had short-barreled Enfields, while others had long-barreled Enfields. Other Confederates used Austrian infantry rifles. A few Rebel cavalry units received the Mississippi rifle, Model 1841, and others used the Model 1817 Common Rifle, a weapon developed by Henry Deringer of Philadelphia, which was popular with pre–Civil War militia units. Crowninshield saw Rebel horsemen who carried long-barreled infantry weapons in a sling hanging from their shoulders while riding.[38]

It is unusual to find Confederate horsemen who were happy with an infantry weapon, but the men of the 4th Kentucky Cavalry proved to be the exception. They captured a number of Enfield rifle muskets from the 100th Ohio in a battle at Limestone, Tennessee, and loved the guns. Later, when given a chance to exchange them, they refused. George Dallas Mosgrove recognized that his comrades typically "looked askance at an infantry musket," but the men of the 4th Kentucky "were much attached" to their Enfields for some reason that he could not explain.[39]

No Federal cavalryman preferred infantry small arms. In fact, the troopers of the 1st Tennessee Cavalry (U.S.) were so unhappy with the infantry weapons they received that "there came near being a [sic] open revolt." One day they stacked their weapons in front of regimental headquarters in an act of near mutiny. It took "a great deal of coaxing" by the officers to convince them to take back their guns and wait for better ones.[40]

Confederate sources rarely report effective use of carbines. William L. Royall of the 9th Virginia Cavalry recalled that he had a great deal of trouble firing his carbine on horseback. He held the rein in his left hand but "as soon as I slackened the pressure on the bit my horse would move forward and disturb my aim." Wet weather often plagued cavalrymen when they needed to use their weapons. During an expedition in Mississippi, only ten men in the 26th Tennessee Battalion could fire in a heavy rain, the others "remained snapping caps and bursting tubes in the enemy's front until ordered to retire." At times Confederate horsemen used their carbines as clubs in a melee to knock opponents off their mounts.[41]

According to Chief of Ordnance Gorgas, there was a lot of resistance to adopting the latest arm for mounted service. "Cavalry officers are not all agreed as to the value of the breech-loading carbine," he wrote in August 1863, "and officers of great experience pronounce in favor of the muzzle-loading carbine." There was little disagreement among Union cavalry officers; most were fervent advocates of breechloaders and repeaters.[42]

Federal cavalrymen universally rejected musketoons and wanted, at the very least, a good carbine; their government listened. Some of the various types of carbines it issued were old, while others were developed just before or during the war. The Hall carbine, originally made in 1833, was readily available in a variant version by the time of the Civil War. A breechloader and percussion weapon, the variant was often called the Side Lever Hall carbine, manufactured from 1844 to 1855 by Simeon North of Middletown, Connecticut. Bondi of the 5th Kansas Cavalry called them "a kind of old fashioned breech loaders" with an effective firing distance of about 200 yards. "Everything about it was big, rough and strong," asserted Phelps of the 3rd Illinois Cavalry, but he noted that powder had a tendency to leak out, leaving only enough to push the ball partway out of the barrel. The 4th Iowa Cavalry received forty Halls in the late spring of 1863. "An inferior gun of short range, taking a paper cartridge," William F. Scott wrote, but the fact that they loaded at the breech made them superior to everything else the regiment possessed, including Austrian infantry rifles, Starr revolvers, and horse pistols.[43]

Many carbines received nothing but criticism from those who used them. Benjamin Franklin Joslyn's carbine, developed by 1855 as a breech-loader and modified in 1861, used a metal rim-fire cartridge; it was "utterly worthless" in the view of Brig. Gen. Judson Kilpatrick. Gilbert Smith developed a carbine by 1857 that also was a breechloader. The barrel broke open for reloading, and the .50-caliber ammunition was encased in rubber. Some 30,000 were manufactured in Massachusetts, but they were not well received. "This was not a good weapon," concluded Crowninshield. When Colonel Grierson landed up at Baton Rouge at the end of his famous raid through Mississippi in the spring of 1863, about half his men used Smith carbines. But he could obtain no ammunition for this weapon in the Department of the Gulf. By June, these troopers were down to no more than eight rounds apiece, so Grierson found Sharps carbines in New Orleans and replaced the Smiths. Col. William D. Hamilton of the 9th Ohio Cavalry also could not easily replace ammunition for the Smith carbine. "I regard the weapon for that reason, and for its liability to get out of repair, as one which should not be used in the service."[44]

The carbine designed by Mahlon J. Gallager and manufactured by Richardson and Overman of Philadelphia from 1861 failed to become popular. It was a breechloader, which involved breaking the barrel to reload, and fired a .52-caliber brass cartridge with a percussion cap. More than 17,000 were sold to the U.S. government even though Chief of Ordnance James W. Ripley knew the men were not happy with it. "They snap often," replied Brig. Gen. Jeremiah T. Boyle when Secretary of War Stanton asked him why the weapon was not popular. "The cartridge hangs in after firing; difficult to get the exploded cartridges out often with [a] screwdriver, men throw them away and take musket or any other arm. They are unquestionably worthless. Can we get Sharp's, or Wesson's, or Ballard's, or some other kind? Sharps best."[45]

But Ballard's carbine also received scathing reviews. Designed by Charles H. Ballard of Worcester, Massachusetts, it was a single-shot weapon using a rim-fire cartridge. More than 6,000 were produced. Lt. Granville C. West referred to "the utter worthlessness of the Ballard rifle," which six companies of his 4th Kentucky Mounted Infantry used in the McCook-Stoneman Raid. "A great many became entirely useless during the action; some bursted from firing; others became useless by the springs, which threw out the old cartridge, getting out of fix." The offering of James H. Merrill of Baltimore, a breech-loading percussion .54-caliber gun with a paper cartridge, fared little better. It was "comparatively worthless," concluded the historian of the 18th Pennsylvania Cavalry, and "a source of discouragement and serious embarrassment to the recruits."[46]

Colt's revolving rifles received mixed reviews. The New Model Revolving Rifle fired a paper cartridge with a percussion cap. Its revolving cylinder carried five to six rounds, depending on the variant, which ranged from .36 caliber to .64 caliber. Produced from 1855 to 1864, the carbine version was fairly well used by Union cavalry regiments. Because it was not easy to reload, especially on horseback, it did not become a universal favorite. Ten companies of the 9th Illinois Cavalry received this weapon in April 1863 and considered it "really a very effective arm," although the men had to fight on foot in order to best manage the reloading process. When the 4th U.S. Cavalry received Colt revolving rifles, the men considered them "so inconvenient for a mounted man that we are going to give them up," as James H. Wiswell reported. Colt's product actually was quite effective when used by men who grew accustomed to its strengths and weaknesses, and that meant hardened veterans, according to Lieutenant Whittaker. "The six shots are fired more rapidly and far more accurately than by any other piece extant, but the loading must be done without flurrying. It is a poor weapon to give to green troops on this account."[47]

A carbine developed by Ambrose Burnside before the war was ranked above most of its contenders by Union cavalrymen. It was a breechloader with a brass cartridge that Burnside also developed, fired with a percussion cap. More than 55,000 carbines of this .54-caliber weapon were produced, making it the third-most-popular shoulder arm for cavalry in the war, bettered only by the Sharps and the Spencer. When the 12th Illinois Cavalry received what Winthrop Allen called "the celebrated Burnside patent" carbine at its organization, the men were happy. It was "a very convenient and pretty as well as destructive and terrible weapon." Soldiers called them their "Burney Rifles," and some bragged about firing eight rounds a minute, although the spent cartridge was at times not easy to extract. Praise, however, was not universal. Capt. Thomas J. Grier of the 18th Pennsylvania Cavalry called the Burnside "a poor arm but superior" to other makes.[48]

The reviews of the Sharps carbine were the most positive of any cavalry shoulder arm; it was the most popular and the most widely distributed carbine of the war. The weapon started in 1848 as a long-barreled firearm, developed principally by Christian Sharps. Nearly 90,000 were manufactured by the Sharps Rifle Manufacturing Company, with Sharps as engineer; it was a breechloader with percussion caps and was easier to reload than any other single-shot breech-loading carbine. Called "one of the most effective arms in the service," it was "much liked" by most cavalrymen. Sharps developed a variant of his carbine and produced it at the company he formed with William Hankins. Known as the Sharps and Hankins Model 1862, it drew praise from the few mounted soldiers who mentioned it. Newel Cheney of the 9th New York Cavalry called the carbine "much more efficient and reliable than the Burnside or Sharp." The Sharps and Hankins fired a .52-caliber metallic cartridge.[49]

The Sharps carbine was the best single-shot breechloader for cavalry service during the Civil War. But a number of men viewed the Spencer repeater as superior to it. A magazine-fed shoulder arm, reloading was effected by working the trigger guard. Some commanders were so convinced that Spencers were the wave of the future that they denigrated its closest rival. Kilpatrick declared that Sharps carbines were, like Joslyn's, "utterly worthless." Custer, Sheridan, and Wilson were among the Spencer's most fervent advocates.[50]

Christopher Spencer designed this new firearm, which became the first military repeater firing a metallic cartridge in global history. More than 200,000 were manufactured from 1860 to 1869. Custer's brigade was among the first to receive this seven-shooter, and "a lighter arm and better adapted for the use of cavalry" could not be found, according to James H. Kidd. In the West John T. Wilder's brigade received Spencers when it converted from infantry to mounted infantry in the spring of 1863. The firearm gained a reputation as the supreme carbine for mounted warfare. Regimental officers requested it for their units and at times were compelled to give them to other units that were assigned to participate in strenuous expeditions. In many regiments Spencers replaced Smiths, Burnsides, and other makes by the early part of 1864.[51]

The Spencer was never universally distributed to the Union mounted arm, but by war's end, many regiments used it. When Wilson took command of the Third Division, Cavalry Corps, Army of the Potomac in April 1864, he counted only two regiments as truly reliable, while the rest were ill armed with Smith carbines. After the Wilson-Kautz Raid of late June and early July, he worked to obtain 2,000 Spencer carbines and claimed that the new arm encouraged his men to fight well. In the West, while Robert H. G. Minty's cavalry brigade refitted in Louisville during December 1864, four of its five regiments received Spencer carbines.[52]

What truly impressed everyone about the Spencer was its rapid rate of fire, a unique experience compared to the single-shot weapons that dominated infantry and cavalry warfare in the 1860s. It could deliver "a greater volume of lead than any other arm then in use," wrote Wilson, "and that is what tells in a fight." Maj. Theodore H. Weed of the 10th New York Cavalry witnessed the fire erupting from Custer's brigade at Cold Harbor, claiming 600 troopers fired 60,000 rounds in seven minutes. "They are wicked," Weed declared of the Spencers, "nothing can stand them . . . , deliver me from charging such hail."[53]

But not everyone so highly praised the Spencer carbine. Lieutenant Whittaker found less difference in the rate of fire between the Sharps and the Spencer. One could shoot off the seven rounds in rapid order, but then it took some time to reload the magazine. With the Sharps, one could maintain a slower but regular rate of fire that Whittaker thought was more effective. "I have fired as many rounds in the course of twenty minutes out of Sharps' as out of Spencers'," he declared.[54]

The Spencer carbine had a problem with the magazine and the firing mechanism that endangered its user. At times, according to William F. Scott, "the pointed bullet of one cartridge struck too hard upon the cap of the one lying before it in the tube. In the shock of riding or other rapid motion, this sometimes occurred, and men were killed or dreadfully wounded by such explosions," which burst the stock wide open.[55]

Surgeon Francis Salter, medical director of Wilson's Cavalry Corps, noted two instances of exploding Spencer magazines. In both cases he thought the problem lay in jostling while riding and for some reason believed the heat was a factor as well. The answer, according to Salter, was to keep the tube completely filled to reduce the possibility of cartridges sliding within it. "Four inches of play on a hot day may explode them, as evidenced in these two cases."[56]

Even the best cavalry arm had some problems, as evidenced by the Spencer. Each of the many types of weapons used by Union mounted regiments had its own list of advantages and disadvantages. Despite clear evidence that Sharps and Spencers were superior to all other makes, all

Civil War cavalryman tried many different types during their war service. For example, the Ordnance Department sent 1,340 Sharps, 630 Smiths, 750 Burnsides, and 439 Colt revolving rifles to various western mounted regiments during the latter months of 1862.[57]

Surprisingly, that kind of variety continued throughout the war. The brigade commanded by Col. La Fayette McCrillis used "at least six different calibers" of shoulder-fired weapons by late 1863. The situation was for some units not much better a year later. Archaeologists working on the Mine Creek battlefield in eastern Kansas, site of a battle mostly involving cavalry units in Price's Missouri Raid, found 275 bullets and cartridge cases. Nearly half of them were fired by breechloaders from at least seven different types of cavalry carbines. When preparing for the March to the Sea, Sherman's chief ordnance officer reported that his 60,000 infantry were armed entirely with either Springfield or Enfield rifle muskets. His lone cavalry division of more than 5,000 men, however, possessed 3,000 Spencer carbines, 2,000 Sharps carbines, and "a few hundred of Burnside, Ballard, Merrill, and Smith carbines and Lindner rifles."[58]

Carbines of all types had their limits as useful cavalry arms. Breech-loaders were easier to load than muzzleloaders, but one still had to handle it on a sometimes unsteady horse. There are examples of ineffective carbine work by Federal mounted units that had dire consequences on the outcome of an engagement. At times this included firing carbines at targets too far to have an effect on them. In a fight at Mount Zion Church, Virginia, during July 1864, a portion of the 2nd Massachusetts Cavalry opened fire with carbines at the Confederates 225 yards away, which proved to be beyond their weapons' effective distance.[59]

Of course, there are many more instances of effective carbine use among Federal units than of failure to utilize it well. The majority of cavalrymen were able to load, aim, and fire on horseback if they had to, and most combat took place at distances closer than 200 yards. As Moses Harris pointed out, much depended on the tactical situation. Carbines were the perfect weapon for dismounted fighting, which was common during the war. Whittaker also pointed out the importance of the individual. Putting any weapon in the hands of a veteran was better than giving even the best carbine to a recruit. "The whole difference in action between green troops and veterans lies only in coolness," he asserted.[60]

Lances

Besides sabers, the only edged weapon issued to cavalry in the Civil War was the lance, and it saw little service. In this the American experience was different from that of European countries. Although it had grown out of favor in most Continental armies by the 1860s, a few still believed in the weapon. McClellan was impressed by the use of lances in the Russian service. "It will be seen that it is a favorite weapon with them," he reported. But it was in Poland that the lance had come into its own during the modern era. Polish lancers were famed across the Continent for their use of the weapon in the recent past. "The lance is a most formidable weapon in the hands of those who know how to use it," wrote Jean Roemer, a former cavalry officer in the Netherlands. But many who admired the lance admitted that its morale effect probably exceeded its ability to physically harm the enemy.[61]

A lancer's manual appeared in New Orleans at the outbreak of the Civil War. Consisting of only twenty-eight pages, it described the weapon as a "a sharp steel blade from 8 to 10 inches long, grooved like a bayonet, with a socket at its base and two iron straps for attaching it to the handle." The shaft was eight to eleven feet long and weighed about five pounds. The end rested in a leather boot attached to the stirrup, and a leather loop was attached to the middle of the shaft, at the center of gravity, so the soldier could use it to control the weapon when deployed or when it rested in the boot. "Lancers are more formidable than other cavalry, because they are able to reach further," declared the anonymous author of this manual.[62]

Very few Confederate soldiers ever read this book because the South failed to create any appreciable number of lancer units. There is an unconfirmed report that Rebel lancers attacked the 98th New York at the Battle of Seven Pines in the spring of 1862. But there is no doubt that Confederate troopers of Company B, 5th Texas Cavalry mounted a lancer attack on a company of the 1st Colorado Infantry, which failed, at the Battle of Valverde in New Mexico Territory on February 21, 1862. It was the only confirmed Southern lancer attack of the war.[63]

The Union army formed a few lancer units. The 3rd Kentucky Cavalry used pikes sharpened on both sides and attached to poles fifteen feet long for a while during the winter of 1861. But as John L. Bruce recalled, "when we got out in the brush and muddy swamps one dark night we broke staffs, cut some horses, and found the weapon altogether useless." The men who formed Company L, 4th Iowa Cavalry initially enlisted for a lancer regiment being organized by a former German officer named Pleyel. When he failed to complete the unit, the few men who had enlisted agreed to join the 4th Iowa Cavalry.[64]

In California the Hispanic heritage of lancer use came into play when Companies A and B, 1st Battalion, Native California Cavalry were organized. More than half the men carried lances. The War Department had authorized the creation of four companies for this battalion, which recruited from the ranches of California men who were native to the state or were Mexican Americans (California vaqueros). The men of Company A soon gave up their lances in favor of Sharps carbines, while those of Company B retained the edged weapons but never used them in battle.[65]

The only full regiment of the Civil War to be armed with lances was the 6th Pennsylvania Cavalry, also known as Rush's Lancers after its first commander, Col. Richard H. Rush. Prompted by his observations in Europe, McClellan specifically asked that this unit be armed with edged weapons in late November 1861, a couple of months after its organization. The men already had pistols and sabers, but Rush conducted a study to see what kind of lance was preferable. After consulting French and German officers on duty with McClellan's army, he chose an Austrian pattern with an eleven-inch blade. The staff, made of Norway fir, was one and one quarter inches in diameter and weighed four pounds, thirteen ounces. A "scarlet swallow-tailed pennon" adorned the lance. The Ordnance Department contracted with a private company to make this weapon, and the men generally liked it even after carbines were issued in a limited way to the regiment.[66]

"I don't think that our Lances will ever be of any use in this war unless we should get a chance to charge in an open Field. In that case, they would be a most Powerful weapon," thought Sgt. Thomas W. Smith. The 6th Pennsylvania had only a few opportunities to try them. Company C charged lances at Confederate pickets during the Peninsula Campaign on May 25, 1862. "It wasn't you we run from," said a captured Confederate to a man in another Union regiment, "it was them fellows with them long Poles." Some limited use of the weapon also took place on June 27. The regiment again utilized it in a small way during a skirmish on April 30, 1863, but less than a month later gave up its lances entirely when carbines were issued to every man. While Thomas Smith tended to believe in the usefulness of the weapon, Chaplain Samuel L. Gracey thought it was "illy adapted to cavalry service, as performed in the wooded country."[67]

Saddles

Other than a weapon, the saddle was a vitally important element in mounted warfare. It had for centuries provided the link between man and horse, the foundation for his "seat," the stable position on the moving animal that offered him mobility. Learning how to use that tool became part of cavalry training and effectiveness in the field.

Mounted warriors needed a particular kind of saddle. Louis E. Nolan, the British Hussar captain, described those needs very well. "That saddle is best for cavalry which, being of a simple construction, brings the soldier close to his horse, in a firm and easy seat. It must be sufficiently strong to carry the necessary kit, easy to repair or replace in the field; it ought to be roomy, and, above all, it ought to give no sore backs."[68]

Since the development of the saddle about 700 BCE, a variety of types had developed across the globe. Many of them acquired cultural or national characteristics that set them apart. A handful of types lasted and spread across regions or continents. The Hungarian saddle tree, for example, became the basis of cavalry saddles widely used in European armies by the nineteenth century. As with any saddle, padding was attached to the tree for the rider, with blankets or a saddle cloth placed underneath to protect the horse's back. A single-size saddle had to fit all for mass distribution among cavalry units, which meant that it fit some horses better than others.[69]

Several basic saddle types were available in the United States. In the East the English saddle influenced American types, while in the region between the Appalachian Highlands and the Mississippi River, saddles used by the Spanish played the major influence. The Mexican saddle, brought to the Western Hemisphere by the Spanish who obtained it from the Moors, was popular in its variants, one of which was called the Texan saddle. According to Frederick Whittaker, the Mexican-Texan saddle had no buckles but used straps and leather thongs to tie things to the pommel, which was the rising part at the front, and the cantle, which was the rising part at the rear. "The broad, flat horn in front is quite a convenience for many purposes, especially to go to sleep on in long night marches."[70]

Before the Civil War, several saddle designs competed with each other for use by the army. Dragoon saddles included the Ringgold saddle of 1844, developed by Maj. Samuel Ringgold, which was replaced by the Grimsley saddle, developed by Thornton Grimsley of St. Louis in 1847, with "lighter and stronger" characteristics. But the saddle that dominated Civil War use was developed by George B. McClellan. While serving on the Delafield Commission to observe the Crimean War, he noticed features of a Prussian saddle based on the Hungarian pattern. It influenced him to modify the Spanish tree used in Mexico. The result was adopted by the U.S. government in 1859 and, through modifications, served the needs of the army to the end of the cavalry era in the middle of the twentieth century.[71]

The Confederates used several types of saddles during the war. Arsenals in Texas manufactured Texan, McClellan, Jenifer, and Hope saddles. Josiah Gathwright, quartermaster on the staff of John Hunt Morgan, developed a saddle he named after his commander and was made at a facility in Alabama.[72]

But the McClellan saddle was the most commonly used by Civil War troopers North and South. Col. John M. Galloway of the 5th North Carolina Cavalry called the McClellan "the best army saddle ever invented by the wit of man." McClellan had shaped the top of the wooden tree to make a more comfortable seat for the rider and the bottom to be more comfortable for the horse. "A narrow slit is cut out over the backbone," observed Capt. Charles C. Nott of the 5th Iowa Cavalry, "which not only saves the horse's spine, but makes it much more cool and comfortable for him." A folded horse blanket provided the padding between saddle and horseflesh. The leather covering had a tendency to crack and split with wetting and drying in field service, but that was a problem with any saddle. The 4th Illinois Cavalry had to use Grimsley saddles during the early period of its service and rejoiced when it could discard them for new McClellans.[73]

Frederick Whittaker evaluated the McClellan saddle in detail. If one

McClellan Saddle.
Capt. George B. McClellan was influenced by several other types
of saddles he observed while serving in the Mexican War and on
the Delafield Commission, which visited Europe during the era of
the Crimean War. From Europe, the influence was the Hungarian
pattern as modified by the Prussians; from the Western Hemisphere,
the influence was the Spanish tree used in Mexico. His saddle was
adopted by the U.S. Army in 1859, and it was the most popular
type used during the Civil War. With modifications, it served
American cavalry needs until the middle of the twentieth century.
Roemer, *Cavalry*, 497.

made sure the horse blanket was adjusted properly and the equipment and supplies were "carefully adjusted, so as not to chafe, there need be no sore backs with this saddle." He found fault with the leather covering, which "always goes just at the edge of the cantle, and, once the rawhide cover is gone, the saddle soon rocks to pieces." It did not have a breast strap that would have prevented the saddle from slipping backward when riding uphill. The saddle bags also were too small; his comrades threw them away and obtained two large canvas bags to "give a man somewhere to put his food." Whittaker both liked and disliked the stirrups. They had a large hood to protect the foot and keep it from slipping forward, but the men often got their foot stuck between the hood and stirrup. The addition of a strip of leather to connect the stirrup and hood would have prevented that problem. The wooden part of the stirrup often rotted and broke apart. This happened twice to Whittaker, and he discovered it only when mounting, suffering a "heavy fall" both times. He tried to use "the open iron stirrup" but found it did not provide "so firm a seat as the hooded wooden one." The best solution, in his view, would have been a hooded and fully iron stirrup. Whittaker asserted that with the McClellan, "you have as good a cavalry saddle as a man need wish for."[74]

The Confederate government initially adopted the Jenifer saddle for its cavalry in December 1861. Developed by Lt. Walter H. Jenifer of the U.S. Army in 1860, it was "basically a streamlined Grimsley with other modifications," according to historian Howard Crouch. At the outset of war, Jenifer resigned from the army and became a captain in the 8th Virginia Cavalry. The Confederates manufactured his saddle with little complaint until the middle of the war, when a flood of criticism fell upon it, probably due to a sudden shift toward shoddy workmanship by the manufacturers. Col. John R. Chambliss Jr. excoriated the saddles in August 1863. They were "dreaded, ridiculed, and avoided by officers and men, and are used only through necessity, seldom without proving ruinous to the back of horses." Josiah Gorgas understood the problem, and the Confederate government officially adopted the McClellan saddle in January 1864.[75]

The saddle blanket had a vital role to play in cushioning the horse's back from sores caused by the tree. It was made of wool, but shortages of that material led to substitutes in the Confederacy. Rebel saddle blankets were made of cotton, old carpet, and even Spanish moss in some parts of the South.[76]

The stirrup gave the rider a more firm seat, increased his control of the horse, and enabled him to stand up while riding. All of these advantages were vital to making an effective mounted warrior. Typically, the stirrup was made of iron or brass, but the McClellan saddle used wood, either oak or hickory, which was steamed and then bent into the proper shape. Fitted with leather hoods to complete the assembly, the McClellan stirrup was distinctive and largely effective.[77]

A good stirrup saved many a cavalryman's foot from severe injury. Capt. George N. Bliss of the 1st Rhode Island Cavalry rode a borrowed horse one day when chased by Confederate cavalrymen. In the frenzied riding, Bliss found it difficult to manage the English saddle. "Frequently my feet would be thrown out of my light stirrups by crowding horses in the narrow road." He slackened his pace and fell to the rear of the Union mass, almost being captured in the process. The McClellan stirrup probably would have prevented this problem. Henry Murray Calvert of the 11th New York Cavalry twice had reason to thank it. One day his horse slipped on a muddy road and "fell flat on his side, pinning me down by the right leg." Fortunately the "tough hickory-wood stirrup of the McClellan saddle saved my ankle, as it has saved others to my knowledge in similar accidents, and the soft mud of the road made a cushion for my leg." On another occasion an irritable horse kicked violently, his hoof hitting Calvert's right stirrup. The blow split the hickory wood and left a hoof print on the leather, but the stirrup saved his foot from being broken.[78]

Even with the best saddle, small problems harried the cavalryman. With long periods of riding, saddles became loose, forcing the trooper to dismount and readjust straps. At times the blanket worked its way back without the rider knowing it. In such cases it was best to attach the blanket to the saddle. This problem often happened with horses that had small abdomens.[79]

Another problem was not with the saddle, but with unscrupulous manufacturers. Complaints about "miserable, worthless saddles that never should have been bought by the Government, or put on a horse's back after they were bought" were common. "The saddles issued to us

Mounted Union Officer. An unidentified but well-appointed officer and his horse are evident in this photograph. The horse has a saddle skirt and crupper.

LC-DIG-ppmsca-31006, Library of Congress.

simply murder horses; it is sure ruin to a horse to put one on his back," complained Brig. Gen. Robert B. Mitchell, chief of cavalry, Department of the Cumberland. They were "worthless, murderous saddles, that dig holes into the backs the first day and break them down. New saddles are worse than old; the hides on them are green, and the first rain they are in pulls it all off. The trees are made of green wood . . . , the iron holding the tree is too weak, and the saddle spreads and settles upon the horse's back, making it set in the worst possible shape."[80]

To a degree, cavalrymen adjusted the saddle and its accoutrements to suit their needs based on experience in the field. Many substituted larger bags for the provided saddlebags to carry their food and personal items. Leather skirts attached to the saddle to protect the horses' sides seemed unnecessary and were easily detached. Adding their personal blankets to the saddle blanket made for a better cushion on the horse's back and was a convenient way for the horseman to carry it as well. All adjustments tended to be along the lines of streamlining the saddle and its attachments, simplifying everything to make traveling more convenient. Albert Brackett thought that adding shoulder belts would have enabled the trooper to more conveniently carry his weapons and cartridge box, but that probably would also have interfered with effective riding.[81]

The cavalryman had access to many pieces of small equipment, most of which were meant to be used in the care of his horse. These included a curry comb, hoof picks, blanket pin, a leather punch or awl, saddler's knife, horse brush, picket pins, and of course horseshoes. "A cavalryman has more equipments than any other branch of the service," concluded Henry Norton of the 8th New York Cavalry. In fact William F. Scott believed that his comrades carried close to fifty pounds of weapons, equipment, and uniform items. The horse probably carried up to seventy pounds of specialized riding equipment, and after adding the weight of the man, Scott estimated the mount had to put up with 200–250 pounds of weight.[82]

"It became a fine art how to lessen the burden of the horse," Scott wrote after the war. Horseshoes and nails were essential, but items considered important for service on the western plains, such as a lariat, were found unnecessary in the eastern part of the continent. Most soldiers did not like to carry a nosebag for feeding their mounts and discarded them. But discarding equipment considered useless always happened with soldiers.[83]

In all three branches of the service there occurred a process of acquisition, trial, and assessment of weapons and equipment. That process was more prolonged and complicated in the cavalry because of the special needs of the mounted arm. Utilizing the horse as a means of mobility and as a fighting platform was the primary factor out of which all the complications arose. Horses played no role in infantry fighting, and they only pulled field guns to the battlefield and then were unhitched and taken to the rear. A cavalryman's outlay of arms and equipment was dominated by the fact that he moved and fought on horseback. He also had to transport all his personal items with him while trying to lessen the load his mount had to carry.

In terms of weapons usage, the Federal cavalry surpassed its counterpart in gray in two types. It had more and better sabers and used them more consistently. The Confederates excelled in the use of pistols for close-distance firing, relying on revolvers as their main weapon by choice or by necessity. But the Federals surpassed the Confederates in the quality and use of shoulder-fired arms, especially breech-loading carbines and repeaters. It took time, but Union mounted forces achieved superiority in most areas that counted when it came to moving toward victory.

10

MOUNTING THE CAVALRY

P utting cavalrymen on horses proved to be one of the most vexing problems of the Civil War for both governments. The initial
mounting was not so difficult. With an abundance of horses in
the civilian economy, mounts were readily available by purchase or by
allowing recruits to bring their private horses to the army. But as the war
lengthened, the problems truly settled in. While many cavalrymen took
care of their horses for long-term use, many more did not. Probably a majority of cavalrymen treated their horses as a machine, and in the Union
cavalry, a machine owned by someone else. Disease became a horrible
problem for both sides, killing more mounts than did combat. Neither
side created a corps of veterinary surgeons; indeed, there were so few
trained veterinarians in the United States that there was little hope of
applying science to the problem of army equine disease. The loss rate of
horses increased the cost and problems of mounting the cavalry.

The huge volunteer armies of North and South tended to be profli-
gate with their horses in contrast to the professional armies of Europe.
George B. McClellan had studied the system of mounting cavalrymen in
Austria. Officials there knew that the men would likely take better care
of their mounts if they owned them. If an Austrian cavalryman rode the
same horse for eight years, he received a gratuity equivalent to $7 plus
$2.50 for each additional year he maintained the mount in good condi-
tion. After twenty years he became the owner of the horse and its equip-

ment. Lower-ranking officers (lieutenants and second captains) were issued government horses and became their owners after eight years of use. All higher-ranking officers, however, were fully responsible for purchasing their own mounts.[1]

Before the Civil War the U.S. Army never instituted a system to allow cavalrymen to become horse owners. But according to Richard W. Johnson, it took pains to mount the cavalry regiments well. A board of officers was created to purchase animals for the 2nd U.S. Cavalry in 1855 and strove to find the best because "a first-class horse will last longer and do more hard work than those purchased by the quartermaster's department at a fixed price." Johnson's company received eighty-five "fine Kentucky horses" that year; after six years of service, forty-four were still in the field.[2]

Even with Johnson's endorsement of the regimental purchasing system, two caveats are required. First, he clearly implied that most horse purchases were not conducted this way but in mass by quartermasters, and those animals were inferior to the ones the 2nd U.S. Cavalry board chose. Second, mounting a small peacetime force was vastly different than horsing a large wartime cavalry.

Confederate Horse Policy

Each side set out on divergent paths to mount their cavalry force. The new Confederate government passed an act calling for 100,000 volunteers to serve for one year on March 6, 1861. Those wishing to join mounted units had to provide their own animal and horse equipment. The government allowed them forty cents per day "for the use and risk of their horses." If a man could not keep a serviceable mount, he would need to serve on foot and lose the forty cents per day. "For horses killed in action volunteers shall be allowed compensation according to their appraised value at the date of muster into service."[3]

The government followed this policy for the rest of the war. It had some short-term advantages, saving the taxpayers a great deal of money and allowing for a quick mobilization of mounted units. For the first year of the conflict it worked well, then the available supply of mounts began to constrict by the summer of 1862. Given the rise of inflation and the depreciation of Confederate currency, assessing the value of the horse at the date of muster in came to hurt the soldier. Also, if his animal died or became disabled due to disease or any reason other than combat, he could not be reimbursed. The problem of finding a replacement soon became a nightmare. Once in service having lost his mount, a Southern cavalryman either had to apply for leave to go home, buy a replacement from someone in the army, or hope to capture a horse from the Federals.[4]

All of these shortcomings became more detrimental to the Confederate army over time. But at the beginning no one thought much of them. "We had our horses valued today & at big figures," reported John H. Ervine of the 1st Virginia Cavalry in June 1861. But many Confederate troopers did not have their mounts or horse equipment appraised until long after they joined the army. J. Kent Langhorne of the 2nd Virginia Cavalry had his horse valued at $650 in June 1863, which gave him a great advantage over having had it appraised on enlistment. Even in January 1864 Joseph Wheeler instructed his division commanders to make sure that all men had their horses mustered and appraised. When this was done early that year, the valuations ranged from $900 to $2,000 in the 3rd Texas Cavalry. The 12th Virginia Cavalry also underwent a thorough appraisal of its horses in April 1864, with valuations ranging from $1,400 to $1,734.[5]

"'When am I to get another horse,'" wrote Col. John R. Chambliss Jr. as he tried to express the problems faced and questions asked by his men in August 1863, "'and how can I buy one at this present price after I have lost so many without any compensation from the Government?'" Chambliss knew that most of his men had "lost from one to five horses, broken down by the hardships of the service." Some were lucky. When George A. Malloy's horse Dora became pregnant, the 3rd South Carolina cavalryman found a replacement for $250 near Grahamville, South Carolina, cheaper than one could be found near his home. In fact, Malloy intended to sell his new horse in a month for $350 "easy."[6]

When faced with the need to find another horse, many Confederate cavalrymen preferred an older mount that had "gone through all the camp diseases," as W. D. Wharton of the 5th North Carolina Cavalry put it. "I am done buying fine horses to take to the Army, I have seen the folly of it." He had already spent $430 on a steed that did not survive very long. Isaac

Norval Baker of the 18th Virginia Cavalry was satisfied with "a little dark sorrel mare" he purchased for $300. "She was a fine runner and jumper and had been in service while young and did not mind the bullets flying around her at all." But the horse died a short time later, making her the fourth mount he lost thus far in the war.[7]

If a man could not find a suitable horse nearby, he tried to have one sent from home. Dunbar Affleck of the 8th Texas Cavalry lost his second horse, which he rode through the Stones River Campaign, to distemper. He then borrowed a mount from a comrade until he had to return it. "I hate to ask you to send me another horse," he wrote his parents in January 1863, but he did not have the cash to pay $300 for one in Tennessee. That price rose to $500 by May. Affleck also needed a new saddle as the one he brought from Texas was "about worne out." He wanted "a regular Mexican tree" that was "Mexican rig[g]ed." Affleck continued, "Texas saddles are in such demand here now I can't get one excepting for an enormous price."[8]

Most Confederate troopers remembered the horses owned by neighbors in their home areas. "I know the Hughs horse can't stand me here," wrote James Michael Barr of the 5th South Carolina Cavalry. "If my Gray won't do, I will swap Pa my Hughs horse for old Pete. I can't care for a fancy horse here and an old horse stands it best." Another factor to consider was the progress of the Union war effort. Almonte T. Dobie of the 13th Virginia Cavalry asked his uncle to "fatten a cavalry horse for me" because his father lived too near Union lines to risk it.[9]

If sending for a mount failed, the final recourse was to apply for a horse furlough. These thirty-day furloughs were often given after a major campaign for travel home to acquire a horse. Officers prioritized, giving them first to unmounted men and second to those whose animals were in bad shape. One company of the 8th Confederate Cavalry had twenty-five to thirty of its members out on horse furloughs in September 1862, which dug deeply into the available manpower of the company.[10]

When the system worked properly, it was a reasonable solution to the problem of remounting the cavalry. Harry S. Dixon's horse suddenly became lame on April 9, 1864, at Montevallo, Alabama. He obtained a certificate from his company commander in the 28th Mississippi Cavalry dated May 10. The furlough allowed him to travel to Demopolis, where his family had taken residence, but he was allowed to be gone only four days. The certificate also verified that Dixon was "a good and faithful soldier, not addicted to straggling and does not shun the battlefield."[11]

That certificate was a key component of the horse-furlough system in Jackson's Division, Department of Mississippi and East Louisiana. Because horse furloughs had been "abused to the detriment of the service," they required a statement "that the applicants are good soldiers, careful with their horses, never straggle, or gallop their horses in camp or on the march," and for the past six months had not "sold or exchanged horses" without the approval of their captain or colonel.[12]

What if a cavalryman became too ill to take care of his privately owned horse? The animal typically was given to a comrade who took charge of it along with his own. But the result all too often was poor care. "I have seen horses that were given to other men to ride in a horrible fix," reported James Michael Barr. "I would hate awfully to give up my horse to any man." Barr had been feeling quite unwell for some time but told his commander, "I would go on my horse sick before I would give him up."[13]

The shrinking horse supply added to the troubles of remounting. Gen. Robert E. Lee encouraged his cavalry commander to spare the horses in July 1862. Four months later he believed his troopers would not find enough mounts to maintain the cavalry by the spring of 1863. Lee suggested dropping the self-mounting system and charging the Richmond government with providing all cavalry horses. "A cavalry soldier cannot perform the terms of his enlistment without a horse," he asserted, "and the Government should be able to control the horse on this ground." Some estimates claim that more than one-fourth of Lee's cavalry was dismounted by the spring of 1863.[14]

What to do with dismounted cavalrymen became a problem. One solution was to keep them with their regiments but in a temporary company or battalion separated from their comrades. The dismounted man was paid as an infantryman while he belonged to this special battalion. In Virginia the special unit was called Company Q, and it "followed the cavalry like a nightmare," wrote John N. Opie. After losing his mount at the Battle of Brandy Station, Opie joined that company while he waited for a horse furlough. Mounts that became disabled for full service but could recover soon also were placed in a special company. W. D. Wharton was put in charge of such a company in the 5th North Carolina Cavalry. "When the Brigade moves, I have to get up all the horses together & lead them together on the march & see that they are attended to properly."[15]

According to William H. Areheart, the dismounted men and disabled horses moved with the wagon trains during the Overland Campaign. The dismounted men of his brigade were formed into a battalion led by a major, with a lieutenant in charge of the seventy troopers from the 12th Virginia Cavalry. They obtained "long range guns" and forty rounds of ammunition. Areheart was one of those assigned to the special battalion. He performed picket duty until managing to secure a horse on May 29 and rejoined his mounted comrades, exchanging his Enfield rifle for a Burnside carbine with a man who was on his way to the special battalion. Areheart lost this horse, however, and was once more sent to the special battalion. Determined to return to mounted duty, he obtained a horse furlough and reached home by July 6, secured a mount, and returned to camp by July 25.[16]

Another way to deal with dismounted troopers was to encourage them to transfer to the infantry or artillery beginning in May 1863. By early spring 1864, the government pushed harder for these transfers, which now could be mandated by unit commanders. In Samuel W. Ferguson's Brigade, "permanently dismounted" troopers were defined as "those who have no horses and can get none or are unwilling to do so." The affected man was allowed to choose his infantry unit. Moreover, the Confederate Congress passed an act on June 7, 1864, authorizing the army to dismount any private or noncommissioned officer guilty of virtually any military wrongdoing. He would receive compensation for his privately owned horse, which now became government property.[17]

The army dismounted many cavalry regiments entirely and compelled them to act as infantry in its effort to get a handle on the horse problem. The 1st Missouri Cavalry (CS), for example, was dismounted in April 1862 for the remainder of the war. Several Texas cavalry regiments were dismounted before they had performed any service on horseback and for the rest of the war carried the term "Dismounted" next to their designation.[18]

Military officials did press horses from unwilling citizens in the South on a sporadic basis in some areas. A quartermaster was required to assess the value of the mount and give the owner a certificate for reimbursement at a future time. When Ferguson's Brigade began to press horses in February 1864, the quartermaster and the owner had to agree on a value that was below $600. If that was not possible, each was to designate "some disinterested persons who will together decide" the amount. Quartermaster S. H. Giles managed to press two horses for $600 each but had to agree on much higher prices ranging from $850 to $1,250 for others.[19]

Confederate troopers could capture horses from the Federals and did so quite often. But that was an uncertain supply, and the animals often were not of the best quality. While Henry Clay Reynolds of the 51st Alabama Mounted Infantry was pleased with the mount he obtained from a Federal trooper, the nearly 2,000 Union horses captured during the McCook-Stoneman Raid were "very much jaded & worn." These animals needed several months of recuperation before offering much to a trooper. This source of supply failed to keep pace with the steady rate of loss in the Southern cavalry.[20]

The system of government horse infirmaries established by the middle of the war also failed to compensate for the loss rate. When a plan was implemented late in 1863 to divide what was left of the Confederacy into four districts for the inspection of field transportation, horse infirmaries appeared in each of the districts to rehabilitate animals for cavalry, artillery, and draft service. The one established at Lynchburg, Virginia, treated 6,875 houses from October 1863 to February 1865; only 1,057 were rehabilitated enough to return to service. Of the rest, 2,844 died, 133 were lost or stolen, 559 were condemned and sold, and 799 were sent to the infirmary in North Carolina, which left 1,483 that remained unserviceable. With a success rate of only 15 percent, the infirmary system could not hope to overturn the many factors that drained Confederate cavalry units of their mounts. Over 4,000 cavalry horses from the Army of Northern Virginia were recovering in the South Carolina infirmary by February 1865. Probably no more than 600 of them could be counted on to return to duty.[21]

In addition to horse shortages, the Confederacy suffered a shortage of horseshoes and nails. Lee noted that nearly half of his cavalry horses were rendered unserviceable due to the lack of horseshoes after the Gettysburg Campaign. The men had to pay for this necessity in the self-mounting system. In one company of Perrin's Cavalry Regiment, Ferguson's Cavalry

Brigade, troopers paid a total of $450.50 for 294 horseshoes, about $1.50 per horseshoe on average.[22]

The Confederate government did not alter its self-mounting policy until nearly the end of the war. In February 1865 Congress passed an act that required the government to provide mounts for dismounted troopers and to purchase all horses of a cavalry unit if a higher-level officer approved. "It is doubtful whether it was ever put into effect at all," concludes historian Charles W. Ramsdell, "but at that late date it could not have relieved the situation to any appreciable extent." According to Thomas T. Munford, horses were selling for as much as $3,000 by the end of the conflict.[23]

Federal cavalry veteran Moses Harris evaluated Confederate horse policy as a fine system to create a large cavalry arm and to sustain it for a few months. But the force "did not possess a cohesive power sufficient to withstand the disintegrating processes of war." Chief among those "disintegrating processes" was the steady erosion of horsepower. Very soon the self-mounting system proved utterly inadequate. As Lt. Robert T. Hubard noted of the 3rd Virginia Cavalry, in the first year or so of the war, only 3–4 men per regiment were in need of replacement mounts at a given time. By the fall of 1862, that rate had sharply increased to 100–200 men per regiment. Moreover, he argued that the system was "subject to *very great abuse.* Men would purposely neglect their horses to break them down" and get a chance to go home.[24]

No one praised the self-mounting system; many were bitter in their condemnation of it. John S. Mosby called it a "vicious policy" that "was the source of continual depletion of the cavalry." Opie believed the Confederate cavalry arm "was absolutely neglected" just when the Federal cavalry was taking great strides forward in its equipment, organization, and morale. "Our imbecile and infantile government permitted the cavalry branch of our army to melt gradually out of existence," he wrote.[25]

Union Horse Policy

At the start of the war, even the U.S. government mandated that all volunteer cavalrymen provide their own horses. Until July 10, 1861, both belligerents followed a self-mounting system. Union authorities also gave an allowance of forty cents per day for the "use and risk" of the horse. The difference was that within four months. Federal administrators realized that self-mounting was unworkable and scrapped it. On July 10 the government authorized quartermasters to provide horses for volunteer cavalry regiments. Nevertheless, "quite a number of the men preferred to own their own horses," noted William H. Beach of the 1st New York (Lincoln) Cavalry.[26]

Before the government dropped self-mounting, several thousand Union cavalrymen rode their own horse and used their own horse equipment, eventually selling all to Uncle Sam. In addition, the Federal government continued to allow units and individuals the choice to provide their own horses at least up to early 1864, adding more men to the roster of the self-mounted. A handful of Northern horsemen such as Frederick Whittaker liked the policy because it encouraged the men to take care of their mounts, which he considered to be "the difference between good and bad cavalry." Isaac Gause also thought self-mounted troopers "usually had the best horses and cared for them the best."[27]

But self-mounting remained a minority method for providing horses to the Union army. By late 1863 and early 1864, the government moved to eliminate the practice by purchasing privately owned horses. The 3rd Indiana Cavalry, which had one battalion serving in the East and the other in the West, was self-mounted until the discontinuation of the forty-cents extra pay in 1864. Members of the 7th Kansas Cavalry tried to negotiate for a continuation of self-mounting when it came time to reenlist in early 1864. William T. Sherman refused to allow it, but most of the men reenlisted anyway. The 9th New York Cavalry had been self-mounting since its organization in the fall of 1861, but that stopped on July 11, 1864, when the government appraised the privately owned mounts and purchased them; prices ranged from $100 to $185. Authorities did not pay the men for their horse equipment because most of them had obtained it from property condemned by the Quartermaster Department. This change in Union policy was accepted gracefully by the troopers, who widely believed the government gave them a fair price for their horses. When officials authorized the creation of some new cavalry units in the spring of 1864, they also allowed the volunteers to bring in their own horses with the idea of purchasing the animals soon after the units were organized.[28]

In the Department of the Missouri, much thought was given to the advantages and disadvantages of self-mounting. Col. John V. Du Bois, chief of cavalry to Maj. Gen. William S. Rosecrans, could not decide if self-mounting was preferable. Some regiments in the department combined "the two systems, and these have all the disadvantages of both with but little of the good, the U.S. horses doing most of the work and receiving but little care." Du Bois estimated that for a regiment of 1,000 self-mounted troopers, the government would have to spend $438,000 during three years to pay the men their forty cents per day plus other costs. He further estimated that it would spend about that same amount to provide horses and equipment to the same regiment for one year alone if it did not use the self-mounting system. On the surface that seems to be proof that self-mounting was more economical, but Du Bois warned that there were additional expenses to be considered. Privately owned horses that were killed or died in service, the latter largely because of disease and shortages of forage, had to be compensated. He believed that an additional $300,000 per year would cover those costs for one regiment. In the end Du Bois argued that the government was better off providing horses from the start. "A regiment can be remounted every six months at the cost now paid by [the] Government for a regiment of private horses," he told Rosecrans. It would cost $850,000 to mount the estimated 6,600 Missouri State Militia troopers who were expected to reenlist for another term of service. The government would save that amount in eleven months simply by not having to pay them forty cents per day for the use of private horses.[29]

The only real drawback to the government-procured system was the horrible waste of horses that accompanied it. The 1st Arkansas Cavalry (U.S.), Du Bois noted, had been issued 2,600 mounts in eighteen months of service. Some of this wastage was caused by battle and hard campaigning with inadequate food, most of it by disease, and some of it by carelessness on the part of the troopers. Brig. Gen. Lewis C. Hunt inspected posts between Rolla and Springfield, Missouri, in April 1864 and found that the privately owned horses of cavalry units were generally "small and apparently unsuited for hard service." But there was a chronic shortage of forage in the area, and this type of animal could survive more readily in that environment than the "larger and stronger class of horses furnished by the Government." Hunt also noted that an added problem was "the neglect and brutality of men who have no personal interest in taking care of" government-provided mounts and "who are so little controlled by their officers." He admitted that there were "some drawbacks connected with" self-mounting, but "upon the whole I think it the preferable plan."[30]

In some circumstances, as Hunt noted, self-mounting probably was the better system. But the peculiar environment of southwest Missouri was not typical of all campaign areas. Moreover, it is obvious that the overwhelming majority of Union troopers and cavalry units, not to mention the government itself, preferred that quartermasters provide all horses to the mounted arm. To the extent that it lasted, the Union self-mounting system worked pretty smoothly. Horse furloughs were given, but there is no evidence they were abused. Although horse shortages occurred in the North, they did not prevent Union troopers from finding mounts. The Northern states had a large farming economy, and Union troops obtained many horses within captured Confederate territory, denying those mounts to their opponents with each successful campaign.[31]

For the majority of Federal cavalry units, the government issued horses from the start of their organization. Often there was time and inclination to sort the mounts according to color. In the 6th Michigan Cavalry, bays went to Company A, browns to Company B, grays to Company C, and blacks to Company D. This presented an impressive sight when the regiment drilled, but such careful apportioning did not last long. "A few months' service sufficed to do away with it and horses thereafter were issued indiscriminately."[32]

Many regiments received good mounts from the government. When horsing the 8th Illinois Cavalry, quartermasters contracted with the partnership of Mix and Sanger of Joliet, Illinois, early in the fall of 1861, paying a reasonable price of $110 per animal. Other quartermasters purchased Canadian horses, called Canucks, for the 1st Massachusetts Cavalry. These "excellent animals" had a "thick mane and tail," wrote Benjamin Crowninshield. Supposedly descended from Norman-French horses although smaller, the mounts as he recalled were "good tempered, and exceedingly hardy. When they could not get hay they would eat the bark of trees, leaves, almost anything." W. L. Curry thought the first issue of horses to the 1st Ohio Cavalry was the best of the unit's war service. At least one of the animals served the regiment to the very end of the conflict.[33]

A good deal of horse trading took place as men tried to secure the best mount. Officers of the 1st Ohio Cavalry instituted a lottery to distribute the first issue of mounts in a random way to avoid the appearance of preferential treatment. A number was assigned to each horse, indicated by a note tied to its halter, with another note to be put into a hat. Each man drew a number, but many were not satisfied with the luck of the draw. "For some weeks" after, a great deal of horse trading took place. Much swapping also took place in the 6th Ohio Cavalry. Thomas M. Covert found his first horse to be small and "very ugly," so he traded with another man, sight unseen, and believed he got the better part of the deal. Covert admitted that his new mount was not handsome, but its gentle nature agreed with him. "I am not afraid of a horse as I was," he told his wife. Two months later the horse died, and his third mount was "a pretty horse." While Covert valued appearance and gentleness, James Riley Weaver of the 18th Pennsylvania Cavalry valued an "easy, loping and racing" horse. He got those qualities when trading his previous mount for a new one, happy to "sacrifice strength for ease." Officers generally allowed horse trading within the regiment, but some warned that if anyone was bested in a trade with a man of another regiment, they would be punished.[34]

Officers were required to purchase their own horses and had the option of buying one from the government. Chaplain Charles A. Humphreys of the 2nd Massachusetts Cavalry picked out "a roan-colored horse and paid the Government one hundred and eighty-four dollars for him." They also could buy one from another officer, as did Lt. E. Willard Warren of the 3rd Pennsylvania Cavalry. "It is a very fine horse indeed but a little too heavy to suit me exactly and I guess that I shall trade him off if I have a good chance," he told his mother.[35]

After using several government-supplied horses, Covert tried mounting himself. In September 1863, when the government still offered it, he estimated that by getting forty cents a day, he could pay off his horse in four months. His only worry was that the animal might die before the four months were up. The mount he purchased was seven years old and "without a blemish. She is real smart" and cost only fifty dollars. A month later he was offered sixty dollars for it but did not sell the mount until December 1863, after earning enough from the government allowance to amount to only thirty-six dollars. He sold the horse just before going to the hospital, uncertain that he would ever return to the regiment. But Covert recovered and continued to self-mount, purchasing a horse for sixty-five dollars just before the government began to shut down the self-mounting system.[36]

In addition to the self-mounting option, Union authorities launched the biggest government procurement of cavalry horses in American history. Dozens of quartermasters in the East, West, and Trans-Mississippi purchased hundreds of thousands of equines to support the huge cavalry force. There were problems and challenges, all of which were more or less met with vigor, intelligence, and innovation.

One source of trouble was the venal attitude of some contractors and even a few quartermasters, which led them to look on the government as a money cow to be milked for their personal profit. There were horrible examples of corruption to be seen early in the war. Many of them became known and were dealt with vigorously by the government to lessen the harmful consequences. In 1862 Secretary of War Stanton issued a directive that allowed the government to try by military law anyone employed by the army or doing business with it accused of wrongdoing. This went a long way toward cleaning up government–private business interaction during the war. Another improvement was the creation of the Cavalry Bureau, which established central control over the process of equine procurement and greatly lessened the latitude exercised by quartermasters across the country.[37]

Other sources of trouble in the procurement system were high-level field commanders who insisted on more horses than was reasonable. Such demands greatly stressed the system. Rosecrans had a habit of wanting everything today, not tomorrow, and greatly pestered everyone until he got it. From November 1, 1862, right after assuming command of the Department of the Cumberland, until April 27, 1863, he turned in 9,119 horses and 1,159 mules as unserviceable. To compensate for this, he arranged for the transfer of 8,212 horses and 11,197 mules from the Department of the Ohio to his own command. That still was not enough; quartermasters purchased an additional 10,305 horses and 7,492 mules for his department. As of March 31, 1863, Rosecrans had 11,478 cavalry horses, 3,939 artillery horses, 2,942 draft horses, and 23,859 mules. Yet he complained that at least one-fourth of the horses were "worn out and unfit for service" and wanted more.[38]

It was time for Quartermaster General Montgomery C. Meigs to comment on what was happening. He assured Rosecrans that the sudden demand for huge issues of animals greatly strained the system. Quartermasters were so pressed that they lowered their standards to meet quotas, introducing marginally fit animals into the pipeline. They could not travel through the countryside looking for the best animals and so had to rely on contractors to bring them into depots for purchase, which was not the best way to ensure quality. The government had already spent $4 million on supplying horses and mules to Rosecrans alone so that Meigs estimated the general had a horse or mule for every two men in the Army of the Cumberland. He pointed out that if one-fourth of the animals were unserviceable, that was a clear sign that the men did not take care of them. "They are either overworked, or underfed, or neglected and abused."[39]

To understand the Rosecrans situation better, one must realize that he labored under conditions common to all field commanders. Brig. Gen. David M. Gregg's Second Cavalry Division went through a total of 5,985 horses from September 18 to October 24, 1863, a period of intense activity by the Army of the Potomac. Of that number 1,433 (23.9 percent) were condemned and turned in to the Quartermaster Department, and another 950 (15.8 percent) were lost in action or abandoned. Gregg was left with 3,144 serviceable and 458 unserviceable horses, the latter representing 12.7 percent of his total. His division had received no hay for the past two weeks, and the general estimated that if he had to make a march of 150 miles in five days, he would lose 20 percent of his usable horses.[40]

As the examples of Rosecrans and Gregg illustrate, there was no simple explanation for the enormous drain of cavalry horses. General in Chief Henry W. Halleck pointed out that, together, the 36 cavalry regiments in the Army of the Potomac averaged 10,000–14,000 men present for duty from May to November 1863. Meigs had issued to those regiments during that time a total of 35,078 mounts. If one counted the approximate number of horses captured in battle or taken from civilians, the total amounted to "an average remount every two months" for each man.

Halleck went on to point out that the entire Union cavalry force consisted of 223 regiments as of November 1863. If the needs for the Army of the Potomac were similar to all of them, then Meigs would have to find 435,000 new horses for the army during 1864. "The waste and destruction of cavalry horses in our service has proved an evil of such magnitude as to require some immediate and efficient remedy," Halleck told Stanton. He believed "the principal fault is in the treatment of their horses by the cavalry soldiers." All he could suggest was a policy of transferring any horse soldier to the infantry if they were found neglecting their mounts. This suggestion probably would not have worked very well, as most officers had more incentives to retain a soldier than to enforce good horse care.[41]

The pressure for more mounts increased in early 1864. For example, Brig. Gen. William Sooy Smith, chief of cavalry in Sherman's Military Division of the Mississippi, warned a subordinate that no government "could keep so much cavalry mounted while animals are so recklessly destroyed." He advised pressing horses from civilians in occupied Southern areas and "endeavor to feed well and insist upon the very best kind of grooming." Yet less than a month later, Smith pleaded with the chief of the Cavalry Bureau for an additional 30,000 horses. "These wants are all immediate and pressing. Eight thousand enlisted men are now idle" due to lack of horses. When Grant, the new general in chief, heard of this, he told Sherman, "it will be impossible to supply half the number." Sherman was embarrassed and admitted that Smith had filed the requisition without consulting him.[42]

The Federals started the campaigns of 1864 with an equine deficit and never really caught up. The 7th Pennsylvania Cavalry acquired 919 horses at Nashville before starting the Atlanta Campaign. Most of the new mounts were "unused to military duty; the majority were young horses, not aged." The regiment also had 300 new men. "Some had never been on a horse before they entered the service, and were without drill." Sherman's cavalry suffered from scarce supplies of forage during several stages of the campaign. No feed of any kind could be issued May 26–June 2, June 11–12, June 19–22, or July 18–19. Half-rations were issued June 13–18 and June 23–July 17. Forage details rode up to thirty miles from the regiment, only to find little if any grain. No wonder that 101 horses of the 7th Pennsylvania Cavalry "were starved to death." The regiment began with 919 horses, captured 42 along the way to Atlanta, but lost 230 to starvation or abandonment, with an additional 171 killed or captured in battle. The total loss of 401 animals subtracted from the 961 in the regiment's possession left 560 horses available when the campaign ended. That was a loss rate of 58.2 percent in four months of hard field service.[43]

Sherman intensified efforts to remount his cavalry after the fall of Atlanta. Col. William Douglas Hamilton took a detail from his 9th Ohio Cavalry to Louisville, Kentucky, where he sought 1,600 horses for his own and other regiments. During late September and most of October 1864, Hamilton carefully selected the animals. He found that many had earlier been rejected more than once "but had been taken back and craftily doped and doctored by the dealers until they looked good enough to be accepted."[44]

The Federals managed to keep enough men mounted to bring the war to a close. As of late 1864, some commands were well off but others were in poor shape. Maj. Gen. Edward R. S. Canby's Military Division of West Mississippi, which embraced most of the lower Mississippi valley, had 30,000 effective cavalrymen, only half of whom were mounted. The Army of the Potomac and the Army of the James, operating against Petersburg and Richmond, had 10,000 horse soldiers. Maj. Gen. Philip Sheridan's Middle Military Division had 12,000 cavalry, while Sherman's Military Division of the Mississippi included 6,500. All of those commands needed replacement horses to some degree. Quartermasters had provided 6,000 horses for the Department of Kentucky, but reportedly 4,000 were lost in a disastrous raid against Confederate salt-making facilities in southwestern Virginia. The Department of Kansas was in good shape, with 4,581 cavalrymen and 4,386 serviceable mounts, but the Department of Arkansas had not received any horses "for several months," which was why half of its cavalrymen were dismounted. Halleck had little regard for the mounted infantry and state militia units that had been organized under Federal authority in Kentucky, Tennessee, and Missouri. To his mind, they had "destroyed a vast number of horses without rendering very efficient service in the field."[45]

Federal authorities were able to find more horses during the early months of 1865. From January 1, 1864, to the cancelation of equine purchases on May 9, 1865, quartermasters bought 193,388 mounts, the largest procurement of cavalry horses in U.S. history. During that same period, 38,277 cavalry horses died at the depots and another 40,070 were considered unserviceable and sold by depot staff. This presented a loss rate of 40.5 percent. Looking at the data for Sheridan's command during the final months of the war, Meigs concluded that "the service of a cavalry horse under an enterprising commander has therefore averaged only four months."[46]

With such a high rate of loss and replacement, it was inevitable that many cavalrymen would be dismounted on a regular and extended basis. If there were prospects of remounting soon, the dismounted trooper tried to keep up with his comrades on foot. "Although I have walked very little for over 2 years," William B. Baker reported, he was able to march with other dismounted men of the 1st Maine Cavalry at the start of the Overland Campaign. At times it seemed as if entire regiments were "frogging it." Col. Louis D. Watkins's brigade in Sherman's command had 1,226 men present for duty but only 295 serviceable and 478 unserviceable horses for them. That left 75 percent of his manpower without a usable mount, which undoubtedly was an unusually high rate.[47]

Finding ways to use dismounted troopers on a scale like this required some innovation. Hugh Judson Kilpatrick ordered Lt. Col. William B. Way of the 9th Michigan Cavalry to organize a temporary brigade of dismounted troopers from his division during the Carolinas Campaign. Way created three regiments so the dismounted troopers of each brigade would have their own unit. A total of 693 men made up this temporary brigade. "The roads were very bad and it was hard upon the men, not being accustomed to marching," reported Way. He employed his command mostly in destroying railroads and other property, but they engaged in combat as well.[48]

Another approach was to assemble dismounted troopers from many commands for centralized control. These "dismounted camps" were on a par with convalescent camps for soldiers who were recovering from illness but were not well enough to return to duty. At times a goodly proportion of any given cavalry command could wind up at the dismounted camp. As of late October 1862 after the Maryland Campaign, 450 men of the 1st Massachusetts Cavalry were in the dismounted camp at Washington, DC, while only about 200 of their comrades were riding serviceable horses in the field.[49]

Cpl. Nelson Taylor of the 9th New York Cavalry was exposed to the major problem of the dismounted-camp system when his horse sprained its foreleg on rough roads. He shifted to a dismounted camp at Pleasant Valley, Maryland, which already had 800 troopers from his division. "Dismounted camp is one of the evils of the Army," he told his sister. On his first night his haversack, portfolio, and housewife were stolen. "There is a class of men that manage some way to get Dismounted and go off to Dismounted Camp they call them Dead Beets, Playouts, Bummers &e."[50]

Higher commanders were well aware of this problem. As early as October 1863, Maj. Gen. George G. Meade agreed "that in many instances the men neglect their horses and lose their arms" so they could have an easy time at the dismounted camp. When Lt. Gen. Jubal Early raided Maryland and nearly entered Washington, DC, in July 1864, a thousand dismounted cavalrymen were sent out to help deal with the threat. There were men from twenty-seven regiments in this group, led by Lt. Col. Samuel Young of the 4th Pennsylvania Cavalry, who had no staff members or company commanders. The men were armed and equipped as infantry, they were not used to marching on foot, and most were complete strangers to their comrades. C. E. McKoy of the 1st Maine Cavalry was among their number. He recalled that the hard marching in pursuit of Early, along with the unfamiliar weapons, the load of equipment, and the lack of company-level organization "was enough to take the fight out of the best troops in the world."[51]

An alternative to the dismounted camp was to keep the horseless men with their units and move replacement mounts and equipment to them. This was often done in many commands, in addition to sending dismounted troopers to the camps. Maj. Gen. George Stoneman suggested sending no more than 500 replacement horses at a time to needy units, which required 150 men "of experience and energy" as an escort, because of the difficulty of controlling larger herds.[52]

Like their Southern counterparts, the Federals transferred chronically dismounted cavalrymen to the infantry service. This was no more popular in the North than in the South. The policy was specifically geared to punish men who did not take care of their government mounts, but it is impossible to estimate how effective this was in curbing neglect and abuse of horses.[53]

The Federals also pressed horses from citizens in occupied Confederate territory, at times doing so thoroughly and systematically. In these cases they cordoned off a town and then sent patrols through the neighborhoods, conducting these sweeps for several days in a row. This practice raised a howl of protest that sometimes resulted in horses returned to their owners, but such concentrated gatherings provided a regiment most of the replacement mounts it needed in quick time.[54]

A marginal source of new mounts was the artillery branch of the army, which required heavy draft animals that were not the best cavalry mounts. But at times a regiment was so desperate for horses that it accepted cast-off artillery animals as a substitute. Mules, however, were not considered a fit substitute for cavalry horses, but a few cavalry regiments resorted to mounting some of their men on them. A quarter of the 5th Iowa Cavalry, for example, used mules by the end of the Atlanta Campaign.[55]

The Federals rehabilitated worn-out horses in convalescent centers located at various places. An estimated 60 percent of them were returned to duty. At times the need for replacements led officers to release convalescent horses too soon. Watkins's brigade, which mostly patrolled and performed garrison duty in northwest Georgia, accepted 762 such replacements from the Chattanooga corral. Most were "nothing but skin and bone, and the very best of them unfit for any kind of use." Regimental commanders tried to fatten them up but with little success. Quartermasters could supply little forage, and there were few opportunities for grazing in the area. Although drawing 238 convalescent horses, the 4th Kentucky Cavalry had to rely on thirty-seven serviceable animals it had captured or pressed from civilians in the area to conduct its patrols.[56]

Despite these problems, the horse-replacement system utilized by the Federals was far superior to the self-mounting policy followed by the Confederates. The latter system faltered by the midpoint of the war, and the Richmond authorities were incapable of fully dropping it in favor of government procurement. They lacked the protean vision that underlay big governmental efforts to sustain the war effort that one can see among

Federal authorities. A system of governmental purchase and distribution became the necessary foundation of effective Union mounted power.

A Federal cavalryman went through an estimated four horses every year of his service. Some French observers thought that rate was more like six horses per year, and they pinpointed the cause—hard service combined with lack of proper care. Horse wastage in the Civil War was unprecedented in the eyes of European observers, who compared it with their own system of grooming, feeding, and resting their expensive animals. The comparison is not entirely fair because peacetime allowed more opportunities to properly care for animals.[57]

Federal authorities had to accept the fact that they could only limit horse wastage, not eliminate it, while compensating by buying and pressing more mounts on a constant basis. They essentially accomplished that goal, in the process reducing the country's horse supply. According to census data, the loyal states possessed 4,288,067 horses and the seceded states 1,743,697 in 1860. While the equine population of the northeastern states declined moderately during the war, it actually increased in the northwestern states. In the states that made up the Confederacy, only Texas experienced an increase in its horse population. More than half of Virginia's horses in 1860 were gone after the war. In the entire South there were 254,208 fewer horses in 1870 than ten years before. In contrast, by 1870, the Northern states had gained 1,205,422 horses compared to 1860.[58]

The Federal government purchased an estimated 650,000 horses during the Civil War. While most of them went into cavalry service, those purchases also supplied animals to artillery service. The average price early in the conflict was $125 each, but it rose to between $145 and $185 by war's end, amounting to a total expenditure of $95,000,000 throughout the war. The Quartermaster Department, which was responsible not only for the purchase of equines but also a wide variety of other war resources, expended a total of $123,864,915 during the war years. In short, horses represented a bit more than 75 percent of the total expenditure of the department. The government recouped a small amount of that expense after the war when it began to sell surplus animals. Eventually, 128,840 horses and mules were sold for about $58 each, amounting to almost $7,500,000.[59]

A cavalry command was of no use unless it was adequately supplied with horses, and the Union army accomplished that goal despite the unprecedented size of its cavalry force. The Confederate army failed to do so. Deep pockets helped the Federal government, but more than just money was involved in the success of the Union horse-replacement story. Federal authorities were willing to rack up a huge long-term debt for needed short-term goals that were considered of vital importance to the country. They valued a large, vital mounted arm more vigorously than did their counterparts in Richmond, and they sacrificed more to create one, firming up one more foundation of Union military success in 1865.

II

—————— • ——————

CAVALRY HORSES

orses are among the most important and widespread domesti-
cated animals on earth. On the eve of the Civil War, the United
States contained 7,434,681 of them, and Europe had an estimated
22,420,000. With an estimated 3,000,000 in Africa and 25,000,000 in
Asia, the world equine population totaled about 58,500,000 to serve an
estimated 1.2 billion people. They were ridden, pulled wagons, ran races,
offered companionship to some humans, and were eaten by other humans. Horses fulfilled a wide variety of human needs, and although often
mistreated, they also flourished in domestication.[1]

Equines of all types also participated in wars around the globe and
across time. A breakdown of the number and type of horses used by the
Army of the Potomac (excluding the Ninth Corps) at the start of the Overland Campaign illustrates this point. The largest contingent was the cavalry horse, at 16,311 mounts. Artillery horses came next, with 5,158, closely
followed by privately owned officer horses, at 4,107. Another 2,684 horses
were used for miscellaneous purposes, making a total of 30,266 horses
for about 75,000 men. Additionally, 20,184 mules pulled 3,451 wagons.
But among horses, cavalry mounts accounted for just over half of those
used by the army.[2]

It is necessary to take equine power into account when trying to understand military operations. Civil War armies could not have operated in
the field without it. It is equally important to understand that the horse

was not just a weaponized animal but a sentient creature with a life of its own. Horses had what the Civil War generation called a "natural history," meaning a psychology, a set of emotions, and a set of habits that made them good partners with man. They have strong bonding tendencies that facilitate the creation of herds, and they understand hierarchical relationships within those herds. Horses respond to authority and obey commands, are capable of forming bonds with trusted handlers, and are responsive to cues and signals from them. All of these natural traits made them amenable to military training, although not all horses performed uniformly within the army regimen. There were individual variations among them, and some horses never became adjusted to the military system or to their trainers. They were animal warriors with possibilities and limitations similar to their human counterparts in the army.[3]

A range of physical characteristics separated the ideal cavalry horse from other equines. With a gestation period of eleven months, a horse had to be at least two years old before it could be used for any purpose and did not become mature until four years of age. Cavalry service demanded horses that were sturdy, responsive to the rider, and capable of quick motion. As Henry W. Halleck estimated, each cavalry horse could be expected to carry from 250 to 300 pounds of weight (including the cavalryman). Horses with other characteristics were best used as draft animals, mainly for ambulance work, because mules were best suited to pull wagon trains.[4]

The ideal way to match a horse with a rider, if there was an opportunity to do so, lay not only in the realm of physical characteristics but also in something deeper and more lasting. Col. Samuel Ringwalt urged cavalrymen to choose a horse by looking "fairly and squarely into his eyes. As the eye of man is the index of his soul, so by the eye of a horse also, all other things being right, you can form a pretty good idea of his character." Sgt. Thomas W. Smith of the 6th Pennsylvania Cavalry knew this because he had created a bond with his mount. "I have one of the best and most Sagacious Horses in the Company and our Officers know that I like it," he told a comrade.[5]

But relatively few troopers seem to have sought an emotional connection with their mounts. Physical considerations tended to dominate their thinking about their horses. For these men, a horse was just a tool to be

White Horse.

This beautiful photograph of a striking animal has a good view of the saddle and skirt. The man is 1st Lt. Frank Vane of the Independent Company Oneida Cavalry from New York. He commanded the guards and orderlies assigned to headquarters, U.S. Engineer Battalion, serving with the Army of the Potomac, when this photograph was taken at Petersburg in December 1864.

LC-DIG-cwpb-03884, Library of Congress.

used. The government wholly paid attention to external physical considerations when issuing horses to cavalrymen. Early in the war the color of the mounts tended to be an important consideration. Many regimental commanders insisted on color coding their companies, with blacks assigned to Company C and grays to Company D in the 1st Tennessee Cavalry (U.S.), for example. Many men were convinced that color denoted aspects of physical stamina, with grays the sturdiest and blacks the least able to endure hard service. Color coding units mimicked the showy nature of European cavalry culture along with colorful uniforms and regular parades through city streets. Like all those other aspects of peacetime martial culture, color coding had little relevance to a long, gritty war, and it soon fell by the wayside.[6]

The horse's age also was a physical consideration. Early in the war quartermasters observed the general rule that a young animal was not fit for field service, but they had to violate it as the war progressed. Horses less than four years old wound up in army service but were found wanting. Ironically, according to Ringwalt, a three-year-old horse could endure a good deal of work in the short term but usually could not outlast an older animal. He believed that all army horses ought to be at least six years of age, but that was impractical in wartime. Four years remained the generally accepted minimum age.[7]

Several other characteristics were considered a detriment for a good cavalry horse. The quartermaster issued a lot of animals to the 8th New York Cavalry that were universally thought too big for their use and were shifted to artillery service. "Dull, sluggish horses can never be trained to the point requisite for efficient cavalry horses," wrote Napier Bartlett of the Washington Artillery. "Almost as much depends, in a successful charge of cavalry, on the horse as on the man. Raw recruits mounted on well-drilled horses, are more serviceable than veteran troops mounted on clumsy, low-spirited animals." Geldings were considered the best for cavalry service, but mares often wound up in the mounted arm. According to Benjamin W. Crowninshield, mares proved to be nearly as durable as geldings.[8]

High-bred or performance horses were scarce in the field. Some mounted soldiers praised the Morgan breed, while others liked animals from the northern parts of New England and across the border in Canada, which "proved to be of superior constitution and metal for cavalry service," according to Frederick Denison. Many of those originally issued to the 1st Rhode Island Cavalry in 1861 were still in service at the end of the war. Crowninshield of the 1st Massachusetts Cavalry recalled a sergeant who rode an originally issued Canadian horse called Ephraim. It had "long hair on the fetlocks, very thick mane and tail, and a large head and heavy neck. He was always fat and well." Unfortunately, someone stole Ephraim in late June 1864. In fact, horse thieves in the army often altered the appearance of the stolen animal by cutting the hair, making an imitation of a brand, or dyeing the hair to cover white patches.[9]

But those cavalrymen who admired performance horses or put their faith in unusual breeds were in the minority. Most troopers were fortunate if their animal met minimum requirements of age, size, physical stamina, and training capacity. Most horses were of a middling class in this regard, just like most human recruits were moderately good soldiers, so there was a workable match-up between the majority of mounts and riders. James Michael Barr of the 5th South Carolina Cavalry told his wife: "We don't want fine horses here. All we want is a horse that will not fall down."[10]

One of the prime characteristics of a cavalry horse was the ability to learn its role in the military machine. If the animal refused to listen to its rider's cues, balked at moving synchronously with other horses, or could not stand the sound of battle, it was useless as a cavalry mount. Some excelled in military service, most acclimated themselves pretty well to cavalry operations, but others utterly failed to do so. Man and horse formed a team; both of them could fail or succeed, depending on their relationship. Training was the key; it separated the apt from the inept men and horses, forging effective partnerships between humans and animals while identifying those recruits and horses that were weak links in the military chain.

The notion that a cavalry horse was little more than a machine has to be heavily revised. As a sentient creature, it had the opportunity to exercise some degree of agency, of choice, even within the military regime. It held a position similar to that of performance animals such as race horses or dolphins at modern theme parks. In both cases the animals are trained for a specific task and generally respond to the trainer's cues. But in each case the animal can vary the performance in small ways, and the rider or trainer has to adjust to those variations. Race horses have been known to ignore the cues of their riders and conduct a race in their own fashion; dolphins have been known to change the routine of a show out of boredom. And if anyone believes that man is supreme, consider this quote from Richard O'Barry, a trainer-performer at a theme park. "If you thought animals were machines, this show would do nothing to dissuade you. But if the dolphins were machines, so was [the trainer]. I was a trained animal as much as they were." In short, O'Barry had to respond to the cues of his managers if he expected to be paid for his work. Former jockey and animal behaviorist Temple Grandin put it well. "A good rider and his horse are a team. It's not a one-way relationship, either; it's not just the human relating to the horse and telling him what to do. Horses are super-sensitive to their riders and are constantly responding to the rider's needs even without being asked."[11]

It is useful to see the relationship between the cavalry horse and the trooper in a similar way. It would be unreasonable to expect the best relationship to exist between every cavalryman and his horse, for individuals varied widely in their emotional, mental, and physical characteristics. But an effective mounted force required a reasonably good relationship between man and horse. The trooper relied on his mount to carry him anywhere he was ordered and to be fearless on the battlefield. The horse relied on the trooper for sustenance, care, and attention.

Training

The training period at the beginning of war service was the first step in creating the bond that was vital in the working relationship between horse and man. All the handbooks relating to horse training and care stressed the essentially gentle and compliant nature of the animal. They also stressed the need to treat it with understanding. Yelling, hitting, and creating an atmosphere of tension were counterproductive. It was necessary to be firm but reassuring. Unsteadiness in mounting or handling instilled a sense of unease in the animal. Horses respected the pecking order of herds, so if they saw the rider as their leader, they usually cooperated.[12]

Without a supportive relationship, training would have been difficult if not impossible. Henry Murray Calvert of the 11th New York Cavalry went out of his way to understand his horse and acclimate it to the army. For example, Calvert rode his mount near infantry regiments that were practicing small-arms firing to accustom it to the sound of battle. He noticed that no one else in his regiment tried to bond with their mounts and criticized the army for not recognizing "the trained intelligence of army horses as a very important factor in war." If the service adopted a better training regimen, "the efficiency of army horses would be largely increased and the insecurity of the men be greatly lessened."[13]

The army training regimen imparted only the basics to cavalry horses. Most of them learned these lessons "in a remarkably short period," reported Stanton P. Allen of the 1st Massachusetts Cavalry. "A majority of the animals became familiar with the bugle calls" and responded to them "without direction from their riders." Cavalry mounts were widely known to respond to bugle calls even when their rider had been unhorsed by combat, keeping up with the unit with empty saddles. Albert Robinson Greene of the 9th Kansas Cavalry rode a horse called Lots of Water that "taught me more than any drill master ever did," he reported. "He knew the difference between the bugle calls of 'right about' and 'left about.'"[14]

Probably the most difficult adjustment of the horse to cavalry service was the unfamiliar sight and sound of weapons and the crowded nature of mounted formations. The first was demonstrated by the 7th Indiana Cavalry when it organized in the summer of 1863. The colonel held a review for Gov. Oliver P. Morton before he had a chance to drill the men or the mounts. Consequently, when everyone drew sabers, many horses bolted, breaking up the review before it began. The second adjustment was noted by W. R. Carter when writing of the training process in his 1st Tennessee Cavalry (U.S.). "Fretful and unruly horses had to get accustomed to the jam and pressure in wheeling and the excitement of the charge."[15]

Horse Characteristics

Some cavalrymen preferred horses with an edge to their personality. Edward Laight Wells of the 4th South Carolina Cavalry was very pleased with his six-year-old mount because she was "just a little vicious, & not well-broken." George E. Flanders of the 5th Kansas Cavalry had a horse that was more vicious than Wells's mount. "He has tried to runaway with me several times and has never succeeded till yesterday. I have a slight remembrance of his dumping me, but justly cant tell *how* it was done."[16]

Other cavalrymen valued grit, stamina, and an appearance of strength and virility in their horses. One horse that served Col. Andrew T. McReynolds of the 1st New York (Lincoln) Cavalry was "clean-limbed, perfectly formed, powerful, intelligent and gentle." W. W. Blackford, adjutant of the 1st Virginia Cavalry, possessed a mount that James E. B. Stuart called "a perfect model of a war horse." Named Cornet, "he was compactly and powerfully built," recalled Blackford, "head and tail carried high in the air and he had a way of tossing his head and chomping his bit, and tossing the foam over his breast that set your blood to tingling in sympathy with his spirit." Another mount called Two-Bits was "well drilled, a thorough soldier and exceedingly intelligent. He seems always to understand what is required of him," wrote an admiring soldier.[17]

Horse Care

No matter how good a horse, it needed the right care to survive the rigors of field service. Col. William Halstead of the 1st New Jersey Cavalry estimated that a cavalry regiment lost 4 horses per 1,000 between battles when "under a commander who understood horse care," but it lost 120 per 1,000 when it was led by a man who had no understanding of that factor. Cleaning the horse was as important as feeding it, which could be simply rubbing the flesh with a handful of straw or hay. Some animals disliked to be cleaned because of mistreatment by previous riders or because they had extra-sensitive skin. In that case, a simple washing with water was better than nothing.[18]

Maj. James A. Congdon of the 12th Pennsylvania Cavalry argued that taking care of his horse was the first duty of every mounted soldier. Some men took this seriously, while others did not. Even reliable soldiers could have an instinctual dislike of feeding and cleaning their mounts. Higher-level commanders who noticed slackness in this duty put pressure on their subordinates to make sure the men performed it. Joseph Wheeler visited his regiments at sunrise to watch the men groom their horses and to make sure regimental officers were supervising the process.[19]

Horses needed a combination of hay and grain to maintain their health, although there was some discussion about how much and what kind of each element was best. The army stipulated fourteen pounds of hay and twelve pounds of grain as the daily ration. "The hay provided nutrition and the bulk required by the horse's digestive system, while the grain afforded high-energy food for muscle and energy," explains historian Ann Norton Greene. "By modern feeding standards, army horses and mules were probably overfed in camp and underfed while working." Ringwalt agreed with the latter part of that conclusion. He thought the combined weight of the hay and grain should have been closer to forty pounds rather than twenty-six while the horses were active in the field. Salt, a necessary part of the horse's diet, was issued on occasion. It was widely believed that the type of grain made a difference. Oats were considered the best food for cavalry horses. "Barley was seldom used" in the war, and wheat, the most expensive grain, was even more rarely issued. Corn was the most common substitute for oats, but Ringwalt thought it was the best grain for horses that worked slowly rather than for those employed in mounted warfare. In contrast, Robert Jennings, a professor in the Veterinary College of Philadelphia, thought that ten pounds of hay per day was the most that should be allowed a cavalry horse. Most equines were fully capable of eating three or four times more if allowed, but that would upset their digestive systems. Jennings thought that as little as eight pounds of hay per day, mixed with the proper ration of grain, was enough to keep a horse in health.[20]

With a well-ordered logistical system, the Union army usually supplied enough hay to fall within the wide variation discussed by Ringwalt and Jennings while mounted units were stationary in semipermanent camps. The hay typically was shipped on river steamers and railroad cars either in bales or piled loosely in containers. Either way it took up an enormous amount of space and at times was damaged in transit. In contrast, the difficulties of providing hay and grain for cavalry horses on active campaign through territory already stripped of resources were far more problematic. To substitute for hay (often referred to as long forage), cavalrymen found corn stalks or straw. Members of the 9th Kansas Cavalry even cut down cottonwood and aspen trees to let horses browse on their leaves during a march through country destitute of hay. Hungry horses chewed the bark off trees or ate dried leaves, even hardtack. Now and then, cavalry regiments had the good fortune to be near a clover field just when it was blooming and could graze their mounts on the fresh forage.[21]

Transporting grain while not wasting it took some effort. During active campaigns, troopers learned how to properly carry their horse's grain ration. In the 6th New York Cavalry, they acquired condemned shelter tents, cut a part of the fabric out, sewed it up to form a pouch big enough to hold three days' rations of grain, and strapped the bag across the cantle of their saddle. Federal cavalrymen during the Atlanta Campaign often rode twenty miles to find hay and grain for their mounts, attaching it to their saddles. But a steady diet of rice as a substitute for oats would not work. Confederate cavalrymen operating near the Atlantic coast suffered losses among their mounts from feeding them rice. Even when good grain was available, it had to be fed in a way to avoid wastage. Wheeler ordered his men to feed their mounts in troughs rather than by piling the ration on the ground while in camp.[22]

Authors of horse-care books asserted that each mount needed four gallons of water daily. James A. Congdon advised watering it three times a day during the summer months and twice during the rest of the year, although not right after it had eaten its meal or when its body temperature was warmer than usual. There may have been a good deal of validity in that last bit of advice. Wells A. Bushnell of the 6th Ohio Cavalry allowed his horse to drink from a stream while overheated, and it became ill with what Bushnell called the "water founder caused by drinking too much water while warm and then standing still taking cold." Forced to drink from whatever source was available, cavalry mounts often made do with muddy, stagnant pools or impromptu wells dug by their riders. But then, even human soldiers drank from such sources of water when pressed.[23]

Emotional Bonds

Taking care of their mounts, feeding them, cleaning them, and rubbing their skin, there is little wonder that an emotional bond developed between many horses and riders. "You know what an attachment one forms for a good horse," James H. Kidd of the 6th Michigan Cavalry told his father. "He will stand until I get on & tell him to go. He learns faster than the men." John E. Brown of the 15th Pennsylvania Cavalry also had a smart horse. "He . . . seemed to know what I said to him and at my command would lie down. It was a mutual love affair between us." Many cavalrymen sacrificed their own comfort to provide for their mount. On long marches troopers walked on foot part of the day to spare them excessive fatigue. They spent time with their horses when not on duty, petting and playing with them. When Julius E. Thomas of the 1st Tennessee Cavalry (U.S.) had to give up his mount to another regiment, he shed a tear and prayed that the new man would take care of it. When William E. Meyer's Billy was hit by two bullets at the Battle of Kelly's Ford, he "boohooed like a child; I cried as if I had lost a brother; he had been my most faithful, playful friend, my good reliable carrier and companion for many months, and to care and feed him with the best and with my own rations when nothing else was left, had been my pleasure." Meyer put Billy out of his misery by saying goodbye and then shooting him "between his ears" with a pistol.[24]

Duty on the picket line deepened the emotional bonds between horses and men. Isaac Gause of the 2nd Ohio Cavalry learned to pay attention to the cues of his horse. "He is a good sentinel; and by watching his ears closely one will never be deceived by an unexpected approach."[25]

The emotional partnership between man and mount could be expressed in horse naming, although even troopers who had no emotional bonds with their horses often named them. These varied widely, from Don Pedro to Maggie, Larry, Bessie, Fanny, Romney, Old Bob, White Eagle, Clodhopper, Brooker, Old Tom, Old Man, Tom Taylor, Ephraim, Lion, Betsy, and Beautiful Dreamer. Edward Laight Wells of the 4th Carolina Cavalry purchased a horse named Brutus but renamed it Dixie. Henry Lee Higginson rode several horses, including Piggy, Nutmeg, and Grater. In one regiment Old Squeezer was "a terror to recruits" because of its rough manner.[26]

Horse Management

Horse management in some units began with an identification mark. While all government-issued mounts in the Union army were branded, some regimental commanders added their own touch. In the 1st Massachusetts Cavalry this was "a small brand on the hoof." But the turnover of mounts was such that this practice became meaningless and was dropped.[27]

Every cavalry horse wore a set of equipment designed to place it under the control of the rider. This set began with bits and bridles. Stanton P. Allen thought it was possible for horses to get an equine form of homesickness, which began the moment a bit was inserted into its mouth. In fact, the horse manuals of the day pointed out that the bit was the most important piece of equipment in terms of controlling the animal. Louis E. Nolan wrote of selecting one to suit the individual mount, so that "to each horse a bit of more or less power, according to the shape of the mouth, the sensitiveness and the temper of the animal," would result. But, of course, in a large cavalry force, a standard-size bit was the only practical option. Frederick Whittaker thought the Union army's standard bit was too heavy, even though it was lighter than that used by the Mexicans, the Turks, the Greeks, and the Arabs. He praised the bits used by the French in Africa and by horsemen in Argentina.[28]

Proper protection for the hooves was the next most important cavalry equipment. Horses have "natural hard hooves in general," according to Ann Norton Greene, but they wear down if the animal works beyond "their natural capacity for regeneration and growth." During the Civil War, cavalry horses were used so frequently and for such hard service that protection for the hoof became a major concern. "A cavalry horse is perfectly useless unless his hoofs are in proper condition," declared C. Armour Newcomer of the 1st Maryland Cavalry (U.S.). Shoes often were lost and had to be replaced on a regular basis. Environmental conditions played a role. Soft soil reduced the need for horseshoes so that the 2nd Iowa Cavalry did not need to keep extra ones while operating in northern Mississippi. But when the regiment moved to Clifton, Tennessee, it found that the soil there required a steady supply of horseshoes. Riding along macadamized turnpikes, paved with crushed rock, also required good shoes.[29]

Whittaker had definite ideas about horseshoes. For summer use, he advocated "plain flat fore shoes . . . , with low heel corks on the hind shoes. These enabled a horse to stop short with much more ease, if suddenly pulled up." For winter use, "both toe and heel corks on all the shoes" were best.[30]

Mass-produced, standard-size shoes were the rule in the Civil War. Henry Burden came to the rescue to supply this need. Born in Scotland in 1791, he arrived in the United States at age twenty-eight and worked for a company that manufactured agricultural equipment in Albany, New York. Then he went to the Iron and Nail Factory at Troy, New York, where he stayed for forty years and eventually purchased the company. By 1834, Burden had invented a horseshoe-making machine that could produce 3,600 shoes per hour in eight different sizes for horses and five sizes for mules. By the outbreak of the Civil War, 11 percent of all horseshoes in the country came from his factory. The heavy demands of the war greatly increased his production.[31]

Each mounted regiment had a farrier whose primary responsibility was shoeing the horses. That was relatively easy while the regiment rested in camp, but on a campaign he earned his salary. Horses tended to throw shoes during heavy marches, and the farrier had to reshoe them during breaks in movement using the two spare shoes and extra nails that each trooper was required to carry in his saddlebags. The farrier also had to deal with the temper of each animal. Horses did not necessarily like to have an iron shoe nailed to their hooves, especially if they had been mistreated by their rider. A different problem was one encountered by Isaac Gause, whose mount had soft hoofs that "would not hold the nails." Once when riding in a hurry, the shoes began to fly off. "I heard every shoe whiz through the air, and one went straight up by my head. The last shoe was gone, and the hoof was liable to break next," but he reached his destination before anything worse happened. If farriers and proper tools were not available, troopers improvised the latter and did the work of the former.[32]

Getting Used to Army Life

Providing equipment was one thing, preparing the mount emotionally for war was another. "Horses are not inherently afraid of battle," Ann Norton Greene has written. "What triggers their fear and flight responses are sights, sounds, and smells, immediate material threats, strange or unexpected events, or encountering something that they remember as dangerous or frightening. Horses can be trained for war so that they are not frightened of the noises or objects they would encounter in combat."[33]

Horses were "very much like men," recalled Richard W. Johnson, "either brave or cowardly, sensible or foolish." Lt. Charles P. Bowditch found that his mount became "blind crazy from fear of my sabre which was dangling against his side and from the spurs." It ran away in a frenzy, hit the barracks building, and went down in a heap with Bowditch. The animal "was always ready to run away." Horses could be terribly frightened by the flash of gunfire in the darkness, had to be blindfolded while led across a narrow fragment of bridging so it could not see the danger of falling, or became "wild and almost unmanageable" when pelted with hail in a summer storm. If most of the other horses bolted for some reason, even normally calm animals became infected with the excitement and joined in.[34]

Another factor in the process of getting used to army life remained the individual characteristics of the mounts. Troopers had to deal with sometimes annoying, even dangerous elements in their horse's make up. Nervousness was often cited as a problem, even in horses that had endured long service. Animals that took it in their heads to start as soon as the rider's foot was in the stirrup but before he had settled securely in the saddle were dangerous. Those that reared up too quickly when the bridle was pulled back could fall over on top of the trooper.[35]

Stress often resulted in horses lashing out to relieve tension. They bit and kicked cavalrymen and other horses alike. It is possible that the army environment caused this reaction. Although herd animals, horses also value close social relations with a handful of other horses. The huge accumulation of equines in army camps, as historian Gervase Phillips has suggested, could have been overwhelming to some individuals separated from those horses with which it had bonded. Perhaps the only reaction one could make in a situation like this was rebellion in the form of violence.[36]

A handful of cavalrymen recorded how viciously their horses acted during the war. John N. Opie of the 6th Virginia Cavalry purchased a black mare, and the first time he rode her, the mount took off at full speed and ran into a barn. Some weeks later while leading her to water, he gave her too much halter. The mare "wheeled, and kicked me with both feet in the face." Opie was knocked out but regained consciousness the next day. On another occasion while riding through woods, the horse ran uncontrollably. Opie lay flat on her back to avoid the many limbs she ran under in what appeared to be a deliberate effort to knock him off. Upon entering open ground, Opie used his spurs to make her run even faster and tire her out as the only way to stop her. During a review, Opie's horse took fright when the artillery fired a salute, "shot out like an arrow" from the ranks, and broke the formation of a neighboring squadron. The black mare literally ran itself to death at the Battle of Brandy Station. Participating in a mounted charge, Opie's horse again shot out of ranks and ran a good distance farther than everyone else. This brought Opie to the Union position all alone. The Federals fired when he was only twenty yards away, hitting his horse four times and placing another bullet in the sole of his right boot. He fell with her, the troubled life of this black mare ending with this bizarre event.[37]

While not necessarily vicious, a horse called Old Sorrel was unwilling to conform to army life. He preferred to trot, bouncing the rider, while other horses cantered easily. Old Sorrel also had "a mouth so tough that no mortal could hold him when he took a notion to run away." The animal had a "total lack of discretion—being as apt to run towards or into the enemy's lines as away from them." He was killed at Chickamauga, and "no tears were shed at his loss."[38]

Horses fought each other in the army too. At times it was because, as herd animals, they respected a pecking order and fought to see which one should be on top. Benjamin Crowninshield noted that when a new mount was added to the picket rope, one could expect a fight to develop between the arrival and the older members of that group. Crowninshield's mount, Old Man, got into a severe fight with Old Tom, which belonged to another officer of the 1st Massachusetts Cavalry. Old Tom suffered a fractured skull but lived. Edward Wall of the 3rd New Jersey Cavalry rode a black mare named Bessy that was very particular about being crowded by other horses. If any came too near, "like a flash her little hoof would be flung out."[39]

Wall called Bessy's effort to keep other horses at arm's length one of her "peculiarities," but animal historians would instead refer to it as agency. In other words, it was an effort by Bessy to control a little bit of the space she occupied in the military machine. Agency can be defined as any sort of behavior in which the animal exercises some degree of control over its relationship with humans or with other animals. There can be little doubt that animal agency existed for warhorses, and the questions are to what extent were cavalry mounts able to exercise it and how did they exert it.[40]

Agency often was gilded, disguised as something else, and thus unrecognized. For example, most horses disliked a tight-laced saddle around their abdomen and learned to "swell out" whenever the troopers "buckled the saddle girths," recalled Stanton P. Allen. "Then, after we had mounted, the horses would materially reduce their circumferences, so much so at times that the saddle would turn when the rider was jolted to one side on the trot or gallop."[41]

Animals that refused the urging of their riders to do something exhibited another example of agency that was blatant rather than disguised. Opie noticed this at the Battle of Upperville in June 1863 when a column was stopped in its tracks because the horses in the front rank refused to jump a stone fence. Wall also noted an instance of agency. One evening when Bessy set out at a rapid pace, he tried to slow her down. She refused and, as he recalled, even "turned and bit at my leg. It was, I thought, more a remonstrance than viciousness. Her means of appealing to me were few, and she used the one that came handy."[42]

The difficulties inherent in interspecies communication inhibited the trooper's ability to realize that his horse was a sentient creature with likes, dislikes, needs, and requests of its own. Insensitive cavalrymen often were treated to violent means of communication because they had no ability to tune in to the animal's means of conveying its needs and desires. Thus, in discussing their horses, many troopers simply believed that they were odd, dangerous, or flighty creatures without realizing that most of the horse's actions probably had a good reason behind them.

For example, Uriah N. Parmelee's mare, "an honest old brute," never seemed to give him a decent ride. Even when walking, he complained, "she would jar my system into tremulousness; she would half stumble every five to six feet and fetch down her fore locks." At each step she bounced Parmelee high in the saddle. He soon got rid of her for a more congenial horse. This troublesome mount may have been just a clumsy animal, but she also may have deliberately and successfully tried to get rid of him.[43]

But there were many acts that could not be mistaken for anything other than deliberate attempts to foil the rider's intent. Once when Charles Francis Adams Jr. dismounted to place a picket for the 1st Massachusetts Cavalry, his horse "turned round, kicked up his heels and ran away. The last I saw of him he was pelting over a distant hill and my man was laboring after him." The horse was later recovered, but it probably enjoyed its little vacation from Adams's control. A horse called Old Bob in the 4th Iowa Cavalry was notorious for "rubbing his master against trees, lying down with him in the water, and other disagreeable pranks," wrote William F. Scott. He called Old Bob "an erratic beast," but really all these actions strongly imply efforts by the horse to get the rider off his back, a not unreasonable objective.[44]

Even more obvious were those mounts that battled with their riders and with all humans. As Gause noted of cavalry horses, there was "an occasional desperado that has to be subjugated; a process which usually breaks his constitution to an extent that renders him worthless." Old Squeezer, mentioned earlier, was such an animal. When issued to a man in the 3rd U.S. Cavalry, he became almost uncontrollable, according to J. A. Arkle. "I had a fight with him in March, 1863, in which he nearly killed me at the picket-line one evening at 'stables,' but I got him down at last on the ground and sat on his neck."[45]

Crowninshield recalled two horses in the 1st Massachusetts Cavalry that never adjusted to army life. One of them, "a light chestnut sorrel" named White Eye, had a habit of doing unexpected things. One day he jumped into a loaded coal wagon on the street with its rider. White Eye was given to a trooper who had been a jockey, and he was able to control him most of the time. But one day the horse bolted from the ranks and "ran for miles" before the former jockey could stop him. White Eye met his end during the Maryland Campaign. While being led with other horses along the towpath of a canal, he suddenly bolted, jumped into a canal boat, and then plunged into the Potomac River, where he drowned. Crowninshield believed White Eye might have been insane, but he could have been so distraught at his enforced servitude in the army that suicide seemed the only recourse. Another horse in Company F absolutely refused to be ridden despite tedious efforts by many men to break him in using a variety of horse-training methods explained in the handbooks. Nothing worked. "The horse was victorious over his enemy, man," concluded Crowninshield.[46]

It should be emphasized that the majority of cavalry horses submitted to human control to a greater or lesser degree, exercising some agency in the process; but it is equally true that a small minority of them could not submit. Fighting back was the only recourse, and possibly even self-destruction, as in the case of White Eye. Persistently stubborn horses should have been released from cavalry service, for they clearly demonstrated their deep resistance to army life and posed a threat to their riders.

Horses on the Battlefield

The ultimate requirement that the army imposed on cavalry horses was participation in battle. The horse and rider were a combat team; both were equally exposed to flying bullets and exploding shells. The experience of combat was in some ways similar for the horse as it was for the trooper.

Gause vividly described the reaction of a cavalry mount to combat based on his impressions of the horse's reactions:

In battle he partakes of the hopes and fears incidental to the occasion. . . . When heavy battles are raging, if standing in line, he becomes nervous with the suspense, and will tremble and sweat and grow apprehensive. At any sound that indicates a move, the rider can feel him working the bit with his tongue. As he moves out he seeks to go faster, and when restrained shows his disapproval by feigning to bolt. He will then grasp the bit afresh, and dash ahead as if to brave the worst and have it over as quickly as possible.[47]

Personal accounts by troopers of both armies are filled with references to battle spirit among cavalry horses, often noting how they continued to ride forward in mounted charges along with other horses even though their riders had been shot off their backs. Two men in the 1st New Jersey Cavalry found that their mounts had become "so crazy with excitement as to be unmanageable." They rode far ahead of others and wound up being killed or captured as a result.[48]

Battle losses could be severe. The horse, after all, represented a large target for flying metal, and it was not unusual for a mounted regiment to lose more animals than troopers in an engagement. The 8th Texas Cavalry took 450 men into the Battle of Shiloh and lost 66 of them killed, wounded, or missing; it also lost fifty-two horses killed and forty more badly wounded. In big battles the number of horses stricken by enemy fire accumulated to an alarming degree. At Gettysburg some 5,000 horses perished, amounting to 2.5 million tons of carcasses.[49]

Gause described a horse's death experience. "If a ball passes through his heart, he will make ten or twelve leaps with even more vigor than at any time during health, and then fall heavily, being dead before falling. If shot through the brain all support is gone, and he falls a dead weight, and straightens out without another move." Gause also described the wounding experience. "If shot through the lungs he will cough one hard choking cough, the blood flowing out of his mouth and nostrils. He will mope away for a short distance and stand with head down. If the wound is a painful one, such as a broken leg, he will utter one piercing shriek or hysterical scream that resembles the cry of the wild panther, and that causes a shudder to run through the frame of the bravest soldier."[50]

Horses faced the wear and tear of heavy campaigning, its emotional as well as its mortal dangers, as did their riders. Col. Charles Russell Lowell, commander of a brigade in Sheridan's army, recorded what happened to his horses during mounted operations in the Shenandoah Valley during the summer and fall of 1864. One horse named Ruksh was hit in the foreleg, and while it seemed possible to save his life, he could not be used anymore. Another mount named Dick also was hit in the leg, so Lowell "left him" somewhere. "Berold is so foolish about bullets and shell now," he told his wife on August 24, "that I really can't ride him under fire." Lowell could not train this gray. The only horse he could rely on was Billy, a true warhorse. In late August a bullet went through the upper part of his neck "very high up," which Lowell counted as "not at all serious." In early September two more bullets caused flesh wounds, "making an ugly cut near the throat" and another that went "crosswise through the point of the withers, cutting the bridle rein and piercing the edge of the blanket, but bullet passing quite above all bones." According to Lowell, this last ball did not bother Billy; it and all the other wounds closed quickly. Whenever Lowell tried other horses, Billy teased him until the colonel gave up and returned to him. But this fruitful relationship ended at the Third Battle of Winchester, September 19, when Billy was mortally wounded by three bullets. Exactly one month later Lowell himself was mortally wounded at the Battle of Cedar Creek. According to one report, he had a total of twelve horses shot under him during the war.[51]

Did horses respect the dead and wounded that littered the battlefields of the Civil War? Most commentators asserted that the animals did not want to step on a man or another horse lying on the ground. But this conclusion has to be modified by the evidence. In the mounted charge by the 5th U.S. Cavalry at Gaines's Mill, Lt. Louis D. Watkins was "severely wounded and also trampled on by several horses of the regiment" as he lay on the ground. And at the Battle of Cedar Mountain, some men in the 1st Pennsylvania Cavalry were injured "by their horses falling over other killed or wounded" animals. If given the opportunity horses probably were careful not to step on prone figures, but in the congestion of battle formations, it at times became unavoidable.[52]

Campaigning

Combat was only the most obvious trial faced by cavalry horses; it was followed by a long list of other stresses that wore away at their constitutions and emotions. Samuel Ringwalt believed that horses were by nature fitful sleepers, and he was certain that the daily circumstances of camp life took its toll on them. "To the loss of proper rest and sleep may in a great measure, be attributed the wearing out and premature death of many horses," he wrote. Excessive heat also stressed them greatly, as did excessive cold. In harsh winter conditions horses were covered with a sheet of ice, had to ford cold streams, and slid on ice-covered roads.[53]

But on rare occasions a commander might decide that bad weather was a good cover for a strike at the enemy. William J. Davis of the 10th Kentucky Cavalry (CS) recalled the pursuit of a Union cavalry force in southwestern Virginia on December 22, 1864. "The necks, breasts, and fore-legs of the horses were covered with clinging sheets of frozen breath, or blood that had oozed from fissures in their swollen nostrils. Often their lips were sealed by the frost to the steel bits, or protruded livid and ragged with icicles of blood." Davis saw a number of Union cavalry horses literally frozen to death. Some of them had legs grossly swollen "to an enormous size, and split open to the bone from knee to hoof; some knelt with muzzles cemented to the hard earth by blood; others lay prone but with heads upraised; I saw two—mates perhaps—which, in the agony of final dissolution, apparently had touched lips in mutual osculation, and stood with their mouths glued together by the killing frost." Davis reported that piles of six to eight carcasses in one heap often obstructed the movement of the Confederate column, and he counted 200 dead horses along a single mile of the route.[54]

Davis's experience represented the worst of all environmental stresses on cavalry horses, but it bears repeating that it was not typical of mounted operations. Normal campaigning offered less deadly but very stressing environmental effects to mounted operations. Moving a cavalry regiment through woods tangled with underbrush was no picnic. When the 4th

Michigan Cavalry advanced in line for two miles "through a dense cedar thicket, over ditches and stones, almost impassable for our horses," close to one-third of the mounts "were ruined by that afternoon's scout," reported Maj. Frank W. Mix. Mounts sometimes became so stuck in sloughs and swamps that their riders simply abandoned them to die. Bad weather made for bad roads, and trying to negotiate a safe footing tired out cavalry horses.[55]

The wear and tear of campaigning posed a threat to equine health. In extreme cases troopers did not remove saddles for two weeks, according to Crowninshield. Continuous saddling severely stressed the mounts, causing sores that, if unattended, ate into the flesh as "great holes," in the words of Jacob W. Bartmess. Frederick Whittaker advocated frequent halts in a long march to unsaddle the horses a couple of times every day. "Plenty of warm water and castile soap" was the best treatment for saddle sores, and one could keep separate "the harsh woollen fibres of the blanket" from the sores by placing gunny bags under the blanket. In addition to long rides under the saddle, intense campaigns often resulted in scant rations for cavalry horses. It was not unusual for mounts to have literally no feed for several days. Reports of cavalry horses dying of starvation during lengthy campaigns were not uncommon.[56]

Because mounted operations often were pushed to extremes, even short campaigns produced heavy suffering. During the Chancellorsville operations, Capt. Charles Francis Adams Jr. lost one-third of the horses in his company even though it engaged in no combat. His men kept them saddled for fifteen hours every day, and Adams inspected each mount after unsaddling to detect sore backs. "Imagine a horse with his withers swollen to three times the natural size, and with a volcanic, running sore pouring matter down each side," he wrote his mother. "The air of Virginia is literally burdened today with the stench of dead horses, federal and confederate. You pass them on every road and find them in every field, while from their carrions you can follow the march of every Army that moves."[57]

In addition to long hours under the saddle, heavy campaigning produced a condition that J. R. Bowen referred to as flutters, "probably a violent palpitation of the heart," that killed many of the mounts in the 1st New York Dragoons. Modern scientists refer to this condition as synchronous diaphragmatic flutter, or "thumps," a contraction of the horse's diaphragm associated with dehydration and electrolyte depletion. Both conditions drain a horse's vitality and endurance.[58]

Deliberate killing by their riders also resulted from intense campaigning. Mounts exhausted by a long march through contested territory often were killed when abandoned because, if left free, the enemy might catch and use them. This seems to have been a feature mostly of the last year of the war. From the beginning of his tenure as commander of the Army of the Potomac's cavalry, Sheridan used this tactic. "The horses which failed were shot by the rear guard, as they could have been easily recuperated and made serviceable to the enemy." He estimated that from 150 to 300 were killed in this way during his first raid in mid-May 1864. Sheridan did the same during the campaign that resulted in the Battle of Trevilian Station the next month. In September 1864 George N. Bliss of the 1st Rhode Island Cavalry estimated that Sheridan's provost guard shot 100 horses every day because they could not keep up with the moving column.[59]

It does not appear that any other cavalry commander made a habit of killing his own horses, but if circumstances seemed to demand it, others were fully capable of such action. During the March to the Sea, the lone Federal cavalry division was hard pressed by the Confederates and found that hundreds of captured horses were "a great incumbrance." During a fearful night's work, each cavalryman selected the best animal he could find, then the rest were deliberately slaughtered. The Second Brigade alone killed more than 500. The men covered the doomed animals' heads with blankets and then used an axe to strike them between the ears. The next morning their carcasses could be seen lined up in ranks where they fell.[60]

Such things may have been seen as a necessity of war, but they certainly were inhumane, wasteful of valuable animals, and cruel to the victims who, despite the blankets, could not have avoided knowing that something dreadful was happening. Whether the slaughter was truly necessary remains a matter of opinion.

Diseases

In contrast to this deliberate killing of animals, the hard service that killed even more, and the inevitable killing of large numbers of horses in combat, Civil War cavalry mounts faced their biggest threat of death from disease. But this should not be surprising—disease was the biggest killer of Civil War soldiers as well. The conflict brought together the largest concentration of equines in American history, collecting them in huge, congested populations that became fertile grounds for the spread of horse ailments and deadly diseases.

Unlike troopers, who could rely on surgeons to curb the effects of human diseases, horses had virtually no professional help. There were a handful of colleges that taught veterinary medicine, but the few graduates tended to be highly paid in the elite centers of American society. Only forty-six veterinarians were listed in the entire United States in the census of 1850, and nearly half of them lived in New York City, where the concentration of urban workhorses was high. Eleven years later there were far too few veterinarians to serve army needs, even though Congress allowed for their employment with cavalry units. Crowninshield noted after the war that his 1st Massachusetts Cavalry never had a true veterinarian, but many men in the regiment claimed to know how to doctor horses. They were farriers or privates with an interest in the subject but without any training and likely as not little real knowledge. The shortage of trained medical aid was even more acute in the Confederate army. "There is a crying want of veterinary surgeons," reported Col. John R. Chambliss Jr. in August 1863. He urged the establishment of a veterinary hospital "where surgeons and farriers might be appointed, with the labor of hired negroes to attend to the horses."[61]

But neither service provided its cavalry with proper medical care. American society as a whole was simply unprepared to offer horses protection from the diseases that assailed them in army service. The riders themselves tried to fill that void but were hampered by their lack of information.

"An officer of cavalry needs to be more horse-doctor than soldier," concluded Charles Francis Adams Jr., "and no one who has not tried it can realize the discouragement to Company commanders in these long and continuous marches. You are a slave to your horses . . . and you see diseases creeping on you day by day and your horses breaking down under your eyes."[62]

Many different equine ailments ranged from the survivable to the deadly. Robert Jennings, a professor at the Veterinary College of Philadelphia whose book on horses appeared in 1860, catalogued 121 horse ailments and diseases. Eleven, or 9.1 percent, were of the mouth; 15, or 12.4 percent, were of the respiratory organs; 13, or 10.8 percent, were of the stomach and intestines; 4, or 3.4 percent, were of the liver; 6, or 4.9 percent, were of the urinary organs; 35, or 28.9 percent, were of the feet and legs; 3, or 2.5 percent, were of the heart; 6, or 4.9 percent, were of the head; another 6, or 4.9 percent, were of the eyes; and 22, or 18.2 percent, were of a miscellaneous type.[63]

Although published the year before the firing on Fort Sumter, Jennings's book made no impression. There are no references to it in official reports, dispatches, or personal accounts produced by the war. Virtually everyone associated with cavalry horses perceived their diseases through the lens of practical experience, folklore, home remedies, and poorly informed common sense. Thus, there were many different terms for the ailments and little real understanding of why they occurred or how to deal with them.

The largest group of ailments and diseases centered on the feet and legs, the parts of the horse's anatomy that met the harsh conditions of the earth and were most used in movements. Various terms such as "foot evil," "hoof rot," and "tetter" were applied to conditions affecting the feet, producing lameness and in some instances causing the hoof to slough off. Eating new corn or not ingesting enough salt were among the assumed causes, along with the effect of limestone dust when marching along turnpikes and the deleterious effects of hot weather. Hoof problems seemed to come in waves, such as when affecting a large percentage of animals in a given unit right after the Maryland Campaign. The 1st Massachusetts Cavalry was "practically unhorsed" two weeks after the Battle of Antietam by this condition.[64]

Capt. Alonzo Gray of the 14th U.S. Cavalry offered a plausible explanation for this disease in his book on cavalry tactics, published in 1910. Hoof rot arose "from constantly standing in the mud" and had been common in the cavalry camp at Huntsville, Alabama, during the Spanish-American War. It was very difficult to cure, but getting the horse onto dry ground helped a good deal. Another post–Civil War cavalryman suggested that the soil of Virginia was conducive to promoting hoof rot, and he may have been on the mark. Chaplain Charles A. Humphreys of the 2nd Massachusetts Cavalry noted that mud infecting a scratch on the hoof or leg led to this problem. Frederick Whittaker of the 6th New York Cavalry understood that wet ground was connected with the disease. He noted that placing the horse on dry ground, carefully cleaning the legs and hooves with warm water and castile soap, then bandaging what he could to keep out the dirt and preserve a scab until new skin could form was an effective treatment. Whittaker called this condition scratches and explained that they were similar to chilblains and chaps for humans. But this healing process was labor-intensive and slow; it was demanding in camp and impossible while on campaign. Some men used chemical applications to treat hoof rot. At the cavalry depots chloride of antimony and even some salt heated on a shovel in the fire were tried.[65]

Jennings identified eleven diseases of the mouth, and Civil War troopers commonly lumped them into the designation "black tongue." This condition caused the tongue to become so sore that the horse could not eat for several days. Lee estimated that three-fourths of Stuart's cavalry mounts were affected with it in November 1862. Treatment consisted of "a decoction of white oak bark" or "borax and alum, half and half, pulverized and mixed with sweet oil and applied with a swab to the tongue." But this required time and unusual ingredients. Attendants at the cavalry depots were better equipped to apply such treatment, which means that horses in the field generally suffered until the ailment went away on its own.[66]

Worse than hoof rot and black tongue were a collection of symptoms that could lead to any one of several diseases. The problem often started with ominous signs. "The horses are dying very rapidly from some cause unknown," wrote August V. Kautz in late July 1862. "They stop eating for a day or two then go down and never get up again. It seems a kind of fever. The disease seems to attack the fittest horses." Often the passage of the animal through various stages of illness wound up with an attack of glanders, a major killer of equines that was but vaguely understood in the Civil War. Samuel Ringwalt knew that hoof rot could lead to farcy and then to glanders, but he believed there were three different kinds of glanders. Forty years later Nelson S. Mayo of the Kansas State Agricultural College reported that "glanders and farcy are different forms of the same disease." If it hit the mucous membranes, it was called glanders; if it hit the lymphatic glands of the body, especially the legs, it was called farcy.[67]

Mayo described the symptoms of farcy as the appearance of firm lumps just under the skin, especially in a string along the legs, that often broke open and spread an amber-colored fluid on the hair. The resulting sores did not heal readily and often spread after bursting. Jennings understood farcy to be "an incipient stage of glanders" but believed it could be cured before getting worse.[68]

Yet Jennings also knew that glanders was an entirely different matter. It was "fatal and much dreaded," and because other less deadly diseases had similar symptoms, the condition was often not identified early enough. It could be communicated to humans and was deadly in them as well. Jennings believed that the chief cause of glanders lay in the "impure air of close, ill-ventilated, and filthy stables" that affected respiration and reduced the horse's natural immunity. The disease was characterized by sticky discharges from the nostrils, often with blood mixed in, and ulcers on the membrane. Jennings admitted that no treatment seemed to be effective against the disease.[69]

Forty years after the war, veterinary science had revealed much about glanders. Mayo noted that it was "caused by a germ (bacillus mallei) that attacks horses, asses and mules." It could not be transmitted through the air but only through touch or via shared water troughs, feed boxes, and hitching posts and infected horse equipment. Flies could transmit it too. The nasal discharges at first were thin and sticky, but as the disease progressed they became "more profuse, thicker, yellowish in color, and sometimes streaked with blood." The ulcers were serious, "raw, depressed in the center, with reddish edges."[70]

But Mayo, like Jennings, could offer no hope for a treatment of glanders. The typical response in the field was to quarantine or kill the affected animals. But Ringwalt reported that killing them was not enough. Anything they had touched with their mouths had to be disinfected. This is exactly what Mayo wrote of the disease nearly half a century after the war. "Glanders and farcy are practically incurable," and the only recourse was destruction of the diseased equines and a thorough cleaning of everything they had touched. Human and horses alike lost their battle with glanders, a disease that was "never eradicated" from any cavalry regiment during the war. It ran its course unimpeded and killed tens of thousands of horses and mules.[71]

An ancient treatment for horse problems resurfaced in the Civil War. The mount that Luman Harris Tenney rode in the 2nd Ohio Cavalry developed a belly ache. "Bled him most to death," Tenney recalled. The next day he reported that the "horse grows stronger," and it eventually became serviceable once more. W. D. Wharton of the 5th North Carolina Cavalry had a horse suffering from what he called yellow waters. "Had to bleed him nearly to death to cure him," Wharton told his father. "Next he took the scratches, has them a little yet, then the distemper."[72]

It was a shame that neither government created a professional health-care system for equines similar to that they had created for soldiers. Animals tended to be ridden until they gave out. "A horse must go until he can't be spurred any further," wrote Adams. No wonder that so few mounts originally issued made it through a unit's war service. In the 5th New York Cavalry, only seven lasted from October 1861 to July 1865, and that seems to have been an unusually high number compared to other regiments.[73]

Some cavalry veterans became aware of this high rate of horse losses only after the war. Moses Harris learned that during the first two years of the conflict, the Federal government purchased 284,000 cavalry horses for about 60,000 cavalrymen, which in his view represented a "terrible waste of horse flesh." George N. Bliss heard that the life expectancy of a cavalry horse during the Civil War amounted to only four months. No wonder that modern historians have calculated that 1,200,000 horses and mules in all branches of service, both Union and Confederate, perished in the Civil War.[74]

Horse deaths declined in the U.S. Army afterward. In World War I the American Third Army lost 32.1 percent of its horsepower, and less than one-third of those deaths were caused by combat. Estimates suggest that this loss rate was less than half that of the Civil War. The British Army did not fare so well, however, when it transported thousands of horses to support operations in the Second Boer War (also known as the South African War) of 1899–1902. It suffered a loss rate of 66.8 percent of horses and 35.3 percent of mules, about the same level as the equine loss rate of American Civil War armies.[75]

Horses versus Mules

Mules were widely believed to have been no substitute for horses in the mounted service. While they were superb at pulling wagons in supply trains, they did not have the temperament or physical characteristics needed for cavalry work. Mules did not satisfy the needs of any horse soldiers who tried them in the field. During the Atlanta Campaign, Capt. Martin Choumee's 5th Iowa Cavalry was partially mounted on mules. The regiment advanced in column along a narrow lane when it received fire, and Choumee ordered the unit to turn about by fours. Because of the narrowness of the lane and "the many obstinate mules on which one-fourth of the men were mounted," the maneuver "was executed with some confusion." The 4th Louisiana Cavalry experimented with mules in the spring of 1864. William B. Mattox reported that the one he rode "ran away with me through the woods." That was enough for him: "I must have a horse and I mean a good one, mules will not do."[76]

As Choumee and Mattox knew too well, only horses could be relied on for cavalry service. They were the only equines with the natural ability to learn how to be animal warriors, and their tendency to bond with their rider was a vital component of their value as war mounts. Their temperament, attitude, and capabilities varied from individual to individual, but that was true of the men who rode them as well. Overwhelmingly, the match up of horse and trooper was the only way that cavalry could operate.

Animal Veterans

For those cavalrymen who were sensitive to their horses, parting with them at war's end was a sad event. "Some of the men were visibly affected when they took final leave" of their mounts, wrote Chauncey S. Norton of the 15th New York Cavalry. "I Shal[l] *always like* a horse *better than Ever* after [my] army life is Over," wrote Lt. Thadeus Packard of the 5th Illinois Cavalry. "They have more intelegence than Some Men," he wrote, "and a Soldier *that does not take good Care* of *his horse, is not a good Soldier* and does *not deserve the name [of] a Man*." Edward Wall of the 3rd New York Cavalry agreed with Packard when he wrote: "Great is the intelligence and willingness of a good horse. They shame sometimes the unreasonableness of their riders."[77]

Some men took their horses home with them. Belle Mosby, the name given a mount captured from the Confederates in 1865 by farrier Joseph R. Phillips of the 18th Pennsylvania Cavalry, remained with him for the rest of her life. Estimated to have been four and a half years old when captured, Belle Mosby lived more than thirty-four years under the tender care of Phillips. A similar story surrounded Fanny, a mare captured from John S. Mosby's partisan command and taken home by Capt. William F. Weller of the 15th New York Cavalry. Fanny lived on Weller's farm near Liverpool, New York, carrying a bullet in her underjaw while mothering two colts. She lived for more than thirty years and was present at several reunions of the regiment. Fanny became a mascot of the regiment and something of a celebrity after the war.[78]

Thus, the cavalry horse ran the gamut from unwilling conscript into war service, through the struggles of adjusting to army regimen and training, and dealing with hard service on long campaigns, bullets and shells on the battlefield, fights with other horses, and the deadly challenge of disease. If lucky, it survived all this; a handful of those survivors were lauded as animal veterans. The war story of the cavalry horse is as full of interest, drama, and poignancy as that of the cavalry trooper, and it deserves greater recognition.

12

CAVALRYMEN

The cavalry service demanded men who were not afraid of horses, who were capable of extended duty in the field, and who were amenable to acquiring the special éclat associated with mounted warfare. Cavalry was an auxiliary branch to infantry, less so than was artillery to be sure, but still it was meant to supplement the core element of infantrymen in every nineteenth-century army. Unlike artillery, the mounted branch could conduct independent operations in the field hundreds of miles from any supporting foot soldiers. It could therefore create a separate identity in a strategic as well as an operational sense, in addition to serving as a close support of infantry formations on the battlefield. The ideal cavalryman was someone who understood all this and took pride in his branch of the national service.

George B. McClellan felt that mounted warriors were unique. "Officers and men should be of a superior order of intelligence, and . . . they should fully understand the care of their horses, which should be active and enduring." Because of these requirements it was "really much more difficult to form reliable cavalry at short notice than to instruct artillery and infantry." Benjamin W. Crowninshield would have agreed with McClellan. He bemoaned the fact that time did not allow for a more careful selection process when organizing the 1st Massachusetts Cavalry. The best horse soldiers were those with extensive riding experience and a familiarity with guns, but few men in that regiment met those requirements.[1]

Affinity for Mounted Service

What made a recruit choose cavalry service over infantry or artillery? Mostly it boiled down to personal preference for its unique characteristics. "I liked its independence; individuality and the self-reliance it imposed," wrote Confederate John C. Wright. Service in the cavalry offered a "display of individual tact, genius and courage. I liked its free and abandoned spirit; its excitement and nervous tension." Cavalry work required "a higher order of personal courage, more individuality to meet the foe, man to man, where but few are engaged, than in serried ranks of thousands." Another Confederate cited the opportunity to forage from the countryside, freeing him from worry about lack of pay and poor commissary supplies. He felt that cavalrymen were generally healthier because their duties kept them actively employed in the field.[2]

While both Union and Confederate horsemen shared a certain affinity for cavalry service, there is no doubt that it was felt more strongly by the men who wore butternut and gray. After Brig. Gen. John Hunt Morgan escaped from a Northern prison and returned to duty, he received many letters from Rebel troops who were eager to join the new brigade he was reported to be organizing. A number of infantrymen, in fact, were itching to transfer to a cavalry unit. They were driven by the lure of excitement and the desire to avoid marching on foot. Switching from infantry to cavalry became such a rage in the Confederate army that it raised alarm in some quarters. Gen. Joseph E. Johnston stopped recruiting for Morgan's new brigade and for Maj. Gen. Nathan Bedford Forrest's command in his Army of Tennessee early in 1864. Maj. Gen. Gideon J. Pillow was especially distraught. Infantrymen went absent without leave and, after a few days of staying at their homes, joined a cavalry unit. "If the evil is not cured the cavalry will swallow up the infantry arm of the service," he warned. Already Pillow believed that two-thirds of the troopers in Brig. Gen. Philip D. Roddey's and Brig. Gen. James R. Chalmers's commands were former infantrymen.[3]

After taking control of Confederate cavalry in the Department of Mississippi and Eastern Louisiana in late 1863, Maj. Gen. Stephen D. Lee was deeply worried that the new mounted units springing up in that area were sucking up all the remaining horses in the region and making it difficult to find replacement animals for the artillery. Moreover, "it takes a long time to make the new cavalry now forming efficient," he pointed out.[4]

But the Southern desire to ride a horse seemed to be so strong that it militated against a rational approach to creating a military machine. "There was something attractive to the younger Southerner in the life of a bold dragoon," wrote Joshua B. Hill of the 3rd North Carolina Cavalry, "especially among those whose circumstances had made them fearless horsemen, and whose life in the open air and participation in field sports had rendered them the finest recruits in the world for this form of military duty."[5]

But two caveats need to be emphasized. First, not all Southern young men fell into the category described by Hill. The overwhelming majority of Confederate recruits preferred infantry service, a fact that too many historians ignore. Second, the lure of mounted service was not by any means the exclusive property of Southerners. Many Northern men also preferred cavalry work for the same reasons as their Southern counterparts.

"But there is something very attractive in the service in spite of all," concluded Crowninshield after the war. "It is more venturesome and varied. Here to-day, there to-morrow; more chance for foraging; sometimes better food, never so much hard-tack and pork, but not unfrequently great hunger and want." Chaplain Charles A. Humphreys of the 2nd Massachusetts Cavalry did not carry a weapon and certainly did not love war, but he understood how some men could get caught up in the excitement of cavalry service. When James Giauque of the 30th Iowa contemplated how the war might come to an end, he assumed that the mounted units would remain in service longer than the infantry to deal with lingering guerrilla activity. He had a desire to rest at home for one month and then rejoin the army, but this time in a mounted unit. "I want to give cavalry service a little trial anyway and oh wouldent [sic] I like it to ride around and clean out the last devil of them," he told his brother.[6]

Motivation played the key role in whether a recruit decided to join a cavalry outfit versus an infantry or artillery unit. But as far as some cavalry officers were concerned, other factors played similarly important roles. Maj. Gen. Philip Sheridan reportedly told an officer of the 17th Pennsylvania Cavalry that his ideal cavalryman was an unmarried man

Better Than Walking.
The title of this illustration from the postwar memoirs of Alfred
Ringgold Gibbons of Company G, 1st Georgia Cavalry expresses
the reason that many men chose cavalry service in the Civil War.
Gibbons, *Recollections of an Old Confederate Soldier*, 17.

eighteen to twenty-two years old weighing not more than 130 pounds. It is quite possible the majority of recruits in mounted units more or less fit that description. When officers of the 4th Illinois Cavalry, with Maj. Gen. Ulysses S. Grant's urging, recruited the 3rd U.S. Colored Cavalry at Vicksburg, they had the opportunity to carefully select men from a large pool. "Young, active men, of medium height," with "a fair amount of natural intelligence" were the criteria. They tried to find those whose physical attributes came as close to the "standard of the ideal cavalrymen as has probably ever been realized," although the regimental historian did not detail what that meant. He also noted that the 3rd U.S. Colored Cavalry was unusual in the quality of its personnel, indicating that the ideal was rarely realized across the board in the war.[7]

It is possible to differentiate between the typical trooper and his counterparts in the infantry and artillery. Historian Joseph T. Glatthaar's social history of the Army of Northern Virginia focuses on a group of 600 members of the army as a sampling of the whole; 150 of them served in cavalry units. More than half of the cavalrymen were farmers, and fewer came from a large city than was average for all recruits in the army. They also tended to come from wealthier slaveholding families and from slave-dense counties than was average for the entire army. Lee's cavalry arm suffered less in battle and on campaign than did the infantry. While 55.7 percent of horsemen were lost to combat during the entire war, the infantry suffered losses of 79.4 percent.[8]

Life in the Cavalry

The key difference in the war service of cavalry compared to infantry and artillery was its life on the go. Horsemen often had to put up with short rations, fatigue, heavy workloads, and a peripatetic lifestyle. "The difference in campaigning lies in the art of making yourself comfortable under any and all circumstances," wrote Lt. Frederick Whittaker of the 6th New York Cavalry as he contemplated the green trooper compared to the experienced veteran.[9]

Based on his own experience, Whittaker advocated rations that were more easily transported, noting that salt pork and hardtack were bulky and heavy. The Confederates often issued flour rather than bread, which made for easier transport but, of course, had to be cooked somehow before eating. Whittaker liked the Prussian policy of issuing a sausage with meal mixed together for easy transport and eating in the field. His comrades did not like the haversack issued to Union cavalry troopers. It was uncomfortable to wear across the shoulders while riding, so they tied it to the saddle where it dangled, "bumping and crashing, till the band gives way, and down comes the load." So the men took out the white inner bag and fashioned three small bags out of it to store their coffee, sugar, and salt. Then they used a piece of old shelter tent to make a bag for their salt pork and strapped everything to the saddle. The hardtack they placed in what was left of the haversack, rolled it up, and strapped it to the saddle, which also had to support the grain bag with the horse's ration. At the end of the day, Whittaker mused, "coffee and a quiet pipe have done more to comfort our men on long raids than anything else."[10]

While all this sounds as if the average trooper barely subsisted in the field, the truth was that many of them thrived on the life of the cavalryman. Lt. Henry H. Belfield informed a friend that there were few sick or despondent troopers in the 8th Iowa Cavalry. "For myself, I never enjoyed such health. I am realey *fat*. The saddle seems to agree with me, and I ride from four a. m. to ten p. m. sometimes, with but little weariness. An ordinary days ride is always a pleasure: and I am not satisfied if I close a day without some miles of fast riding."[11]

Belfield's attitude was shared by many of his mounted comrades. In fact, some relished the image of a horse warrior as a swashbuckler. Before the war, James Albert Clark envisioned a trooper as one "who rode terrifically with his sabre gripped by his teeth, a revolver in each hand and his breath almost aflame and spurted from his nostrils." Another aspect of that romantic imagery involved the trooper's hair. "With the affectation of many young cavalry men of that day, I wore my hair hanging down to my shoulders," recalled Capt. John P. Rea of the 1st Ohio Cavalry. This was in violation of army regulations, but officers could more easily get away with flaunting those rules than enlisted men. George A. Custer and Frederick W. Benteen were among those who wore their hair long.[12]

According to Crowninshield, the regulation army uniform for cavalry service was modified to some degree by individual taste. In his words, "utility and common sense" dictated such alterations. Footwear and headgear were the most common articles of clothing to be adjusted in this way. "Boots of various kinds" found their way into cavalry service, and at least in the 1st Massachusetts Cavalry, the tendency was to tuck the ends of trouser legs into them. Cavalry boots tended to be substantial affairs, going almost up to the knee.[13]

Some units sported huge felt hats with feathers. The 6th Ohio Cavalry received hats with "one side turned up and fastened to the crown and a long drooping black feather in each Hat." But these showy pieces were not popular with the men. In the 6th New York Cavalry, similarly gaudy headgear was thrown away, and the men obtained a variety of hats and caps as substitutes. Most horse soldiers preferred cloth forage caps of varied quality and utility. Sheridan mandated forage caps, in fact, during the last year of the war, but those issued by the government tended to be unsatisfactory in quality. "Nine-tenths of the men preferred paying two dollars for a decent and serviceable cap," recalled Whittaker. The government cap took only sixty cents off the clothing allowance of each man, but they considered the extra $1.40 to be well spent if they could obtain headgear that was not "literally worthless."[14]

While there may have been some disagreement on the best type of headgear, everyone agreed that the trousers issued by the government were useful. They were reinforced at the seat for longer wear, but exactly what to reinforce them with was a debatable question. In Europe leather was used as the reinforcing material, but in the United States it was cloth. Whittaker, never at a loss for an opinion, suggested that canvas or sailcloth would have been more durable and should have been used for the entire pair of pants. If that was not possible, he preferred leather to cloth. But no matter how the campfire discussion went, everyone agreed that a reinforced pair of trousers was necessary. It would be better if that pair fitted tightly, according to Whittaker, who pointed out that loose-fitting pants tended to get caught on things associated with the horse equipment and reduced the leg control a cavalryman exercised with his mount.[15]

Utility was the key in this regard; therefore, it is a bit surprising that some horsemen tried to make a showy thing of their pants. Crowninshield noted that many troopers in the prewar army borrowed this concept from Texans and Mexicans. They "cut open the trouser legs" to "ornament them with brass buttons down the seam, or else they would have them cut over, with very wide spring bottoms." This not only was unnecessary but also wasteful, considering the muddy conditions of Virginia and the states west of the Appalachian Highlands. More than any other part of the cavalryman's uniform, trousers bore the brunt of wear and tear because they covered the parts of the man's anatomy most in touch with the horse. "My blue trousers are ragged from contact with the saddle and so covered with grease and dust that they would fry well," joked Charles Francis Adams Jr.[16]

Even more than for the infantry and artillery, a cavalryman's feet had to be protected by proper gear. Two incidents illustrate this point. One day a horse lashed out and kicked Benjamin H. Grierson near the knee. He was sure that "the high-topped, heavy-legged boots" he wore prevented a serious injury, even though the kick produced "a severe sprain" that constituted the worst personal wound he received during the war. It could have been a crippling injury without the protection of the boots. In another incident, during Joseph Wheeler's raid on Union boats traveling the Cumberland River in January 1863, the weather turned freezing. A private in the 8th Confederate Cavalry lost the soles of his shoes and "had his feet frozen to his iron stirrups and could not dismount until warm cloths had been applied."[17]

Men and Horses

A cavalryman's life was centered on his mount, and taking care of it consumed a large portion of his daily routine. The first duty on waking in the morning was to feed his horse even before he ate breakfast, grooming it as the animal munched its hay and oats. In well-ordered units an officer superintended feeding and grooming. "Keep to work there!" he yelled if someone slacked off. After feeding and grooming, the troopers watered their animals. Then they ate breakfast and tended to many other chores in camp until evening brought another round of horse care. Often someone had to feed and water two mounts, his own and another belonging to a comrade who was absent sick. If his mount happened to be ill or was suffering from saddle sores, the trooper invested even more time and effort in treatment.[18]

Many aspects of life in the mounted service took place from the back of a horse. Troopers were "always on the move," as R. S. Whitehead of the 1st Georgia Cavalry put it. Henry Belfield exaggerated a bit when he told a friend that a cavalryman did not know if he would be allowed to stay on one spot for even five minutes. No wonder that many official reports and personal accounts by horse soldiers tend to be imprecise, blurred, and incomplete due to the quick nature of cavalry movements. "Hear to day. There to morrow," recalled Robert Milton McAlister, a Confederate Tennessee cavalryman. "Most all ways on the go. Either running to or from the foe, and having to hustle. There was but little time for observations." Writing to his wife, Thomas M. Covert often stopped in the middle of his long letters to answer a call. "Cant write any more, boots and saddles is sounding."[19]

Even when resting in camp, cavalrymen had to be on the move. They often held impromptu races that raised concern among officers. These races wore on the horses and presented a danger if held too near the tents. Even if held far from quarters, they resulted in physical injuries to horses and men, which is why officers tried to clamp down on them. Sheridan ordered subordinates to arrest anyone found "riding their horses faster than a trot or slow canter and dismount them unless they can show proper authority for such riding." Nevertheless, many officers allowed their men to have a little fun now and then. The presence of a well-maintained turnpike near camp was often too much of a temptation, serving as a good venue for a fast race that would determine which trooper had the speediest mount.[20]

But the government did not issue mounts to cavalrymen to hold races. As the platform for the trooper, the horse had to bear a substantial burden of 225 pounds on average. That included the saddle, riding equipment, the man, his weapons, food, cooking utensils, and a few personal belongings. At the start of their war service, horsemen typically loaded themselves and their mounts with a lot of material they thought necessary for comfort in the field. Hard experience soon taught them the least they took along the better. Weight was "a penance" to the horse, as Whittaker put it. Troopers learned to economize by deciding what was essential to keep and devising ways to carry it. Only experience could teach them this important rule of army life. Whittaker believed it was possible to reduce the load to 200 pounds per mount.[21]

Horses surely appreciated this streamlining. The benefits were best seen when conducting long marches, which often started in the middle of the night and proceeded at a steady walk to conserve the horses. George N. Bliss of the 1st Rhode Island Cavalry thought a rate of three and a half miles per hour was ideal. If the weather was dry and the roads dusty, huge clouds were raised before a shower turned that dust into mud. All of this settled on the troopers "until his own mother could not have recognized him." Dust could be so dense that the rider was unable to see his comrades in the column—sometimes even to see his own hand held in front of his face. "It came near suffocating us and I spit out great mouthfuls of pure mud," recalled Charles Crosland, a South Carolina cavalryman, of one notably dusty march.[22]

Campaigning led to heavy demands on the personal comfort of troopers. It was not unusual for them to keep their boots on for days at a time and to have no opportunity to wash their faces, much less bathe. But sleep deprivation was the worst problem. Being in the saddle eighteen to twenty hours each day for weeks at a stretch, as during the Atlanta Campaign, taxed their endurance to the limit. Men were fortunate to snatch three hours of sleep per night on some campaigns.[23]

Circumstances made effective sleepers of these men; they could nod off almost anywhere. "The art of balancing oneself while asleep on horseback is easily acquired," recalled Henry Murray Calvert of the 11th New York Cavalry, "but it is even less comfortable than sleeping in church, because inequalities in the road constantly disturb the sleeper." But George Tilton believed that an experienced trooper could adjust so well to sleeping on horseback that it was more comfortable than sleeping in a chair at home. Some cavalrymen preferred to lean forward, inclining the upper part of their bodies almost horizontally, but most remained vertical while dozing. Some men reported being sound asleep while in the saddle, although only for a few minutes at a time. "It is fitful, broken, unsatisfactory sleep," wrote George Dallas Mosgrove.[24]

When a trooper slept in the saddle, he had to rely on his horse to keep moving. If he woke up every few minutes to correct the mount's movements all was well, but if he dozed off for any length of time, the horse often strayed from its place in the column. It was not unusual for a handful of sleeping troopers at the head of a column to stop the entire command when their horses decided to slow down or stop. Sometimes while their riders were fast asleep, mounts would move faster than those around them or leave the column entirely. Even officers got lost because their horses took advantage of the freedom from commands to exercise a bit of agency. In following Lee's retreat from Pennsylvania, Capt. James H. Kidd slept in the saddle for some time during the late night, and when dawn broke he woke up. Kidd could recognize no one around him. "A moving mass of horses with motionless riders all wrapped in slumber" greeted his view, and none of them were familiar. "The horses were moving along with drooping heads and eyes half-closed. Some walked faster than others," and all were out of synchronization with their units. When a halt was finally called, it took an hour for Kidd's company to reassemble.[25]

Henry C. Meyer, a clerk for Brig. Gen. David M. Gregg's adjutant general, typically rode ahead of the column and just behind the staff officers. On the march one day during the Stoneman Raid of the Chancellorsville Campaign, he fell sound asleep. His horse had a habit of going ahead every time Meyer dozed, and the staff found it amusing, encouraging the

Played Out.

Troopers faced unusual difficulties in their effort to catch some sleep during a strenuous campaign since they were responsible for their horses. Many learned how to sleep while holding the reins if they did not have time or opportunity to set up a picket rope to tie them to, as was normal practice. This illustration comes from the postwar reminiscences published by Pvt. Henry H. Eby of Company C, 7th Illinois Cavalry.

Eby, *Observations,* 51.

animal forward to see how far it would go. This day Meyer rode on until he was even with Gregg, and the division commander had to wake him. Meyer always suffered in these saddle sleeps—tree branches scratched his face, and he often lost his cap—but he willingly endured the mishaps in exchange for catching a nap while on the move.[26]

Sleep deprivation was one of the major problems of cavalry life in the Civil War, something the trooper could only curb rather than eliminate. To a far lesser degree, yet still worth noting, were problems between horse and man. It would be misleading to overemphasize this issue because the majority of troopers controlled their mounts well enough to get by, and some of them were superb horsemen who developed close bonds with their animals. But a minority of horses found the military regimen difficult to accept, which caused trouble for their riders.

"I had had some experience with horses on a farm," recalled Stanton P. Allen of the 1st Massachusetts Cavalry, "but I had never struggled for the mastery with a fiery, untamed war-horse." When he and his comrades initially tried to groom the horses, they "kicked us around the stables *ad libitum*. One recruit had all his front teeth knocked out." That stormy introduction smoothed out until, according to Allen, most of his fellow soldiers created a calm, cooperative relationship with their mounts.[27]

Even after they got used to each other, the horse-human combination was fraught with potential danger to the trooper. Fast movements in tight formations produced dangerous accidents. During a charge at Stones River, Wilmon W. Blackmar nearly was injured when his horse stumbled in a hole and "turned a somersault. I was under him, freed from my saddle and lying on my back, protected from his full weight by an arch formed by my saddle with my blanket strapped on the cantle and my overcoat on the pommel. I was partially stunned, but remember perfectly looking up and seeing my horse's feet in the air and Jack Horn's horse making a flying leap right over me." Fortunately, Blackmar's horse "rolled over, jumped to his feet," and allowed the dazed trooper to stand up, miraculously unhurt.[28]

But the number of cavalrymen injured by their horses could be counted in the thousands. Most were relatively minor issues, but there also were many serious injuries inflicted by nervous or severely stressed animals. When the 8th Illinois Cavalry settled into its first camp in the Washington, DC, area, Surgeon Abner Hard began treating "quite a number" of men for horse kicks. The incidents happened when troopers took their mounts to water in Rock Creek half a mile from camp, and the kicks usually landed four to six inches below the knee, "frequently laying bare the bone," as Hard put it. Even when sleeping during the night, "it was no uncommon thing for horses to get loose and endanger the limbs and lives of the soldiers, by running over them." The 1st Maine Cavalry experienced much the same thing early in its war service. "A number of the boys have been kicked and some knocked over," wrote Sgt. William B. Baker, "yet not but one has been hurt seriously."[29]

But serious accidents occurred in many regiments. A kick in the head killed a man in the 9th Pennsylvania Cavalry, while a fall from his mount led to the death of a trooper in the 1st Massachusetts Cavalry. At times horse-related incidents led to the wounding or death of the trooper indirectly. In the 15th New York Cavalry, Myron Ostrander was dismounting when the hammer of his carbine caught "in some manner" and discharged the weapon, putting a bullet in his right leg. That limb was later amputated. And in the 8th Illinois Cavalry, Sidney Sessions's horse fell while jumping a ditch, and the trooper's carbine went off, killing him.[30]

Accidents combined with deliberate acts of violence by the animal made for an unusual slice of danger in the mounted service. "In the cavalry regiments," wrote the medical director of the Army of the Potomac, "the sick report is swollen considerably in consequence of injuries to the men received from the horses." Sergeant Baker thought the men could avoid all or most of this "if they will only be carefull [*sic*]."[31]

It was very difficult to manage the horses if a regiment had to bivouac for the night but keep the mounts handy for quick use. Typically each man held the reins and slept on the ground, or they could have one man remain awake and hold his own and three other horses at a distance, being relieved in shifts by his comrades. Chaplain Humphreys of the 2nd Massachusetts Cavalry thought most horses were careful not to trod on prone men during night bivouacs. They sometimes "got lonesome" and "would poke us with their noses" or lay down next to the rider. But Wells A. Bushnell of the 6th Ohio Cavalry was nearly killed by one horse during a night bivouac. He awoke to find that as the mount was wandering about, "his shod hoof struck me farely [*sic*] on the head cutting and bruising it quite seriously."[32]

Riding and Human Health

Another set of problems arising from the relationship between animal and human involved the health of the trooper. Constant, intense riding produced an array of medical conditions in the human body. In the short term these were rarely noticed. But medical conditions caused by long-term horse riding raises the question as to whether the horse-man combination was ever meant to be.

William F. Scott of the 4th Iowa Cavalry described the effect of long marches on the frame of the trooper. "A cavalryman suffers a slowly increasing pain, from his cramped position and the unceasing motion of his horse, a pain that is often very hard to bear hour after hour. It is an indescribably general keen ache and rasping of the nerves." With continued riding, the trooper's "sensations are exquisite tortures. Every bone aches fiercely and seems ready to crack with pain, and every muscle feels as sore and tender as if it had been separately scourged." Abner Hard, surgeon of the 8th Illinois Cavalry, treated many men for "chafing or excoriations on the inside of thighs or legs, caused by riding." But he had little guidance in this. "Such things as these we had to learn from experience." In his book *Hints on Health in Armies, for the Use of Volunteer Officers,* medical professor John Ordronaux of Columbia Law School warned cavalrymen of more serious effects of long, hard riding. "Hernias, and inflammations of the testicles often testify to the effects of incessant jolting in the saddle, and it is advisable for all horsemen to protect themselves against these accidents by wearing a suspensory bandage."[33]

Modern medicine, allied with osteoarchaeology, has proven that repeated horseback riding has serious consequences for the spine and other bone structures of the rider. Examination of skeletal remains found in a Scythian royal burial mound of about 325 BCE shows the same type of bone deformation one sees in horsemen and women today. A team research project headed by Clayton N. Kraft and published in 2009 conducted magnetic resonance imaging of fifty-eight riders. It was found that 88 percent of them had "lumbar disk degeneration" and other conditions, while only thirty-three percent of the control group of nonriders exhibited the same issues. Competitive riders "frequently complain of orthopaedic problems" such as pain in the lower back, hip joint, or hamstring muscle. They have 73 percent more chance of developing back pain than nonriders. All horsemen and women have to absorb a good deal of shock from virtually every movement of the horse. It resonates from the animal and through the stirrup, foot, knee, and hip. "Horseback riding is one of the most dangerous recreational sports," conclude the authors of this study, dangers that include a range of accidents. Falls from the mount and horse kicks account for most of the overt danger, and the effect of those incidents "range from mild bruising to fatality."[34]

The type of riding performed today by dedicated horse people, especially competitive riders, mimics that done by Civil War cavalrymen. Troopers liked to jump their mounts over ditches and fences, often raced them when given the opportunity, and certainly spent more time in the saddle than even the most dedicated horseman or woman of today. While osteoarchaeology and magnetic resonance were things of the future, evidence emerging from the Civil War assure us that troopers were not immune to the skeletal problems or the horse-related accidents common to modern horse culture.

When the Mason family of Pulaski, Tennessee, authorized the exhumation of a grave in their family cemetery, purportedly that of Pvt. Isaac Newton Mason of the 1st Tennessee Cavalry (CS), osteoarchaeologist Douglas Owsley and his team thoroughly examined the contents of the iron casket that was dug up. They could prove that the remains belonged to a cavalryman between thirty-three and thirty-seven years old who was five feet ten inches tall and had brown hair. Several telltale conditions of his skeletal structure clued in the researchers to his life-long riding. One of these related to his gluteus muscle attachment sites. "The gluteus maximus extends the hip in order to keep the individual upright in unstable conditions, such as horseback riding." If an individual is a habitual rider from early in life, the riding habit influences how the muscle is attached to the skeletal structure.[35]

Osteoarchaeological analysis of the remains of eight men recovered from the Little Bighorn battlefield in 1991 provides further reference points for understanding the effect of long rides on cavalrymen during the Civil War. A good many stresses were evident in the skeletal structure, beginning with invertebral disk degeneration mostly located "in the mid-to lower back." This degeneration led to severe lower back pain. Some of the individuals had evidence of osteoarthritis in the base of the skull, "perhaps from head bobbing and shaking during horse riding." Osteoarchaeologists consider Schmorl nodes to be the most reliable indication of habitual riding. They are "small depressions in the vertebral bodies indicating disk problems, which are frequent among the skeletons of the Little Bighorn." Repeated squatting led to hyperflexion of the hips and ankles, resulting in alterations of the skeletal structure for some of the individuals. The examiners speculated that they may have had a habit of riding with their toes "high in the stirrups and the heels low" or of "hunching beside campfires and many other, even less dignified activities."[36]

In addition to the reins and verbal coaxing, cavalrymen used their legs to control their mounts. Hip and thigh adductors are the muscles used to do this. They "squeeze the rider's thighs and knees against the animal's back." While only two of the eight individuals found on the Little Bighorn battlefield showed exaggerated development of the thigh adductors, the examiners assumed that such overdevelopment must have been more widespread than this small sample would indicate. That may well be true, but the evidence from these eight individuals also indicates that the skeletal alterations that arise from habitual horseback riding are not uniform for all riders. Some of the conditions seem to rely heavily on whether an individual rides properly or improperly, as in the hyperflexion of hips and ankles, while others such as degenerative disk effects seem to be universal.[37]

In addition to the osteoarchaeological evidence from these eight unidentified casualties of the battle at Little Bighorn, medical records of the 7th U.S. Cavalry reveal that forty-four horse-related injuries were treated by the surgeon of that regiment from 1866 to June 25, 1876. Of that number thirty-three were contusions resulting "from kicks and falls," seven were sprains, three were fractures, one was a laceration, and one was a dislocation of the thumb. In other words, post–Civil War troopers found their horses just as dangerous to work with as did their predecessors in blue or gray.[38]

On the Battlefield

"Whoever heard of a dead cavalryman?" was a famous saying of the Civil War. It carried the smell of interservice rivalry, as infantrymen and artillerymen denigrated the fighting ability of horsemen. But it was a foolish phrase because cavalry actually did more service in the field than either infantry or artillery, even though their combat-loss ratio was lighter than that of the other two arms. Maj. Gen. Joseph Hooker was generally credited (or discredited) as the originator of that question. James H. Kidd of the 6th Michigan Cavalry called it "so pointless a saying, devoid alike of sense and of wit."[39]

Many troopers were aware that they suffered fewer casualties than their comrades in the other two services. "Although we are kept very busy and fight every day we don't get many hurt," reported Harden Perkins Cochrane of the 2nd Alabama Cavalry. In part this was because the horse often took bullets that might otherwise have hit the trooper. This happened to William L. Wilson of the 12th Virginia Cavalry, who lost several horses. "I ought to be thankful that the bullets which [hit] them do not strike me," he told his mother and aunt. Horses of unusual colors tended to draw special fire from the enemy. George Knox Miller of the 8th Confederate Cavalry believed that white horses were at least four times more likely to be targeted than those of any other color, although his own light-gray mount also "attracted the aim" of Federal soldiers.[40]

Cavalrymen were more visible targets when they rode horses as opposed to fighting on foot. As a result it was not unusual for them to literally die in the saddle. Sgt. Frederick Herring of the Anderson Troop (later redesignated as the 15th Pennsylvania Cavalry) was shot through the head at Stones River. "He lingered in the saddle a moment," recalled John G. Marshall, who rode next to him," then fell with a thud to the ground, and his blood saturated my shoulder." In some cases the body of a slain trooper was transported on his own horse by laying it across the saddle, the head on one side and the legs on the other.[41]

The high level of mobility that characterized cavalry operations created special problems for the care of wounded troopers. Sheridan reported the results during his first raid in Virginia. His formation lost 250 men wounded and had to leave 30 of them behind in various farmhouses. During the raid that resulted in the Battle of Trevilian Station, his command lost 160 wounded on June 11, and the surgeons were able to take along all but 36 of them. The next day Sheridan's command lost 366 wounded, leaving 94 behind. On both days one or two surgeons, several attendants, food, and medical supplies were left behind along with the men. The rest of the injured were transported in ambulances, empty ammunition wagons, and civilian buggies and carts.[42]

Once engaged in combat, horses allowed troopers to quickly flee if they chose to do so. "A demoralized cavalryman is far more unmanageable than an infantryman in the same situation," concluded Chaplain Humphreys, "for himself and his horse are both bent on flying, and the rider easily satisfies his conscience by shifting the responsibility of retreat on his unmanageable steed."[43]

The often-shrill tone of inspirational orders issued by mounted commanders stemmed from the easy ability to flee the battlefield. "Cavalry knows no dangers, knows no failures," read a typical order; "what is ordered to do it must do." Any mounted unit failing in a charge "will be disgraced." Orders such as these, which mixed inspiration with threat, had little effect because mounted combat had a life of its own. "There occurred one of those unfortunate stampedes which are always inexplicable," admitted Confederate William P. Roberts of a fight at Hanover Court House in May 1864. "The best officers and men seemed to be demoralized. Everything was in a perfect rout, myself with the rest." One company of the 7th Tennessee Cavalry (CS) bolted in a fight during September 1862. "The demoralization was imparted from man to man and the scare from horse to horse till it became a rout," observed John Milton Hubbard.[44]

Night fighting, which occurred more often with the cavalry than with the infantry and artillery, greatly challenged the stamina of the trooper. "It required more nerve for a night fight than for a daylight encounter," wrote Lt. John M. Porter of the 9th Kentucky Cavalry (CS). Darkness enclosed the trooper, hid from him the nearness of danger, and prevented him from taking advantage of the terrain. And yet there were some instances where men rose to the challenge. A battalion of the 1st Maryland Cavalry (U.S.) was surprised by John S. Mosby's partisans, who attacked their bivouac without warning. Even though awakened from a deep sleep, the Unionists grabbed their weapons and fought back. "Every man was for himself," wrote C. Armour Newcomer, although they yelled out to each other to kill Mosby's horses to disable their enemy. The Marylanders repelled the attack despite their many disadvantages.[45]

Cavalrymen and Plunder

"The peculiar character of the cavalry service affords facilities and temptations greater than in the other arms of the service," wrote August V. Kautz. He meant that horses allowed the men to wander about the countryside and pillage from citizens. To be sure, pillaging was endemic among infantrymen and artillerymen, but those servicemen had to search for food on foot. Also, because they often were posted in isolated positions, cavalrymen were less subject to the control of officers.[46]

All cavalry commanders made efforts to curb this tendency among their men, with limited effect. On June 8, 1864, Maj. Gen. William H. Jackson reminded the troopers of his division that the Confederate Congress had allowed company and regimental commanders to transfer "lawless and refractory cavalry soldiers" to infantry service. By June 28, he issued another order complaining of "the extensive depredations that are being daily practiced on the farming interest of the surrounding country." Officers were the key to doing something about it. "Before leaving an encampment, Brig Commanders will see that all damages are promptly settled & charged to the guilty parties." After he assumed command of the Military Division of the West in the fall of 1864, Gen. P. G. T. Beauregard issued a general order expressing pain at the number of cavalrymen absent from their units who pillaged civilians. All troopers caught from their units without authority were to be arrested and sent to depots, their horses to be confiscated for the use of the government. Even stringent measures such as these failed to stop plundering.[47]

Commanding Cavalry

Whenever trouble with managing the rank and file cropped up, commanders always looked to their subordinate officers as the key to dealing with it. The officer was the foundation of unit effectiveness. He could set an example of personal attention to duty or show his men that he did not care for military detail, and most of his subordinates would take their cue from his attitude. Many officers were not up to the challenges of small-unit command, while others became superb at it.

What was needed for a good cavalry officer? In answering that question many observers have focused on the officers' role as a combat leader. "With the cavalry officer," wrote Louis E. Nolan of the British Army, "almost everything depends on the clearness of his *coup-d'oeil*, and the felicity with which he seizes the happy moment of action, and, when once action is determined upon, the rapidity with which his intentions are carried into effect. There is little time for thought, *none* for hesitation." By coup-d'oeil, Nolan refers to the ability to size up troop positions as they relate to the topography of the battlefield. This had to be almost instantaneous. Nolan praised the "inspiration of genius" rather than "the result of calculation and rule" as the key to a good cavalry officer. James H. Kidd, who commanded a company, a regiment, and a brigade during the Civil War, also focused on combat leadership. The mounted officer needed "great personal daring and the rare ability to handle men in action, keeping them well together so as to support each other and accomplish results." In mounted service "all officers had to act for themselves and on their own responsibility," wrote Capt. Charles Francis Adams Jr. "We were always in the face of the enemy and generally in small force."[48]

Col. Robert Williams described a man capable of handling himself in such situations to Gov. John Andrew after he took charge of the 1st Massachusetts Cavalry. "A man of comparatively light, active figure, of quick, active intellect, and, in addition, capable of leading his men, if necessary, into the most desperate encounters with coolness, but at the same time with the greatest rapidity. He should be the first in every charge, the last in every retreat; and, above all, should admit nothing, in the power of man and horse to accomplish, as impossible." A graduate of and later a cavalry instructor at the U.S. Military Academy, Williams, as he told the governor, had "made cavalry and its duties the study of my life."[49]

Federal commentators also were swayed by the personal touches, the urbanity, and the geniality of their commanders. James Albert Clark of the 17th Pennsylvania Cavalry thought John Buford "was really and truly the terrific cavalryman of our war history" because he was an "old school gentleman." Clark also thought well of Theophilus F. Rodenbough, "a right down royally good cavalryman, yet as graceful and accomplished . . . and as genial in greeting on all times and occasions as if a comrade with his playfellows. How we provincial youngsters from the country aped those cosmopolitan, well-bred men." Looking back from the perspective of postwar years, he thought the example of officers like Buford and Rodenbough "was the making of us in our department in after life."[50]

Regimental commanders especially impressed their men. "The conduct of a colonel stamps itself on the character of a regiment," concluded Francis Colburn Adams of the 1st New York Cavalry. "You cannot have good men, unless a colonel shows by his character that he is fit to properly shape their conduct while in an enemy's country." Capt. William H. Powell of the 2nd Loyal Virginia Cavalry asserted that "an army of soldiers are but a photographic, or characteristic, fac-simile [*sic*] of its commanders."[51]

Confederate commentators agreed that personality and character counted a great deal in a good cavalry officer. Pvt. Harry S. Dixon effused in his description of Frank Armstrong, a West Pointer who commanded the brigade to which his 28th Mississippi Cavalry belonged. "He showed himself to be second to no cavalry officer in the West, and won the blind devotion of his men. One of the finest specimens of the physical man, he had a sort of brusque, half-savage air which, coupled with his dash and daring and undoubted capacity, endeared him to his men. They soon dubbed him 'Old Strong-Arm.'" Sidney S. Champion, an officer in the same regiment, agreed with Dixon's judgment of Armstrong and contrasted it with the division commander, William H. Jackson. He was "an old Granny, hence have no use for him, however is not much in the way of Armstrong, or any one else."[52]

Most troopers wanted officers with dash, courage, daring, and even recklessness. "Here goes for hell or promotion" was the favorite motto of Confederate brigade commander Pierce M. B. Young when going into action.[53] The men ignored everything else that made for an effective commander, such as attention to paperwork, making sure supplies were brought forward, and rewarding good deeds and punishing bad ones. Ability to command in battle, for most cavalrymen, was the only important job description.

13

FROM DISPERSION TO CONCENTRATION

T he history of Civil War cavalry mimicked that of Civil War field artillery in one important way. During the early part of the conflict, resources in both branches were dispersed, with the assignment of individual mounted regiments and artillery batteries to operate with infantry brigades. Much complaint ensued from cavalry and artillery officers who felt that concentrating mounted forces and cannon into larger groupings to be commanded by cavalry and artillery officers was a more effective way to manage them. As time went on, dispersion weakened and concentration became a reality in both branches by about the midpoint of the war.

In the Union army that meant creating brigades, divisions, and eventually corps of mounted units. This was unprecedented in American cavalry history. No such large mounted formations had been created before 1861 and would not be seen after 1865. The Civil War was unique in American history for witnessing something that was common in European warfare. The Confederate army did not go so far as their opponents in this regard. It formed many brigades and divisions of mounted troops but did not match the Federals in the strength and persistency of corps-level cavalry organizations. The corps led by Philip Sheridan and James H. Wilson during the last year of the conflict were the premier examples of large cavalry concentrations in American history.

A debate ensued as to whether dispersion or concentration was the better course to take in cavalry organization. Dispersion was heavily favored by the infantry commanders, who valued having a regiment of troopers attached to every division for picket, outpost, screening, and reconnaissance duties. Concentration was largely favored by mounted officers, who were eager for a chance to prove what large formations of cavalry could do under their own commanders. Concentration greatly aided the mounted commander's desire to strike out on independent operations and fulfilled ambitious cavalry officers' yearning for promotion.

As far as the debate over dispersion and concentration centered on cavalry effectiveness, it really was misguided. There can be no question that cavalry was responsible for many roles in military operations. It was the best branch of the service to perform picket, outpost, screening, and reconnaissance duties because of its high level of mobility. At the same time, there could be no question that, concentrated into divisions and corps under the right leader, it could be quite effective by striking out on its own. In truth, both dispersion and concentration were legitimate ways to organize mounted power as they were for organizing artillery power. The only problem lay in extremes; complete dispersion or complete concentration were bad policies, and neither should have been tolerated. The kind of dispersion practiced in the Union and Confederate armies during the early war months was something close to complete, but the kind of concentration practiced during the latter war months was not extreme. Thus, the last half of the conflict witnessed something like an effective balance between the two methods of organizing cavalry power.

The trend from dispersion toward concentration led to an increase in effectiveness, at least in the Federal cavalry arm. On the Confederate side the trend toward effectiveness was largely cut short by worsening supply problems that severely affected the mounted force in 1863. With diminished numbers of men and horses and growing shortages of provisions and good weapons, Confederate cavalry atrophied during the last half of the war at the same time that it reached its potential as far as concentration was concerned.

Dispersion to Concentration in the East

The Confederate cavalry arm in the eastern theater, which essentially was the mounted units attached to the Army of Northern Virginia, enjoyed its glory time in 1862. Under James E. B. Stuart and organized as a brigade and later into divisions, it startled the North with daring exploits such as riding around the lumbering Army of the Potomac. Stuart also was adept at close cooperation with the army's commander, at screening infantry formations from prying Union cavalry, and at gathering information useful to infantry operations. He was an all-around cavalry commander who was effective at every role mounted forces were called on to perform.[1]

But the apparent superiority of Lee's cavalry over that attached to the Army of the Potomac began to change in 1863. Capt. Rufus Barringer of the 1st North Carolina Cavalry had been wounded in the face at Brandy Station in June 1863 and, when he returned to duty the following October, was surprised at the change in Stuart's command. It had been "so completely reduced & demoralized by the Pa. Campaign, that a general re-organization had taken place." His regiment had only 150 men available for duty, and the brigade it now belonged to could count only 500 troopers. Looking back from a postwar perspective, Col. William A. Morgan of the 1st Virginia Cavalry saw 1863 as a pivotal year in the history of Lee's horsemen. "Our cavalry retrograded, after the depleting campaigns of 1863, our government being too poor to furnish horses or even feed them, and our general quartermasters and commissaries too inefficient, and worthless to sustain them in a proper manner." In May 1864, when the Federal cavalry in Virginia was being armed with the latest breech-loading carbines, many Confederate horsemen made do with captured Union weapons or "miserably made Richmond breaches." Other Rebel cavalrymen "either had muzzle loading Enfield rifles or only their pistols and sabres," reported Robert T. Hubard Jr.[2]

Facing a Union cavalry force surging forward in numbers, morale, weaponry, and large organization at a time of their own steep decline in all of those areas, Lee's cavalrymen faced their greatest struggle during the almost nonstop operations of 1864 and 1865. At times they held their own and at other times inflicted tactical defeats on the Federals. But mostly the Rebel horsemen were worn down, failed to stop the Unionists from inflicting damage on Lee's railroads, or were soundly trounced on the battlefield. By the fall of 1864, Confederate cavalry in the East had so withered as to suffer one of the worst battlefield defeats of any mounted force in the war at the Battle of Tom's Brook on October 9. Ten days later at Cedar Creek, Union mounted formations played a key role in another Confederate defeat. "It is fast becoming equal to that of Europe," wrote Confederate artillery officer Thomas Henry Carter of the Union cavalry at Cedar Creek. "I saw them charge Infantry & break it repeatedly, while ours has dwindled down to a mere handful by straggling & they run at the sound of their horses hooves."[3]

This impressive achievement, to go from almost complete dispersion in 1861 to large concentrations of well-equipped, well-supplied, and well-officered Federal cavalrymen in 1864, was difficult. Resistance to concentration was strong at the top, and it took many months of embarrassing setbacks to change that policy.

Ironically, dispersion was firmly implanted by a man who had once been a captain in the mounted force of the prewar army. George B. McClellan saw the mounted arm only as a source of screening and intelligence for the infantry, calling it "the antennae of the army." When organizing the Army of the Potomac in the fall of 1861, he assigned a cavalry regiment to each division for these purposes. Only gradually did McClellan organize mounted brigades when the number of units justified it, but he limited his chief of cavalry to administrative duties rather than command in the field.[4]

McClellan was not loved by his mounted officers. Wesley Merritt criticized "his ignorance of the proper uses of cavalry." Asa B. Isham thought "he destroyed its efficiency, as an arm of the service by distributing the regiments among the infantry corps, where the dismemberment process was continued further by breaking up the regiments into detachments as escorts for Generals." McClellan partially defended himself by noting in his memoirs that he had only 4,000 cavalrymen during the Peninsula Campaign, "less than one-fourth of what it should have been."[5]

John Pope could not complain about too few cavalrymen during the Second Bull Run Campaign. He reported 5,000 horsemen serving with his Army of Virginia, which totaled 38,000 infantry and artillery troops. But Pope did complain that his troopers were "badly mounted and armed and in poor condition for service." He tried to balance dispersion with concentration, allowing corps leaders to detach troopers as personal escorts or orderlies but intending all spare troopers to mass and report to the chief of cavalry in each corps. Left to their own decision, however, the three corps leaders heavily leaned toward dispersion. Franz Sigel divided his cavalry and sent them to division and brigade leaders to use as they wished. The 1st Maryland Cavalry was "so much scattered it was prevented from accomplishing as much as might have been otherwise," reported Lt. Col. Charles Wetschky.[6]

The Federal cavalry did little better during the Maryland Campaign of September 1862. In fact, when Lincoln tried to push McClellan into a follow-up movement to Lee's defeat at Antietam, the question of cavalry effectiveness was one of the topics that cropped up. "Stuart's cavalry outmarched ours, having certainly done more marked service on the Peninsula and everywhere since," the president told his general. McClellan admitted that on two occasions Stuart outmarched the Federals. Otherwise, he declared, "I am unconscious of a single instance where the rebel cavalry has exhibited any superiority over ours."[7]

McClellan was fooling only himself. Lee maintained a better balance between the needs of dispersion and concentration, viewing them as equally valid ways to organize cavalry rather than the extreme views of his opponent. That was the most fundamental reason for Rebel mounted supremacy in Virginia during 1862, not the supposed superiority of Southern young men in horsemanship.

McClellan's successor, Ambrose E. Burnside, failed to effect any change in this situation, but Joseph Hooker, who replaced Burnside, moved toward a balanced cavalry organization. On February 5, 1863, Hooker created a Cavalry Corps consisting of three divisions and named George Stoneman to command it. Gathering mounted regiments together into divisions within the corps suddenly made everyone realize "what a capital mounted force there was," recalled Lt. Col. Frederick C. Newhall. "Superb regiments seemed to creep out of every defile within the lines of the army." Grouping them allowed for more intensive training on the brigade and division levels. Schools were established for noncommissioned officers to study tactics and recite to the senior captains of each company, and commissioned officers also studied and recited to their majors, who in turn recited to their colonels. No one from corporals to lieutenant colonels were exempt from these schools. Boards of examination also were established to weed out incompetent officers.[8]

A grand review of Stoneman's command held on April 8, 1863, surprised and exhilarated everyone. It was the first time that 11,000 cavalrymen had been grouped into one formation in the history of the Western Hemisphere. "Nobody was more astonished than the troopers themselves when they saw the face of the country swarm with cavalry," wrote Newhall.[9]

Stoneman's review took place three weeks after the first of two pivotal battles in which the Potomac army's cavalry proved its worth. In the first, at Kelly's Ford on March 17, 1863, a division of Union horsemen under William W. Averell attacked a Confederate force that had been harassing Federal units. The engagement witnessed attacks and counterattacks by both sides and was noteworthy for the aggressive, persistent nature of Union action. Although Averell broke contact and retired, the major result of this fight was an upsurge of confidence among his troopers and a grudging admission by his opponents that the Federals had never fought so well. Observers on both sides commented on how well Averell's men had used the saber, driving home mounted charges with spirit and determination. As a captain in the 3rd Pennsylvania Cavalry put it, "the baton of superiority was wrested from the enemy never to be recovered."[10]

The second important battle took place at Brandy Station on June 9. Again the Federals challenged Lee's mounted arm, but the forces were larger, with about 10,000 troopers on each side. Once again a swirling action on open terrain resulted in attacks and counterattacks. And once again the Federals withdrew in the end, although only after the Confederates narrowly averted a tactical disaster. The Union cavalry came off with increased confidence and prestige. Even their opponents admitted it. "They exhibited marked and wonderful improvement in skill, confidence and tenacity," wrote John N. Opie. Many Federals saw Brandy Station as their coming of age, having "whipped them out of their conceit," as one wrote of the Rebel attitude. They believed that their cavalry arm was not only the equal of Lee's but also the equal of any mounted force in Europe.[11]

Brandy Station was followed by an extended series of battles at Aldie on June 17, Middleburg on June 19, and Upperville on June 21. Give and take were the order of each days' fight, with the result that more respect was accorded the Union mounted arm. "I had never known the enemy's cavalry to fight so stubbornly or act so recklessly," wrote James W. Watts of the 2nd Virginia Cavalry about Aldie. The Gettysburg Campaign continued this progression. The big cavalry fight on July 3 duplicated the earlier battles with charge and countercharge, both sides fighting each other to a tactical standstill that benefited the Federals more than the Confederates.[12]

Stoneman had been replaced by Alfred A. Pleasanton as head of the Cavalry Corps, Army of the Potomac after the Battle of Chancellorsville, and thus Pleasanton was at its head during most of the action that did so much to elevate the arm to prominence. He continued to urge more concentration, wanting a force of 15,000 troopers and the opportunity to select more of his high-level officers. Although he did not mention it, there was an important administrative reason for concentration. A cavalry company assigned to an infantry unit had to rely on infantry quartermasters and commissaries for its needs, and the mounted officer often complained that his wants were not properly understood by them. A battalion of the 11th New York Cavalry was detached from its regiment in the summer of 1863. "We shared the fate of all small detachments in the field in not having anyone whose authority could protect our interests," complained Henry Murray Calvert, "and so we roughed it a great deal more than we should have done."[13]

One of the advantages of improving the organization of mounted power in the East was that it could contribute more readily to the operational power of the Army of the Potomac. As historian Ethan S. Rafuse has noted, concentrated cavalry forces were useful elements in creating mobile operations—that is, a war of maneuver rather than positional warfare.[14] With the creation of the Cavalry Corps, the main Union army in the East now was as capable of maneuvering across large swaths of territory as the Army of Northern Virginia had been up to that time.

What the Federal mounted arm had achieved in Virginia by 1863 was at least parity with its principal opponent, but whether that would translate into supremacy was not entirely clear. Union officials could not know how rapidly the Confederate mounted arm was deteriorating, and most of the engagements of 1863 turned out to be tactical draws. Neither Stoneman nor Pleasanton proved to be the right man to lead the Cavalry Corps to further accomplishments, and it was possible the eastern cavalry might have remained at this level for the remainder of the conflict.

Sheridan

This changed when Ulysses S. Grant was elevated to the position of general in chief in early March 1864. In one of his early talks with Lincoln, Grant expressed his view that the Union cavalry arm in the east was capable of accomplishing more than it had thus far in the war—it only needed the right man at the top. Newly appointed chief of staff Henry W. Halleck, the former general in chief, overheard this conversation and recommended Philip H. Sheridan to lead the Potomac army's mounted arm. Grant, who was familiar with Sheridan, agreed to order him from Tennessee, where his infantry division was part of the Army of the Cumberland.[15]

Sheridan, a West Point graduate, had served as a quartermaster under Halleck in the western theater before securing command of the 2nd Michigan Cavalry. His fame started as the result of a fight near Booneville, Mississippi, on July 1, 1862, in which he skillfully maneuvered a small command against a larger Confederate force. That led to promotion and infantry command. Sheridan did well in battles at Perryville, Stones River, and Missionary Ridge.[16]

But the order to take over the cavalry attached to the Army of the Potomac was a complete surprise. It "staggered me at first," Sheridan confided in his memoirs. He knew few officers in that army and was so conscious of the responsibility that it "momentarily upset me." But it did not take long for him to accept the challenge. By the time he was ready to leave in late March 1864, Sheridan had adopted an aggressive attitude toward his new assignment. "Doctor, I'm going to take the cavalry away from the bob-tail brigadier-generals," he told Surgeon John H. Brinton. "They must do without their escorts. I intend to make the cavalry an arm of the service." At his first meeting with Lincoln on April 4, Sheridan found confirmation for his attitude. The president told him that the Army of the Potomac cavalry "had not done all it might have done."[17]

With his job clearly defined, Sheridan found that the mounted force was stressed by excessive outpost and picket duty protecting the infantry camps of the Army of the Potomac. The picket lines were unusually long; David M. Gregg's division covered eighteen miles, while James H. Wilson's division protected a sector that was twenty-eight miles long. Sheridan estimated that, laid out on a straight line, the entire picket line would have been sixty miles long. Many men were dismounted, a total of 754 of 2,692 troopers in Wilson's division alone. Sheridan's solution was to arrange for the infantry to do much of their own picketing, allowing most cavalrymen to rest, feed, and groom their mounts. He also found that the regiments were armed with a variety of weapons. Wilson's division sported four different types of carbines and two different types of pistols. Sheridan tried to streamline the array by obtaining Spencer repeater carbines, the best shoulder arm for cavalry service.[18]

When he had a conference with Army of the Potomac commander George G. Meade, Sheridan first brought up his idea that the Cavalry Corps should be massed to fight Lee's troopers. "My proposition seemed to stagger General Meade not a little. I knew that it would be difficult to overcome the recognized custom" of "wasting cavalry for the protection of trains, and for the establishment of cordons around a sleeping infantry force." For a time, he admitted, Meade "would hardly listen to my proposition, for he was filled with the prejudice that, from the beginning of the war, had pervaded the army regarding the importance and usefulness of cavalry." In addition to the operational argument for massing the troopers into a large striking force, Sheridan pointed out that if he could defeat Lee's troopers in a couple of battles, it would infuse new spirit in the ranks of the Federal horsemen. Meade was not convinced, forcing Sheridan to later admit, "we had to bide our time" before getting approval for the course of action he wished to pursue.[19]

Adding to Meade's hesitance was the fact that Sheridan had never commanded a mounted force above the regimental level, and even that for only a brief time in 1862. Wilson, a new division leader, had had no experience commanding cavalry in the field at all. These two westerners (Wilson had been on Grant's staff for much of the early war period and had briefly served as head of the Cavalry Bureau) also were unknown quantities to the Army of the Potomac. But as Wilson pointed out after the war, his and Sheridan's lack of experience with cavalry probably was an advantage, for neither of them had any prejudices against using horsemen as an independent arm. Both men brought fresh perspectives to the task of managing cavalry formations, Sheridan's to be felt quickly in the East, and Wilson's to be felt later in the West.[20]

Sheridan had to endure a frustrating start of the Overland Campaign. During the Wilderness phase, Meade used his mounted units for close support of infantry formations. For example, the 2nd Ohio Cavalry shifted around so much that it took orders from eight infantry commanders on the brigade, division, and corps levels. Worse, Meade issued orders directly to two of Sheridan's divisions without informing the corps commander, which prevented those two divisions from helping the third division hold Spotsylvania Court House on May 8. Then Meade called Sheridan to his headquarters to complain that the cavalry had gotten in the way of the Fifth Corps march to Spotsylvania. Sheridan exploded. He pointed out that this had been caused by Meade's interference, and both men exchanged angry words, with Sheridan telling his commander that he could whip Stuart if given a chance. Meade told Grant of this conversation and repeated Sheridan's boast about beating Stuart. "'Did he say so?'" Grant asked, according to Sheridan. "'Then let him go out and do it.'" Meade thus was forced to authorize the cavalry to act independently.[21]

When Sheridan told his three division leaders what was going to happen, they were a bit surprised but soon warmed to the idea. "Our move would be a challenge to Stuart for a cavalry duel behind Lee's lines, in his own country," as Sheridan put it. The corps started on May 9, marching along one road past Lee's right flank. Sheridan intended to keep his command well in hand rather than move along widely separated lines of advance because he expected and wanted a confrontation with Stuart. When that confrontation took place near Yellow Tavern on May 11, the Federal horsemen inflicted the worst defeat on Lee's cavalry thus far in the war by breaking the Confederate position and mortally wounding Stuart. Afterward, Sheridan headed straight for Richmond, threatening the Confederate capital. He veered off to the east before hitting the city's defenses and had some difficulty getting back to Union lines, but his first raid had fulfilled his promise to Meade.[22]

Sheridan later interpreted the first raid as primarily important in an emotional sense. It greatly encouraged his men and discouraged his opponents. "We Can whip their Ca'l'y," exulted the surgeon of the 3rd Indiana Cavalry. On the other hand, Confederates viewed the Battle of Yellow Tavern as a major defeat. "Its effect was very bad, demonstrating, as it did, to *the men* that our cavalry with its paucity of arms of improved patterns and half-starved horses couldn't hope to contend successfully with the larger, splendidly mounted and equipped command" of Sheridan.[23]

It would not be easy for the Federal horsemen to maintain their relative position with Lee's mounted arm for the rest of the war. There were victories and defeats for the remainder of the Overland Campaign and into the early phases of the Petersburg Campaign that followed. But the operations of May and June brought the Cavalry Corps to its full potential as a large formation. Sheridan succeeded in proving its ability to strike out on independent campaigns. "If there were any honest doubts as to the efficiency and fighting qualities of the Potomac cavalry," wrote James H. Kidd, "they were dissipated by the campaign of 1864."[24]

In August much of the Cavalry Corps shifted to the lower Shenandoah Valley when Sheridan was elevated to command the newly created Middle Military Division. His job was to deal with Lt. Gen. Jubal A. Early whose Second Corps, Army of Northern Virginia had threatened Washington, DC, in mid-July. This led to a concentration of Union power in the lower valley that included two divisions and a brigade of mounted troops from Meade's army plus the equivalent of another division of cavalry from the Department of West Virginia. With added infantry forces from three departments, Sheridan assembled the Army of the Shenandoah and placed Alfred T. A. Torbert in charge of the mounted arm. His seven mounted brigades matched the same number of cavalry brigades in Early's command, but Sheridan used his cavalry effectively both in independent action and in close cooperation with his infantry.[25]

The first major battle, outside Winchester on September 19, occurred on a largely open and level battleground "such as all good cavalry officers long to engage in," thought Wesley Merritt. Sheridan massed his horsemen for attacks on weakening Confederate positions to win a smashing victory. "It was the first time that proper use of this arm had been made in a great battle during the war," commented Kidd. Sheridan "was the only general of that war who knew how to make cavalry and infantry supplement each other in battle." Early admitted that the Union mounted arm was better than his own. "The enemy's great superiority in cavalry and the comparative inefficiency of ours turned the scale against us."[26]

Another victory occurred at Fisher's Hill on September 22, with a further retreat up the valley by the Confederates. Federal strategic needs did not require Sheridan to follow too far, so his army turned and fell back a short distance, harassed by a division of Early's cavalry. Frustrated by this, Sheridan ordered Torbert to ride out and chastise the Rebels. As Benjamin W. Crowninshield recalled the order, it was given early on the morning of October 9, when Torbert met Sheridan over a log fire at their bivouac site. After saying "Good morning, general," Torbert received his orders. "General Torbert, get upon your horse, and don't let me see you again until either you have beaten the rebel cavalry, or they have beaten you!" The chastened general said nothing and left to organize a strike that resulted in the worst defeat of Lee's cavalry in the war at Tom's Brook. In a two-hour fight the Federals crushed the Confederate position and captured eleven pieces of artillery as well as the entire wagon train. "There could hardly have been a more complete victory and rout," Torbert reported with a sigh of relief.[27]

Early's entire command struck back by attacking the Federals in their camps at Cedar Creek on October 19, when Sheridan was attending conferences at Washington, DC. The Confederates drove Union forces back but then stalled. As the Federals regrouped a short distance away, Sheridan arrived and infused new energy and direction into operations. Once everything was in order, he moved both infantry and cavalry in close coordination to inflict a battlefield disaster on the Confederates. "I found it impossible to rally the troops," Early reported. "They would not listen to entreaties, threats or appeals of any kind. A terror of the enemy's cavalry had seized them and there was no holding them. They fled in the greatest confusion."[28]

In addition to close cooperation on the battlefield, Torbert's men kept busy with outpost, picket, and reconnaissance work and were the main agents in the destruction of resources in the Shenandoah ordered by Grant. The purpose was to create a zone denuded of the food and fodder necessary to sustain Confederate forces in the valley. In addition, the cavalry was the main force used to combat the growing guerrilla problem.

While not all irregular fighters used horses, the most effective of them were mounted. The only real chance of countering a mounted irregular force was by the use of cavalry.[29]

By early 1865, replacing mounts had become a serious problem. Quartermaster General Montgomery C. Meigs complained that he had to replace three-fourths of Sheridan's cavalry horses every three months. That amounted to 8,265 new mounts sent to his army from December 1, 1864, to February 20, 1865, creating "a most serious expense." Torbert declared on March 2 that preserving their horses should be the first priority of subordinate commanders. The key was in finding enough fodder for them, providing proper grooming and rest, and preventing the men from abusing their animals by fast riding. "The strength of the horses . . . must be husbanded," Torbert declared.[30]

By this time, most of Early's command had rejoined the Army of Northern Virginia and only a scratch force stood in Sheridan's path at Waynesboro as the Federals started to move back to the Army of the Potomac. Union horsemen conducted a mounted charge there, riding over their opponents and field fortifications alike. After joining Grant's concentration at Petersburg, Sheridan was given the major role of conducting operations with joint mounted and infantry forces in the final effort to turn Lee's right flank in the long fortified line that had shielded the city and Richmond for months. At the Battle of Five Forks, on April 1, another mounted charge broke open a fortified Confederate position. Afterward the cavalry played a key role in heading off Lee's retreat westward from Petersburg and compelling the surrender of the Army of Northern Virginia at Appomattox on April 9.[31]

The Union cavalry arm in the eastern theater achieved the most impressive display of operational and tactical effectiveness of any mounted formation in American history. From being a derided and dispersed force from 1861 to 1863, it reached a stage of improvement and equilibrium with its Confederate opponent by the midpoint of the war and then far exceeded that opponent during 1864–65. The Federal cavalry excelled at all functions of the mounted arm, from outpost duty to mounted charges against enemy infantry, and in close cooperation with friendly foot soldiers. Part of the reason for this lay in the resources of men, arms, equipment, and horses more readily available to the Federals, but those advantages had been available ever since the start of the war. It was the selection of the right man to lead the concentrated force that was the key ingredient, as well as the selection of effective division and brigade leaders under him, that advanced the Union horsemen of the East to the next level of effectiveness.

Sheridan was not an easy officer to work with, as many men could testify. He was demanding, even threatening, in his insistence on a high level of performance. While most historians praise him, Eric Wittenberg, the prominent cavalry scholar, is highly critical of the general as a glory hog protected by Grant's patronage. Nevertheless, Sheridan's influence on success during the last year of the war is undeniable. According to Isaac Gause, Sheridan told a group of officers from the 2nd Ohio Cavalry in the winter of 1863–64 that he believed cavalry could become "an independent command" and operate against the enemy without being tied to infantry formations. "I was prepared to do something effective" upon arriving in Virginia, as the general told an interviewer from the *National Tribune* years after the war. Secretary of War Stanton praised Sheridan when he told him, "your cavalry has become the efficient arm in this war that it has proved in other countries."[32]

From Dispersion to Concentration in the West

In the western theater, mounted forces also went from dispersion to concentration but at a slower and less certain pace. The much larger geographic extent of the region inhibited concentration and placed a higher premium on parceling out mounted units to infantry formations between the Appalachian Highlands and the Mississippi River. In the Trans-Mississippi a combination of geography, sparse population density (which made living off the countryside more difficult than usual), and the widespread nature of infantry deployment further inhibited concentration. No cavalry corps appeared in the Trans-Mississippi. East of the Mississippi River, the Confederates experimented with cavalry corps with little success, while the Federals organized one only late in the war.

Both Union and Confederate cavalry assets were dispersed during 1861 and 1862, rarely rising to the existence of divisions. One of the rare examples of using mounted forces in close cooperation with infantry in the West occurred at Stones River on December 31, 1862. Braxton Bragg's Army of Tennessee had a cavalry division of four brigades led by Joseph Wheeler. Bragg effectively used the two strongest brigades for close support of his operations, sending one of them under Wheeler to ride around the Union army, destroying hundreds of wagons and severely stressing Union logistics. Another brigade led by John A. Wharton rode with the left flank of Bragg's infantry as his left wing advanced early on the morning of December 31, driving the Union right wing in bloody fighting for three miles. Wharton captured many Federal infantrymen after their formations had been broken up. The Federals had only two mounted brigades, which barely managed to counter some of Wharton's and Wheeler's actions.[33]

At the same time that the Stones River Campaign played out in Middle Tennessee, Grant was conducting a drive south through northern Mississippi. That offensive came to a halt when a brigade of Confederate horsemen under Earl Van Dorn rode around his left flank and destroyed the major Union supply depot at Holly Springs on December 20. This strike, coupled with an even more destructive raid by Nathan Bedford Forrest on long stretches of railroad line in western Tennessee, compelled the Federals to cancel their overland drive toward Vicksburg. This was one of the few clear successes of a mounted force playing a decisive role in changing the opponent's campaign. On January 13, 1863, Van Dorn took command of all Confederate cavalry in the Department of Mississippi and Eastern Louisiana, and soon afterward Joseph E. Johnston pushed through a plan to combine Van Dorn's horsemen with the cavalry in Bragg's Department of Tennessee. On January 19 the Adjutant and Inspector General's Office in Richmond also tried to limit the dispersion of cavalry strength. It mandated that mounted regiments were to be kept intact and that courier service should be performed by detailed infantrymen who could obtain a horse.[34]

But the concentration of Confederate cavalry in the West led to some weaknesses while failing to provide much in the way of benefits. The shifting of Van Dorn's corps to Middle Tennessee in the spring of 1863 denuded the Department of Mississippi and Eastern Louisiana of mounted assets. Van Dorn was killed in April by a civilian over a personal issue, and command was then divided between Wheeler and Forrest, each of whom led a small corps consisting of four brigades grouped into two divisions. For the Chickamauga Campaign, William S. Rosecrans also organized his cavalry into a corps, but it consisted of two divisions with a total of five brigades. These were weak corps at best, and at least on the Confederate side, the limited concentration failed to pay dividends. Despite their experience and undeniable skills, both Forrest and Wheeler made many mistakes during the campaign that contributed to the Confederate loss of Chattanooga.[35]

Federal commanders in the West also dispersed their mounted arm during the first half of the war. The 7th Pennsylvania Cavalry, for example, had one of its three battalions assigned to infantry formations at each of Columbia, Kentucky; Nashville; and Murfreesboro, Tennessee. The morale of troopers serving in dispersed units suffered. Grenville M. Dodge complained that Union cavalrymen "sometimes act timidly and run at the sight of a horseman, without stopping to see what there is."[36]

Rosecrans tried to improve this situation by creating a larger and separately organized cavalry force for the Army of the Cumberland. Soon after assuming command, he brought in David S. Stanley to take charge of his mounted arm. "The cavalry had been badly neglected," reflected Stanley, an old trooper in the prewar army. "It was weak, undisciplined, and scattered around, a regiment to a division of infantry. To break up this foolish disposal of cavalry, and to form brigades and eventually divisions, was my first and difficult work." Rosecrans supported him when infantry commanders protested the loss of their mounted units.[37]

The Stones River Campaign demonstrated that he needed more cavalrymen, Rosecrans argued, but the Union force structure in the West could not provide them. He then tried to increase his mounted power by putting foot soldiers on horses, but Washington disapproved his plan to mount 8,000 infantrymen. It did authorize him to mount a brigade commanded by John T. Wilder and arm the men with the latest breechloaders. This was accomplished by scouring Middle Tennessee for horses. "We paid no attention to age, color, size, sex, or previous condition of servitude," wrote George W. Wilson of the 17th Indiana. "Whenever we found an animal, hornless and with deck-room for a saddle, we took it."[38]

In May Rosecrans engaged in a spirited debate with Quartermaster General Meigs because his vision of mounted power knew no bounds. He argued that with 20,000 cavalrymen, he could achieve wonders, but Meigs pointed out the near impossibility of mounting, equipping, and feeding such a host. "I doubt the wisdom of building up such masses, which crumble under their own weight," he counseled Rosecrans. "Rely more upon infantry and less upon cavalry, which in this whole war has not decided the fate of a single battle rising above a skirmish, which taxes the resources of the country and of which we have now afoot a larger animal strength than any nation on earth. We have over one hundred and twenty-six regiments of cavalry, and they have killed ten times as many horses for us as for the rebels."[39]

Rosecrans was driven by his knowledge that Bragg's Army of Tennessee fielded a larger and more effective cavalry force than his own. Only by making a pest of himself with the Washington authorities could he hope to build up the Cumberland army's mounted assets. Yet the debate between Rosecrans and Meigs illustrated an important point. No doubt that large formations, if handled effectively, could make a difference, but those large formations demanded a very high level of logistical support.[40]

The other major Union formation in the West, the Army of the Tennessee, never advanced as far as Rosecrans's in terms of its mounted assets during the first half of the war. Dispersal was the order of the day, with only small concentrations amounting to brigades by late 1862. Even so, the readiness of those mounted units was not high in the eyes of James H. Wilson. At this time a lieutenant serving on Grant's staff, he found the cavalry to be "green and badly organized." The men "were excellent material, but all untrained and badly deficient in discipline. In the advance they did well, but in the retreat they were entirely unmanageable. . . . [T]he entire organization was lacking in coherence, coöperation, and steadiness."[41]

William T. Sherman developed a negative view of the horse soldiers operating with the Army of the Tennessee. The Confederates' "cavalry is so much better than ours, that in all quick movements they have a decided advantage." His assistant adjutant general, John Henry Hammond, echoed Sherman's view when criticizing the action of mounted units during the Jackson Campaign of July 1863. On one occasion the cavalry "showed the most ridiculous cowardice (as they always do)." He allowed that the troopers were good, but the officers were "the damndest [sic] cowards alive."[42]

The largest concentration of mounted troops thus far in the West took place during the four-month-long campaign for Atlanta. Sherman's army group fielded an awkward mounted organization. Most of it belonged to the Army of the Cumberland, which was primarily responsible for this territory. Its Cavalry Corps fielded three divisions with a total of nine brigades. The Army of the Tennessee, which had been transferred from its home department along the Mississippi River, had no organic mounted units. George H. Thomas loaned it one of his Cumberland cavalry divisions for much of the campaign. The Army of the Ohio, which also was transferred from its home department in Tennessee and Kentucky, had brought along one division of three brigades (with a small reserve brigade attached). Unevenly distributed among the three infantry armies and lacking a unified command structure, Sherman's mounted arm typically failed whenever it launched efforts to disrupt enemy supply lines. The disastrous raids of late July, which largely wrecked his cavalry arm, were stunning indications that Sherman had a right to expect more of his mounted force than it achieved.[43]

In contrast, the Confederate cavalry was more effectively organized and often performed better than the Federal arm during the Atlanta Campaign. The Army of Tennessee's Cavalry Corps consisted of three divisions with a total of eight brigades, which supported the army's two infantry corps. The equivalent of a third infantry corps, consisting of troops from the Department of Mississippi and Eastern Louisiana and called the Army of Mississippi, joined the Army of Tennessee in mid-May. It brought along one cavalry division of three brigades that cooperated with Joseph Wheeler's Army of Tennessee troopers. The Army of Mississippi was incorporated into the Army of Tennessee structure as a corps in late July, upon which its cavalry division was placed under Wheeler's command. Unity of command, pretty consistent cooperation with the infantry formations, and aggressive responses whenever Union cavalry threatened railroad communications were the keys to a higher level of effectiveness delivered by western Rebel cavalrymen in the summer of 1864.[44]

Sherman had definite ideas about how to use his mounted power during the Atlanta Campaign. "Cavalry is most effective when appearing suddenly on the flank or rear of the enemy, as it usually is the advance of a column of infantry, . . . but if it hesitates in acting the effect is lost." He despaired, however, of fielding a large force. The general had 52,000 cavalrymen on the rolls in the Military Division of the Mississippi but could commit no more than three divisions of 5,000 men each to the campaign, having to disperse mounted forces across his command for rear-area defense.[45]

The problem was not really numbers, it was the lack of a unified command and the absence of an aggressive spirit at the top. Grant recognized this and told Sherman that he wanted to send someone "whose judgment and dash could both be relied on." The general in chief relieved Wilson from command of the Third Division in Sheridan's corps on October 1. Wilson stopped at Washington three days later and wrote Grant about his plans for the western cavalry. "I am confident a corps organization will be extremely beneficial—in fact, nearly indispensable to efficiency."[46]

When Wilson joined Sherman at Gaylesville, Alabama, on October 23, the latter was chasing John Bell Hood's Army of Tennessee through northern Georgia to protect his rail link with Chattanooga. The next day Sherman issued an order announcing Wilson as chief of cavalry, Military Division of the Mississippi. He also abolished the position of chief of cavalry in the three departments that made up his military division. "Wilson will reorganize the forces under his command and will bring into the field the greatest number of mounted troops possible," read the order. What Sherman hoped for was a mounted force of up to 20,000 men that could penetrate "the richer parts of Alabama and Georgia for the purpose of destroying the railroad communications and supplies of the rebels." In other words, he wanted the cavalry to have a deep influence on the strategic course of the war.[47]

From the beginning, Sherman was unable to give Wilson the time needed to refurbish the cavalry arm. He sent him to Nashville to cooperate with Thomas on organizing forces to defend Middle Tennessee against the expected invasion by Hood's army. This meant that Wilson had to work with whatever was available after Sherman detached from his command Judson Kilpatrick's division for his march from Atlanta into the heart of the Confederacy.[48]

Wilson found the cavalry arm depleted and in need of replacement mounts and better weapons. Nearly 10,000 troopers in the seven mounted divisions of the Military Division of the Mississippi had been dismounted by late October due to horse shortages. In addition to finding horses, Wilson wanted to streamline the varied types of firearms the troopers used. For this, he sought 10,000 Spencer carbines along with 10,000 sabers.[49]

Wilson fully adopted Sheridan's perspective. He criticized the previous tendency to disperse mounted power. The military division's horsemen needed unitary organization and intense training. "Cavalry is useless for defense," he exaggerated in writing to John A. Rawlins, Grant's chief of staff. "It's only power is in a vigorous offensive. Therefore I urge its *concentration* south of the Tennessee and hurling it into the bowels of the South, in masses that the enemy can't drive back."[50]

Dissatisfied with the mounted commanders in the West, Wilson also told Rawlins of "the absolute necessity of my having good officers." He arranged to have Joseph Knipe, Washington Elliott, and Kenner Garrard transferred to infantry commands "for which they are better suited." He looked to the Army of the Potomac for fresh faces. Wilson asked for George Custer, Marcus Reno, and Alexander C. M. Pennington Jr. but managed only to obtain Emory Upton, who moved from an infantry brigade command in the East to lead one of the western cavalry divisions by early 1865. Wilson reorganized his divisions so that most of them had two brigades each.[51]

It proved impossible to complete the preparation of a concentrated mounted force before Hood's invasion of Middle Tennessee. Reaching Nashville on November 6, Wilson took 4,500 troopers to join John M. Schofield's two infantry corps at Pulaski, Tennessee, by November 23. Only days later Hood crossed into the state. Wilson cooperated with Schofield in the retreat to Nashville, although his men played no role in the battle at Franklin on November 30.[52]

In the Battle of Nashville on December 15–16, Thomas planned to use the Federal mounted force in close cooperation with his infantry, and Wilson's men turned in the best example of this kind of cavalry work ever performed by the Union horsemen in the West. Pushing aggressively against Hood's left flank, many of his troopers fought dismounted on the first day. They contributed more on the second day, overrunning Confederate earthworks and helping break Hood's position. Then Wilson led the Union pursuit of the Rebels into northern Alabama, but bad weather and shortages of fodder hampered the effort.[53]

Wilson reported that his nascent cavalry corps had captured thirty-two guns, eleven caissons, twelve flags, and 3,232 prisoners at Nashville and during the pursuit. The proper use of large cavalry concentrations, he declared, "is now well understood, while the necessity for its complete organization in masses is becoming, as the war progresses, a matter of the first importance."[54]

In late December Wilson laid plans to concentrate and rejuvenate the military division's cavalry power. He sent entire brigades to Louisville for remounting, rearming, and reequipping. Wilson also tried to rehabilitate jaded horses, correctly believing that older, experienced mounts were more reliable than fresh and inexperienced animals. To that end he established corrals where 7,500 horses could recuperate during the winter months. The general also received permission to base his concentration in northwestern Alabama, at Gravelly Springs, to be closer to Deep South targets.[55]

Wilson began with only 5,831 men but promised Thomas that he could field 25,000 by the spring if enough horses and weapons for them could be found. He continued to oppose "the reckless and ill-advised system of scattering the cavalry of this military division in small squads over the country" because it had "been productive of more harm than good." The only way to win the war was "to excel the rebels in the power of offense and in the capacity to use this power."[56]

Wilson appointed Capt. John Green as a special inspector of cavalry for the military division, charging him with managing the evaluation of existing mounts and hurrying the acquisition of new ones. The general also issued new orders for the careful feeding of animals and charged all officers with devoting personal attention to horse care. Wilson stripped serviceable horses from some units performing occupation duties and gave them to units he intended to use in the planned offensive.[57]

The large concentration of troopers at Gravelly Springs underwent "a thorough system of instruction" that winter. Men had grown rusty or were stuck in their ways, and Wilson also wanted to revert to the two-rank formation, deviating from Cooke's official manual that emphasized one rank.

He ordered all units to begin with the school of the trooper dismounted to learn the two-rank system. Wilson never really explained why he thought two ranks were better than one, but the change was criticized by his men. "Have had three years practice in cavalry service," complained brigade leader Robert H. G. Minty to his diary, and "have now to try *theory*."[58]

Wilson's push for more Spencer carbines bore fruit with a shipment of 1,200 arriving in mid-January 1865, but subsequent issues appeared more slowly. Unlike his views on the two-rank system, the general explained why he preferred Spencer carbines. He thought no other weapon could compete "for economy of ammunition and maximum effect, physical and moral." Subordinates told him one man with a Spencer was equal to three with any other weapon. He saw that using the carbine had inspired confidence during the Tennessee campaign, and now every regiment in his command was requesting it. Wilson asked for 10,000–15,000 Spencers "as soon as possible."[59]

A number of items relating to horse equipment flowed into the camps at Gravelly Springs. They began with 2,000 horseshoes in early January and moved into several items designed to stabilize the saddle on the horse's back. After months of observation Wilson noticed that most troopers misused the surcingle, a strap designed to wrap around the girth of the horse to keep the saddle in place. Not more than one out of ten men tied it that way, while the rest wrapped it around the breast of their horses. All troopers were issued cruppers, a loop designed to wrap around the tight bundle of the tail just as it emerges from the horse's body to keep the saddle from slipping forward. But Wilson suggested that the crupper be abandoned and a breast collar be substituted for the surcingle. This collar was a more complicated piece of equipment that wrapped around the horse's chest, with another extension that went between its legs designed to keep the saddle from slipping backward. Since few troopers used the surcingle properly and seemed to prefer a breast attachment rather than a tail attachment, this proved to be a logical solution of the problem. Finally, since Wilson anticipated a good deal of dismounted fighting, he wanted something that could secure sabers to the saddle. James E. B. Stuart had developed a simpler way of attaching the weapon to the saber belt for quick and easy access when he had been a lieutenant in the U.S. Army in 1859. This was incorporated into the cavalry equipment system developed by Col. William D. Mann that was widely used by the Federal cavalry during the Civil War. Wilson thought that Stuart's device, along with Mann's system, was the best way for his men to leave their sabers and belts attached to the saddles and requested 20,000 of them for his command.[60]

Supplying a large concentration of cavalry was a relatively new operation in the West. Chief of Staff Halleck scoffed at the idea of moving 20,000 troopers into the Deep South. "Like all extravagant undertakings, its very magnitude will defeat it. The horses will starve, the equipments be lost, and the men left on foot along the road." To avoid such a fate, Wilson hoped to find enough food and fodder along the way, reducing his train to no more than 250 wagons escorted by 1,500 dismounted men from three divisions. He organized a pontoon train of thirty boats escorted by a battalion of mounted troops to accompany his column.[61]

Even before setting out, logistics played a huge role in the preparation phase of Wilson's operation. The Tennessee River valley had been decimated by military operations since early 1862. The only way he could support his training camps at Gravelly Springs was by the constant arrival of river steamers to northwestern Alabama. He knew that during the early part of his strike into the Deep South, his column would traverse mountainous country with little fodder or provisions. But Wilson calculated that only a few days' riding would get him past that sterile zone and into a region of middle Alabama rich with agricultural products. Therefore, he planned to stock his wagon trains with so-called small rations like hardtack, coffee, sugar, and salt. He also could take enough feed for the horses to last the first five days and enough ammunition to provide 90 rounds per man in the wagon train with an additional 100 rounds carried on the trooper. The Federals could rely on scouring the countryside for the bulk of their provisions and horse feed once in the middle part of the state.[62]

Despite his well-formed opinion about concentration, Wilson was compelled to break up some of his command. His troop strength at Gravelly Springs rose to a maximum of 22,000 men by early February, but operational needs in other areas compelled him to divert much of that strength until he had only 12,000 left. That number represented about half of all troopers serving in the Military Division of the Mississippi at this time. When he left Gravelly Springs on March 22, Wilson commanded the largest, best-mounted, best-armed, and best-equipped cavalry concentration of the Civil War.[63]

The Federal column quickly moved through the sterile zone in north Alabama to emerge into the productive central part of the state. The troopers achieved their first victory at Ebenezer Church over Confederate forces commanded by Nathan Bedford Forrest on April 1. Not only did they outnumber them by almost three to one, but Wilson's training and requipping also paid off in a stunning attack that crushed their opponents. "We literally rode over their rail barricades," recalled Charles O. Mitchell.[64]

The Federals arrived at Selma, their first major target, the next day. The town had become the industrial heart of what was left of the Confederacy, producing most of the ordnance supplies and other military materiel, with a strong earthwork system around it. The Federals could not simply ride over these fortifications, for they included a deep ditch and large parapet. Wilson planned an assault spearheaded by a dismounted brigade. When the Federals went in late on April 2, they cracked open the defenses, exploited the breach, and collapsed the entire defensive perimeter of the city. They captured thirty-two guns and 2,700 prisoners. Because he had earlier detached some units to strike other targets in the state, Wilson used 9,000 men to accomplish this. "I regard the capture of Selma the most remarkable achievement in the history of modern cavalry," he proudly reported, "and one admirably illustrative of its new powers and tendencies."[65]

This "decisive fight of the campaign," as division commander Eli Long put it, opened up the entire Deep South to the Federals. They destroyed the productive capacity of the city and constructed a bridge over the Alabama River, crossing to the south side on the night of April 8–9. Wilson's objective now was to move east and wind up in Virginia to help Grant and Sherman deal with Lee's army.[66]

The capture of Montgomery, the state capital, was almost anticlimactic. Confederate forces evacuated the city as the mayor and city council surrendered the place on April 12. Two days later the Federals continued east toward Columbus, Georgia, while detaching a brigade toward the northeast to hit West Point, Georgia, as well. A fight developed at Columbus, which was protected by an earthwork system on the west side of the

Chattahoochee River in Alabama. Once again dismounted Federal cavalry penetrated the Rebel fortifications and sent defending troops retreating in disorder across the bridge on the late evening of April 16. The Federals closely pursued and secured the bridge before it could be set afire, thereby capturing Columbus. They then destroyed enormous amounts of stores and production facilities, including gunboats. Crushing the 3,000 Confederate defenders, Wilson's men captured 1,200 prisoners and fifty-two field guns at a loss of only twenty-four men. They were now 400 miles from their starting point at Gravelly Springs.[67]

In nearly one month Wilson's Cavalry Corps had accomplished the most destructive expedition of the war. Living largely off the countryside, it penetrated Deep South areas previously untouched by Union troops and smashed what was left of the Confederate armaments industry. The regiments moved a total of 500 miles from Gravelly Springs, Alabama, to Macon, Georgia, when measured on a straight line but an estimated 610 miles when factoring in the scouting, foraging, and other side trips. They captured five fortified towns, twenty-three flags, 288 pieces of artillery, and 6,820 prisoners. Wilson compiled a long list of the resources his men destroyed, mostly at Selma and Columbus. This was in addition to many privately owned industrial plants scattered along the line of advance. Just one of the six brigades in Wilson's command destroyed an estimated $11 million worth of property. Moreover, with the war nearing an end, Wilson paroled 59,878 Confederates. He lost only 725 men in the expedition.[68]

Lewis M. Hosea correctly argued that Wilson's Raid, as it generally is termed, was not really a raid. It did not involve mounted troops making a mere dash behind enemy lines and returning after inflicting modest damage. Instead, Wilson conducted "a legitimate military campaign, planned and executed with rare ability, directed against fortified points," and with the intention of staying in the territory it penetrated.[69]

Wilson credited the retraining and refitting at Gravelly Springs for his impressive achievement and bragged that the three divisions were "the model cavalry of the world for discipline, organization, drill and battle." He was not far off the mark. "Our cavalry is cavalry at last," Wilson crowed in dispatches to Sherman. It was "the most coherent organization" of mounted power the war had seen, arguably stronger than Sheridan's Cavalry Corps in the Army of the Potomac. "Without your carte blanch and the admirable assistance of General Thomas," he told Sherman, "nothing could have been accomplished."[70]

The Union cavalry in the West had indeed come a long way from the days of dispersal early in the war to the smashing success of Wilson's campaign through Alabama and Georgia. Expanding our view beyond the confines of the war, Wilson's command was arguably the largest, most powerful concentration of mounted power in the history of the Western Hemisphere and the equal of anything seen in Europe. The Confederates never assembled a cavalry force that could equal Wilson's or Sheridan's, both of which were not only the best examples of large cavalry concentrations in the Americas but the first and the last as well. No subsequent war in American history required large mounted forces. Sheridan and Wilson orchestrated the pinnacle and the swansong of large cavalry power in the New World.

14

WORKING TOWARD EFFECTIVENESS

Many seemingly diverse elements contributed to the level of effectiveness of cavalry units during the Civil War. They ranged from interservice rivalry to the problems associated with mobility, the enormous expense of mounted power, and the thorny problems associated with administering a huge cavalry force to ensure proper supply and transportation. Other elements of this complicated picture included how to resupply ammunition to units heavily engaged in combat and the level of horsemanship achieved by individual troopers. The never-ending work of the cavalry led to exhaustion, draining losses of manpower and horses that could best be detected and remedied by thorough systems of inspections and by the management ability and leadership qualities of officers on all levels of command. Concentration of mounted power, the versatility that enabled troopers to fight mounted or dismounted, and the problem of approaching some degree of combined-arms operations with infantry contributed to the mounted arm's effectiveness in the Civil War.

With a total of 232 cavalry regiments in the Union and 127 in the Confederate armies, the Civil War witnessed the creation of the largest mounted force ever to be assembled in the Americas. On the Federal side only 6 of those regiments were part of the U.S. Army, while the rest had been raised by state governments and constituted a separate force called the Volunteer Army. Only a handful of volunteer regiments were commanded by regular officers. In other words, the majority of all mounted troopers and their officers were new soldiers without prior experience in the military. They had much work to do if they hoped to become good cavalrymen. The same was even more true of the Confederate mounted arm, for none of those units had been part of a regular army.

Much discussion had taken place by 1861 as to how long it took to train a recruit. Moses Harris heard that the time was one year, but Charles Russell Lowell considered four months long enough to impart the basic skills before a regiment was sent into the field. Lowell was astonished at the thought of fielding a cavalry regiment for only nine months of service, which he considered "an injustice to the Government." Still, if it had to be, he thought that two months of training followed by two months of field experience would at least "make a regiment of some account."[1]

Interservice Rivalry

It was common in the Civil War for infantrymen and artillerymen to make fun of their cavalry comrades. From the start to the end of the war, interservice rivalries spurred an unwarranted view that mounted soldiers did little more than ride around the countryside living off the fat of the land, while the foot soldiers and the gunners did the heavy work. Andrew Jackson Neal of the Marion Light Artillery of Florida was amused to "hear the jaunts and sneers of the infantry. Cavalry never has and never will fight and is heartily despised by the men who do the fighting. I had rather run any gauntlet than be a Cavalry man and ride by a brigade or battery."[2]

In part this jibing was due to the peculiar nature of cavalry service. Unlike the infantry and artillery, which operated closely with each other, the cavalry typically operated independently. Benjamin F. Boring of the 30th Illinois wrote that cavalry units usually "passed us on the line of march, splashed mud upon us, and galloped on."[3]

Mobility and Its Problems

But the infantry belief that cavalry's mobility made it unreliable had some validity. "Calvary soldiers was allways on the goe," recalled J. W. Andes of the 4th Tennessee Cavalry (CS), with little regard for spelling. Daniel Harvey Hill reportedly said that "it takes a good man to stand and fight against heavy odds, when he has only two legs under him; but that if you put six legs under him to run away with, it required the best kind of a man to stand and fight." Hill was not far from wrong. Cavalry operations tended to be highly mobile because of the horse. This had a tendency to lessen cavalry losses and to increase the disdain felt by infantrymen and artillerymen who were firmly rooted to one spot in a fight. Braxton Bragg recognized this problem even before the war broke out. He predicted just after the start of the secession crisis that if war developed, most Southern men would opt for cavalry service. "But it is a great error to suppose it adds to their efficiency," he informed an acquaintance. "As a general rule it is only an excuse and a means for running."[4]

An added challenge lay in the deeply rooted problems of logistics and supply in the Confederate army. When the system failed, the cavalry had an advantage over the infantry and artillery with its horsepower. Troopers had greater opportunities to seek food from civilian sources, which often led to a breakdown of discipline. The consequent pillaging grew to epidemic proportions in the latter part of the war. Southern civilians came to fear their own cavalrymen more than Federal soldiers, and even Confederate infantrymen and artillerymen grew to detest their mounted comrades for the suffering they created.

"I detest the sight of mounted men," wrote Benedict Joseph Semmes, an Army of Tennessee commissary officer in January 1863. "They are the worst and most useless soldiers in the Army, and annoy the people almost as much as the yankees." When Albert G. Grammer, a member of Swett's Mississippi Battery, talked with Patrick R. Cleburne about transferring to the cavalry, he got an earful of criticism. "He does not like cavalry," Grammer told his diary, "and says they are a 'nuisance to the country.'"[5]

When Stephen D. Lee took command of the mounted forces in the Confederate Department of Mississippi and Eastern Louisiana, he was appalled at the depredations. "I regret to state that our people at times suffer as much from our own troops, as the Enemy, . . . and it is injuring our Cause seriously." Lee understood that mobility was a part of the problem. "Put a new man on a horse and he has a confused idea of riding over every body & every thing," he told Congressman William Porcher Miles.[6]

Even in the far-better-supplied Union cavalry, riding a horse tended to show off how limited the mounted arm could appear to some observers.

Artillery officer Charles Wainwright criticized the appearance of George Stoneman's cavalry during the review of the new Cavalry Corps, Army of the Potomac in April 1863. "Some of the regiments looked quite well, but many were little better than ridiculous," he wrote. "Our men are far too slouchy, the 'setting up' and bearing of the real soldier showing much more on horseback than on foot."[7]

The Burden of Expense

Another aspect of cavalry service lay in the enormous expense of maintaining a force that inherently tended to be wasteful of resources. Samuel W. Ferguson's mounted brigade was guilty of "shameful waste of ammunition," in the words of its commander, a problem apparent to him ever since the brigade had been organized. He estimated that from October 7, 1863, to April 22, 1864, his men wasted 200,000 rounds of precious ammunition. Previously the excuse had been the shortage of cartridge boxes, but that problem was remedied long before April 22. Ferguson instructed his subordinate officers to hold their men accountable by stopping their pay. He would allow for "the inconveniences of marches and campaigns," but no more than a reasonable percentage of loss should be tolerated.[8]

On the Federal side Henry W. Halleck bemoaned the expense of maintaining a large mounted arm. In 1864 his government had expended $125 million on cavalry alone. That amount included horses, forage, rations, pay, clothing, ordnance, equipment, and transportation costs. It was "certainly a pretty large sum for keeping up our cavalry force for one year," he told Grant. This included purchasing 90,000 sabers, 93,394 carbines, 71,000 pistols, and 180,000 horses issued to mounted units. All this to support a force of 105,434 men present for duty, 160,237 present and absent. These numbers dwarfed any accumulation of cavalry in all previous wars in America.[9]

Cavalry Bureau

The Federal government created a unique bureau to handle management problems associated with cavalry by issuing General Orders No. 236 on

July 28, 1863. The most important task of the Cavalry Bureau was to procure and distribute horses and equipment by directing the work of quartermasters, maintaining an archive of inspection reports and procurement requisitions, and managing the system of horse care. The bureau established new depots for recruits, dismounted men, and sick horses. Neither the infantry nor the artillery had any such organization overseeing management and supply. "The enormous expense attending the maintenance of the cavalry arm points to the necessity of greater care and more judicious management on the part of cavalry officers," stated the general order.[10]

General Orders No. 237, issued the same day as No. 236, specified in more detail the duties of inspectors. Their reports were to indicate not only the condition of horses in the field but also what kind of service the mounts had performed in the past month, the miles they had traveled, the quality and quantity of their feed, and how troopers had treated them. Inspectors had to categorize cavalry horses into four groups: those to be condemned, those in poor shape for cavalry service but suitable for team or draft purposes, those currently unfit but capable of rehabilitation for cavalry use, and those immediately serviceable for mounted duty.[11]

The first head of the Cavalry Bureau, George Stoneman, established it on a firm basis. He selected the site for its flagship depot at Giesboro Point at the confluence of the Eastern Branch of the Potomac River with the main channel in the eastern part of the District of Columbia. Giesboro became a massive depot capable of handling up to 12,000 sick and well horses plus a dismounted camp. Stoneman and his staff of twenty-one officers planned for a large cavalry depot at St. Louis and smaller ones at Louisville and other cities. Quartermasters continued purchases, paying from $120 to $145 per horse, cheaper in the West than in the East. By October 15, 1863, the Cavalry Bureau had already spent $1,400,000 on infrastructure, horse purchases, equine care, and other expenses. But Stoneman pointed out that the value of the 2,500 horses that were lost to the service since July 10, 1863, was more than the cost of building the stables at Giesboro for 10,000 animals.[12]

Control of the Cavalry Bureau changed hands frequently. Brig. Gen. Kenner Garrard relieved Stoneman on January 2, 1864, then Brig. Gen. James H. Wilson replaced Garrard on January 26. Wilson targeted unscrupulous contractors with a rigorous system of inspection, branding rejected horses with an "R" on their left shoulder or near their hooves to prevent shysters from passing them through the system again. He mandated that all cavalry mounts had to be fifteen to sixteen hands high and five to nine years old.[13]

Lt. Col. James A. Ekin relieved Wilson on April 7, 1864, so the latter could command a mounted division in the Army of the Potomac. A week later Chief of Staff Halleck agreed to run the Cavalry Bureau in addition to his many other duties. Halleck appointed an officer to oversee "the organization, equipment, and inspection of cavalry," while Ekin took charge of purchasing and inspecting horses. Under Halleck's guidance, the bureau did its best work. Rather than have an ambitious cavalry general who yearned for service in the field, it was best to have a good administrator as superintendent, relying on seasoned staff officers to do the actual work.[14]

At its peak the bureau employed 5,355 men. An estimated 60 percent of the worn-out horses and mules it handled were rehabilitated to take the field again. The centralized administrative system created more consistent policies and oversight of practices. The Confederates created nothing like the Cavalry Bureau.[15]

The alternative to a centralized administrative system was assigning responsibility for maintaining mounted units in the field to the regimental commanders. Benjamin W. Crowninshield noted that Continental European armies retained a battalion of each regiment on home territory and relied on it to recruit men and secure remounts for the other two battalions in the field. This often was called the depot system of regimental support. He envisioned an American version of it since Union mounted regiments had a battalion organization. But Americans never attempted to replicate this system.[16]

Supply and Transportation

Managing resources became an important goal with such huge mounted forces. Despite its highly mobile nature, cavalry always needed to have wagon trains to haul ammunition and other stores. Substituting pack trains was not an option, for as Frederick Whittaker asserted, one army wagon pulled by six mules could convey as much ammunition as twenty-four pack mules. The artillery accompanying cavalry also could not convey enough of its ammunition and necessary ordnance stores in a pack train. Whittaker estimated that a corps of 14,000 troopers would need a total of at least twenty-six wagons exclusive of additional vehicles to haul baggage for the troops and officers. As with the infantry, the number of wagons allowed mounted units in the Union army was reduced over time. The 1st Ohio Cavalry started the war with ten wagons but winnowed that number down to just one in the latter part of the conflict. But cavalry always retained some pack mules in addition to wagons. In the Army of Tennessee, the ratio was one mule for every ten men late in 1862. Two or three pack mules were led by one man on horseback in the 9th New York Cavalry. It took experience and skill to know how to position the material on the pack saddle for maximum efficiency.[17]

Both sides scavenged war material from the battlefield, but this was more important for the resource-starved Confederates. Thorough resupply from combat could best be done by capturing enemy troopers and stripping them of everything they possessed, which the Confederates regularly did during the latter part of the war. But Federal troopers also used captured material "in accordance with established usages in the cavalry," as Col. Oscar H. La Grange put it. The difference was that they often found Confederate equipment to be so poor in quality as not to be worth appropriating. After the Battle of Kelly's Ford, Union troopers selected only nine Confederate sabers that lay on the field, the others "being of so many patterns, and without scabbards," reported J. Irvin Gregg, "I did not deem them worth picking up."[18]

Resupplying Ammunition

Resupplying ammunition in battle became an important problem to solve. It started with trying to regulate firing so as not to waste ammunition. Whittaker was highly critical of cavalry officers for encouraging their men to fire rapidly during a fight. This strongly tended to degrade the quality of their shooting as well. If an officer bothered to test fire a carbine in battle, Whittaker argued, he would be better able to direct the fire of his men so as not to needlessly expend rounds.[19]

The widespread use of repeaters during the last year of the war in-

Losses and Ammunition Expended in Winslow's Brigade during the Tupelo Campaign, July 1864

Regiments	Men	Horses	Carbines	Pistols	Sabers	Saddles	Carbine Rounds Expended
3rd Iowa Cavalry	19	47	8	4	10	6	35,000
4th Iowa Cavalry	17	29	2	4	Not reported	2	21,494
10th Missouri Cavalry	1	15	2	4	1	1	8,000

Source: *OR*, 39(1):307.

creased the rate of fire and deepened the problem of resupply. A trooper could not carry more than sixty or eighty rounds on his person. Lt. Col. George A. Purington's 2nd Ohio Cavalry fired all available rounds near Hanover Court House on May 31, 1864, while its trains were nine miles away. Purington had to send a detachment to bring more rounds forward, each returning man carrying an ammunition box weighing eighty-five pounds on his horse. The resupply took half a day, the detachment rode a total of twenty-seven miles because it had to search for the train, and it lost three boxes captured by Confederate patrols along the way. A cavalry regiment could not rely on a haphazard resupply system like this.[20]

How many rounds a unit fired in any given battle varied widely, complicating the work of ordnance officers. The 8th Indiana Cavalry, with 366 troopers, fired 5,000 rounds in a battle late in the Atlanta Campaign, averaging out to thirteen rounds per man. In contrast, the 4th Iowa Cavalry, with 625 men, fired twenty-five to forty rounds per trooper during a fight near the end of the Tupelo Campaign. This is why Lt. Stephen Carr Lyford, Grant's chief ordnance officer, considered 150 rounds per cavalryman to be "a liberal supply" of ammunition in the Vicksburg Campaign.[21]

The problem lay in finding effective ways to get fresh rounds from the field transportation (wagon trains and pack trains) to the firing line when they were most needed. No general system was ever created to solve this problem. Thus, regimental, brigade, and division commanders worked out methods on their own. Usually the ordnance officer kept a close watch on remaining supplies, aided by his unit commander, and detailed men to bring up more rounds or have the men responsible for the trains bring them up.[22]

Horsemanship

In addition to issues of supply, the quality of a mounted force depended to a degree on the level of horsemanship attained by the troopers. In fact, some Civil War veterans asserted that this was paramount. "No soldier can become a good cavalryman unless he is a good horseman," wrote William L. Curry of the 1st Ohio Cavalry. For many regiments, the raw recruits started at a very low point. Chauncey S. Norton of the 15th New York Cavalry believed that "scarcely one out of a hundred of the men . . . had ever rode a horse to any great extent while at home." Accomplished Confederate horsemen denigrated the low level of horsemanship they observed in their opponents. Col. William A. Morgan of the 1st Virginia Cavalry claimed that he actually saw "raw Dutchmen strapped on the horses by straps buckled around their waists and legs fastened to the saddle, and I have witnessed in battle their horses going to the rear, with their dead or wounded riders hanging by these straps to their saddles." It is possible Morgan was writing truthfully, but there is no corroboration for this highly questionable way to keep a man on a mount. As Curry put it, if one trained to be a good rider as a young adult, "he has a certain amount of recklessness and has no fear, for a person that is timid and has no confidence in his ability to control his horse never can become a good rider."[23]

It has long been accepted that Confederate cavalrymen were better riders than Union troopers. They learned from an early age how to handle horses and enjoyed riding. This has often been cited as the key reason why Rebel cavalry dominated their opponents in the field and is buttressed by the success of James E. B. Stuart's mounted command in the eastern theater.[24]

But like all readily accepted explanations for complicated issues, the superiority of Confederate horsemanship needs to be reevaluated. There is ample proof that a certain portion of the Rebel cavalry force consisted of superb riders. H. V. Redfield, a civilian living in East Tennessee who observed Union and Confederate cavalrymen, marveled at the tricks Texans could perform. He saw them "riding at full gallop, leaning over toward the ground, picking up a stone and throwing it, and dropping hats on the ground and coming back at full gallop and picking them up without the least abatement in speed." Early in the war the 8th Texas Cavalry's proficiency at riding tricks preceded it, and citizens brought stubborn horses to the regiment, asking the men to break the animals for riding. The civilians placed coins on the ground and allowed the men to keep them if they could snatch the currency while galloping by.[25]

But this image of the Southerner as a natural rider must be modified. It is clear that not all Confederate troopers were adept horsemen. Chaplain Robert F. Bunting of the 8th Texas Cavalry, the regiment often cited for excellent horsemanship, distinguished between true cavalrymen such as the men of his regiment and what Braxton Bragg said were merely "'men on horseback.' Poorly mounted, poorly armed, and shamefully poor horsemen, they are often a reproach to this honorable arm of the service." In other words, even honest Confederates admitted that most of their troopers were as inept with their horses as they claimed Union cavalrymen to be.[26]

Bunting's comment, which was written for publication in a Texas newspaper, is convincing. The superb horsemen were a small and elite proportion of Confederate troopers. Moreover, there is ample evidence that an equally small proportion of Federal troopers were adept at riding. Curry noted that during the early months of 1863, a lot of horse racing took place in the cavalry camps of the Army of the Cumberland at Murfreesboro, Tennessee. There were small "scrub races" as well as bigger, thoroughly planned races. He mentioned that many men could snatch a hat or a saber from the ground while galloping by. According to Southern theory, trick riding like this could only be learned by early experience with horse riding, so we must conclude that even in Northern society many young men enjoyed riding and excelled at it.[27]

The majority of men in both cavalry forces needed a certain amount of instruction to become horsemen. The level of necessary training may have been lower in the South than in the North, but the idea that Confederate troopers were universally better riders than their opponents does not ring true. Stuart's exploits in 1862 were due more to the poor management displayed by Union cavalry leaders than to poor horsemanship by their men.

David M. Gregg, one of the best cavalry commanders in the East, argued that by the time of the Peninsula Campaign, "the volunteer regiments . . . were in a surprising state of serviceability," and the "regular regiments were in their habitual state of efficiency." That was not a universal opinion among Federal officers. Crowninshield maintained that the Army of the Potomac cavalry was inferior to that of the Army of Northern Virginia throughout 1861 and 1862. It rose to become its equal by the spring of 1863 and then dominated Lee's cavalry in the spring of 1864, nearly annihilating it by the spring of 1865. But much of this stemmed from cavalry management from the top down rather than good horsemanship from the bottom up. Moreover, some men argued that western troopers were better horsemen than their compatriots in Virginia. Francis Colburn Adams noticed this when he compared the 8th Illinois Cavalry, which served throughout the war in the Virginia theater, with regiments raised in the northeastern states. And there were those who believed that, no matter how inexperienced recruits happened to be with horses, intensive training for a few months turned most of them into effective riders and serviceable cavalrymen.[28]

Good horsemanship certainly could play a role in the level of effectiveness, but it by no means was the key factor. Training, doctrine, proper equipment and weapons, and effective leadership by officers on all levels spelled success or failure in the field. What does picking up one's hat from the ground while galloping by have to do with conducting a mounted saber charge, performing outpost duty, or fighting dismounted? One did not need to do circus tricks in order to become a good cavalryman. Trick riding was good for show but unnecessary for hard cavalry work.

The Most Complicated Branch of the Service

Being able to perform hard and varied work in the field was the key to cavalry effectiveness. The wear and tear of mounted service was severe because of the never-ending role of cavalry in military operations. Between campaigns, troopers remained busy with outpost, picket, and reconnaissance duties. During combat operations, they were pushed to the limit of their endurance in long, hard rides through contested territory, engaging in spur-of-the-moment skirmishes and wearing out their horses and their own physical and mental resources. All three branches of the service endured wear and tear during campaigns, but the cavalry suffered more in this way than the infantry or artillery.

"The duties of cavalry are as arduous, complex and diversified as it is possible for any branch of the military service to be," commented Col. Smith H. Hastings of the 5th Michigan Cavalry. Theophilus F. Rodenbough listed all the roles played by Union cavalry forces during the Gettysburg Campaign. Within the space of thirty days, they fought "a great cavalry battle" at Brandy Station on June 9; conducted screening and intelligence gathering at Aldie, Upperville, and Middleburg June 15–21; secured a good position for infantry and reinforced an infantry line on July 1; and defeated Confederate attempts to gain the rear of the Union position in severe mounted combat on July 3. Rodenbough did not go on to enumerate the many tasks involved in following up Lee's retreat from Gettysburg, but that work prolonged the stress and exhaustion felt by all Union troopers.[29]

Losses

Finding ways to compensate for the inevitable loss of manpower, horses, and equipment became important to cavalry effectiveness. Manpower casualties tended to be lower than the loss of infantrymen, but they were not inconsiderable. Much depended on the circumstances of any particular operation. Col. Edward F. Winslow's brigade suffered what might be called "normal" casualties during the Tupelo Campaign of July 1864 in Mississippi. The 3rd Iowa Cavalry lost nineteen men and forty-seven horses; the 4th Iowa Cavalry lost seventeen men and twenty-nine horses; and the 10th Missouri Cavalry suffered only one man lost and fifteen horses put out of service.[30]

In attacking fortifications, an unusual role for cavalry, troopers could suffer higher losses than normal. At Selma Col. Abram O. Miller's brigade advanced dismounted against the earthworks and lost 155 men out of 856 engaged, a loss ratio of 18.1 percent. The 17th Indiana Mounted Infantry in Miller's command suffered a ratio of 21.8 percent in that attack, while another brigade commanded by Col. Robert H. G. Minty lost 17.4 percent of its men in the engagement. These casualty ratios would not have been unusual in infantry units engaged in heavy fighting, but they were a bit higher than normal for mounted units. There were times, however, when cavalry formations suffered quite high losses. The 1st Maine Cavalry fought to slow down a Confederate infantry assault at Dinwiddie Court House on March 31, 1865. "We thought that was fighting," commented Edward P. Tobie, as the regiment lost 28.7 percent of its men engaged.[31]

Confederate cavalry officers were less careful to report the numbers of men engaged compared to the number lost in a particular battle. Isaac Norval Baker of the 18th Virginia Cavalry knew that mounted men made pretty good targets; "sometimes it seems strange that so many can ride away" after they "draw a heavy fire" on the battlefield.[32]

Inspections

The first step in maintaining mounted regiments at a level of effectiveness was the process of careful inspection. Officers had no idea what to requisition or how much materiel was needed unless subordinates reported their needs. The quality of inspection reports probably was lower in the cavalry than in the other two branches of the service, mostly because of the mobile nature of mounted service combined with constant calls for duty in the field. The former made it difficult to store records and paperwork, and the latter robbed inspectors of time to look over the troopers and their equipment; it could take half a day to properly inspect a regiment of cavalry. Moreover, there was an element of administrative culture that placed a higher regard for proper administration in the Union army than in the Confederate force. Some Rebel mounted formations, such as Wheeler's command late in the war, were pitifully administered compared to the average Union cavalry unit.[33]

The condition of Wheeler's command was thoroughly documented because it deteriorated so much that several outside inspectors were sent to examine the formation. At the start of 1864, the Cavalry Corps, Army of Tennessee seemed to be in fine shape. Lt. Col. Gustavus A. Henry Jr. found it in good camps and clothing when he visited in April, concluding that everything had improved since his last inspection a month before.[34]

But then the four-month-long campaign for Atlanta, followed by the hopeless endeavor to oppose Sherman's army group during the March to the Sea, eroded the Cavalry Corps. The latter campaign produced reports of rampant destruction of civilian property by its members. The troopers retained most of their fighting spirit, but their discipline was deteriorating, and Southern civilians became more afraid of their own army than of the Federals. Lt. Col. Alfred Roman conducted a thorough inspection of the cavalry in January 1865 and reported frankly about the problems. He listed them as "negligence and incompetency of many" company and regimental commanders, "want of system and good administration" in the Commissary Department, lack of pay, the self-mounting policy, and finally Wheeler's "excessive leniency."[35]

"Too much familiarity exists between officers and men," Roman concluded. "Discipline is thereby greatly impaired. It has become loose, uncertain, wavering. Orders are not promptly obeyed. Inspections of arms and ammunition are carelessly attended to by Company Commanders." Troopers on picket duty had less than half the rounds of ammunition they should have carried, and when Roman questioned their officers about it, those commanders were not at all concerned. "Roll-calls are neglected. In many cases, officers would be at a loss to find a list of their men." Most brigades also failed to appoint an officer of the day to supervise camp routine and security.[36]

Nothing was done in response to Roman's report because the Carolinas Campaign soon occupied Wheeler's attention. Discipline continued to drop during the early months of 1865, producing strident complaints from hundreds of civilians. William J. Hardee sent Lt. Col. Charles C. Jones Jr. to inspect the cavalry in February. Jones found a bewildering variety of weapons, ranging from Spencers to Burnsides, Sharps, and Maynards plus "various kinds of pistols." Most of the better weapons were claimed by the men as private property, either through capture, purchase, or exchange. This created a nightmare for the ordnance officers, who could not obtain the right kind of ammunition for such an array of guns. Jones criticized the lack of sabers in the command and bemoaned the lack of attention paid to saber charges. In fact, he found that many troopers had no weapons at all, a natural consequence of relying so heavily on battlefield captures. Those who were armed had only about forty rounds of ammunition available, which they carried in their pockets or haversacks because they did not have cartridge boxes. The command lacked a number of saddles, saddle blankets, curry combs, and brushes. A "considerable" number of troopers were dismounted, and it was "exceedingly difficult" to remedy that problem. So many of Wheeler's men had lost their privately owned mounts due to combat that the Confederate government owed them a total of $967,465 as compensation, and there seemed no prospect of receiving it. Many of Wheeler's men needed jackets, pants, overcoats, shoes, and blankets. Acts of vandalism could never be controlled unless mobile courts accompanied the corps to mete out swift justice. Men recommended for advancement because of bravery on the battlefield waited for months to have their promotions approved by the clogged bureaucracy in Richmond.[37]

Jones's report revealed how far Wheeler's Cavalry Corps had deteriorated from its comparatively good state in April 1864. Most of the problems were administrative in nature, compounded by the universal problem of scarce resources in the Confederacy. Yet another inspection, this one by Col. E. E. Portlock Jr. on behalf of Adjutant and Inspector General Samuel Cooper, took place in April 1865 as the war drew to a close. He noted a problem also identified by Jones, that many of Wheeler's units had been detached to various duties away from the corps. In other words, even though this was very late in the war, the policy of dispersion still weighed heavily on Confederate cavalry operations. Portlock mentioned the shortage of officers of proper rank to fill responsible positions on the regimental and brigade levels, and he bemoaned shortages of clothing and soap.[38]

The picture we derive from Roman, Jones, and Portlock is of a cavalry command that retained a basic element of effectiveness despite enormous and widespread problems. That fundamental element of usefulness rested on the quality of individual troopers, who managed to retain enough spirit and determination to continue their duties. Portlock, in fact, highly praised Wheeler's men as caring little for the trappings of army service but were highly reliable when it came to riding, fighting, and hoping for the best to result from their efforts.[39]

In fact, one could argue that it made little difference whether the administration of the Cavalry Corps was good or whether it was properly supplied as long as the troopers fought well. That position is valid to an extent. But a force such as this had essentially no hope of competing with an opponent who not only was in good spirits but also had the best of weapons, clothing, and other supplies at their disposal in addition to enjoying a high degree of proper administration to manage all those resources. And that is exactly what Wheeler's cavalry faced in 1864 and 1865. While one could say that the opposing Union and Confederate cavalry were on a level of rough parity in these important ways during the first half of the war, by mid-1864, that was a thing of the past. During the last months of the Civil War, Confederate cavalry rapidly declined, while the Union cavalry rapidly improved. The result was a triumph of mounted warfare, and all of it was due to improvements in administration, supply, spirit, and organization in the Federal mounted force.

Officers

It would be a mistake to denigrate paperwork and the effect of good officers simply because the privates were able to continue soldiering without those assets. Many Confederates fully understood the importance of regular reports, returns, and inspections, viewing them as the foundation of unit effectiveness. A string of general orders and circulars issued by the headquarters of Samuel W. Ferguson's brigade in March and April 1864 testifies to the importance placed on those records. They contain very detailed instructions about how to fill out all manner of paperwork combined with assurances that Ferguson needed the information on those documents to understand the needs of his regiments. The orders stressed the importance of submitting this paperwork on time because "a delay with them, necessarily impairs & delays the returns from Corps & Department Hd Qrts, and may, at a critical juncture, interfere with the operation and disposition of troops very seriously."[40]

Good paperwork depended on good officers, and the latter seemed to be the key to good cavalry in the eyes of observers. Gov. Henry T. Clark of North Carolina certainly felt that way. "I think that the teachings of experience show that a long and thorough trainage of both men and horses is absolutely required to make cavalry effective," he wrote in July 1862, "and a rare combination of talent is required for officers to drill or command or use cavalry to advantage. Without these advantages they are useless except for couriers or pickets. They are very expensive and contribute far more than any other corps to exhaust the resources of a country."[41]

Clark's viewpoint was echoed by other observers in both armies. Wheeler felt that the problems of straggling and plundering indicated "many inefficient officers" were in his command, and he created examining boards to weed out such men. According to one report, the boards were lenient on some and harsh on others. Capt. George Knox Miller of the 8th Confederate Cavalry was given an oral exam of about two dozen questions, while other men were grilled with written examinations "of several hours length." The difference in severity was spurred by the board members' view of the worth of these officers, for all of them had been in service for a long while and were known to the examiners. Benjamin Crowninshield noted that for several months in the winter of 1863–64, the 1st Massachusetts Cavalry had no field officers present, and only eight of twenty-eight line officers in eight of its companies were on duty. The result was "great demoralization" in the regiment, and the temporary filling of those positions with noncommissioned officers did not mitigate the problem. Historian Stephen Starr has argued that the improvement of Union cavalry units during the latter part of the war owed much to the quality of their officers. He noted that in the 7th Kansas Cavalry, the officer slots were kept full with qualified individuals, most of whom had worked their way up from the ranks. But the turnover among officers in most regiments was high. The 5th New York Cavalry started with 50 officers in October 1861, and a total of 124 officers served in the regiment by war's end, with only 4 of the original contingent remaining by July 19, 1865.[42]

Why did one mounted regiment excel another, wondered James Albert Clark. "The making of the men is all in the officers," he decided. "There is a something which permeates, as does the psychic force of a man transmitted to the horse he rides. Fear begets fear; confidence begets confidence. The lack of initiative in small matters betrays itself and the men feel it." Col. William H. Palmer certainly felt that his 15th Pennsylvania Cavalry could not do without his guidance. He informed a friend in February 1865 that he could not even think of resigning. "I have guarded its honor with constant vigilance," he declared, and could not trust it in the "hands of anybody else whatever."[43]

Versatility

Most mounted officers agreed that an important element of effectiveness was versatility, which was seen mostly in the ability to fight dismounted when needed. It was not an invention of the Civil War, having taken place regularly during the republican period of Roman history. But dismounted combat took place more widely and more intensely during the Civil War than in any previous conflict. Theophilus F. Rodenbough praised this trait, referring to it as the "superiority of the so-called 'hybrid' variety of cavalry." Moses Harris believed that a unit capable of fighting on foot and conducting a saber charge on horseback could take on enemy infantry or cavalry.[44]

The cavalry's ability to capture enemy fortifications was another aspect of its versatility. While this was not a normal part of its operational mode, it happened on more than one battlefield. Union troopers overran Confederate earthworks at Falling Waters in July 1863 and at Selma, Five

**Union Cavalry Charge across Confederate Earthworks
at the Battle of Falling Waters, July 14, 1863.**
One might think that earthworks represented an impassable barrier
to a mounted charge, but such was not necessarily the case. If the
parapet was small, there was no ditch, and the defenders were
few, it was quite possible for mounted troopers to cross the works
and continue charging forward. Falling Waters was only one of
several engagements in which this unusual feat took place.
Frank Leslie's Scenes and Portraits, 395.

Forks, and Columbus in 1865. During the March to the Sea, Judson Kilpatrick's mounted division attacked and defended rail barricades in duels with Wheeler's cavalry near Waynesboro, Georgia. Both sides constructed and used those hasty field defenses.[45]

Combined-Arms Operations

Cavalry's ability to mount combined-arms operations remained limited during the Civil War. While infantry and artillery had a natural affinity on the battlefield, cavalry was the odd man out. Its high level of mobility was the chief reason why it was so difficult to meld its operations with that of the slow, foot-powered infantry and the horse-drawn carriages of the artillery. It is true that European armies had developed very effective methods of combining the battlefield operations of cavalry with infantry and artillery, but that was a major lesson unlearned by Americans. In other words, American commanders had never felt the need to combine the services of all three arms in the field. When the Civil War gave them the opportunity, they mostly failed to take advantage of it.

"The fact is we have no general who has shown himself able to handle infantry, artillery, and cavalry so as to make them co-operate together," wrote Capt. Charles A. Phillips of the 5th Massachusetts Battery after the Battle of Fredericksburg in December 1862. Mounted forces "have not been of the slightest use in a single pitched battle," he argued."[46]

If Phillips had been patient, he would have seen a few exceptions to the rule. Bragg effectively used his cavalry forces at Stones River later that month, and Sheridan did so in the lower Shenandoah Valley in September and October 1864. In fact, Wilson called Third Winchester "the first battle fought in the United States where cavalry was handled as it ought to have been, and where it took its proper part as a factor in the movements of the three arms." He also pointed to his own handling of troopers, both on horse and dismounted, at the Battle of Nashville. He could also have pointed to Sheridan's work during the final phase of the Petersburg Campaign and the pursuit of Lee's army to Appomattox.[47]

But these examples of combined-arms operations failed to start a consistent doctrine applicable to all Union or Confederate armies. The overwhelming majority of opportunities to craft a combined-arms doctrine were overlooked, and the Civil War contributed little to the global development of cavalry theory as it related to cooperation with the other arms.

Never Resting

All mounted regiments were extremely busy nearly all the time. The 2nd Ohio Cavalry, for example, served in all three theaters of war, traveled 27,000 miles, and fought in ninety-seven engagements. After the war a regimental comrade told James Albert Clark of the 17th Pennsylvania Cavalry that he counted himself as engaging in 101 fights, not considering the skirmishes. But Clark replied that he recognized fifty-six engagements and more than eighty skirmishes. "I do not count sniping and pot shooting," he explained. "I call it an engagement when a good battle line was formed and fought on, and where artillery was used. What I call a skirmish is where a determined and well defined line was shooting to kill an equally deployed and persistent line though the reserves were not wholly called into action." Clark admitted that they were hesitant to tell anyone all this for fear they would not be believed.[48]

But Clark's telling has credence, as many Civil War mounted units racked up undeniably huge numbers of engagements. The 5th New York Cavalry saw fifty-two battles and 119 skirmishes from October 1861 to July 19, 1865. The 9th New York Cavalry was in a total of 141 engagements of all types. Cole's Cavalry, which started as a battalion of four companies in 1861 and then was added to the 1st Maryland Cavalry (U.S.), fought in nearly 200 battles by muster out in June 1865.[49]

Confederate mounted units engaged in roughly similar numbers of battles. The 6th Texas Cavalry formed a line of battle 112 times during the Atlanta Campaign alone and fought from 85 of them. In contrast, E. M. Cooksey of the 8th Mississippi Infantry stated that his regiment fought in seventeen battles and skirmishes during that campaign. In the eastern theater Rufus Barringer claimed that the 1st North Carolina Cavalry engaged in nearly 150 combats during its war service.[50] These unusually large numbers of cavalry engagements compared to infantry and artillery fights were due to the constant duty imposed on mounted units.

Hard service produced casualties that may not have equaled those of the infantry but still challenged unit effectiveness. Even Confederate cavalrymen heard of Hooker's quip about never seeing a dead trooper. "I have seen piles of dead cavalrymen, in heaps," wrote F. J. Quarterman of the Jeff Davis Legion in response to that ungenerous phrase. John C. Wright, who commanded an Arkansas infantry regiment in the Trans-Mississippi, admitted that he had "a very mistaken opinion of the cavalry" for much of the war. "It was thought that the cavalry had an easy time; had a horse to ride, got the best there was to eat and did but little fighting." Then Wright served for ten months in a cavalry unit and concluded, "it is the infantry that has the good time."[51]

The Civil War produced the largest mounted force in American history. According to Thomas M. Vincent, the assistant adjutant general of the U.S. Army, the Federal government fielded a total of 232 cavalry regiments, nine battalions of cavalry, and 122 independent companies of cavalry.[52] The Civil War witnessed not only the largest mounted force ever raised in America but also the most effective cavalry force in the country's history despite many problems and limitations.

So many factors affected the level of effectiveness that it is difficult to pinpoint any one as of supreme importance. But an argument can be made that management and administration were the keys. No matter how little or how much material an army could access, officers on all levels of command had to smartly use it if the force could be expected to perform properly. Federal officers clearly surpassed their Confederate counterparts in cavalry management. Abundant resources mean nothing in fighting a war unless they are utilized well and combined with many other assets to create an effective fighting force.

15

AFTER THE WAR

The army that the United States had created to fight the Civil War virtually disappeared after Appomattox. From 232 regiments, mostly volunteer, the Union mounted force contracted to only ten regular cavalry regiments. The original five that existed before the outbreak of the war were retained, as was the sixth regiment authorized soon after the war began. Congress authorized four new cavalry regiments, two of them consisting of Black enlisted men officered by whites. From 1873 to the Spanish-American War in 1898, cavalry amounted to about 20 percent of the entire U.S. Army. Of course, all 127 Confederate mounted regiments dispersed at war's end.[1]

During the postwar period, the War Department went back and forth when it came to officially labeling the subunits of the cavalry regiment. In July 1862 it had required companies to be officially called "troops" but changed that back to "company" in June 1873. Then in May 1881 the department mandated the use of "troop." The source of this waffling stemmed from the use of the term "company" in the infantry branch of the service. Cavalrymen wavered on the question of having a distinctive term to distinguish their organization from that of the foot soldiers.[2]

Lessons from the American Perspective

Given the size and significance of the mounted arm in the Civil War, many veteran horse soldiers looked for important lessons to derive from its operations. Theophilus F. Rodenbough identified the key characteristics of Civil War cavalry as independent action, boldness of execution, and versatility of methods. By independent action he meant "operating at a distance, cutting an enemy's communications, anticipating his occupation of strategic points, and engaging his infantry, with improved firearms, on more advantageous terms than ever before." Boldness seemed to him self-evident; he was a proponent of the school that taught cavalry leaders to fear nothing, make quick decisions on the battlefield, and accept risks rather than throw away chances of success. Rodenbough also wrote of "the superiority of the so-called 'hybrid' variety of cavalry over soldiers taught to leave their saddles only under protest." In other words, his view of mounted versatility embraced both the saber charge and dismounted fighting.[3]

Rodenbough believed modern firearms such as the breechloader and repeater empowered cavalry rather than circumscribed its role. In fact, he foresaw the continued importance of mounted force in future wars. Writing in the *Journal of the United States Cavalry Association* in 1889, Rodenbough argued that the Battle of Brandy Station could be taken as a model for the kind of mounted clash that he expected would open any future war. He envisioned large cavalry forces leading the infantry armies of both belligerents, preparing the offensive and aiding the defensive, and assumed those mounted formations would conduct the initial battles.[4]

As members of the defeated side, former Confederate cavalry officers were not often called upon to offer their views on lessons learned from the Civil War. But when it happened, Joseph Wheeler tended to be the one asked. This was in part because he had authored a cavalry tactics book published in 1863 and partly because he lived a long life, serving with high profile in the American forces during the Cuban campaign of the Spanish-American War. Despite those apparent qualifications, Wheeler could offer little more than to summarize the role of cavalry in the Confederate Army of Tennessee rather than foresee the future of mounted operations. He listed five major roles in the war: to lead the army's advance and protect its retreat; to hold Union infantry advances while the Confederates prepared to meet them; to pursue Union raiding forces behind Confederate lines; to keep the army commander "constantly informed" of Union positions; and "to seek battle with the enemy's cavalry" in order "to weaken that arm of the opposing forces." None of this would have struck students of mounted warfare as new or insightful. Moreover, Wheeler grossly exaggerated when he asserted that most of his officers had "studied cavalry tactics and brought their troops to an excellent condition of drill and discipline."[5]

When Capt. Matthew F. Steele, editor of the *Journal of the United States Cavalry Association,* asked Wheeler to write an article about "the work of your cavalry corps in the great war," the former general began by recalling that "the disparity in numbers of the Confederates were so great that we were driven to our wit's end to prevent disaster." Rather than screen the Army of Tennessee with a curtain of videttes and outposts close to friendly positions, which would have required large numbers of mounted men, Wheeler preferred to post small groups as close to Union positions as possible "and watch them and thus learn of movements, or if possible of preparations for movements." He also stressed the ability of his men to fight on foot as well as on horseback and emphasized close cooperation with infantry formations.[6]

But Wheeler devoted most of his attention to gathering intelligence. "It took me but a short time and a few hard knocks to learn that the A, B, C's of warfare was to know, All about your own army, All about that of the enemy, And all about the country," he told Steele. Wheeler could always capture a few Union horsemen, and they often were forthcoming with information such as how many days' rations they carried and who commanded their column. He also sent scouts to talk with civilians who lived along the route of the Federal march to see what they could tell of the column. Wheeler kept a book "in which a page was devoted to information regarding each regiment" in the opposing force. A separate page was devoted to each brigade and division. "When a prisoner was captured, or a deserter came in, he was subjected to a regular set of questions, and his answers were entered." Those questions dealt with an array of topics, including how many men were on duty in his company and how that company compared with others in the same regiment. Some of those captives and deserters were well informed, while others were not, and some even tried to deceive the Confederates. Often, however, Wheeler could produce evidence from other captives or deserters to contradict an attempt at deception that then compelled the man "to tell accurately all he knew."[7]

Wheeler also relied on other means of gathering information. He employed spies, apparently civilians, some of whom he knew were double agents receiving pay from both Union and Confederate authorities. "It was sometimes difficult to determine to which side they were truly loyal, but such men I met at the outpost and never let them know much to communicate to the enemy." At times his men would capture Union returns and ordnance papers. He found information in Northern newspapers helpful, especially when the editors published official reports by Union commanders. Wheeler relied heavily on a "young officer who had been a bookkeeper" to organize all this disparate bits of intelligence "in a very clear and satisfactory manner." As time went by, the amount of information built up. "Each separate piece of information seemed but little in itself but taken all together it was very valuable." Wheeler could compile a table of organization of the Union army, and Braxton Bragg, Joseph E. Johnston, and John Bell Hood each, he believed, "seemed to place implicit confidence in my reports."[8]

This detailed description of the important role that Wheeler's cavalry played in intelligence gathering is informative. But it did not address the equally important question of how the Civil War could point to cavalry's role in future wars.[9]

Lessons from the European Perspective

As a general rule European military observers derived few lessons from the Civil War. They tended to be overly influenced by the improvised nature of the Union and Confederate mounted force, assuming that negated any important lessons applicable to European standing armies. They also tended to be appalled at the waste of both Union and Confederate horses; Europeans enjoyed long-established systems of horse care to avert callous waste of precious animals. They also tended to ignore the huge level of improvement achieved by the Federal mounted force near the end of the war.[10]

There were exceptions to the rule, especially among the British. A number of writers praised Civil War cavalry for its ability to fight dismounted or on horseback as needed. It could operate independently and in concert with large infantry formations, construct field fortifications, hold its own against enemy infantry, and perform picket and outpost duty. Those perceptive students of the Civil War tended to believe that British cavalry was incapable of such versatility but hoped to improve it. Douglas Haig wrote a book on cavalry in which he expressed support for the concentration of mounted power into larger units—at least divisions and even corps when called for—and cited the effectiveness of Sheridan's command in the Army of the Potomac to support his views.[11]

But Moses Harris, veteran of the 1st U.S. Cavalry, bemoaned the fact that no European army used its cavalry force as Sheridan had done in 1864–65. Speaking in 1891, he expressed frustration that many English writers simply did not understand a key point. They praised the ability of Union horsemen to fight on foot but "with stupid persistency call it mounted infantry" rather than cavalry that could do everything. "They appear to be ignorant of the fact that the same cavalry which fought so efficiently dismounted, charged successfully with the sabre against intrenched lines of veteran infantry, and that it was in this combined efficiency that its remarkable strength consisted."[12]

European Wars

Whether Harris's criticism was justified is unclear, but what is not in question is the fact that European armies failed to use their cavalry forces well in wars during the later nineteenth century. In the Austro-Prussian conflict of 1866, both sides held back large cavalry reserves to use them at a decisive moment, much as Napoleon had done half a century before. As a result they never used them at all except as a last resort to save a deteriorating situation because the commander had no infantry reserves available. Observers tended to blame the use of modern weapons for this cavalry failure, but it really was the result of commanders mishandling their resources. They tended also to neglect outpost, picket, and reconnaissance work by the mounted arm.[13]

After 1866 the Germans worked to improve their mounted doctrine.

They focused on the division level rather than creating corps organization and allowed those divisions more latitude to conduct reconnaissance duties rather than tying them too closely to infantry operations. They also allocated at least one mounted regiment to serve the needs of every infantry division, combining concentration with dispersion in measured ways. In contrast, the French army remained stuck in the cavalry doctrine it had created in 1829, thus their horse power was outperformed by the German cavalry early in the Franco-Prussia War of 1870–71. French commanders tended to hold their mounted forces in abeyance until it was too late to do anything with them except conduct desperate mounted attacks against intact German infantry flushed with success. In contrast, through careful handling, the German cavalry arm conducted at least sixteen examples of mounted attacks during the latter phase of the war; twelve of them were "completely successful," although conducted by relatively small forces of mounted men.[14]

But the Franco-Prussian War initiated a significant change in how European armies, especially that of the Germans, managed their mounted power in war. The trend was now toward greater versatility, as the Civil War had already indicated, and improving the quality of horses, men, equipment, and training to meet the ever-growing challenges of the modern battlefield. Improved infantry small arms and especially artillery seemed to be the most important problems faced by the mounted arm during the last three decades of the nineteenth century. The ability to fight on foot seemed a viable way to deal with those developing challenges.[15]

Among the more conservative of military systems, the Russian cavalry arm was not used well in the war with the Ottomans in 1877–79. Lt. Francis Vinton Greene, a graduate of the U.S. Military Academy in 1866, was sent as an American observer and wrote scathingly of Russian cavalry operations. He complained that Russian officers knew virtually nothing of the American Civil War except to be fascinated by long-range mounted raids deep into enemy territory. They "constantly question me about them," Greene reported, while ignoring "the true use of cavalry in modern warfare." According to the lieutenant, that true use was to scout, to follow up an enemy retreat, and to fight on foot, in addition to conducting the admired independent raids. "Since 1865 there has been nothing new on the subject," Greene concluded. The Russians did successfully mount a large raid of 5,000 cavalry, 5,800 infantry, and forty guns that rampaged through Turkish territory somewhat like Wilson's Raid of 1865. But their cavalry was quite poor at the essential roles of reconnaissance and screening.[16]

During the late nineteenth century, the theme that increasingly dominated the work of cavalry theorists was the role played by new weapons as negating the effectiveness of mounted power on the battlefield. Unfortunately latter-day historians have accepted that idea at face value and have created a line of interpretation based on it. They strongly tend to see cavalry as in a state of decline during the last few decades of the nineteenth and into the first years of the twentieth century because of breechloaders, repeaters, and improved field artillery. Historians have often considered the continued fielding of large cavalry formations during this period as anachronistic and wasteful.[17]

But in recent years a handful of cavalry historians, mostly in the United Kingdom, have upended this old interpretation. They point out that the situation was far more complex, as cavalry theorists in several nations, especially Great Britain, worked during this period to adjust to the changing battle conditions. By the outset of World War I, those changes resulted in quite a bit of improvement in their mounted forces, with the American Civil War becoming something of an inspiration for many of them. The day of mounted power on the battlefield was far from over.[18]

The Second Boer War of 1899–1902 was a pivotal event in this ongoing self-evaluation among British cavalry officers. Taking place in an environment not so very different from the frontier regions of the United States and against an opponent who largely resorted to guerrilla operations, British theorists took away from the conflict a resolve to create a more versatile mounted force capable of fighting on foot as well as on horseback. On occasion British horse soldiers successfully charged mounted against Boer infantry armed with modern rifles, indicating that the naysayers who argued that modern weapons would inevitably deny cavalry an opportunity to succeed on the battlefield were wrong. Advocates of a hybrid role for mounted forces were countered for years by those who continued to believe in specialization (that is, maintain one cavalry force for mounted action and another for foot combat), but by 1914, those who supported a versatile role for one cavalry force prevailed. The Boer conflict also pointed out that British cavalry needed to improve its ability to conduct scouting, picketing, and reconnaissance duties. A shoulder arm capable of longer-distance firing than the carbine was introduced after the South African war, and theorists argued that machine guns could be used to support a mounted charge. The tradition of government-sponsored horse-breeding establishments became even more important as Continental nations sought to improve the quality of their cavalry mounts.[19]

To a degree, cavalry reform also took place in Russia during the turn of the century, but in Germany the discussions about how to improve the mounted arm assumed proportions nearly as important as in Great Britain. The Germans focused much on dismounted combat but were leery of the details. Some pointed out that horse soldiers carried only half the number of cartridges as infantrymen, that mounted units tended to have fewer men than infantry units, and that cavalry had to win a dismounted fight with infantry early or all the advantages would accrue to their opponents. German theorists also continued to value mounted charges, although they were fully aware that the modern battlefield made that tactic more dangerous. One had to prepare the target beforehand with heavy artillery fire and carefully select the right circumstances; hitting unshaken infantry with a mounted charge had even less chance of success than it had in Napoleon's day or during the American Civil War. German regulations continued to stress the importance of reconnaissance for a versatile mounted force, which would remain relevant in the new era. Many German theorists looked to the Civil War for guidance and were impressed by that conflict's experience of strategic raids. But they did not believe such operations would be possible to replicate in a major European war due to logistical difficulties. They also pushed for dismounted fighting, another lesson learned from the Civil War.[20]

American Trends

To a significant degree, American cavalry officers of the late nineteenth century could boast that the Civil War held significant lessons for the future of European warfare. They contributed in some ways to a more general effort among the major powers to modernize their mounted arm. It is arguable, as asserted by historian Gervase Phillips, that the effectiveness level of cavalry in world history reached its peak in the decades preceding the onset of World War I, at least in terms of theory, doctrine, and preparation for future conflict. In the United States that assertion was just as relevant as it was for the European powers. American cavalry officers continued to value a versatile role, stressing dismounted fighting and shock action when needed. They also stressed open-order formations and taking cover whenever possible. "The U.S. cavalry regulations had thus achieved a balance between mounted and dismounted actions and between the strategic and tactical uses of cavalry," as historian Antulio J. Echevarria has put it.[21]

But the United States would never have an occasion for fielding a large mounted force again. The Spanish-American War of 1898 was too short to justify such action. Out of 125,000 state volunteers, only eight states fielded any mounted units, totaling three regiments and nine companies. Only three companies of that volunteer force actually went overseas, specifically to Puerto Rico and the Philippines. In addition to the state volunteers, the U.S. government raised three new regiments of cavalry and utilized five existing regiments of cavalry in the regular army, fighting dismounted, in the Cuban campaign. None of those units had an opportunity to fight on horseback.[22]

Nevertheless, American cavalry theorists continued to adhere to their strong conviction in favor of a versatile mounted force. Capt. Alonzo Gray of the 14th U.S. Cavalry looked to the Civil War to bolster that argument. While serving in the Philippines in 1910, he scoured the *Official Records* for cavalry reports and compiled excerpts, adding commentary about the lessons to be learned from them. The U.S. Cavalry Association published his work that year. Gray firmly believed that modern weapons would simply alter the importance of cavalry, not destroy it, and that the sphere of work would be enlarged rather than diminished by the new battlefield conditions. In fact, he argued that automobiles and motorcycles would be a blessing to the cavalryman because they could be used to deliver dispatches and save horseflesh.[23]

Gray was a good student of the Civil War. He carefully sifted through the reports and offered wide-ranging commentary on the nature of mounted operations in that conflict. Gray examined Cooke's tactical manual, McClellan's writings on cavalry, and Wheeler's tactical book to understand theoretical formations and maneuvers as compared with the actual tactics used in the field. He carried that discussion through into the post–Civil War era and up to the drill regulations of 1896. "Wheeler was, without doubt, the best Confederate cavalry leader in the west," Gray contended. "He was always ready to work in the team and play a subordinate part to his commanding general." That comment was a direct criticism of independent-minded cavalry commanders like Nathan Bedford Forrest and John Hunt Morgan, who had tremendous difficulty subordinating themselves to the orders of infantry commanders. "He could not bear restraint," Gray concluded of Forrest, "and did not work well to the central idea."[24]

Reading Civil War reports, Gray was impressed that his predecessors had utilized a wide variety of formations and maneuvers in the field. This indicated thorough training, a careful selection of tactical formations by officers, and a professional view of cavalry operations among the mass of volunteers. "The formation depended altogether on the conditions," he correctly observed. When given a choice, it seemed to Gray as if the column of squadrons was preferred, which gave the formation a front of two companies and a depth of six ranks if the regiment was deployed in one rank for each company.[25]

In terms of weapons, it seemed to Gray that his Civil War predecessors often fired their carbines while mounted, especially on the skirmish line. He understood that at any distance this fire tended to be inaccurate because of the man's need to control his horse. Gray noted that pistols were widely used in individual shooting but rarely fired in unison. He liked to see evidence of mounted saber charges but observed that troopers had difficulty switching from saber use to firearm work. There were only three ways to dispose of one's saber, none of which were good options when in a melee. The trooper could not return it to the scabbard while fending off opponents; if he dropped it on the ground, he lost its future use; and he dare not let it hang loosely from his wrist for fear of cutting himself or his horse. Gray admitted that even in 1910 there was no solution to this problem. The need to switch from cold steel to hot lead in a melee was evident to Gray, who believed that if handled well, the revolver was more effective in close combat. He concluded from the reports and from conversations with Civil War veterans that they strongly preferred to cut rather than thrust with their sabers. Gray still believed in the continued utility of mounted saber charges in 1910. To achieve the maximum shock effect, it was important that the formation be tightly massed, "boot-to-boot," as he put it, at the point of impact.[26]

Gray's book is interesting from more than one perspective. It shows how thoroughly he took the Civil War as an object lesson in mounted warfare. On another level Gray also accepted those lessons as still relevant for cavalry operations half a century after Appomattox. World War I, the first truly modern conflict in global history, was only four years in the future when Gray's book was published, yet the Civil War seemed to point to a continuance of cavalry's importance.

European Trends

To many observers, the Great War of 1914–18 seemed to prove that cavalry's importance had ended permanently. Locked in static, positional warfare for four years on the Western Front, the major belligerents struggled to find the proper role for their huge infantry and artillery forces, much less for mobile cavalry formations. Yet it probably would surprise many to learn that every European belligerent of that conflict not only fielded large mounted forces but also used them effectively whenever the conditions allowed it. A total of 100 cavalry divisions were formed by those countries, containing about 7,000 men in each, and many independent smaller units were organized as well. Mounted operations were more frequent and widespread in theaters where mobile warfare predominated, as in the Middle East, yet they also took place in Belgium and France during the early, highly mobile phase of the Western Front and on the long, much less static Eastern Front. All the major powers had invested effort for decades before 1914 in altering cavalry doctrine, modernizing training, and improving the quality of horses, so that in many ways the Great War witnessed the apogee of mounted warfare in Europe. The Germans used mounted troops to help stabilize their front during the final Allied offensives that ended the war, the cavalrymen riding to the scene of disaster and then fighting on foot as in the Civil War. But an obsession with modern weapons use, not to mention the horrors of static trench warfare, has tended to overshadow the varieties of operational modes to be seen in this complex war. Thus, cavalry's role has been muted, misunderstood, and overlooked by most contemporaries and historians alike. Yet cavalry observers were certain World War I proved that mounted operations were still important.[27]

National governments continued to fund large cavalry forces during the interwar years and into World War II. Poland, for example, trained its mounted formations to deal with the threat of mechanization. Cavalrymen were issued antitank weapons and taught to attack enemy foot formations that had become disorganized and were vulnerable to mounted charges. Germany and the Soviet Union also fielded cavalry formations during the interwar years. Many of the conflicts of that era, including the Russian Civil War of 1918–20, the Soviet-Polish War of 1920, and the Spanish Civil War of 1936–39, involved mounted operations. In World War II, the most highly mobile conflict thus far in global history, thousands of cavalrymen rode horses. The Soviets used thirty cavalry divisions of 5,000 men each while they also worked to mechanize infantry divisions. Germany fielded eight cavalry divisions and France deployed three cavalry divisions when the war began. The British and Americans phased out mounted formations as they worked to mechanize their infantry, but an American cavalry regiment did conduct mounted operations in the Philippines, and the British had a handful of small mounted units in the Middle East.[28]

The true demise of mounted warfare took place after 1945. The major belligerents had finally achieved something like full mechanization of large infantry formations by the end of World War II. In other words, the Civil War had taken place just before developments began that would ultimately negate cavalry's role in operations. During the 1860s, no one could anticipate the widespread use of heavy artillery along a static front stretching across national borders, as in World War I, or the rapid pace of mechanized warfare, as in World War II. The Civil War was one of the last major conflicts in which the conditions of campaign and battle were far closer to Napoleon's day fifty years before than to the twentieth-century wars fifty years later. It was one of the last major conflicts in which cavalrymen could shine among the three branches of the military system.

With the exception of the Plains Indian Wars to come, the Civil War also was far and away the most important conflict as far as cavalry operations were concerned. The rise to effectiveness in the Union mounted arm contributed significantly to Federal victory, and the decline in effectiveness of Confederate mounted formations contributed significantly to Southern defeat. In no other American conflict—again, save for the Plains Indians Wars—could this be said of mounted power.

CONCLUSION

If one wanted to see how Americans waged mounted warfare on a large scale commensurate with the European cavalry heritage, they would need to focus on the Civil War alone. In no previous conflict had Americans created anything that could be considered a large mounted force. None of those earlier wars represented a true test of American cavalry, with the same holding true of all conflicts after 1865 as well. The Civil War stands out as the only event in American history that deserved to be considered as a true example of American mounted warfare on the level achieved by world powers of the mid-nineteenth century.

By 1861, cavalry officers in the United States had full access to the doctrine of mounted warfare. The army had a good training manual, and the country was capable of producing the equipment and arms needed to outfit a large cavalry force. It also had an ample supply of suitable horses. Thus, the country possessed all the basic knowledge and material for supporting large cavalry formations—it just needed the desire to do so.

When the Civil War began, the willingness to create large mounted forces came at a halting pace in the North but with enthusiasm in the South. Federal authorities were initially hesitant to endorse the expenditure of funds to create cavalry regiments and to shoulder the continued expense of maintaining them. They justified this hesitancy not only by a desire to save money but also on the assumption that the wooded nature of Southern terrain would impede the use of mounted formations. This was a foolish way of thinking; cavalry forces were by definition more expensive per regiment than infantry, but every infantry army needed a certain number of mounted units if for no other reason than to screen, escort, perform outpost and picket duty, and provide fast couriers for infantry commanders. Even if the authorities were not interested in forming large columns of mounted power for operations independent of infantry armies, they had to create enough cavalry units to perform those tiresome tasks closely linked with serving infantry. In the early months of the war, Federal authorities hardly allowed the creation of enough cavalry regiments for even those duties.

Fortunately for the Union war effort, Federal authorities soon relented, and more cavalry regiments were accepted for service. This melting away of reluctance snowballed until the Union army supported the largest concentration of mounted power in American history, significantly outnumbering the cavalry supporting its opponent in the South. That large Federal cavalry force experienced a clear trajectory of improvement in its performance throughout the war. It seemed to be outperformed by the Confederate cavalry early in the conflict but improved a lot by its midpoint. The most important factor in its success lay in the high command's willingness to reduce the mounted arm's commitment to serving the infantry and to create large concentrations of cavalry power for large-scale independent action. This increased the pride and sense of importance among horse soldiers of all ranks. Coupled with continued improvement in arming the cavalry (breechloaders and repeaters), in addition to readily supplying the mounted arm with traditional weapons (good sabers), the Union cavalry reached a pinnacle of performance during the last year of the Civil War. It outperformed its Confederate opponent, more consistently dominating it than in any previous period of the conflict.

The rise of Union mounted power was based on wise decisions on the part of high-level administrators in Washington, DC. It was supported by good officers on all levels who used the available doctrine to train their recruits in the complicated formations and maneuvers involved in cavalry operations. When the administrators in Washington provided the money to purchase good weapons and equipment, especially to support the expense of replacing worn-out horses, all that was needed was to find a handful of aggressive and smart commanders for the few large concentrations of cavalry power created during the latter half of the war. Despite their limitations, Philip Sheridan and James H. Wilson proved their worth as chieftains of mounted warfare.

Confederate cavalry started strong at the beginning of the war but failed to maintain its quality, resulting in a steady decline by the mid-point of the conflict. Confederate officials adopted policies that worked initially but soon came to haunt Rebel horse power. From the start the Richmond government mandated that its cavalrymen had to provide their own horses. If the war had lasted only a few months, it would have been considered a wise move. But in a long, drawn-out conflict, self-mounting was worse than foolish, especially considering the Confederate government's inability to maintain a stable currency and to pay its cavalrymen regularly. How could they be expected to replace their worn-out horses if they did not receive pay for months at a time? How could the readiness of the regiment be maintained if half the men had to be given furloughs to go home and try to scrounge up a replacement mount? Confederate cavalry had access to the same tactical and training system that the Union cavalry used, but it did not have access to the weapons and equipment available in the North. Material shortages, financial weaknesses, and short-sighted policies hampered the creation and maintenance of a large Confederate mounted force. Rebel authorities experimented with creating large concentrations, but those combinations never worked because no one truly capable of controlling them was found at the right time. Commanders such as Wade Hampton might have been capable, but the many and varied duties assigned to cavalry, plus the relative shortage of numbers, meant that the Confederates could not assemble large concentrations easily and give men like Hampton the chance to prove themselves at the highest level of command.

Cavalry Dominance

Many themes present themselves when considering the history of cavalry in the Civil War. Perhaps the most salient to modern students of the subject is the idea that Confederate cavalry thoroughly outperformed Union cavalry at least during the first half of the war. Like most popular notions, this one has some truth and some falsehood about it. It is true that in the

Virginia theater the Confederate cavalry under James E. B. Stuart outperformed its opponent. That was largely due to the spirited leadership of Stuart, his vision of what mounted forces could do, and his daring efforts to implement that vision. Riding completely around the Army of the Potomac on two occasions more than any other exploit sealed his reputation as a dashing cavalry commander. This took place at the same time that, under George B. McClellan's deadening hand, the Federal cavalry in the East was so deeply entrenched in the dispersion of its resources to serve the needs of infantry units that it was difficult to create a sizeable mobile force to counter him.

But there is little reason to believe that Confederate cavalry in the western theater achieved a similar level of dominance over their Union opponents during the first half of the war. Here the two mounted forces were far closer to par, with each side trading success and failure. Even Earl Van Dorn's successful raid against Holly Springs on December 20, 1862, does not necessarily denote dominance. Van Dorn was helped enormously by one of the most inept defenses of a Union-held town to be seen in the war, and his further attempts to capture other Union-held towns along the same railroad during the next few days were defeated by spirited defensive action. The many successful raids of Nathan Bedford Forrest also do not necessarily denote Confederate cavalry superiority. The key to his success was to carefully plan to avoid major concentrations of Union power, hit towns and railroads and bridges where the Federals were most vulnerable, and then move on quickly, mostly staying one or two steps ahead of his pursuers. When forced to do battle, he almost always fought dismounted like infantry, and his battlefield victories often owed as much to lack of expertise among his opponents as to anything else.

True cavalry dominance is most clearly seen when two mounted forces, able to conduct all the varied roles of horse soldiers, confront the main force of their opponents. That was not fully seen until the creation of the Cavalry Corps in the Army of the Potomac in the East and its counterpart during the Atlanta Campaign in the West. By then, the trajectory of cavalry development among the eastern Federals gave them a decided advantage over the mounted force of the Army of Northern Virginia. Union cavalry dominance came late in the western theater, although not clearly until Wilson forged his powerful command early in 1865.

In short, it is not a simple proposition that the Confederate cavalry was better than the Union cavalry even during the first half of the conflict, and it is not at all true of the second half. Differences between East and West were real and have to be taken into consideration. Whatever superiority Confederate cavalry enjoyed during the Civil War was ephemeral. The cavalry system created by the Richmond government was geared for short-time effectiveness, not for a long, exhausting war, which was in direct contrast to the system created by the Federal government. That was the most fundamental fact affecting cavalry performance during the Civil War.

Horsemanship

Another common belief is that Confederate cavalry was superior to Union cavalry because Southern young men were better horsemen than Northerners. This is a major idea that even some Union cavalrymen believed and that Confederate cavalrymen liked to brag about. Most modern students and historians tend to accept that notion, but it is important to question the point for the sake of being thorough about the issue of mounted effectiveness.

As broached in chapter 14, how much advantage being a good horseman conveyed to a mounted soldier is an open question. If one defines good horsemanship as the ability to perform impressive tricks in the saddle, such as being able to grab a hat from the ground while galloping past it, then that notion becomes irrelevant. A cavalryman had no need of such skills. All he had to do was to become familiar enough with horsemanship to be able to handle his steed according to the formations and maneuvers explained in Cooke's tactical manual. He also had to be able to keep the horse calm in dangerous surroundings. As long as he created a supportive relationship with his horse so that both could cooperate to be effective on campaign and in battle, the trooper had achieved all that was necessary in the way of horsemanship. It is clear that the overwhelming majority of Union and Confederate cavalrymen achieved that level; otherwise their failure to do so would have been more commonly noted.

The ultimate point is that we should not be so ready to rely on simple conclusions to explain complicated issues such as cavalry dominance. Native ability to ride horses probably was more widespread among Southerners but could not have applied to literally all of them. Nor could it hope to overcome shortages of horses along with poor weapons and equipment. In the long run the Federals had all the advantages in keeping an effective mounted force in the field, and they did not hesitate to use those advantages.

Saber Charges and Dismounted Fighting

Knowing how to manage a horse effectively was important for all cavalry duties but none more so than the mounted charge. This action had long been the ultimate role of mounted soldiers, utilizing their horse mobility to create a powerful column of steel-armed warriors that swept across the battlefield and smashed into opposing formations. No other branch of the military could do anything like this, and cavalrymen naturally took pride in their ability to conduct saber charges. While some historians have argued that Civil War cavalry dropped the mounted charge halfway through the conflict because of the widespread use of modern firearms, that argument simply is not convincing.[1] The reports and personal accounts fully confirm that saber charges never went out of style; they occurred during the last year of the war as often as before and were just as successful or not, according to the circumstances of each individual charge, as they had been during the early part of the conflict.

Dismounted fighting was a very marked feature of Civil War cavalry operations and rightly so. But one must keep the subject in context. Civil War horsemen certainly did not invent the idea of riding to the battlefield, dismounting, and fighting on foot. That had taken place sporadically throughout the long history of mounted warfare dating back thousands of years. Now and then dismounted fighting rose to prominence, and one must see the American Civil War as another one of those periods. In fact, American cavalrymen deserve credit for bringing dismounted fighting to a fine point of effectiveness. They did so not because of the adoption of modern rifles, as some historians have assumed, but because it was an obviously practical method of combat. Mixing dismounted action with mounted action added a vital element of versatility to the cavalry arm, giving it a chance to deal with opposing infantry. It was standard practice to form a cavalry command so that some units were dismounted while other units supported them by remaining on horse. The mounted units could be thrown into the fight if an opportunity arose to break up a disordered enemy formation or to pursue a retreating foe. Mounted columns seldom were used to attack a well-formed infantry force. The few times this was attempted in the Civil War led to disaster for the mounted attackers. This was not at all surprising, and it had nothing to do with the widespread adoption of modern firearms because, even before the Civil War, mounted charges against well-ordered infantry had typically failed—even when the infantry used smoothbore muskets.

Civil War cavalrymen were proud of their ability to fight on foot and on horseback. They sometimes referred to themselves as hybrid cavalry; by whatever name, Civil War mounted forces became distinguished by their ability to fight in two different but complementary modes of combat. No other cavalry force in other countries and other time periods could match Union and Confederate horsemen in their versatility.

Given the emphasis on dismounted fighting, one would assume that mounted infantry would become an important component of Civil War armies. But that was not really accurate. Taking infantry units, giving the men horses, and training them how to use their mounts was done, of course, but those units melded smoothly into the larger cavalry forces. They did not retain any distinctiveness in their modes of operation because originally organized cavalry units were already fighting dismounted on a regular basis. Those mounted infantrymen simply became cavalrymen for all practical purposes. The only thing that distinguished them was their designation—17th Indiana Mounted Infantry, for example—but in the way they marched and fought, there was nothing to tell them apart from cavalrymen.

Moreover, the Civil War can claim no distinction for initiating the concept of mounting infantrymen, transporting them to the battlefield by horse, and then making them fight on foot. That concept also had a long pedigree in world military history. European cavalry forces had long before the American Civil War organized mounted infantry units, and even the U.S. Army had a regiment of such men before 1861. But with the impressive versatility of the hybrid cavalry of the Civil War, there simply was no need to continue mounting infantrymen after 1865.

Another tradition of mounted power that seemed to have little consequence during the Civil War was to accompany cavalry units with fast-moving artillery support. This also had a long pedigree in European history and had been a feature of American cavalry organization before 1861. Despite the generally good quality of the so-called horse artillery, there is little evidence that they played much of a role in the outcome of cavalry battles. The primary reason for this was the high level of mobility cavalry enjoyed, rarely remaining at one place very long during an engagement. In contrast, artillery needed time to establish itself in advantageous positions and further time to damage enemy artillery and men with its fire. The slower pace of infantry battles allowed artillery enough time to support foot soldiers, but mounted operations rarely settled for long at one spot before the units were off on a charge, retreat, or change of position. Still, the chances of doing some good always remained, and this led cavalry commanders to keep their guns handy even though there were many times when the artillerymen had to scramble so as not to be left behind.[2]

Mobility

Mobility was the chief characteristic of mounted warfare. Cavalry was the fastest arm, far more so than infantry, artillery, and naval action. Movement distinguished mounted operations, imparting a sometimes dizzying pace, and all good cavalry officers tried to take advantage of it. After the war William Brooke-Rawle cautioned John Bachelder about his hopes for pinpointing cavalry positions at Gettysburg with monuments. "You will find that the location of the monument in a cavalry fight is a far different thing from that of infantry. Cavalry are flying all over the field, never for long in any one spot and it is hard to put ones' hand on them."[3]

Making best use of that horse-based mobility involved separating part of the available mounted force from duties associated with closely supporting the infantry. While outpost and picket duty, providing couriers for infantry commanders, and protecting flanks during a battle were all legitimate roles for mounted troops, raiding, long-range reconnaissance, and independent action were equally legitimate roles that made the best use of the mounted arm's horse power.

The dual role of cavalry, to serve as support for infantry and to conduct independent action, was a major story of mounted warfare during the

Civil War. Of course, that conflict did not originate the idea of massing cavalry units; such a concept had deep traditions in European cavalry history. The United States had never created a cavalry force large enough to allow a dual role before 1861, and it took some time for the idea of massing mounted power to take root. When it finally happened, the results proved the wisdom of the experiment. Sheridan's and Wilson's campaigns stand tall in the long sweep of American military history as exemplars of what can be accomplished with the right combination of numbers, training, leadership, weapons, and supplies.

But in one area Civil War cavalry cannot take pride in its accomplishments. That lies in the abominable care too many soldiers administered to their mounts. Even though it should have been obvious that the horse played a key role in their military service, far too many Union and Confederate cavalrymen rode their mounts into the ground, took inadequate care of them in camp, and callously discarded them when unserviceable. They cannot be held completely at fault; neither side provided personnel trained in horse doctoring, nor did they thoroughly establish procedures to prevent the spread of horrible diseases or establish proper rehabilitation facilities for mounts. Horse care was too largely left to happenstance and the inclinations of individual soldiers.

It is true that many cavalrymen appreciated, loved, and understood their horses, taking very good care of them. Those emotions often extended to other mounts in their regiment. "My recollection of some of the horses of my comrades is more distinct than it is of the men who rode them," admitted one of Wheeler's troopers after the war.[4] These men could be counted on to do all they could to preserve their mounts for effective service. An equally sizeable group of cavalrymen would have obeyed orders to take adequate care of their horses out of a sense of duty to their officers. But the rest looked upon their horses as little more than tools to be used, abused, neglected, and discarded. This combination of individual attitudes and institutional inadequacy led to extremely high levels of horse wastage in the Civil War. The result was huge expenditures of public funds by the Federal government to replace mounts, an expense that caused much worry for responsible officials, and it contributed greatly to the steady decline in Confederate abilities to find proper replacement horses. It also represented an environmental disaster for the sentient creatures shoved against their will into a military system in which so much was demanded of them and so little given in return.

The high level of horse wastage shocked European observers. The major powers had a long tradition of maintaining large peace establishments of cavalry forces, and with that tradition had developed effective systems of horse care and housing mounts in well-constructed masonry barracks to endure the harsh winters. Maintaining proper systems of care, housing, grooming, feeding, and exercise preserved horse flesh and reduced overall expenditures on large permanent cavalry forces. The Americans had no such experience prior to the Civil War and, North and South alike, were caught unprepared to care for a huge population of horses. The military systems were overwhelmed, just as they had been with providing medical care for soldiers during the early months of the war before human health care improved. But the limited effort to establish horse-rehabilitation camps, about the only thing either army did in the way of health care for equines, achieved limited results at best.

Although appalled by horse wastage, European observers were very impressed by the concentration of Union cavalry power late in the war. They also were taken by the long-range mounted expeditions. Mounted raids to strike at enemy lines of communication captivated the imagination of European cavalry officers as much as it had captured the spirit of American officers. For many reasons, however, Europeans did not think it was possible to conduct such affairs in their own wars, and it rarely was attempted. Finally, the other component of Civil War cavalry operations that caught the attention of European observers was the versatility of American mounted operations. The ability of a Union or Confederate horse soldier to fight equally well on foot or mounted was something new to Europeans of the mid-nineteenth century. This they could do something about. At least in the British cavalry, training mounted men to become hybrid cavalry, capable of both types of combat on demand, became apparent.

American cavalry veterans were very proud of their achievements in the Civil War and assumed that their example had set a new standard for mounted warfare. In that assumption they were only partially right. Europeans studied Civil War cavalry and came away with differing opinions of its performance, adopting only a part of its lessons. But for that matter even American cavalrymen of the post–Civil War era could take seriously only part of that heritage after the U.S. government largely reverted back to its pre-1861 policies of maintaining a mounted force of minimal size to accomplish its frontier duties while saving as much money as possible. There also would be no more big wars for American cavalrymen to fight after 1865. The Spanish-American War was too short and too small, and World War I ushered in dramatic changes in overall military operations that limited but did not yet eliminate mounted warfare. While several European belligerents maintained huge mounted formations during that war, there were many reasons why the Americans did not. By the time they entered the conflict, it had been mired in static trench systems for years, and the cost of sending a large mounted force across the Atlantic would have been staggering.

As with so many other aspects of the Civil War when set within the context of the European military heritage, Union and Confederate cavalry fits comfortably within that framework for the most part. As far as its size, training, utilization, and accomplishments were concerned, Europeans found little different in Civil War mounted forces than that of their own. The key differences were the waste of horses, the level of dismounted fighting, and the strategic raids. Those anomalies can best be seen as variations on the European example rather than radical departures from it, and European cavalry authorities failed to fully copy two of them while shunning the other.

But when comparing Civil War cavalry with prior and subsequent American experience at war, the conflict stands out as unique. In all aspects—the size of the mounted force, its intensive training, the enormous demand the cavalry exerted on resources of manpower, horses, weapons, and equipment—the Civil War occupied a category of its own within the framework of American military history. The influence of cavalry on shaping the nature and trajectory of operations during that war also stood out when compared to any other American conflict. Cavalry certainly did not decide victory or defeat in this long, complicated war, but it just as certainly played a larger role in it than in any previous or subsequent conflict. In the long sweep of American cavalry history, the Civil War was the ultimate test of mounted warfare.

NOTES

Abbreviations

ADAH	Alabama Department of Archives and History, Montgomery
CHM	Chicago History Museum, Chicago, IL
DPL	Detroit Public Library, Special Collections, Detroit, MI
DU	Duke University, David M. Rubenstein Rare Book and Manuscript Library, Durham, NC
FHS	Filson Historical Society, Louisville, KY
KHS	Kansas Historical Society, Topeka
LC	Library of Congress, Manuscript Division, Washington, DC
NARA	National Archives and Records Administration, Washington, DC
OR	*The War of the Rebellion: A Compilation of the Official Records of the Union and Confederate Armies*, 70 vols. in 128 pts. (Washington, DC: Government Printing Office, 1880–1901); all citations are to series 1 unless otherwise stated
SOR	*Supplement to the Official Records of the Union and Confederate Armies*, 100 vols. (Wilmington, NC: Broadfoot, 1995–99)
UC	University of Chicago, Special Collections Research Center, Chicago, IL
UNC	University of North Carolina, Southern Historical Collection, Chapel Hill
USC	University of South Carolina, South Caroliniana Library, Columbia
UTK	University of Tennessee, Special Collections, Knoxville
VMI	Virginia Military Institute, Archives, Lexington
WRHS	Western Reserve Historical Society, Cleveland, OH

1. The Cavalry Heritage

1. Drews, *Early Riders*, 1, 128; Wentz and De Grummond, "Life on Horseback," 107; Sidnell, *Warhorse*, 1, 6, 12, 15, 17. For a good overview of cavalry history, tracing several themes, see Black, *Cavalry*.

2. Drews, *Early Riders*, 121–22, 128; Sidnell, *Warhorse*, 23–25, 28–29, 42–51.

3. Sidnell, *Warhorse*, 20–21, 33, 36, 142–43.

4. Sidnell, *Warhorse*, 39–40, 75–77, 79–80, 86, 125, 135–36; Sears and Willekes, "Alexander's Cavalry Charge," 1017–35; Drews, *Early Riders*, 124–25.

5. McCall, *Cavalry of the Roman Republic*, 1–2, 11–12, 70, 72; Sidnell, *Warhorse*, 155, 157, 171, 180, 194–95, 254–56, 281, 283.

6. Sidnell, *Warhorse*, 303, 305–8, 310, 312–13, 329–30.

7. Gassman, "Thoughts on the Role of Cavalry," 149–77.

8. Phillips, "'Of Nimble Service,'" 4, 6–8, 12–15, 18–19.

9. Lynn, *Giant of the Grand Siècle*, 490–92, 494–98, 528–30.

10. Robinson, "Horse Supply," 121–40.

11. Robinson, "Equine Battering Rams?," 722–23, 725, 728n, 731.

12. Duffy, *Military Experience*, 116–17.

13. Duffy, *Military Experience*, 118–20.

14. Duffy, *Military Experience*, 222–27.

15. Showalter, *Wars of Frederick the Great*, 72–73, 81, 114, 190, 205.

16. Houlding, *Fit for Service*, 265–266, 285.

17. Quimby, *Background of Napoleonic Warfare*, 26–27, 34–35, 37–38, 40–41, 50–54, 88.

18. Quimby, *Background of Napoleonic Warfare*, 106, 122, 133.

19. Quimby, *Background of Napoleonic Warfare*, 134–40, 164, 252.

20. Lynn, *Bayonets of the Republic*, 195–96, 200, 203; Nosworthy, *With Musket, Cannon. and Sword*, 14–15, 305–6; Muir, *Tactics and the Experience of Battle*, 105–8.

21. Muir, *Tactics and the Experience of Battle*, 108–11; Nosworthy, *With Musket, Cannon. and Sword*, 280–83, 287–95, 297–98, 351–52; Duffy, *Military Experience*, 228.

22. Nosworthy, *With Musket, Cannon. and Sword*, 133–34, 263–67, 270, 334–35; Muir, *Tactics and the Experience of Battle*, 120–21, 131.

23. Muir, *Tactics and the Experience of Battle*, 114, 117–18, 122, 135, 137; Nosworthy, *With Musket, Cannon. and Sword*, 409.

24. Muir, *Tactics and the Experience of Battle*, 122, 124, 126–27; Nosworthy, *Bloody Crucible*, 293.

25. Duffy, *Austerlitz*, 44, 92.

26. Weigley, *Age of Battles*.

27. Duffy, *Borodino*, 85, 87.

28. Mikaberidze, *Battle of Borodino*, 121–25, 168–69, 172–87; Zemtsov, "Battle of Borodino," 103–6, 109–10.

29. Hamilton-Williams, *Waterloo*, 297–303, 320–24.

30. Gerges, "Command and Control," 400–401, 405–6; Muir, *Salamanca*, 23–24, 43–44, 126–36, 213.

31. Muir, *Tactics and the Experience of Battle*, 112.

32. Lieven, "Mobilizing Russian Horsepower," 153–55.

33. McClellan wrote a long report as part of his duties on the Delafield Commission. A short time later parts of it were reprinted for the trade-book market. McClellan's *European Cavalry*, which includes the report's segment on that arm of the service, was published in the latter months of 1861.

34. McClellan, *European Cavalry*, 13–214.

35. McClellan, *European Cavalry*, 13–14, 109, 111–12, 115–16; *OR*, ser. 3, 1:304.

36. McClellan, *European Cavalry*, 118, 137, 161–63; Roemer, *Cavalry*, 18.

37. McClellan, *European Cavalry*, 175, 191, 193–94, 200–202; Roemer, *Cavalry*, 18.

38. McClellan, *European Cavalry*, 205, 213.

39. Roemer, *Cavalry*, 18, 25; Bonin, "Challenged Competency," 113.

40. Roemer, *Cavalry*, 18; Bonin, "Challenged Competency," 113; *OR*, 46(2):546.

41. Spring, *With Zeal and with Bayonets Only*, 270–74; Halleck, *Elements of Military Art*, 272; Bonin, "Challenged Competency," 110–11.

42. Upton, *Military Policy of the United States*, 137; Brackett, *History of the United States Cavalry*, 14, 20–23, 32–35, 37, 60, 123, 140–41; Bonin, "Challenged Competency," 111; Gray, *Cavalry Tactics*, 5.

43. Nelson, "General Charles Scott," 219–51; Gilpin, *War of 1812 in the Old Northwest*, 214–34; Murphy, *Two Armies on the Rio Grande*, 222–23.

44. Brackett, *History of the United States Cavalry*, 158–60; Halleck, *Elements of Military Art*, 264, 270; *OR*, ser. 3, 1:304; Welcher, *Union Army*, 508; Nosworthy, *Bloody Crucible*, 286–87; Wheeler, *Revised System of Cavalry Tactics*, 22–24; Scott, *Military Dictionary*, 154; Gray, *Cavalry Tactics*, 6.

45. *Napoleon's Maxims of War*, 114–16; Jomini, *Art of War*, 304–5, 360; Nolan, *Cavalry*, 69; Phillips, "'Who Shall Say,'" 17.

46. Morrison, "Educating the Civil War Generals," 108–9; Boynton, *History of West Point*, 226, 274.

47. Taylor, *Destruction and Reconstruction*, 37.

48 Nosworthy, *Bloody Crucible*, 287–88; Mahan, *Elementary Treatise*, 19; Scott, *Military Dictionary*, 156; Halleck, *Elements of Military Art*, 126–27.

49. Halleck, *Elements of Military Art*, 125, 270; Mahan, *Elementary Treatise*, 18–21.

50. Halleck, *Elements of Military Art*, 263–64, 270.

51. Halleck, *Elements of Military Art*, 263.

52. Scott, *Military Dictionary*, 154–15; Nosworthy, *Bloody Crucible*, 282; Halleck, *Elements of Military Art*, 127–28.

2. Organizing the Cavalry

1. Kempster, "Early Days of Our Cavalry," 61–62; Crowninshield, *First Regiment of Massachusetts Cavalry*, 40–41; Dornblaser, *Sabre Strokes of the Pennsylvania Dragoons*, 9, 11; Farrar, *Twenty-Second Pennsylvania Cavalry*, 11–12, 14, 24.

2. Scott, "Black Horse Cavalry," 590–92; Peck, *Reminiscences*, 2; McMurry, *Uncompromising Secessionist*, 306–7; Deupree, "Noxubee Squadron," 12–13.

3. McClellan, *Regulations and Instructions*, 9; Nolan, *Cavalry*, 64–67; McClellan, *European Cavalry*, 116.

4. O'Brien and Diefendorf, *General Orders*, 1:100–101.

5. Gregg, "Second Cavalry Division," 115.

6. Halleck, *Elements of Military Art*, 272; O'Brien and Diefendorf, *General Orders*, 1:32–33; *OR*, ser. 3, 1:921.

7. *OR*, ser. 3, 1:304, 456.

8. *OR*, ser. 3, 1:580, 608, 622, 728, 735, 873.

9. *OR*, ser. 3, 1:909, 912–13, 2:183–84.

10. *OR*, ser. 3, 2:859–60.

11. Gray, *Cavalry Tactics*, 6–7; *OR*, ser. 3, 2:518; Cheney, *Ninth Regiment, New York Volunteer Cavalry*, 12–13.

12. Crowninshield, *First Regiment of Massachusetts Cavalry*, 47; *History of the Service of the Third Ohio*, 15; *OR*, 10(1):735; Cheney, *Ninth Regiment, New York Volunteer Cavalry*, 21–22; Moyer, *Seventeenth Regiment Pennsylvania Volunteer Cavalry*, 56.

13. Bouvé, "Battle at High Bridge," 404; Crowninshield, *First Regiment of Massachusetts Cavalry*, 270.

14. Crowninshield, *First Regiment of Massachusetts Cavalry*, 300; Cooke, *Battle of Kelly's Ford*, 6; Thatcher, *Hundred Battles*, 25; Scott, *Story of a Cavalry Regiment*, 11, 49; [Tenney], *War Diary*, xi.

15. McClellan, *Regulations and Instructions*, 12; Gray, *Cavalry Tactics*, 6; O'Brien and Diefendorf, *General Orders*, 1:85; *OR*, 42(1):644; Harrison, "Personal Experiences," 232; Carter, *From Yorktown to Santiago*, 20; Schlotterbeck et al., *James Riley Weaver's Civil War*, 24; Graham, "Nineteenth Regiment," 90; Opie, *Rebel Cavalryman*, 145.

16. OR, ser. 3, 3:175; Kidd, *Riding with Custer*, 57.

17. Dickenson, "Fifth New York Cavalry," 147–49; Preston, *Tenth Regiment of Cavalry, New York State Volunteers*, 15, 33; Reader, *Fifth West Virginia Cavalry*, 25.

18. Francis Reiley to mother and friends, October 19, November 13, December 9, 1861, and February 2, 1862, Francis and John Reiley Papers, WRHS.

19. Wells A. Bushnell Memoirs, 11–12, 24–25, 30–31, 36–39, WRHS.

20. Clark, "Making of a Volunteer Cavalryman," 462; *History of the Eighteenth Regiment of Cavalry Pennsylvania Volunteers*, 13–14.

21. Hamilton, *Recollections*, 41.

22. Hamilton, *Recollections*, 41–43, 68.

23. Kirk, *Fifteenth Pennsylvania Volunteer Cavalry*, 13–15, 601–2, 605–8, 615–17, 622.

24. Kirk, *Fifteenth Pennsylvania Volunteer Cavalry*, 15, 30–31, 33–34, 37, 40, 68–69, 178–80; [Williams], *Leaves from a Trooper's Diary*, 89, 93.

25. Kirk, *Fifteenth Pennsylvania Volunteer Cavalry*, 180–81, 187–90, 204–5, 211–12, 214, 619–20.

26. Crowninshield, *First Regiment of Massachusetts Cavalry*, 255–58, 267–68, 282.

27. Crowninshield, *First Regiment of Massachusetts Cavalry*, 196–97, 200.

28. Ewer, *Third Massachusetts Cavalry*, 53, 79, 99, 277.

29. The 39th Indiana received horses in April 1863 and by October was redesignated as the 8th Indiana Cavalry. The 4th Tennessee Infantry (U.S.) converted to cavalry service in October 1862 and was renamed the 1st Tennessee Cavalry (U.S.). Bowen, *First New York Dragoons*, 7–9, 86, 96, 98–99; Carmony, "Jacob W. Bartmess Civil War Letters," 62; Carter, *First Regiment of Tennessee Volunteer Cavalry*, 57, 59–60.

30. *OR*, 32(2):520–21.

31. Bergeron, *Guide to Louisiana Confederate Military Units*, 39–68.

32. Pickerill, *Third Indiana Cavalry*, 40, 42, 44.

33. Pickerill, *Third Indiana Cavalry*, 9, 55, 100, 111, 120, 124–25; McCain, *Soldier's Diary*, 5.

34. "Letters of a Civil War Surgeon," 134; Pickerill, *Third Indiana Cavalry*, 40, 182.

35. Ladd and Ladd, *Bachelder Papers*, 1:652; Brooke-Rawle, "Gregg's Cavalry in the Gettysburg Campaign," 159n; Denison, *Sabres and Spurs*, 428–29; Crowninshield, *First Regiment of Massachusetts Cavalry*, 248.

36. Rein, *Second Colorado Cavalry*, 219; Hastings, "Cavalry Service," 260; [Tenney], *War Diary*, xi–xii; Scott, *Story of a Cavalry Regiment*, 11.

37. Crowninshield, *First Regiment of Massachusetts Cavalry*, 300; Clark, "Making of a Volunteer Cavalryman," 474; Whittaker, *Volunteer Cavalry*, 96.

38. Gleason, "U.S. Mounted Bands," 102, 107–8, 111, 113, 117.

39. *OR*, ser. 3, 3:605–6, 886.

40. *OR*, ser. 3, 3:990–92.

41. *OR*, ser. 3, 4:86–87.

42. *OR*, ser. 3, 4:549; Vincent, "Greatest of Military Nations"; Bonin, "Challenged Competency," 127.

43. Crowninshield, "Cavalry in Virginia," 5; [Adams], *Trooper's Adventures*, 30; Congdon, *Cavalry Compendium*, 14.

44. *OR*, ser. 3, 4:1167.

45. Receipt, June 28, 1861, and memorandum of expenses, June 24–July 20, 1861, Boykin Family Papers, UNC.

3. Books, Doctrine, and Training

1. *Abstract of Colonel Herries's Instructions;* Duane, *Hand Book for Cavalry*, i, vi.

2. Brackett, *History of the United States Cavalry*, 48; *Cavalry Tactics, First Part*, 3, 12, 53–54, 72–81; *Cavalry Tactics, Second Part*, 114, 143–54, 197, 200–203, 232–36, 244, 252–53; *Cavalry Tactics, Third Part*, 15, 22, 86.

3. *Cavalry Tactics, First Part*, 77, 79, 85–97, 100–124, 133–56, 159–98.

4 Brackett, *History of the United States Cavalry*, 48; Cooke, *Cavalry Tactics*, vol. 1, frontispiece.

5. Cooke, *Cavalry Tactics*, 1:3–4.

6. Cooke, *Cavalry Tactics*, 1:4, 6.

7. Cooke, *Cavalry Tactics*, 1:10.

8. Cooke, *Cavalry Tactics*, 1:22, 24–29, 31–32, 38.

9. Cooke, *Cavalry Tactics*, 1:39.

10. Cooke, *Cavalry Tactics*, 1:39–40.

11. Cooke, *Cavalry Tactics*, 1:40.

12. Hess, *Civil War Infantry Tactics*, 212.

13. Cooke, *Cavalry Tactics*, 1:41.

14. Cooke, *Cavalry Tactics*, 1:42.

15. Cooke, *Cavalry Tactics*, 1:43–44.

16. Cooke, *Cavalry Tactics*, 1:52–71.

17. Cooke, *Cavalry Tactics*, 1:73–78, 87.

18. Cooke, *Cavalry Tactics*, 1:121, 132, 142–43, 154–55.

19. Cooke, *Cavalry Tactics*, 1:166–67.

20. Cooke, *Cavalry Tactics*, 1:167, 171–75, 194–96.

21. Cooke, *Cavalry Tactics*, 1:207–8, 211–12.

22. Cooke, *Cavalry Tactics*, 1:215.

23. Cooke, *Cavalry Tactics*, 2:1–27.

24. Cooke, *Cavalry Tactics*, 2:59.

25. Cooke, *Cavalry Tactics*, 2:62–63, 65–66.

26. Cooke, *Cavalry Tactics*, 1:4.

27. Lord, "Army and Navy Textbooks," 95, 101; Nolan, *Cavalry*, 193–94, 225, 287–88.

28. McClellan, *Regulations and Instructions*, 3–4.

29. Roemer, *Cavalry*, 24, 138.

30. Congdon, *Cavalry Compendium*, 65–155.

31. Davis, *Trooper's Manual*, iii–v; Longacre, *Soldier to the Last*, 94.

32. Maury, *Skirmish Drill for Mounted Troops*, frontispiece.

33. Patten, *Cavalry Drill*, 3, 6, 11, 68, 70–72, 75.

34. Wheeler, *Revised System of Cavalry Tactics*, 41–45; Longacre, *Soldier to the Last*, 95.

35. Frank to mother, September 5, 1861, Francis and John Reiley Papers, WRHS; Force to Mr. Kebler, August 1, 1863, M. F. Force Papers, University of Washington, Special Collections, Seattle; Blackford, *War Years*, 13; Beale, *Ninth Virginia Cavalry*, 16.

36. *OR*, 27(1):45.

37. *Revised Regulations*, 105.

38. Wheeler, *Revised System of Cavalry Tactics*, 22.

39. Cooke, *Cavalry Tactics*, 2:60–62; *Revised Regulations*, 105.

40. Cooke, *Cavalry Tactics*, 2:36; Nolan, *Cavalry*, 295.

41. Bowen, *First New York Dragoons*, 97; Moyer, *Seventeenth Regiment Pennsylvania Volunteer Cavalry*, 28; Frank to Mother, September 27, 1861, Francis and John Reiley Papers, WRHS.

42. McClellan, *Regulations and Instructions*, 13; Curry, *Four Years in the Saddle*, 22.

43. Hamilton, *Recollections*, 83; Cooke, *Battle of Kelly's Ford*, 9.

44. Curry, *Four Years in the Saddle*, 21; Harrison, "Personal Experiences," 232; [Tenney], *War Diary*, 143–44.

45. Tobie, *First Maine Cavalry*, 15; Foster, *Reminiscences and Record*, 98.

46. Norton, *"Red Neck Ties,"* 17.

47. Flanders to brother, July 1, 1863, George E. Flanders Civil War Letters, KHS; Coles and Engle, *Yankee Horseman*, 22; Ezell, "Excerpts from the Civil War Diary of Lieutenant Charles Alley," 246.

48. Pickerill, *Third Indiana Cavalry*, 13; Crowninshield, *First Regiment of Massachusetts Cavalry*, 297–98; Rowell, *Yankee Cavalrymen*, 36.

49. Bowen, *First New York Dragoons*, 97–98.

50. *History of the Service of the Third Ohio*, 14.

51. *History of the Service of the Third Ohio*, 15; Foster, *Reminiscences and Record*, 98.

52. Scott, *Military Dictionary*, 154; Reminiscences, 15, August Bondi Papers, KHS; Avery, *Fourth Illinois Cavalry*, 47.

53. Cooke, *Cavalry Tactics*, 1:117–18; Taylor, *Saddle and Saber*, 138; Avery, *Fourth Illinois Cavalry*, 47–48.

54. *History of the Service of the Third Ohio*, 18; Tobie, *First Maine Cavalry*, 17; Pierce, *Second Iowa Cavalry*, 11.

55. Bowen, *First New York Dragoons*, 97.

56. Allen, *Down in Dixie*, 144–45.

57. Whittaker, *Volunteer Cavalry*, 6; Starr, "Cold Steel," 149.

58. Ezell, "Excerpts from the Civil War Diary of Lieutenant Charles Alley," 247; Maness and Combs, *Do They Miss Me?*, 28.

59. Coles and Engle, *Yankee Horseman*, 22; Pierce, *Second Iowa Cavalry*, 11–12.

60. Davis, *Trooper's Manual*, vii.

61. Lee to William Porcher Miles, January 28, 1864, Stephen D. Lee Service Record, M331, RG 109, NARA; Cutrer, *Our Trust*, 71.

62. Davis, *Trooper's Manual*, viii–ix; William H. Areheart Diaries, August 10, 1864, DU; Wharton to father, November 28, 1862, W. D. Wharton Papers, UNC.

63. Roberts, "Additional Sketch Nineteenth Regiment," 105–6; Barringer to V. C. Barringer, January 27, 1866, Rufus Barringer Papers, UNC.

64. Deupree, "Noxubee Squadron," 15; McMurry, *Uncompromising Secessionist*, 195.

65. Wheeler, *Revised System of Cavalry Tactics*, 52. George W. Patten said the same things about moulinet and thrusting in *Cavalry Drill*, 27–28.

66. McMurry, *Uncompromising Secessionist*, 308; Brown, *War Years*, 221.

67. Clark, "Making of a Volunteer Cavalryman," 474.

4. Formations and Maneuvers

1. Duane, *Hand Book for Cavalry*, iv–vi; Nolan, *Cavalry*, 331, 338.

2. Nolan, *Cavalry*, 328–29; McClellan, *European Cavalry*, 119.

3. McClellan, *Regulations and Instructions*, 10; Scott, *Military Dictionary*, 156; Mahan, *Elementary Treatise*, 19; Maury, *Skirmish Drill*, 4.

4. Cooke, *Cavalry Tactics*, 1:1–2.

5. Tobie, *First Maine Cavalry*, 16; Crowninshield, *First Regiment of Massachusetts Cavalry*, 297; Carpenter, "Sheridan's Expedition around Richmond," 301.

6. *History of the Eleventh Pennsylvania*, 24; Kidd, *Riding with Custer*, 48, 232–33.

7. Scott, *Story of a Cavalry Regiment*, 14–15; *History of the Service of the Third Ohio*, 14.

8. *OR*, 12(2):275; Fitzsimmons, "Hunter Raid," 396; Kidd, *Riding with Custer*, 332.

9. *OR*, 45(2):589.

10. Whiting, "Diary and Personal Recollections," 92; Scott, *Story of a Cavalry Regiment*, 427.

11. Scott, *Story of a Cavalry Regiment*, 427–28.

12. Bahde, *Story of My Campaign*, 219.

13. *OR*, 40(1):721; Vance, *Report of the Adjutant General*, 6:419.

14. Davis, *Trooper's Manual*, iv; Gilmor, *Four Years in the Saddle*, 247–48; *SOR*, pt. 1, 3:312.

15. Dodson, *Campaigns of Wheeler*, 375; Wheeler, *Revised System of Cavalry Tactics*, i; Longacre, *Soldier to the Last*, 94.

16. Hess, *Civil War Infantry Tactics*, 208–10.

17. "Sketches of the Field and Camp in a Series of Letters from a Sanitary Inspector to the Little Folks at Home, Vol. 1, Washington, Feb. 1862," 78–79, Folder 1, Box 37, Franklin Benjamin Hough Papers, New York State Library, Albany; *OR*, 38(2):839; Ladd and Ladd, *Bachelder Papers*, 2:916; Julius E. Thomas Civil War Diary, May 11, 1864, UTK. For references to flankers, see *OR*, 12(1):589; Wells A. Bushnell Memoirs, 269, WRHS; Pratt diary, September 21, 1862, Richard Henry Pratt Papers, LC; and *OR*, 47(1):869.

18. Kidd, *Riding with Custer*, 264–266. For columns of regiments, see *OR*, 42(1):640. For columns of battalions, see *OR*, 30(2):675; Wittenberg, *One of Custer's Wolverines*, 63; and Kidd, *Riding with Custer*, 297, 422. For columns of squadrons, see Ladd and Ladd, *Bachelder Papers*, 1:652, 2:1124, 1279; Joseph Wheeler to Johnston, May 16, 1864, Joseph E. Johnston Papers, Huntington Library, San Marino, CA; Griffin, *Three Years a Soldier*, 220; Athearn, "Civil War Diary of John Wilson Phillips," 102; and *OR*, 43(1):445, 47(1):888. For columns of companies, see Wells A. Bushnell Memoirs, 46, WRHS. For columns of platoons, see Carter, *From Yorktown to Santiago*, 29; Greene, "Campaigning in the Army of the Frontier," 303; and *OR*, 43(1):485, 518. For columns of half platoons, see *History and Roster of the Seventh Pa. Cavalry*, 8. For columns of eights, see *OR*, 18:8. For columns of fours, see *OR*, 32(1):75, 144, 313, 12(1):679–80, 40(1):612–13, 44:390; *History of the Service*

of the Third Ohio, 163; and Thomas, *Some Personal Reminiscences*, 4. For columns of twos, see *SOR*, pt. 1, 4:32; and McClellan, *Regulations and Instructions*, 13.

19. McClellan, *Regulations and Instructions*, 13; Ladd and Ladd, *Bachelder Papers*, 2:1219.

20. McClellan, *Regulations and Instructions*, 13; *SOR*, pt. 1, 5:236–37; Kidd, *Riding with Custer*, 294; Kidd, "Michigan Cavalry Brigade," 234; *OR*, 27(1):946.

21. Rea, "Kilpatrick's Raid around Atlanta," 165; *OR*, 38(2):814.

22. *OR*, 43(1):450, 456, 533; Kidd, *Riding with Custer*, 416.

23. *OR*, 43(1):523, 27(2):973, 20(1):649; Beach, *First New York (Lincoln) Cavalry*, 424; Kidd, *Riding with Custer*, 418.

24. Ford, "Charge of the First Maine Cavalry," 276, 283; McClellan, *Regulations and Instructions*, 13; *SOR*, pt. 1, 3:239–40; Gause, *Four Years with Five Armies*, 345; Starr, "Wilson Raid," 235.

25. McClellan, *European Cavalry*, 145; *OR*, 49(1):482, 39(1):37, 46, 38(2):824, 42(1):607, 648, 32(1):299–301; Tobie, *First Maine Cavalry*, 260.

26. *OR*, 27(1):985, 44:382, 10(1):736; Cheney, *Ninth Regiment, New York Volunteer Cavalry*, 221.

27. For references to columns of fours, see Dixon diary, May 20, 1864, Harry St. John Dixon Papers, UNC. For columns of squadrons, see Giles, *Terry's Texas Rangers*, 46; Graham, "Nineteenth Regiment," 91–92; and Cooke, *Battle of Kelly's Ford*, 28–29. For columns of battalions, see Cooke, *Battle of Kelly's Ford*, 22–23. For the use of the gallop, see Roberts, "Additional Sketch Nineteenth Regiment," 104. For deploying from column to line, see *OR*, 34(1):608; and *SOR*, pt. 1, 3:312. For distance within the column, see Wheeler, *Revised System of Cavalry Tactics*, 26; *OR*, 27(2):732; and Ladd and Ladd, *Bachelder Papers*, 2:1078. For flankers, see *OR*, 40(1):614. For the mix of mounted and dismounted units within a formation, see Means, "Additional Sketch Sixty-Third Regiment," 605–6.

28. *OR*, 41(1):332–33, 336; Scott, "Last Fight," 321–22, 324–25; *SOR*, pt. 1, 7:382–83; Scott, *Story of a Cavalry Regiment*, 334–35.

29. *OR*, 32(1):295, 20(1):647.

30. Curry, "Raid of the Union Cavalry," 273.

31. Barron, *Lone Star Defenders*, 44.

32. Beach, *First New York (Lincoln) Cavalry*, 420; Greene, "Campaigning in the Army of the Frontier," 291.

33. Kidd, *Michigan Cavalry Brigade*, 11–13; Crowninshield, *First Regiment of Massachusetts Cavalry*, 209.

34. Gardiner, "Incidents of Cavalry Experiences," 439; *OR*, 44:376, 391.

35. Trowbridge, *Stoneman Raid*, 107.

36. McClellan, *Regulations and Instructions*, 13; *OR*, 43(1):482.

37. McMurry, *Uncompromising Secessionist*, 298; Beale, *Lieutenant of Cavalry*, 184; Means, "*Additional Sketch Sixty-Third Regiment,*" 649.

38. Munnerlyn to sister, October 9, 1862, James Keen Munnerlyn Papers, UNC; Nanzig, *Civil War Memoirs of a Virginia Cavalryman*, 205; *OR*, 11(1):429; Wells A. Bushnell Memoirs, 186, WRHS; Foster, *Reminiscences and Record*, 47; Gause, *Four Years with Five Armies*, 345; Crowninshield, *First Regiment of Massachusetts Cavalry*, 126.

39. Bliss, "Reminiscences," 60–62.

5. Mounted Operations

1. Cooke, *Cavalry Tactics*, 1:157–58.
2. Cooke, *Cavalry Tactics*, 1:158; *OR*, 30(2):683, 25(1):57.
3. Mitchell, *Letters of Major General James E. B. Stuart*, 329–30; Kidd, *Riding with Custer*, 418; *OR*, 27(1):956, 43(1):483, 541; Wells A. Bushnell Memoirs, 184, WRHS.
4. *SOR*, pt. 1, 5:233; *OR*, 42(1):609, 645, 30(2):683.
5. Carpenter, "Sheridan's Expedition around Richmond," 302.
6. Nosworthy, *Bloody Crucible*, 303; Cutrer, *Our Trust*, 53–57; *OR*, 17(1):243–44, 38(4):336.
7. Hitchcock, "Recollections," 779.
8. Hitchcock, "Recollections," 779.
9. C. F. James to editor, January 3, 1899, *Confederate Veteran* Papers, DU; Hitchcock, "Recollections," 779; *OR*, 11(2):45–47.
10. McWhiney and Jamieson, *Attack and Die*, 128.
11. Thomas, *Some Personal Reminiscences*, 4, 7; *OR*, 12(2):141.
12. *OR*, 17(1):556–59.
13. *OR*, 42(1):645–46.
14. *OR*, 32(1):90.
15. Brooke-Rawle, "Gregg's Cavalry in the Gettysburg Campaign," 178.
16. Nosworthy, *Bloody Crucible*, 301.
17. West, "McCook's Raid in the Rear of Atlanta," 32; *OR*, 36(1):821, 30(2):748, 23(2):155.
18. Hess, *Civil War Field Artillery*, 233, 236–37; Dyer, "Fourth Regiment of Artillery," 852, 854; Collier and Collier, *Yours for the Union*, 259; *OR*, 25(1):55.
19. Hess, *Civil War Field Artillery*, 235–36; "Correspondence of Ira Butterfield," 278; Kaplan, *Artillery Service*, 88–89, 236; *OR*, 29(2):130–31, 410, 26(1):721, 38(1):121, 185, 25(1):694; Birkhimer, *Historical Sketch . . . of the Artillery*, 206; *SOR*, pt. 2, 50:513; Trout, *Memoirs of the Stuart Horse Artillery*, 191; Maxwell, *Perfect Lion*, 235; Wiley, *Norfolk Blues*, 45; Ladd and Ladd, *Bachelder Papers*, 2:1252; Daniel, *Cannoneers in Gray*, 89; Morton, *Artillery of Nathan Bedford Forrest's Cavalry*, 161–62.
20. *Brief History of the Fourth Pennsylvania*, 37; *OR*, 29(1):397; Crowninshield, *First Regiment of Massachusetts Cavalry*, 218; *SOR*, pt. 1, 3:518.
21. *OR*, 32(1):147.
22. *OR*, 34(1):448, 25(1):55.
23. Trout, *Memoirs of the Stuart Horse Artillery*, 206.
24. McDonald, *Laurel Brigade*, 32; *OR*, 25(1):54.
25. Maass, *Defending a New Nation*, 27–34.
26. "List of American Civil War Legions," Wikipedia, https://en.wikipedia.org/wiki/List_of_American_Civil_War_legions. This Internet source offers a handy list of Union and Confederate legions with information on primary and secondary sources about them.
27. Bennett and Haigh, *Thirty-Sixth Regiment Illinois Volunteers*, 720–21.
28. *OR*, 38(4):439.
29. Barringer, "Ninth Regiment," 418.
30. Mahan, *Elementary Treatise*, 49–50, 53–58.
31. Clark, "Making of a Volunteer Cavalryman," 472–73.

32. Rae, "Four Weeks," 38; *History of the Eleventh Pennsylvania*, 52–53; Baker to Mercie, September 3, 1863, William B. Baker Papers, UNC; Wells A. Bushnell Memoirs, 202, WRHS.

33. Ford, *Cycle of Adams Letters*, 2:69, 104–5, 1:282–84.

34. *OR*, 39(1):305, 42(1):642–43.

35. Crowninshield, *First Regiment of Massachusetts Cavalry*, 33, 285; Whittaker, *Volunteer Cavalry*, 98–100.

36. Graham, "Nineteenth Regiment," 81; Hill, "Forty-First Regiment (Third Cavalry)," 772–73.

37. *OR*, 20(1):958.

38. Wheeler, *Revised System of Cavalry Tactics*, 46–47; Circular, Wheeler's Cavalry Corps, April 22, 1864, General Orders, Civil War, 982, Box 130, Joseph Wheeler Family Papers, ADAH.

39. Mays, *Let Us Meet in Heaven*, 165; J. A. Cooper to Morgan, January 21, 1864, John Hunt Morgan Papers, UNC; Hubbard, *Notes of a Private*, 49; Munnerlyn to sister, October 9, 1862, James Keen Munnerlyn Papers, UNC; *OR*, ser. 4, 2:720; Mosby, *War Reminiscences*, 213.

40. Mosby, *War Reminiscences*, 218.

41. Reader, *Fifth West Virginia Cavalry*, 249.

42. Circular, Headquarters, Wheeler's Cavalry Corps, July 2, 1864, General Orders, Civil War, Box 130, and J. R. Rion to Wheeler, September 25, 190a [*sic*], Joseph Wheeler Family Papers, ADAH.

43. McMurry, *Uncompromising Secessionist*, 344.

44. Taylor, *Saddle and Saber*, 69; *OR*, 30(2):673; Newcomer, *Cole's Cavalry*, 66; Berkenes, *Private William Boddy's Civil War Journal*, 122; Norton, *Deeds of Daring*, 34.

45. Brown, *War Years*, 222–23; Norton, *Deeds of Daring*, 52.

46. McClellan, *Regulations and Instructions*, 33–34; Halleck, *Elements of Military Art*, 266.

47. Brown, *War Years*, 166–67.

48. Ford, *Cycle of Adams Letters*, 2:70; Pratt diary, August 18, 1862, Richard Henry Pratt Papers, LC; Humphreys, *Field, Camp, Hospital and Prison*, 24–25; *OR*, 32(1):282; Bliss, "Cavalry Service," 201.

49. Opie, *Rebel Cavalryman*, 171.

50. Allen, *Down in Dixie*, 155–56.

51. Ford, *Cycle of Adams Letters*, 1:227; Norton, *Deeds of Daring*, 28–29.

52. [Tenney], *War Diary*, 42; Graham, "Nineteenth Regiment," 90; *Brief History of the Fourth Pennsylvania*, 39.

53. *OR*, 44:376, 38(2):811–12; *SOR*, pt. 1, 5:243.

54. Tobie, "Service of the Cavalry," 129; *OR*, 36(2):174, 36(1):792, 41(1):392; Wittenberg, *"We Have It Damn Hard,"* 114; Scott and Angel, *Thirteenth Regiment Tennessee Volunteer Cavalry*, 229.

55 Beard, "With Forrest," 307; *OR*, 30(2):670–72.

56. Kennedy and Parker, "Seventy-Fifth Regiment," 84; Graham, "Nineteenth Regiment," 96–97; Nanzig, *Civil War Memoirs of a Virginia Cavalryman*, 103; Dodson, *Campaigns of Wheeler*, 57, 250n; Hastings, "Cavalry Service," 262; Newcomer, *Cole's Cavalry*, 90.

57. McClellan, *European Cavalry*, 143; *SOR*, pt. 1, 4:206; Connelly, "Recollections," 463.

58. Curry, "Raid of Union Cavalry," 271.

59. Gilmor, *Four Years in the Saddle*, 33; Hubbard, *Notes of a Private*, 158; Beard, "With Forrest in West Tennessee," 304.

60. Humphreys, *Field, Camp, Hospital and Prison*, 216–17.

61. Gause, *Four Years with Five Armies*, 353–56.

62. *SOR*, pt. 1, 4:212; *OR*, 32(1):286.

63. Opie, *Rebel Cavalryman*, 118.

64. Baker to parents, April 19, 1863, William B. Baker Papers, UNC; Cooke, *Battle of Kelly's Ford*, 19.

65. Barringer, "Ninth Regiment," 439–41; Barringer to brother, January 27, 1866 Rufus Barringer Papers, UNC.

6. Mounted Charges and Personal Combat

1. Cooke, *Cavalry Tactics*, 1:207–8, 211–12; Halleck, *Elements of Military Art*, 266; McClellan, *European Cavalry*, 121.

2. Meyer, "Sailor on Horseback," 206; "A Chat with Sheridan."

3. Vale, *Minty and the Cavalry*, 5; Rea, "Kilpatrick's Raid around Atlanta," 153; Bouvé, "Battle at High Bridge," 409.

4. Mitchell, *Letters of Major General James E. B. Stuart*, 330–31.

5. Cooke, *Battle of Kelly's Ford*, 10.

6. Wells A. Bushnell Memoirs, 213–14, WRHS; Gilmor, *Four Years in the Saddle*, 68; Gause, *Four Years with Five Armies*, 292–93; *SOR*, pt. 1, 5:244; Kidd, *Riding with Custer*, 147.

7. *OR*, 36(1):822; George W. Hunt to friend, November 26, 1864, Basil Wilson Duke Papers, UNC.

8. Barron, *Lone Star Defenders*, 208–9, 213–14.

9. Beach, *First New York (Lincoln) Cavalry*, 37; Curry, "Raid of the Union Cavalry," 252.

10. McDonald, *Laurel Brigade*, 65; Mosby, *War Reminiscences*, 88, 90; Cheek, "Additional Sketch Ninth Regiment," 458.

11. *OR*, 38(2):876; *SOR*, pt. 1, 5:238–39.

12. Beach, "Some Reminiscences," 282; *OR*, 49(1):475; Mahan, *Elementary Treatise*, 20.

13. Cooke, *Battle of Kelly's Ford*, 29–31.

14. Turchin, "Bayonet and Saber."

15. Ladd and Ladd, *Bachelder Papers*, 2:1267; *OR*, 25(1):1093 (emphasis original); Gilmor, *Four Years in the Saddle*, 35.

16. Gilmor, *Four Years in the Saddle*, 249; Taylor, "Bayonets and Sabers"; Treichel, "Major Zagonyi's Horse-Guard," 241–45; Lewis to father, May 3, 1863, William A. Lewis Letters, 15th Illinois Cavalry Folder, Vicksburg National Military Park, Vicksburg, MS; *OR*, 31(1):637–38, 34(1):448, 38(2):752, 36(1):790.

17. Galloway, "Sixty-Third Regiment," 532–33; Bouvé, "Battle at High Bridge," 409; Holt, "Additional Sketch Seventy-Fifth Regiment," 96; *OR*, 29(1):394, 32(1):274; Crane, "Bugle Blasts," 248.

18. *OR*, 27(1):947–48, 1018–19, 10(1):736–37; Opie, *Rebel Cavalryman*, 153; *SOR*, pt. 1, 1:717.

19. *OR*, 38(2):825, 44:384; Isaac Norval Baker Civil War Memoirs, 12, VMI; Ladd and Ladd, *Bachelder Papers*, 2:1117, 1201.

20. *OR,* 38(2):814; Ladd and Ladd, *Bachelder Papers,* 3:1533, 2:1207, 1299; Kidd, *Riding with Custer,* 149–50.

21. *OR,* 27(1):1018–19; Mitchell, *Letters of Major General James E. B. Stuart,* 346–47.

22. Lloyd, "Battle of Waynesboro," 203.

23. Vale, *Minty and the Cavalry,* 5.

24. Brooke-Rawle, *Right Flank at Gettysburg,* 20–21; *OR,* 12(2):274; *SOR,* pt. 1, 5:257, 473–74; Ladd and Ladd, *Bachelder Papers,* 3:1491–92; Rea, "Four Weeks with Long's Cavalry," 39–41; Wittenberg, *One of Custer's Wolverines,* 50.

25. Pierce, *Second Iowa Cavalry,* preface.

26. Brooke-Rawle, *Right Flank at Gettysburg,* 21; Mosby, *War Reminiscences,* 105, 107.

27. Kirk, *Fifteenth Pennsylvania Volunteer Cavalry,* 118–19; Rodenbough, *From Everglade to Cañon,* 289n; Gilmore, "Cavalry," 41.

28. Hess, *Civil War Infantry Tactics,* 165.

29. Calvert, *Reminiscences,* 82–83. For an example of mounted close-range combat depicted on a letterhead, see letter of March 23, 1862, Rapp-Idleman Family Papers, FHS. For a similar scene, see *Frank Leslie's Illustrated Newspaper,* January 31, 1863, 301.

30. *OR,* 27(1):1015, 41(1):336; Ladd and Ladd, *Bachelder Papers,* 3:1436.

31. Opie, *Rebel Cavalryman,* 176; McMurry, *Uncompromising Secessionist,* 284–85.

32. M'Minn, "Service with Van Dorn's Cavalry," 385; Heermance, "Cavalry at Chancellorsville," 224.

33. Bliss, "Cavalry Service," 215–18, 286.

34. Bliss, "Cavalry Service," 218–19, 221, 277.

35. Bliss, "Cavalry Service," 286–87.

36. Bliss, "How I Lost My Sabre," 83–84, 87–88.

37. Bliss, "How I Lost My Sabre," 83, 88–89, 92–94.

38. Bliss, "Cavalry Service," 217.

39. Bliss, "How I Lost My Sabre," 128.

40. Bouvé, "Battle at High Bridge," 408–9; Ladd and Ladd, *Bachelder Papers,* 1:659; Bliss, "First Rhode Island Cavalry," 166; *OR,* 45(1):604, 47(1):879.

41. Brown, *One of Morgan's Men,* 74–75; Ladd and Ladd, *Bachelder Papers,* 3:1492; *OR,* 23(1):559, 49(1):500, 38(2):826, 43(1):521; Mosby, *War Reminiscences,* 90; *SOR,* pt. 1, 3:313; White, "First Sabre Charge of the War," 28; Bliss, "First Rhode Island Cavalry," 170–71; Nanzig, *Civil War Memoirs of a Virginia Cavalryman,* 96–97.

42. Baker to sister, June 21, August 11, 17, 1863, William B. Baker Papers, UNC.

43. Gilmor, *Four Years in the Saddle,* 35–36, 46–47, 88, 109.

44. Gilmor, *Four Years in the Saddle,* 110.

45. Williams and Wooster, "With Terry's Texas Rangers," 312; Gill, *Reminiscences,* 73–74.

46. Berkenes, *Private William Boddy's Civil War Journal,* 170; *Memoir of Thomas H. Malone,* 170–72, 174–75.

47. Rockwell, "With Sheridan's Cavalry," 230–31; Crowninshield, *First Regiment of Massachusetts Cavalry,* 123–24.

48. Meyer, *Civil War Experiences,* 29; McMurry, *Uncompromising Secessionist,* 298.

49. Calvert, *Reminiscences,* 79.

7. Dismounted Fighting

1. Whittaker, *Volunteer Cavalry*, 16.

2. Galloway, "Sixty-Third Regiment," 537; Means, "Additional Sketch Sixty-Third Regiment," 602–3; *OR*, 30(2):677–78, 38(3):998, 42(1):631, 641, 648, 44:369, 392, 34(1):819–20; Morgan to D. G. Reed, March 25, 1863, John Hunt Morgan Papers, UNC; Kidd, *Riding with Custer*, 300–305; Champion to wife, May 31, 1864, Sidney S. Champion Papers, DU; Fenton, "From Petersburg to Appomattox in 1865," 7–8, Alcinus Ward Fenton Papers, Regimental Papers of the Civil War, Box 17, Folder 2, WRHS.

3. *OR*, 38(2):808, 34(1):842.

4. Robinson, *"With Kilpatrick,"* 4; Graham, "Nineteenth Regiment," 90.

5. Robinson, *"With Kilpatrick,"* 4; *OR*, 43(1):559.

6. Kidd, *Riding with Custer*, 281–82.

7. Hess, *Civil War Field Artillery*, 149–56.

8. Hess, *Civil War Infantry Tactics*, 53–55, 95–102.

9. *OR*, 42(1):609, 27(1):925, 929, 43(1):471.

10. *OR*, 11(1):435; Weed to sister, July 3, [1864], Theodore H. Weed Papers, DU.

11. *OR*, 30(2):683, 31(1):805; Ford, "Charge of the First Maine Cavalry," 282.

12. *OR*, 49(1):503, 10(1):835, 38(2):750, 36(1):821, 839, 848, 886, 39(1):132, 43(1):471–72; Galloway, "Sixty-Third Regiment," 538; Beale, *Lieutenant of Cavalry*, 184.

13. Wells A. Bushnell Memoirs, 301, WRHS; Kidd, *Riding with Custer*, 324–26; Peck, *Reminiscences*, 21; Means, "Additional Sketch Sixty-Third Regiment," 597; *OR*, 31(1):659; Wittenberg, *One of Custer's Wolverines*, 88; Hess, *Civil War Infantry Tactics*, 148–61.

14. Dixon, "Recollections of a Rebel Private," 72; Foster, *Reminiscences and Record*, 53–54; Dodson, *Campaigns of Wheeler*, 295n; Osborn, "Sherman's Carolina Campaign," 112; Champion to wife, June 5, 1864, Sidney S. Champion Papers, DU.

15. Tobie, "Service of the Cavalry," 157–58.

16. Robinson, *"With Kilpatrick,"* 12; *OR*, 40(1):729, 49(1):448, 31(1):552–53.

17. Thomas, *Some Personal Reminiscences*, 21; Ladd and Ladd, *Bachelder Papers*, 2:1193, 1205, 1222; *OR*, 42(1):647, 823, 36(1):840, 897, 46(1):1255; Wells A. Bushnell Memoirs, 313, WRHS.

18. Berkenes, *Private William Boddy's Civil War Journal*, 139; Mosgrove, *Kentucky Cavaliers*, 156.

19. *OR*, 42(1):833, 38(3):1005–8, 32(1):90, 38(2):927; Capron, "Stoneman Raid," 412; Sowle to father and mother, March 6, 1863, Charles H. Sowle Papers, DU.

20. *Reminiscences of the South Carolina Confederate Cavalry*, 30–31.

21. *OR*, 46(1):1253, 38(3):955, 34(1):617; *SOR*, pt. 1, 4:190.

22. Allen, *Down in Dixie*, 224, 226; McMurry, *Uncompromising Secessionist*, 57; *OR*, 39(1):326, 42(1):824.

23. *OR*, 45(1):606, 36(2):363.

24. Ryan, "Letters of Harden Perkins Cochrane," 286; Robinson, *"With Kilpatrick,"* 6–7.

25. Munford, "Confederate Cavalry Officer's Views," 198.

26. Guild, *Fourth Tennessee Cavalry*, 169.

27. Robinson, *"With Kilpatrick,"* 4; *OR*, ser. 4, 2:718; Barringer, "Ninth Regiment," 430.

28. Dodson, *Campaigns of Wheeler*, 336–37; Carpenter, "Sheridan's Expedition around Richmond," 302.

29. *OR*, 27(1):944, 36(1):816–18.

30. Humphreys, *Field, Camp, Hospital and Prison*, 257 (emphasis original); Gracey, *Sixth Pennsylvania Cavalry*, 274; *OR*, 38(2):836; Hood, *Advance and Retreat*, 132.

31. *OR*, 27(1):944, 17(2):484–85; Newhall, "With Sheridan," 212; Robinson, *"With Kilpatrick,"* 4.

32. Allen, *Down in Dixie*, 224.

33. Whittaker, *Volunteer Cavalry*, 16.

8. Raiding

1. Curry, "Raid of the Union Cavalry," 253.

2. Mitchell, "Field Notes of the Selma Campaign," 175–76.

3. Dodson, *Campaigns of Wheeler*, 249n; *OR*, 19(2):56.

4. Wall, "Raids in Southeastern Virginia," 80; Tobie, "Personal Recollections," 194.

5. *OR*, 41(1):338; *SOR*, pt. 1, 6:628; Baker to father, March 20, 1864, William B. Baker Papers, UNC; Wells A. Bushnell Memoirs, 273, WRHS.

6. *OR*, 38(3):960; Wall, "Raids in Southeastern Virginia," 72; Wilson, "Wilder's Brigade," 76; Pyne, *First New Jersey Cavalry*, 261.

7. Taylor, *Saddle and Saber*, 159.

8. Mitchell, "Sanders Raid," 245.

9. Calvert, *Reminiscences*, 296–97; Mosgrove, *Kentucky Cavaliers*, 150.

10. *OR*, 24(1):522, 525, 528.

11. Dinges and Leckie, *Just and Righteous Cause*, 154–55, 179; *OR*, 24(1):521–22.

12. Dinges and Leckie, *Just and Righteous Cause*, 153, 156; Woodward, "Grierson's Raid," 686–87; Surby, *Grierson's Raids*, 60–65.

13. *OR*, 24(1):524; Dinges and Leckie, *Just and Righteous Cause*, 166–67.

14. *OR*, 24(1):527; Dinges and Leckie, *Just and Righteous Cause*, 179.

15. *OR*, 25(1):115, 120–21.

16. *OR*, 25(1):119–20. For the history of the Burning Springs oilfield, see Geiger, "Burning Springs Oil Field," West Virginia Encyclopedia, last rev. October 18, 2023, https://www.wvencyclopedia.org/articles/726. For oil prices during the Civil War, see History of Oil Prices, https://thecrudechronicles.com/history-of-oil-prices/#:~:text=And%20this%20is%20where%20our%20story%20begins.%20In,by%20the%20blue%20line%20along%20the%20right%20axis, accessed November 10, 2023. Internal problems render this webpage inaccessible in 2024, but similar information can be gleaned from Holodny, "Energy Transition: 155 Years of Oil Prices—in One Chart," World Economic Forum, December 22, 2016, https://www.weforum.org/stories/2016/12/155-years-of-oil-prices-in-one-chart/, accessed November 15, 2024.

17. *OR*, 25(1):119–20, 129, 133.

18. *OR*, 25(1):120.

19. *OR*, 38(2):910–11.

20. *OR*, 38(2):904–7; Hamilton, *Recollections*, 136–37.

21. *OR*, 38(2):907; Hamilton, *Recollections*, 134–35.

22. *OR*, 38(2):907–9.

23. *OR*, 17(1):503.

24. *OR*, 17(1):592–93.

25. *OR*, 23(1):285–86.

26. *OR*, 23(1):286–87.

27. *OR*, 23(1):288, 292.

28. *OR*, 23(1):293; Kniffin, "Streight's Raid," 199.

29. *OR*, 23(1):639–45.

30. Allen, "In Pursuit of John Morgan," 230–33, 235; Gause, *Four Years with Five Armies*, 169.

31. Connelly, "Recollections," 77.

32. *OR*, 40(1):620–22, 625–26; Wilson, "Cavalry of the Army of the Potomac," 61.

33. *OR*, 40(1):637, 642, 733; Starr, "Wilson Raid," 219, 221, 226.

34. *OR*, 40(1):623, 627–30, 642–43, 735, 738; Starr, "Wilson Raid," 237.

35. *OR*, 40(1):732, 740, 40(3):17; Starr, "Wilson Raid," 223–24, 228–29.

36. "Letters of a Civil War Surgeon," 160; *OR*, 37(2):300.

37. *OR*, 38(2):775, 875, 915, 919–20, 925–26, 928–29.

38. *OR*, 38(2):916–19, 921, 925–26, 928; Kniffin, "General Capron's Narrative," 117.

39. *OR*, 38(2):761–64.

40. Pierce, *Second Iowa Cavalry*, 58.

41. Pierce, *Second Iowa Cavalry*, 60–61.

42. Curry, "Raid of the Union Cavalry," 253; Preston, "Cavalry Raid to Richmond," 498–99, 503; Hastings, "Cavalry Service," 261.

43. *OR*, 17(2):484–85, 23(2):302–3.

44. *OR*, 36(3):199.

45. *OR*, 39(2):365; Nevins, *Diary of Battle*, 324–25.

46. Cox, *Military Reminiscences*, 2:290.

47. *OR*, 39(1):76.

48. *OR*, 39(1):398; newspaper clipping of article based on report by a *Montreal Gazette* correspondent, November 3, 1865, John B. Hood Papers, RG 109, NARA.

49. *OR*, 32(3):504; Smith to Lue, September 9, 1864, J. M. Smith Letters, Texas A&M University, Special Collections, College Station; *OR*, ser. 3, 5:988–89; Hess, *Supply and Strategy*, 184–95.

50. Wilson, "Cavalry of the Army of the Potomac," 74–75; Bearss, "Grierson's Winter Raid," 37.

51. Cutrer, *Our Trust*, 212–13.

9. Weapons and Equipment

1. Nosworthy, *Bloody Crucible*, 290–91.

2. Gray, *Cavalry Tactics*, 7.

3. *OR*, ser. 3, 1:355, 363, 485; Blackburn, "Reminiscences of the Terry Rangers," 41.

4. Graham, "Nineteenth Regiment," 82; *SOR*, pt. 2, 69:713, 789; Crane, "Bugle Blasts," 235.

5. Brown, *War Years*, 220; *SOR*, pt. 2, 69:778–79.

6. *OR*, 5:13; Starr, *Jennison's Jayhawkers*, 82–83; Crowninshield, *First Regiment of Massachusetts Cavalry*, 295; Pierce, *Second Iowa Cavalry*, 26–27; Thomas, *Some Personal Reminiscences*, 6; Connelly, "Recollections," 463; Sperry to sister, March 6, 1864, Isaac L. Sperry Letters, DU.

7. Starr, "Cold Steel," 145; Gray, *Cavalry Tactics*, 8.

8. Starr, "Cold Steel," 144–46.

9. Parmelee to mother, March 16, 1862, Samuel Spencer Parmelee Papers, DU; Crowninshield, *First Regiment of Massachusetts Cavalry*, 295; Scott, *Story of a Cavalry Regiment*, 370.

10. Crowninshield, *First Regiment of Massachusetts Cavalry*, 295; Mosgrove, *Kentucky Cavaliers*, 183; Starr, "Cold Steel," 144; *OR*, ser. 4, 2:719.

11. Farlow and Barry, "Vincent B. Osborne's Civil War Experiences," 196.

12. Crowninshield, *First Regiment of Massachusetts Cavalry*, 35, 294–95; McClellan, *European Cavalry*, 146–47.

13. McClellan, *European Cavalry*, 146–47; McClellan, *Regulations and Instructions*, 13.

14. Calvert, *Reminiscences*, 81–82; Bowen, *First New York Dragoons*, 30; Clark, "Making of a Volunteer Cavalryman," 473; Curry, *Four Years in the Saddle*, 27.

15. Starr, "Cold Steel," 146; Whittaker, *Volunteer Cavalry*, 7–8; Crowninshield, *First Regiment of Massachusetts Cavalry*, 35, 187, 295; Lloyd diary, March 5, 1862, William Penn Lloyd Diary and Notebooks, UNC; Norton, *"Red Neck Ties,"* 65.

16. Brooke-Rawle, *Right Flank at Gettysburg*, 21; Mosby, *War Reminiscences*, 89.

17. Wiley N. Nash account, Folder 3, J. F. H. Claiborne Papers, UNC.

18. Wilson, "Cavalry of the Army of the Potomac," 85–86; Sutton, *Second Regiment West Virginia Cavalry*, 49; *SOR*, pt. 1, 4:389; William Sooy Smith to Sherman, February 26, 1864, William T. Sherman Papers, LC; *History of the Service of the Third Ohio*, 18–19.

19. Greene, "Campaigning in the Army of the Frontier," 286–87.

20. Harris, "Union Cavalry," 354–55.

21. Beach, "Some Reminiscences," 282; Beach, *First New York (Lincoln) Cavalry*, 37; Norton, *Deeds of Daring*, 93–94; Kidd, *Riding with Custer*, 170; *OR*, 44:362–63, 365, 17(1):501.

22. Meyer, "Sailor on Horseback," 214–15.

23. Blackburn, "Reminiscences of the Terry Rangers," 76; Wiggins, *Journals of Josiah Gorgas*, 128.

24. *OR*, 30(2):683, 52(1):112; Starr, "Cold Steel," 157; Lemmon, "5th Iowa Cav"; Pierce, *Second Iowa Cavalry*, 27–28; Pickerill, *Third Indiana Cavalry*, 26; Ladd and Ladd, *Bachelder Papers*, 1:653; Meyer, *Civil War Experiences*, 55.

25. Ford, *Cycle of Adams Letters*, 2:28.

26. Crowninshield, *First Regiment of Massachusetts Cavalry*, 285; Boudrye, *Fifth New York Cavalry*, 38; Norton, *"Red Neck Ties,"* 85.

27. *SOR*, pt. 2, 69:725–26; record book, March 14–15, 1863, Albert Clayton Swindler Papers, LC; Epps to wife, children, mother, and sisters, August 17, 1862, Commodore D. Epps Papers, UNC; McMurry, *Uncompromising Secessionist*, 343; Crowninshield, *First Regiment of Massachusetts Cavalry*, 295.

28. Giles, *Terry's Texas Rangers*, 101.

29. Williams and Wooster, "With Terry's Texas Rangers," 313, 317–18; Williams and Wooster, "With Wharton's Cavalry," 257–58.

30. *OR*, 20(1):969.

31. *OR*, 32(1):365; Ladd and Ladd, *Bachelder Papers*, 3:1436; Mitchell, *Letters of Major General James E. B. Stuart*, 331.

32. Reminiscences, 15, August Bondi Papers, KHS; *OR*, 17(2):282; Scott, *Story of a Cavalry Regiment*, 25.

33. Scott, *Story of a Cavalry Regiment*, 25–26.

34. Phelps, "Cavalry"; Pickerill, *Third Indiana Cavalry*, 12; Sutton, *Second Regiment West Virginia Cavalry*, 49.

35. Crowninshield, *First Regiment of Massachusetts Cavalry*, 295; Whittaker, *Volunteer Cavalry*, 13; Harris, "Union Cavalry," 354.

36. *OR*, 31(1):654, 27(1):933, 941, 36(1):848; Taylor, *Saddle and Saber*, 168; Whittaker, *Volunteer Cavalry*, 14; Wells A. Bushnell Memoirs, 269, WRHS.

37. Bahde, *Story of My Campaign*, 27, 59; Reminiscences, 6, 15, August Bondi Papers, KHS.

38. Sutton, *Second Regiment West Virginia Cavalry*, 49; Mays, *Let Us Meet in Heaven*, 217; *Reminiscences of the South Carolina Confederate Cavalry*, 12; *SOR*, pt. 1, 4:717; *OR*, 27(1):908; Gilmor, *Four Years in the Saddle*, 32; Crowninshield, *First Regiment of Massachusetts Cavalry*, 295.

39. Mosgrove, *Kentucky Cavaliers*, 157.

40. Julius E. Thomas Civil War Diary, September 15, 1864, UTK.

41. Royall, *Some Reminiscences*, 55; *OR*, 39(1):397–98, 31(1):547.

42. *OR*, ser. 4, 2:720.

43. Gause, *Four Years with Five Armies*, 42; Tarrant, *Wild Riders*, 26; Reminiscences, 15, August Bondi Papers, KHS; Phelps, "Cavalry"; Scott, *Story of a Cavalry Regiment*, 63.

44. *OR*, 44:361. 26(1):134, 47(1):890; Crowninshield, *First Regiment of Massachusetts Cavalry*, 72; Wells A. Bushnell Memoirs, 68, WRHS; Dinges and Leckie, *Just and Righteous Cause*, 191.

45. *OR*, 16(1):750.

46. *OR*, 38(2):780; *History of the Eighteenth Regiment of Cavalry Pennsylvania Volunteers*, 14–15.

47. Thatcher, *Hundred Battles*, 30; Davenport, *Ninth Regiment Illinois Cavalry*, 58, 93; Wiswell to father, January 8, 1862 [1863], James H. Wiswell Papers, DU; Whittaker, *Volunteer Cavalry*, 15.

48. Pratt, "Civil War Letters of Winthrop S. G. Allen," 558; Maness and Combs, *Do They Miss Me?*, 142; *History of the Eighteenth Regiment of Cavalry Pennsylvania Volunteers*, 38; *History of the Service of the Third Ohio*, 19.

49. Carter, *From Yorktown to Santiago*, 105; Tarrant, *Wild Riders*, 26; *SOR*, pt. 1, 4:389; Brackett, *History of the United States Cavalry*, 166; Carpenter, "Sheridan's Expedition around Richmond," 301; *History of the Service of the Third Ohio*, 19; Cheney, *Ninth Regiment, New York Volunteer Cavalry*, 59.

50. *OR*, 44:361; Wilson, *Life of Charles A. Dana*, 345.

51. Kidd, *Riding with Custer*, 77–78; Wilson, "Wilder's Brigade," 49; *SOR*, pt. 1, 5:271; Carmony, "Jacob W. Bartmess Civil War Letters," 67; Davenport, *Ninth Regiment Illinois Cavalry*, 108–9, 117; Emerson, *Life and Letters of Charles Russell Lowell*, 316–17; Gause, *Four Years with Five Armies*, 219; *History and Roster of the Seventh Pa. Cavalry*, 11; Pierce, *Second Iowa Cavalry*, 97; Robinson, *"With Kilpatrick,"* 6; *History of the Eleventh Pennsylvania*, 141–42; Brackett, "Cavalry Bureau"; Dornblaser, *Sabre Strokes of the Pennsylvania Dragoons*, 149; Scott, *Story of a Cavalry Regiment*, 369; *OR*, 44:361.

52. Wilson, "Cavalry of the Army of the Potomac," 77–78; Minty diary, January 1, 1865, Robert Horatio George Minty Papers, DPL; Hamilton, *Recollections*, 206.

53. Wilson, "Cavalry of the Army of the Potomac," 85; *OR*, 39(1):318; Weed to sister, July 3, [1864], Theodore H. Weed Papers, DU.

54. Whittaker, *Volunteer Cavalry*, 15.

55. Scott, *Story of a Cavalry Regiment*, 283.

56. *OR*, 49(1):409.

57. *History and Roster of the Seventh Pa. Cavalry*, 3; *OR*, 45(1):630, 17(2):282; Scott, *Story of a Cavalry Regiment*, 25; Farlow and Barry, "Vincent B. Osborne's Civil War Experiences," 127, 129; Sipes, *Seventh Pennsylvania Veteran Volunteer Cavalry*, 9; Pratt diary, March 24, 1862, Richard Henry Pratt Papers, LC; Cyrus Bussey Civil War Reminiscences, 20, Iowa State University, Special Collections, Ames.

58. *OR*, 30(2):746, 39(3):713; Lees, "When the Shooting Stopped," 49–50.

59. *OR*, 27(1):1015, 39(1):317, 46(1):465, 32(1):310, 37(1):359.

60. Harris, "Union Cavalry," 354; Whittaker, *Volunteer Cavalry*, 16.

61. McClellan, *European Cavalry*, 116; Nolan, *Cavalry*, 131, 135; Roemer, *Cavalry*, 54.

62. *Lancer's Manual*, unpaginated.

63. Morey, "Torpedoes at Yorktown"; Norris, "Lancers in the Rebel Army."

64. Bruce, "Lances in the Union Army"; Scott, *Story of a Cavalry Regiment*, 8.

65. Prezelski, "Lives of the Californio Lancers," 29, 33, 37.

66. Gracey, *Sixth Pennsylvania Cavalry*, 20, 26, 34–35.

67. Wittenberg, *"We Have It Damn Hard,"* 41; Gracey, *Sixth Pennsylvania Cavalry*, 45, 66, 138, 154–55.

68. Nolan, *Cavalry*, 140.

69. Roemer, *Cavalry*, 484, 490.

70. Roemer, *Cavalry*, 494; Whittaker, *Volunteer Cavalry*, 42–43; Crouch, *Horse Equipment*, 77.

71. Crouch, *Horse Equipment*, 33, 38; Roemer, *Cavalry*, 494;

72. Crouch, *Horse Equipment*, 77.

73. Galloway, "Sixty-Third Regiment," 543; Brackett, *History of the United States Cavalry*, 161; Nott, *Sketches of the War*, 33; Harris, "Union Cavalry," 354; Avery, *Fourth Illinois Cavalry*, 87.

74. Whittaker, *Volunteer Cavalry*, 38, 41–45.

75. Crouch, *Horse Equipment*, 50, 64, 68; *OR*, ser. 4, 2:719–21.

76. Crouch, *Horse Equipment*, 129.

77. Crouch, *Horse Equipment*, 137.

78. Bliss, "First Rhode Island Cavalry," 143; Calvert, *Reminiscences*, 94–95, 132.

79. Morgan, "For Our Beloved Country," 47; Whittaker, *Volunteer Cavalry*, 43.

80. *OR*, 30(2):673, 31(1):835–36.

81. Crowninshield, *First Regiment of Massachusetts Cavalry*, 294; Brackett, *History of the United States Cavalry*, 166.

82. Crouch, *Horse Equipment*, 154, 156 58, 171; Norton, *Deeds of Daring*, 107–8; Scott, *Story of a Cavalry Regiment*, 26–27.

83. Scott, *Story of a Cavalry Regiment*, 28–29; Crowninshield, *First Regiment of Massachusetts Cavalry*, 294; *SOR*, pt. 1, 4:389.

10. Mounting the Cavalry

1. McClellan, *European Cavalry*, 154–55.

2. Johnson, *Soldier's Reminiscences*, 95.

3. *OR*, ser. 4, 1:126–27.

4. Nanzig, *Civil War Memoirs of a Virginia Cavalryman*, 66; Ramsdell, "General Robert E. Lee's Horse Supply," 759–60; Munford, "Confederate Cavalry Officer's Views," 199.

5. Ervine to Ellen, June 18, 1861, John H. Ervine Letter, VMI; Langhorne to Papa, June 1, 1863, Jacob Kent Langhorne Papers, VMI; voucher, December 10, 1863, Samuel H. Craun Papers, VMI; Circular, Headquarters, Wheeler's Cavalry Corps, January 11, 1864, General Orders, Civil War, Box 130, Joseph Wheeler Family Papers, ADAH; Barron, *Lone Star Defenders*, 276; William H. Areheart Diaries, April 21, July 27, 1864, DU.

6. *OR*, ser. 4, 2:719; George A. Malloy to Pa, April 1, [1862], Malloy Family Papers, USC.

7. Wharton to father, November 28, 1862, W. D. Wharton Papers, UNC; George A. Malloy to Pa, November 6, [1863], Malloy Family Papers, USC; Isaac Norval Baker Civil War Memoirs, 4, VMI.

8. Williams and Wooster, "With Terry's Texas Rangers," 315–16, 319.

9. Langhorne to Mama, May 19, 1863, Jacob Kent Langhorne Papers, VMI; Mays, *Let Us Meet in Heaven*, 222; Almonte T. Dobie to Uncle, September 28, 1864, Edward George Washington Butler Papers, DU.

10. Stonebraker, *Rebel of '61*, 89; Means, "Additional Sketch Sixty-Third Regiment," 591; George A. Malloy to Pa, April 3, [1863], Malloy Family Papers, USC; McMurry, *Uncompromising Secessionist*, 86.

11. Dixon, "Recollections of a Rebel Private," 205–6.

12. Brown, *War Years*, 242.

13. Mays, *Let Us Meet in Heaven*, 237.

14. *OR*, 12(3):916, 19(2):709, 29(2):853–54; Ramsdell, "General Robert E. Lee's Horse Supply," 763.

15. E. I. Burford to W. T. Martin, April 18, 1864, Letters and Telegrams, 1863–1865, Box 131, Joseph Wheeler Family Papers, ADAH; Brown, *War Years*, 243; Opie, *Rebel Cavalryman*, 158–59; Wharton to cousin, August 21, 1864, W. D. Wharton Papers, UNC.

16. William H. Areheart Diaries, May 5–29, July 2–25, 1864, DU.

17. *OR*, ser. 4, 2:568, 719, 3:499, 503; John W. Lockett to Morgan, April 18, 1863; R. I. Singleton, H. T. Ball, and A. B. Smith to Morgan, February 4, 1864; and Samuel J. B. Fair to Morgan, January 21, 1864, John Hunt Morgan Papers, UNC; Brown, *War Years*, 243, 258; Mays, *Let Us Meet in Heaven*, 237.

18. Calkin, "Elk Horn to Vicksburg," 14–15, 25, 27.

19. Blackburn, "Reminiscences of the Terry Rangers," 43–44; Wheeler to George W. Brent, August 25, 1863; and Wheeler to A. P. Mason, April 30, 1864, Letters and Telegrams, 1863–65, Box 131, Joseph Wheeler Family Papers, ADAH; Brown, *War Years*, 200–202, 209.

20. Reynolds to Mary, January 31, 1863, H. C. Reynolds Papers, ADAH; McMurry, *Uncompromising Secessionist*, 244.

21. Ramsdell, "General Robert E. Lee's Horse Supply," 765, 772–73; Brown, *War Years*, 319.

22. *OR*, ser. 4, 2:720; *OR*, 27(2):302; Brown, *War Years*, 226.

23. Ramsdell, "General Robert E. Lee's Horse Supply," 775; Munford, "Confederate Cavalry Officer's Views," 199.

24. Harris, "Union Cavalry," 356; Nanzig, *Civil War Memoirs of a Virginia Cavalryman*, 66–67.

25. Mosby, *War Reminiscences*, 214; Opie, *Rebel Cavalryman*, 158.

26. Gerleman, "War Horse!," 49; O'Brien and Diefendorf, *General Orders*, 1:61, 82; Beach, *First New York (Lincoln) Cavalry*, 24, 47.

27. Whittaker, *Volunteer Cavalry*, 26; Rankin, "Brave Band"; Tarrant, *Wild Riders*, 11; Curry, *Four Years in the Saddle*, 23; Gause, *Four Years with Five Armies*, 27.

28. Kohl, *Prairie Boys*, 13, 157; Starr, *Jennison's Jayhawkers*, 283–84; Cheney, *Ninth Regiment, New York Volunteer Cavalry*, 195; William G. Hills Diary, July 11, 1864, LC; Pickerill, *Third Indiana Cavalry*, 157; McCain, *Soldier's Diary*, 16; Bahde, *Story of My Campaign*, 194; *OR*, ser. 3, 4:228–29.

29. *OR*, 34(2):453.

30. *OR*, 34(2):453, 34(3):226.

31. William G. Hills Diary, April 23, 1864, LC.

32. Dornblaser, *Sabre Strokes of the Pennsylvania Dragoons*, 32; Calvert, *Reminiscences of a Boy in Blue*, 18; Kidd, *Riding with Custer*, 48.

33. Hard, *Eighth Cavalry Regiment, Illinois Volunteers*, 37, 39; Crowninshield, *First Regiment of Massachusetts Cavalry*, 36; Norton, *Deeds of Daring*, 9, 17, 24; Curry, *Four Years in the Saddle*, 22–23.

34. Curry, *Four Years in the Saddle*, 23; Rowell, *Yankee Cavalrymen*, 33–35; Covert to wife, May 20, 23, 31, July 4, 1862, Thomas M. Covert Papers, WRHS; Schlotterbeck et al., *James Riley Weaver's Civil War*, 10, 14; Allen, *Down in Dixie*, 380.

35. Humphreys, *Field, Camp, Hospital and Prison*, 374; Warren to mother, May 26, 1863, E. Willard Warren Correspondence, DU.

36. Covert to wife, September 2, 11, October 22, December 21, 1863, January 15, 1864, Thomas M. Covert Papers, WRHS.

37. Barton, "Procurement of Horses," 17–20; Hess, *Civil War Logistics*, 29–30; O'Brien and Diefendorf, *General Orders*, 2:289–90.

38. *OR*, 23(2):282.

39. *OR*, 23(2):300–301, 303.

40. *OR*, 29(2):400–401.

41. *OR*, ser. 3, 3:1041–42.

42. *OR*, ser. 3, 4:1168; *OR*, 26(1):719, 32(3):70, 300–301, 398.

43. *OR*, 38(2):832–33.

44. Hamilton, *Recollections*, 146; Brackett, "Cavalry Bureau."

45. *OR*, 46(2):546–47; *OR*, ser. 3, 4:1167–69.

46. *OR*, ser. 3, 5:220–21.

47. Maness and Combs, *Do They Miss Me?*, 156; Collier and Collier, *Yours for the Union*, 341; Baker to father, May 1, 1864, William B. Baker Papers, UNC; *OR*, 38(2):794–95.

48. *OR*, 47(1):902–5.

49. Crowninshield, *First Regiment of Massachusetts Cavalry*, 84; Field Report, 2nd Brigade, 3rd Division, Cavalry Corps, June 13, 1863, William Penn Lloyd Diary and Notebooks, UNC; William G. Watson Memoirs, VMI.

50. Taylor, *Saddle and Saber*, 179–80.

51. *OR*, 29(2):400–401; McKoy, "Dismounted Cavalry."

52. *OR*, 29(2):400, 402.

53. Parmelee to mother, March 16, 1862, Samuel Spencer Parmelee Papers, DU; William G. Hills Diary, April 14, 1864, LC; Julius E. Thomas Civil War Diary, December 21, 1864, UTK; Engerud, *1864 Diary of Lt. Col. Jefferson K. Scott*, 23; *OR*, 32(3):407.

54. Avery, *Fourth Illinois Cavalry*, 170; *OR*, 38(2):799; *History of the Service of the Third Ohio*, 183.

55. *OR*, 49(1):649–50, 38(2):873, 878, 17(2):375.

56. *OR*, ser. 3, 5:256; *OR*, 38(2):792–93, 796–97.

57. Wilson, "Cavalry of the Army of the Potomac," 38; Edmonds, "Wastage of Cavalry Horses," 250–51.

58. Gerleman, "War Horse!," 48, 60–61.

59. *OR*, ser. 3, 5:220, 254, 527; Gerleman, "War Horse!," 47.

11. Cavalry Horses

1. Ringwalt, "Horse," 322; "World Population by Year," Worldometer, 2024, https://www.worldometers.info/world-population/world-population-by-year/. For the topics covered in this chapter, see also Hess, "Animal-Human Relationship in War," 1–20.

2. *OR*, 36(2):355.

3. Phillips, "Writing Horses," 165–67; Pooley-Ebert, "Species Agency," 150–52; Waran and Casey, "Horse Training," 186; McGreevy and McLean, "Behavioural Problems with the Ridden Horse," 198–99; Scott, "Racehorse as Protagonist," 45–65.

4. Greene, *Horses at Work*, 134; Ringwalt, "Horse," 328; Halleck, *Elements of Military Art*, 265.

5. Ringwalt, "Horse," 326; Wittenberg, *"We Have It Damn Hard,"* 41.

6. Carter, *First Regiment of Tennessee Volunteer Cavalry*, 61; Sutton, *Second Regiment West Virginia Cavalry*, 49; Connelly, "Recollections," 458–59.

7. Ringwalt, "Horse," 328; Mays, *Let Us Meet in Heaven*, 230.

8. Norton, *Deeds of Daring*, 37; [Bartlett], *Soldier's Story*, 74; Crowninshield, *First Regiment of Massachusetts Cavalry*, 292.

9. Crowninshield, *First Regiment of Massachusetts Cavalry*, 289–91; Denison, *Sabres and Spurs*, 31; Reminiscences, 6, August Bondi Papers, KHS.

10. Mays, *Let Us Meet in Heaven*, 236.

11. Scott, "Racehorse as Protagonist," 50–55, 57–59.

12. Jennings, *Horse and His Diseases*, 200–201, 219.

13. Calvert, *Reminiscences*, 92–93, 232–33.

14. Allen, *Down in Dixie*, 145; Billings, *Hardtack and Coffee*, 186, 328–29; Greene, "Campaigning in the Army of the Frontier," 284.

15. Cogley, *Seventh Indiana Cavalry*, 65; Carter, *First Regiment of Tennessee Volunteer Cavalry*, 61.

16. Edward Laight Wells to Sabina, January 21, 1864, Smith and Wells Family Papers, USC; Flanders to mother, March 25, 1864, George E. Flanders Civil War Letters, KHS.

17. Baker to father, August 10, 1863, William B. Baker Papers, UNC; Beach, *First New York (Lincoln) Cavalry*, 40; Perry, *Life and Letters of Henry Lee Higginson*, 160; Gilmor, *Four Years in the Saddle*, 88; Blackford, *War Years*, 21–22; Curtis, "Cavalry Veteran," 31–43.

18. Greene, *Horses at Work*, 158; Whittaker, *Volunteer Cavalry*, 40; Ringwalt, "Horse," 330; Jennings, *Horse and His Diseases*, 207–8.

19. Congdon, *Cavalry Compendium*, 23; Baker to father, December 23, 1861, William B. Baker Papers, UNC; Julius E. Thomas Civil War Diary, January 9, 1865, UTK; McMurry, *Uncompromising Secessionist*, 195, 333; Brown, *War Years*, 243.

20. Greene, *Horses at Work*, 135; Ringwalt, "Horse," 329, 331–32; Jennings, *Horse and His Diseases*, 138–39, 143, 145–47, 149.

21. Ringwalt, "Horse," 330; Robinson, *"With Kilpatrick,"* 7; Ford, *Cycle of Adams Letters*, 1:246, 2:4; Baker to parents, April 19, 1863; and Baker to father, August 10, 1863, William B. Baker Papers, UNC; Taylor, *Saddle and Saber*, 120; *OR*, 29(2):419; Greene, "Campaigning in the Army of the Frontier," 296; McMurry, *Uncompromising Secessionist*, 319; Stickney to Rose, June 26, 1864, Clifford Stickney Collection, CHM; Flanders to brother, March 20, 1864, George E. Flanders Civil War Letters, KHS.

22. Whittaker, *Volunteer Cavalry*, 36; *OR*, 38(2):832, 39(1):313; McMurry, *Uncompromising Secessionist*, 267; Wall, "Raids in Southeastern Virginia," 72; Circular, Headquarters, Wheeler's Cavalry Corps, April 1, 1864, General Orders, Civil War, Box 130, Joseph Wheeler Family Papers, ADAH.

23. Congdon, *Cavalry Compendium*, 24–27; Wells A. Bushnell Memoirs, 42–43, WRHS; Ford, *Cycle of Adams Letters*, 2:4; Legg to mother, July 7, 1864, Charles A. Legg Correspondence, DU.

24. Wittenberg, *One of Custer's Wolverines*, 20; Kirk, *Fifteenth Pennsylvania Volunteer Cavalry*, 244–45; Gardiner, "Incidents of Cavalry Experiences," 424; Foster, *Reminiscences and Record*, 83; *OR*, 49(1):499; McMurry, *Uncompromising Secessionist*, 44; Calvert, *Reminiscences*, 233; Langhorne to Mama, May 19, 1863, Jacob Kent Langhorne Papers, VMI; Morgan, "For Our Beloved Country," 82–83; Julius E. Thomas Civil War Diary, January 31, 1865, UTK; Meyer, "Sailor on Horseback," 208, 212.

25. Gause, *Four Years with Five Armies*, 383.

26. McMurry, *Uncompromising Secessionist*, 44; Langhorne to Mama, May 19, 1863, Jacob Kent Langhorne Papers, VMI; Ryan, "Letters of Harden Perkins Cochrane," 287; Edward Laight Wells to Sabina, January 21, 1864, Smith and Wells Family Papers, USC; Wall, "Raids in Southeastern Virginia," 72; Norton, *"Red Neck Ties,"* 87; Perry, *Life and Letters of Henry Lee Higginson*, 161; Arkle, "Old 'Squeezer'"; Calvert, *Reminiscences*, 93; Baker to Fannie, March 10, 1864, William B. Baker Papers, UNC; Scott, *Story of a Cavalry Regiment*, 392; Crowninshield, *First Regiment of Massachusetts Cavalry*, 287, 289–90; Kirk, *Fifteenth Pennsylvania Volunteer Cavalry*, 253.

27. Crowninshield, *First Regiment of Massachusetts Cavalry*, 293.

28. Allen, *Down in Dixie*, 380–381; Nolan, *Cavalry*, 137; Whittaker, *Volunteer Cavalry*, 45,

29. Greene, *Horses at Work*, 138; Newcomer, *Cole's Cavalry*, 66; Pierce, *Second Iowa Cavalry*, 120–21; *OR*, 12(1):733.

30. Whittaker, *Volunteer Cavalry*, 40–41.

31. Gates, "For Want of a Shoe," 18–19; Greene, *Horses at Work*, 139–40; Crowninshield, *First Regiment of Massachusetts Cavalry*, 293.

32. Robert Dandridge Jackson to wife, January 25, 1863, Jackson Family Papers, ADAH; Crowninshield, *First Regiment of Massachusetts Cavalry*, 293; Jennings, *Horse and His Diseases*, 209; Gause, *Four Years with Five Armies*, 198; Whittaker, *Volunteer Cavalry*, 40; Congdon, *Cavalry Compendium*, 28; *OR*, 45(1):581.

33. Greene, *Horses at Work*, 153.

34. Johnson, *Soldier's Reminiscences*, 190; Ford, *Cycle of Adams Letters*, 1:111, 256; "War Letters of Charles P. Bowditch," 472–73; Mosby, *War Reminiscences*, 15; *History of the Service of the Third Ohio*, 189; Davenport, *Ninth Regiment Illinois Cavalry*, 70.

35. Covert to wife, June 23, 1863, Thomas M. Covert Papers, WRHS; Wells A. Bushnell Memoirs, 203–4, WRHS.

36. Jennings, *Horse and His Diseases*, 203–5; Phillips, "Writing Horses," 167.

37. Opie, *Rebel Cavalryman*, 94, 115–16, 145–48.

38. Dodson, *Campaigns of Wheeler*, 310–12.

39. Crowninshield, *First Regiment of Massachusetts Cavalry*, 289–90, 292; Wall, "Raids in Southeastern Virginia," 72.

40. Wall, "Raids in Southeastern Virginia," 72. Agency is an important topic in the academic discussion of animal history. See, for example, the essays in McFarland and Hediger, *Animals and Agency*.

41. Jennings, *Horse and His Diseases*, 214–15; Allen, *Down in Dixie*, 146.

42. Opie, *Rebel Cavalryman*, 160, 162; Wall, "Raids in Southeastern Virginia," 72.

43. Parmelee to Sammy, August 2, 1862, Samuel Spencer Parmelee Papers, DU.

44. Ford, *Cycle of Adams Letters*, 2:24; Scott, *Story of a Cavalry Regiment*, 392.

45. Gause, *Four Years with Five Armies*, 383; Arkle, "Old 'Squeezer.'"

46. Crowninshield, *First Regiment of Massachusetts Cavalry*, 287–89.

47. Gause, *Four Years with Five Armies*, 383–84.

48. Chalaron, "Battle Echoes from Shiloh," 219; Pyne, *First New Jersey Cavalry*, 49.

49. Cutrer, *Our Trust*, 57; Blackburn, "Reminiscences of the Terry Rangers," 146; Greene, *Horses at Work*, 161.

50. Gause, *Four Years with Five Armies*, 384.

51. Emerson, *Life and Letters of Charles Russell Lowell*, 325–26, 338, 347–48; Warner, *Generals in Blue*, 285.

52. Gause, *Four Years with Five Armies*, 383; *OR*, 11(2):46–47, 12(2):141.

53. Ringwalt, "Horse," 332–33; Munnerlyn to sister, August 8, 1862, James Keen Munnerlyn Papers, UNC; Baker to mother, January 29, 1863, William B. Baker Papers, UNC; Berkenes, *Private William Boddy's Civil War Journal*, 93; Gause, *Four Years with Five Armies*, 345.

54. Davis, "Winter Raid," 33.

55. *OR*, 23(1):560; Augustus C. Houts diary, December 19, 1862, January 19, 1863, Houts Family Papers, University of California, Bancroft Library, Berkeley; Stickney to Rose, June 26, 1864, Clifford Stickney Collection, CHM; Berkenes, *Private William Boddy's Civil War Journal*, 106.

56. Crowninshield, "Cavalry in Virginia," 25–26; Carmony, "Jacob W. Bartmess Civil War Letters," 65; Whittaker, *Volunteer Cavalry*, 38, 59–60; Gardiner, "Incidents of Cavalry Experiences," 427; *OR*, 38(2):833, 38(4):287, 39(1):307, 311.

57. Ford, *Cycle of Adams Letters*, 1:287, 295, 2:4–5.

58. Bowen, *First New York Dragoons*, 167; "Synchronous Diaphragmatic Flutter," Equinews: Nutrition and Daily Health, December 1, 2005, https://ker.com/equinenews/synchronous-diaphragmatic-flutter/.

59. *OR*, 36(1):792; *SOR*, pt. 1, 6:802; Bliss, "Reminiscences," 77.

60. Atkins, "With Sherman's Cavalry," 389–90.

61. Crowninshield, *First Regiment of Massachusetts Cavalry*, 293–94; McShane and Tarr, *Horse in the City*, 157; O'Brien and Diefendorf, *General Orders*, 2:327–28; *OR*, ser. 4, 2:719–20.

62. Ford, *Cycle of Adams Letters*, 2:3–4.

63. Jennings, *Horse and His Diseases*, 221–339.

64. McCain, *Soldier's Diary*, 8; *OR*, 29(1):353, 19(2):709, 29(2):401; Newhall, "With Sheridan in Lee's Last Campaign," 208; Crowninshield, *First Regiment of Massachusetts Cavalry*, 77.

65. Gray, *Cavalry Tactics*, 166; Edmonds, "Wastage of Cavalry Horses," 251; Humphreys, *Field, Camp, Hospital and Prison*, 222; Whittaker, *Volunteer Cavalry*, 38; *OR*, 29(2):419.

66. Taylor, *Saddle and Saber*, 74–75; *OR*, 19(2):709, 29(2):401, 419.

67. *SOR*, pt. 1, 2:131–32; Ringwalt, "Horse," 333; Mayo, "Glanders and Farcy," 193.

68. Mayo, "Glanders and Farcy," 194; Jennings, *Horse and His Diseases*, 327.

69. Jennings, *Horse and His Diseases*, 325–26.

70 Mayo, "Glanders and Farcy," 193–94.

71. Ringwalt, "Horse," 333; Mayo, "Glanders and Farcy," 194; Crowninshield, "Cavalry in Virginia," 24.

72. [Tenney], *War Dairy*, 35, 44; Wharton to father, November 28, 1862, W. D. Wharton Papers, UNC.

73. Ford, *Cycle of Adams Letters*, 2:4; Wells A. Bushnell Memoirs, 99, 358, WRHS; Boudrye, *Fifth New York Cavalry*, 206.

74. Harris, "Union Cavalry," 352; Bliss, "Reminiscences," 77; Phillips, "Writing Horses," 167.

75. McShane and Tarr, *Horse in the City*, 156; Swart, *Riding High*, 103–4, 121.

76. *OR*, 38(2):873; Fowler, "'Mules Won't Do!,'" 66.

77. Norton, *"Red Neck Ties,"* 85; Packard quoted in Kohl, *Prairie Boys*, 158 (emphasis original); Wall, "Raids in Southeastern Virginia," 81.

78. *History of the Eighteenth Regiment of Cavalry Pennsylvania Volunteers*, 31; Norton, *"Red Neck Ties,"* 87–88; Jordan, "Has He Not Been in the Service of His Country?," 211–27.

12. Cavalrymen

1. McClellan, *McClellan's Own Story*, 110; Crowninshield, *First Regiment of Massachusetts Cavalry*, 284.

2. Wright, *Memoirs*, 164; Brown, *One of Morgan's Men*, 131–32.

3. Chestteen M. Sabbett to Morgan, January 21, 1864, John Hunt Morgan Papers, UNC; Isaac Norval Baker Civil War Memoirs, 4, VMI; Munnerlyn to sister, August 8, September 8, 1862, James Keen Munnerlyn Papers, UNC; Ryan, "Letters of Harden Perkins Cochrane," 286; Joseph E. Johnston to James A. Seddon, January 23, 1864, "Records Cleburnes Div Hardees Corps A of Tenn," chap. 2, no. 265, RG 109, NARA; *OR*, ser. 4, 2:775–76, 794.

4. Thomas Austin to Morgan, January 25, 1864, John Hunt Morgan Papers, UNC; *OR*, ser. 4, 2:4; *OR*, 31(3):743.

5. Hill, "Forty-First Regiment," 768.

6. Crowninshield, "Cavalry in Virginia," 25–26; Humphreys, *Field, Camp, Hospital and*

Prison, 26–27; James Giauque to brother, June 24, 1863, Giauque Family Papers, University of Iowa, Special Collections, Iowa City.

7. Clark, "Making of a Volunteer Cavalryman," 466; Main, *Third United States Colored Cavalry*, 12, 58.

8. Glatthaar, *Soldiering in the Army of Northern Virginia*, 33–38, 41.

9. Whittaker, *Volunteer Cavalry*, 16.

10. Whittaker, *Volunteer Cavalry*, 34–36.

11. Belfield to James H. Trowbridge, July 25, 1864, Henry H. Belfield and Belfield Family Papers, UC.

12. Clark, "Making of a Volunteer Cavalryman," 481; Rea, "Kilpatrick's Raid around Atlanta," 163; Scott, "Last Fight," 324; *Revised Regulations*, 21.

13. Crowninshield, *First Regiment of Massachusetts Cavalry*, 296; Kidd, *Riding with Custer*, 48; Ford, *Cycle of Adams Letters*, 2:70.

14. Crowninshield, *First Regiment of Massachusetts Cavalry*, 296; Kidd, *Riding with Custer*, 48; Wells A. Bushnell Memoirs, 31, WRHS; Whittaker, *Volunteer Cavalry*, 46.

15. Whittaker, *Volunteer Cavalry*, 47–49.

16. Crowninshield, *First Regiment of Massachusetts Cavalry*, 296; Ford, *Cycle of Adams Letters*, 2:30.

17. Dinges and Leckie, *Just and Righteous Cause*, 199; McMurry, *Uncompromising Secessionist*, 321–22.

18. Taylor, *Saddle and Saber*, 123; George Tilton to friend, March 6, 1863, Walter M. Howland Papers, DU; Norton, *"Red Neck Ties,"* 18, 107–8; Maness and Combs, *Do They Miss Me at Home?*, 27; Wells A. Bushnell Memoirs, 66–67, WRHS; Isaac Norval Baker Civil War Memoirs, 3, VMI.

19. R. S. Whitehead reminiscences, in Yeary, *Reminiscences of the Boys in Gray*, 792; Henry H. Belfield to James H. Trowbridge, July 25, 1864, Henry H. Belfield and Belfield Family Papers, UC; Robert Milton McAlister reminiscences, in Elliott and Moxley, *Tennessee Civil War Veterans*, 4:1409; Covert to wife, July 2, 9, 1863, Thomas M. Covert Papers, WRHS.

20. Sheridan to James H. Wilson, July 23, 1864, Philip Henry Sheridan Papers, LC; Norton, *"Red Neck Ties,"* 59; Warren to mother, January 1, 1862, E. Willard Warren Correspondence, DU.

21. Ford, *Cycle of Adams Letters*, 2:4; Bliss, "Reminiscences," 77; Wells A. Bushnell Memoirs, 39, 63, WRHS; Isaac Norval Baker Civil War Memoirs, 2, VMI; Whittaker, *Volunteer Cavalry*, 57.

22. Kidd, *Riding with Custer*, 88; Bliss, "Reminiscences," 76–77; Wells A. Bushnell Memoirs, 279, WRHS; Cheek, "Additional Sketch Ninth Regiment," 468–69; Charles Crosland memoirs, in *Reminiscences of the South Carolina Confederate Cavalry*, 20.

23. Brooke-Rawle, "Gregg's Cavalry in the Gettysburg Campaign," 178; Bahde, *Story of My Campaign*, 179; *OR*, 38(2):752, 875; *SOR*, pt. 1, 3:232; Ford, *Cycle of Adams Letters*, 2:101; Powell, "Sinking Creek Valley Raid," 201.

24. Calvert, *Reminiscences*, 119; George Tilton to friend, March 6, 1863, Walter M. Howland Papers, DU; Henry Clay Reynolds to wife, May 25, 1864, H. C. Reynolds Papers, ADAH; Gardiner, "Incidents of Cavalry Experiences," 425–26; Mosgrove, *Kentucky Cavaliers*, 150.

25. Barron, *Lone Star Defenders*, 225–26; Ford, *Cycle of Adams Letters*, 2:29; Kidd, *Riding with Custer*, 171–72.

26. Meyer, *Civil War Experiences*, 25–26.

27. Allen, *Down In Dixie*, 92–93.

28. Kirk, *Fifteenth Pennsylvania Volunteer Cavalry*, 112–13.

29. Hard, *Eighth Cavalry Regiment, Illinois Volunteers*, 47, 122; Baker to parents, October 24, 1861, William B. Baker Papers, UNC.

30. *OR*, 10(1):531, 12(1):587; Hard, *Eighth Cavalry Regiment, Illinois Volunteers*, 106, 120; Rowell, *Yankee Cavalrymen*, 185; Ford, *Cycle of Adams Letters*, 1:247; Norton, "Red Neck Ties," 56–57.

31. *OR*, 5:713; Baker to parents, October 24, 1861, William B. Baker Papers, UNC.

32. Wells A. Bushnell Memoirs, 312–13, WRHS; Bouldin, "Last Charge at Appomattox," 251; Baker to Mercie, May 10, 1863, William B. Baker Papers, UNC; Humphreys, *Field, Camp, Hospital and Prison*, 29.

33. Scott, *Story of a Cavalry Regiment*, 266–67; Hard, *Eighth Cavalry Regiment, Illinois Volunteers*, 47–48; Ordronaux, *Hints on Health*, 31.

34. Wentz and De Grummond, "Life on Horseback," 112; Kraft et al., "Magnetic Resonance Imaging Findings of the Lumbar Spine," 2205–6.

35. Owsley et al., "Man in the Iron Coffin," 89, 92, 94.

36. Scott and Willey, "Little Bighorn," 155–58, 162–63; Scott, Willey, and Connor, *They Died with Custer*, 277–79.

37. Scott, Willey, and Connor, *They Died with Custer*, 275, 279.

38. Scott, Willey, and Connor, *They Died with Custer*, 272.

39. Lewis, *War Sketches*, 47–48; Kidd, *Riding with Custer*, 329.

40. Ryan, "Letters of Harden Perkins Cochrane," 287; Summers, *Borderland Confederate*, 83; McMurry, *Uncompromising Secessionist*, 244.

41. John G. Marshall, "What I Saw of Stone River," in Kirk, *Fifteenth Pennsylvania Volunteer Cavalry*, 109; Wells A. Bushnell Memoirs, 315–16, WRHS.

42. *OR*, 36(1):776–78, 798; *SOR*, pt. 1, 6:550.

43. Humphreys, *Field, Camp, Hospital and Prison*, 99.

44. Brown, *War Years*, 168; Roberts, "Additional Sketch Nineteenth Regiment," 101; Hubbard, *Notes of a Private*, 36–38.

45. Brown, *One of Morgan's Men*, 90; Newcomer, *Cole's Cavalry*, 93–95.

46. *OR*, 36(3):596.

47. Brown, *War Years*, 287, 311; Circular, Headquarters, Wheeler's Cavalry Corps, March 16, 1863, Box 130, Joseph Wheeler Family Papers, ADAH; *OR*, 45(2):658–59.

48. Nolan, *Cavalry*, v–vi, 226; Kidd, *Riding with Custer*, 282; Ford, *Cycle of Adams Letters*, 1:269–70, 272.

49. Crowninshield, *First Regiment of Massachusetts Cavalry*, 41, 43–44.

50. Ford, *Cycle of Adams Letters*, 1:206; Meyer, *Civil War Experiences*, 97; Bouvé, "Battle at High Bridge," 405; Clark, "Making of a Volunteer Cavalryman," 481–82.

51. [Adams], *Trooper's Adventures*, 28; Powell, "Sinking Creek Valley Raid," 203.

52. Dixon, "Recollections of a Rebel Private," 203; Champion to wife, June 11, 1864, Sidney S. Champion Papers, DU.

53. Galloway, "Sixty-Third Regiment," 537–38.

13. From Dispersion to Concentration

1. *OR*, 11(1):1036–42.

2. Gilmor, *Four Years in the Saddle*, 72; Rufus Barringer to V. C. Barringer, January 27, 1866, Rufus Barringer Papers, UNC; *OR*, 27(3):1068–69; Ladd and Ladd, *Bachelder Papers*, 2:1275; Nanzig, *Civil War Memoirs of a Virginia Cavalryman*, 162–63.

3. Dozier, *Gunner in Lee's Army*, 251, 253, 259.

4. Harris, "Union Cavalry," 350–51; *OR*, 5:13–14, 19, 21, 19(1):80; Welcher, *Union Army*, 509–10.

5. Wesley Merritt quoted in Rodenbough, *From Everglade to Cañon*, 283–84; Isham, "Cavalry of the Army of the Potomac," 301–2; Thomas, *Some Personal Reminiscences*, 2; Harris, "Union Cavalry," 353; McClellan, *McClellan's Own Story*, 119.

6. *OR*, 12(2):20, 271–75, 12(3):581.

7. *OR*, 19(2):490–91.

8. Welcher, *Union Army*, 515; Wittenberg, *With Sheridan in the Final Campaign*, 20; Bliss, "Reminiscences," 64; Wells A. Bushnell Memoirs, 159, WRHS.

9. Nevins, *Diary of Battle*, 177–78; Wittenberg, *With Sheridan in the Final Campaign*, 20; Wells A. Bushnell Memoirs, 159, WRHS.

10. Bliss, "Reminiscences," 69; Gilmore, "Cavalry," 40; *OR*, 25(1):49–50, 52, 55; Griffin, *Three Years a Soldier*, 122; Cooke, *Battle of Kelly's Ford*, 11–12.

11. Shaw, "Fifty-Ninth Regiment," 461; Gregg, "Union Cavalry at Gettysburg," 376; Rodenbough, "Cavalry War Lessons," 108–9; Opie, *Rebel Cavalryman*, 157; Ford, *Cycle of Adams Letters*, 2:69–72; Griffin, *Three Years a Soldier*, 121.

12. Wittenberg, *With Sheridan in the Final Campaign*, 21n; *SOR*, pt. 1, 5:472.

13. Pleasanton to "General," June 23, 1863, Alfred Pleasanton Collection, LC; Calvert, *Reminiscences*, 124.

14. Rafuse, "Culture and Cavalry," 76.

15. Grant, *Personal Memoirs*, 2:133–34.

16. See Sheridan, *Personal Memoirs*, vol. 1.

17. Sheridan, *Personal Memoirs*, 1:342–43; Brinton, *Personal Memoirs*, 267.

18. Sheridan, *Personal Memoirs*, 1:347; Crowninshield, *First Regiment of Massachusetts Cavalry*, 33; Wittenberg, *"We Have It Damn Hard,"* 120; Sheridan to Seth Williams, April 19, 1864; and Sheridan to Andrew A. Humphreys, April 11, 1864, Philip Henry Sheridan Papers, LC; *OR*, 36(1):787, 875; Wilson, "Cavalry of the Army of the Potomac," 37–38.

19. Sheridan, *Personal Memoirs*, 1:354–56.

20. *OR*, 36(1):787; Wilson, "Cavalry of the Army of the Potomac," 76.

21. *OR*, 36(1):894–95; Sheridan, *Personal Memoirs*, 1:366–70.

22. Sheridan, *Personal Memoirs*, 1:370–71, 378; *OR*, 36(1):789.

23. Sheridan, *Personal Memoirs*, 1:387; "Letters of a Civil War Surgeon," 158; Nanzig, *Civil War Memoirs of a Virginia Cavalryman*, 162.

24. *OR*, 36(1):793–97, 852, 40(1):620–24; Kidd, *Riding with Custer*, 329, 344; Sheridan, *Personal Memoirs*, 1:445.

25. *OR*, 43(1):110–12, 421–423, 566–67.

26. *OR*, 43(1):443, 555; Kidd, *Riding with Custer*, 393–94.

27. Crowninshield, "Sheridan at Winchester," 686; *OR*, 43(1):431.

28. *OR*, 43(1):562.

29. *OR*, 43(1):436, 442–43, 477, 486, 489, 508–11, 510, 529; William G. Hills Diary, October 1, 1864, LC.

30. *OR*, 46(2):658, 793.

31. Norton, *Deeds of Daring*, 109; Thomas, *Some Personal Reminiscences*, 23; *OR*, 46(1):1100–1110; Hsieh, "Lucky Inspiration," 127–34.

32. Gause, *Four Years with Five Armies*, 213; "A Chat with Sheridan"; *OR*, 43(1):62. For a critical assessment of Sheridan, see Wittenberg, *Little Phil*.

33. *OR*, 10(1):531, 20(1): 182, 661, 958–59, 966–68.

34. *OR*, 17(1):503, 593–97, 17(2):835; *OR*, ser. 4, 2:364.

35. *OR*, 30(1):178–79, 30(2):20; Powell, *Failure in the Saddle*, xii–xiii, 200–205, 207–8, 210–11, 213–18.

36. Vale, *Minty and the Cavalry*, 2–3; Rae, "Four Weeks with Long's Cavalry," 17; *History and Roster of the Seventh Pa. Cavalry*, 4; Dinges and Leckie, *Just and Righteous Cause*, 104–5; Scott, *Story of a Cavalry Regiment*, 50–51, 53; Simon, *Papers of Ulysses S. Grant*, 6:269.

37. Stanley, *Personal Memoirs*, 120–21; *OR*, 17(2):154, 281, 20(2):31; *History and Roster of the Seventh Pa. Cavalry*, 6.

38. *OR*, 20(2):326, 331; Wilson, "Wilder's Brigade," 48–49; *Ninety-Second Illinois Volunteers*, 90.

39. *OR*, 23(2):302–4.

40. Kniffin, "Cavalry of the Army of the Cumberland," 419–20, 431.

41. Smith, "Mississippi Raid," 379–81; Wilson, *Under the Old Flag*, 1:143.

42. Simpson and Berlin, *Sherman's Civil War*, 491; Hammond diary, July 8–9, 1863, John Henry Hammond Papers, FHS.

43. *OR*, 38(1):101-2, 110, 114.

44. *OR*, 38(3):642, 646, 665–66.

45. *OR*, 32(3):497, 504.

46. *OR*, 39(2):438, 45(1):554; Simon, *Papers of Ulysses S. Grant*, 12:195.

47. *OR*, 39(3):414–15, 45(1):554, 49(1):371; Johnson, *Soldier's Reminiscences*, 334–35; Simon, *Papers of Ulysses S. Grant*, 12:197.

48. Simon, *Papers of Ulysses S. Grant*, 12:197; *OR*, 49(1):371.

49. *OR*, 39(3):414, 439–40, 45(1):555.

50. *OR*, 49(1):355; Simon, *Papers of Ulysses S. Grant*, 12:197.

51. *OR*, 39(3):441, 443–44, 45(1):555, 598; Simon, *Papers of Ulysses S. Grant*, 12:195, 197.

52. *OR*, 45(1):555–57, 560–62.

53. *OR*, 45(2):190, 45(1):563–64, 589, 45(2):513; Pierce, *Second Iowa Cavalry*, 146; Stanley, *Personal Memoirs*, 132.

54. *OR*, 45(1):554, 568, 45(2):431.

55. *OR*, 45(2):276, 430–31.

56. *OR*, 45(2):430–32, 518–19, 49(1):354–55.

57. *OR*, 45(2):489, 516–17, 536, 547, 582, 49(1):355.

58. *OR*, 49(1):355, 45(2):589; Minty diary, January 26, 1865, Robert Horatio George Minty Papers, DPL.

59. *OR*, 45(2):488, 583, 49(1):758; Davenport, *Ninth Regiment Illinois Cavalry*, 175.

60. *OR*, 45(2):487, 489.

61. *OR*, ser. 3, 4:1169; *OR*, 49(1):356. According to Charles A. Dana, Halleck believed the maximum size of a supportable cavalry column was 15,000 men and horses. Wilson, *Life of Charles A Dana*, 353.

62. *OR*, 49(1):356, 758, 45(2):513.

63. *OR*, ser. 3, 4:1168, 5:505.

64. *OR*, 49(1):359; Mitchell, "Field Notes of the Selma Campaign," 182.

65. Scott, *Story of a Cavalry Regiment*, 434–35; *OR*, 49(1):351, 357, 359–61; Minty diary, April 2, 1865, Robert Horatio George Minty Papers, DPL.

66. *OR*, 49(1):362, 439.

67. *OR*, 49(1):362–65, 498.

68. *OR*, 49(1):369, 385, 478, 499, 501.

69. Hosea, "Campaign of Selma," 104–5.

70. *OR*, 49(1):355, 49(2):663; Jones, "'Your Left Arm,'" 245; James H. Wilson to Sherman, June 16, 1865, William T. Sherman Papers, LC.

14. Working toward Effectiveness

1. Vincent, "Greatest of Military Nations"; Bonin, "Challenged Competency," 127; Harris, "Union Cavalry," 350; Emerson, *Life and Letters of Charles Russell Lowell*, 230, 287–88.

2. Wittenberg, *With Sheridan in the Final Campaign*, 17n; Galloway, "Sixty-Third Regiment," 542; Cannon, *Inside of Rebeldom*, 109; Opie, *Rebel Cavalryman*, 54; "History of Company B, 40th Alabama Infantry," 199; Lewis, *War Sketches*, 48; Neal to Ella, March 3, 1864, Andrew Jackson Neal Letters, Emory University, Manuscript, Archives, Rare Book Library, Atlanta.

3. Boring, "Some Reasons Why the Cavalry and Infantry Did Not Fraternize."

4. J. W. Andes reminiscences, in Elliott and Moxley, *Tennessee Civil War Veterans*, 1:212; Stiles, *Four Years under Marse Robert*, 66–67; Bragg to Dear Sir, December 7, 1860, Braxton Bragg Letters, Louisiana State University, Louisiana and Lower Mississippi Valley Collections, Special Collections, Baton Rouge.

5. Semmes to wife, January 3, 1863, Benedict Joseph Semmes Papers, UNC; Albert G. Grammer Diary, February 8, 1864, Old Court House Museum, Vicksburg, MS.

6. Lee to William Porcher Miles, January 28, 1864, Stephen D. Lee Service Record, M331, RG 109, NARA.

7. Nevins, *Diary of Battle*, 178.

8. Brown, *War Years*, 246.

9. *OR*, ser. 3, 4:1167.

10. *OR*, ser. 3, 3:580.

11. *OR*, ser. 3, 3:580–81.

12. *OR*, ser. 3, 3:884–86.

13. *OR*, ser. 3, 4:2, 47; "Inspection of Cavalry Horses," 404–5; Poulter, "Cavalry Bureau," 70–71.

14. *OR*, ser. 3, 4:219, 228–29; *OR*, 42(3):1090–91; Brackett, "Cavalry Bureau."

15. *OR*, ser. 3, 5:221, 527.

16. Crowninshield, *First Regiment of Massachusetts Cavalry*, 121–22.

17. Whittaker, *Volunteer Cavalry*, 71–72; Curry, *Four Years in the Saddle*, 326; *OR*, 20(2):424; Cheney, *Ninth Regiment, New York Volunteer Cavalry*, 259–60; Julius E.

Thomas Civil War Diary, January 1, 1865, UTK; Circular, Headquarters, Wheeler's Cavalry Corps, March 18, 1863, Box 130, Joseph Wheeler Family Papers, ADAH.

18. Roberts, "Additional Sketch Nineteenth Regiment," 106; *OR*, 49(1):430, 25(1):57–58.

19. Whittaker, *Volunteer Cavalry*, 19, 21.

20. *OR*, 36(1):894–95.

21. *OR*, 38(2):875, 883, 39(1):312–13; *SOR*, pt. 1, 4:385.

22. For information about how the infantry and artillery managed ammunition resupply on the battlefield, see Hess, *Rifle Musket*, 17, 104–7; and Hess, *Civil War Field Artillery*, 99, 278–81.

23. Curry, *Four Years in the Saddle*, 23–24; Norton, *"Red Neck Ties,"* 17; Ladd and Ladd, *Bachelder Papers*, 2:1274–75.

24. Bonin, "Challenged Competency," 114–15, 119; Gilmore, "Cavalry," 39–40; Mosby, *War Reminiscences*, 213.

25. Redfield, "Characteristics of the Armies," 368; Blackburn, "Reminiscences of the Terry Rangers," 45.

26. Cutrer, *Our Trust*, 127–28.

27. Curry, *Four Years in the Saddle*, 305.

28. Gregg, "Union Cavalry at Gettysburg," 373; Crowninshield, *First Regiment of Massachusetts Cavalry*, 3; Gregg, "Second Cavalry Division," 116; [Adams], *Trooper's Adventures*, 31; Acken, *Service with the Signal Corps*, 192.

29. Hastings, "Cavalry Service," 261; Leeland Hathaway Recollections, UNC; *History of the Service of the Third Ohio*, 210; Griffin, *Three Years a Soldier*, 121; Rodenbough, "Cavalry War Lessons," 106.

30. *OR*, 39(1):307.

31. *OR*, 49(1):448, 457, 462–63; Tobie, "Service of the Cavalry," 167.

32. Isaac Norval Baker Civil War Memoirs, 4, VMI; Galloway, "Sixty-Third Regiment," 542.

33. For examples of Union focus on good inspection of cavalry, see *OR*, ser. 3, 2:380, 844.

34. Dodson, *Campaigns of Wheeler*, 407.

35. Inspection report, January 22, 1865, 1–5, Alfred Roman Papers, LC.

36. Inspection report, January 22, 1865, 12–14, Alfred Roman Papers, LC.

37. Charles C. Jones Jr., inspection report, February 1865, in Dodson, *Campaigns of Wheeler*, 408–13, 417–18.

38. E. E. Portlock Jr., inspection report, [April 1865], in Dodson, *Campaigns of Wheeler*, 422, 425.

39. E. E. Portlock Jr., inspection report, [April 1865], in Dodson, *Campaigns of Wheeler*, 425.

40. Brown, *War Years*, 221–22, 252.

41. *OR*, ser. 4, 2:4.

42. Circular, Headquarters, Wheeler's Cavalry Corps, December 7, 1864, Box 130, Joseph Wheeler Family Papers, ADAH; McMurry, *Uncompromising Secessionist*, 185; Crowninshield, *First Regiment of Massachusetts Cavalry*, 197; Starr, *Jennison's Jayhawkers*, 311–12; Boudrye, *Fifth New York Cavalry*, 205–6.

43. Clark, "Making of a Volunteer Cavalryman, 476–77; Kirk, *Fifteenth Pennsylvania Volunteer Cavalry*, 726.

44. Wilson, "Cavalry of the Army of the Potomac," 87; Rodenbough, "Cavalry War Lessons," 106; Harris, "Union Cavalry," 371–72.

45. *OR*, 44:364–65, 376, 383, 391–92, 402.

46. *History of the Fifth Massachusetts Battery*, 499.

47. Wilson, "Cavalry of the Army of the Potomac," 81, 84.

48. Gause, *Four Years with Five Armies*, 379; Clark, "Making of a Volunteer Cavalryman," 479–80.

49. Boudrye, *Fifth New York Cavalry*, 206; Cheney, *Ninth Regiment, New York Volunteer Cavalry*, 282; *History of the Sixth New York Cavalry*, 30; Newcomer, *Cole's Cavalry*, 11, 160.

50. E. M. Cooksey and D. W. Fulton accounts, in Yeary, *Reminiscences of the Boys in Gray*, 151, 245; Barringer, "Ninth Regiment," 419.

51. Quarterman, "Defending the Cavalryman," 170; Wright, *Memoirs*, 162–63.

52. Vincent, "Greatest of Military Nations."

15. After the War

1. Bonin, "Challenged Competency," 127–28.

2. Carter, *From Yorktown to Santiago*, 130n; Kidd, *Riding with Custer*, 43.

3. Rodenbough, "Cavalry War Lessons," 104, 106.

4. Rodenbough, "Cavalry War Lessons," 105, 108.

5. Ed. L. Godfrey to Wheeler, November 12, 1881: and Wheeler to editor *Nashville Daily News*, June 11, 1904, Box 127, Joseph Wheeler Family Papers, ADAH.

6. M. F. Steele to Wheeler, October 4, 1904; [Wheeler] to [M. F. Steele], n.d.; and Wheeler to editor *Nashville Daily News*, June 11, 1904, Box 127, Joseph Wheeler Family Papers, ADAH.

7. [Wheeler] to [M. F. Steele], n.d., Box 127, Joseph Wheeler Family Papers, ADAH.

8. [Wheeler] to [M. F. Steele], n.d., Box 127, Joseph Wheeler Family Papers, ADAH.

9. [Wheeler] to [M. F. Steele], n.d., Box 127, Joseph Wheeler Family Papers, ADAH.

10. Phillips, "'Who Shall Say,'" 11–12; Comte de Paris, *History of the Civil War*, 1:295.

11. Phillips, "'Who Shall Say,'" 12–13; Havelock, *Three Main Military Questions*, 78–79; Haig, *Cavalry Studies*, 3–4.

12. Harris, "Union Cavalry," 372.

13. Phillips, "'Who Shall Say,'" 15–16.

14. Phillips, "'Who Shall Say,'" 18–21; Wawro, *Franco-Prussian War*, 61–63; Echevarria, *After Clausewitz*, 24–28.

15. Phillips, "'Who Shall Say,'" 23.

16. Greene, *Russian Army and Its Campaigns in Turkey*, 453; O'Connor, "Vision of Soldiers," 278; Echevarria, *After Clausewitz*, 62.

17. Phillips, "'Who Shall Say,'" 5; Phillips, "Scapegoat Arm," 37–38.

18. Phillips, "'Who Shall Say,'" 5; Phillips, "Scapegoat Arm," 37–38.

19. Phillips, "'Who Shall Say,'" 24–25; Phillips, "Scapegoat Arm," 40–41, 45–46, 48; Badsey, "Boer War," 75–97; Jones, "Scouting for Soldiers," 496, 498; Echevarria, *After Clausewitz*, 74–75.

20. Phillips, "'Who Shall Say,'" 27; Echevarria, *After Clausewitz*, 42–43, 47, 130, 137, 140; De Pardieu, *Critical Study of German Tactics*, 58–62.

21. Phillips, "'Who Shall Say,'" 5; Echevarria, *After Clausewitz*, 137–38.

22. Bonin, "Challenged Competency," 128–29.

23. Gray, *Cavalry Tactics*, 3.

24. Gray, *Cavalry Tactics*, 9–14.

25. Gray, *Cavalry Tactics*, 44–45.

26. Gray, *Cavalry Tactics*, 24–26, 45, 49.

27. Phillips, "'Who Shall Say,'" 6–10; Phillips, "Scapegoat Arm," 51 54.

28. Czarnecki, "Rebirth and Progress of the Polish Military," 758–59, 767–68; Phillips, "Scapegoat Arm," 51, 56–57, 59.

Conclusion

1. Starr, "Cold Steel," 155.

2. Hess, *Civil War Field Artillery*, 233–38.

3. Ladd and Ladd, *Bachelder Papers*, 3:1950.

4. Dodson, *Campaigns of Wheeler*, 310.

BIBLIOGRAPHY

Archives

Alabama Department of Archives and History, Montgomery
Jackson Family Papers
H. C. Reynolds Papers
Joseph Wheeler Family Papers

Chicago History Museum, Chicago, Illinois
Clifford Stickney Collection

Detroit Public Library, Special Collections, Detroit, Michigan
Robert Horatio George Minty Papers

*Duke University, David M. Rubenstein Rare Book
and Manuscript Library, Durham, North Carolina*
William H. Areheart Diaries
Edward George Washington Butler Papers
Sidney S. Champion Papers
Confederate Veteran Papers
Walter M. Howland Papers
Charles A. Legg Correspondence
Samuel Spencer Parmelee Papers
Elisha A. Peterson Papers
Charles H. Sowle Papers
Isaac L. Sperry Letters
E. Willard Warren Correspondence
Theodore H. Weed Papers
James H. Wiswell Papers

*Emory University, Manuscript, Archives,
Rare Book Library, Atlanta, Georgia*
Andrew Jackson Neal Letters

Filson Historical Society, Louisville, Kentucky
John Henry Hammond Papers
Rapp-Idleman Family Papers

Huntington Library, San Marino, California
Joseph E. Johnston Papers

Iowa State University, Special Collections, Ames
Cyrus Bussey Civil War Reminiscences

Kansas Historical Society, Topeka
August Bondi Papers
George E. Flanders Civil War Letters

Library of Congress, Manuscript Division, Washington, DC
William G. Hills Diary
Alexander Newburger Diary
Alfred Pleasanton Collection
Richard Henry Pratt Papers
Alfred Roman Papers
Philip Henry Sheridan Papers
William T. Sherman Papers
Albert Clayton Swindler Papers

Louisiana State University, Louisiana and Lower Mississippi Valley Collections, Special Collections, Baton Rouge
Braxton Bragg Letters

National Archives and Records Administration, Washington, DC
John B. Hood Papers, RG 109
Stephen D. Lee Service Record, M331, Compiled Service Records of
    Confederate General and Staff Officers and Non-Regimental Enlisted
    Men, RG 109
"Records Cleburne's Div. Hardees Corps A of Tenn," chap. 2, no. 265, RG 109

New York State Library, Albany
Franklin Benjamin Hough Papers

Old Court House Museum, Vicksburg, Mississippi
Albert G. Grammer Diary

Texas A&M University, Special Collections,
College Station
J. M. Smith Letters

University of California, Bancroft Library, Berkeley
Houts Family Papers

*University of Chicago, Special Collections Research Center,
Chicago, Illinois*
Harry H. Belfield and Belfield Family Papers

University of Iowa, Special Collections, Iowa City
Giauque Family Papers

University of North Carolina, Southern Historical Collection, Chapel Hill
William B. Baker Papers
Rufus Barringer Papers
Boykin Family Papers
J. F. H. Claiborne Papers
Harry St. John Dixon Papers
Basil Wilson Duke Papers
Commodore D. Epps Papers
Leeland Hathaway Recollections
William Penn Lloyd Diary and Notebooks
Lucas Family Papers
John Hunt Morgan Papers
James Keen Munnerlyn Papers
Benedict Joseph Semmes Papers
W. D. Wharton Papers

University of South Carolina, South Caroliniana Library, Columbia
Malloy Family Papers
Smith and Wells Family Papers

University of Tennessee, Special Collections, Knoxville
Julius E. Thomas Civil War Diary

University of Washington, Special Collections, Seattle
M. F. Force Papers

Vicksburg National Military Park, Vicksburg, Mississippi
15th Illinois Cavalry Folder

Virginia Military Institute, Archives, Lexington
Isaac Norval Baker Civil War Memoirs
Samuel H. Craun Papers
John H. Ervine Letter

Jacob Kent Langhorne Papers
William G. Watson Memoirs

Western Reserve Historical Society, Cleveland, Ohio
Wells A. Bushnell Memoirs
Thomas M. Covert Papers
Alcinus Ward Fenton Papers. Regimental Papers of the Civil War
Francis and John Reiley Papers

Websites

Geiger, Joe. "Burning Springs Oil Field." e-WV: The West Virginia Encyclopedia. Last revised October 18, 2023. https://www.wvencyclopedia.org/articles/726.

History of Oil Prices. https://thecrudechronicles.com/history-of-oil-prices /#:~:text=And%20this%20is%20where%20our%20story%20begins.% 20In,by%20the%20blue%20line%20along%20the%20right%20axis (page discontinued).

Holodny, Elena. "Energy Transition: 155 Years of Oil Prices—in One Chart." World Economic Forum. December 22, 2016. https://www.weforum.org /stories/2016/12/155-years-of-oil-prices-in-one-chart/.

"List of American Civil War Legions." Wikipedia. Last edited June 16, 2024. https://en.wikipedia.org/wiki/List_of_American_Civil_War_legions.

"Synchronous Diaphragmatic Flutter." Equinews: Nutrition and Daily Health. December 1, 2005. https://ker.com/equinews/synchronous-diaphragmatic -flutter/.

"World Population by Year." Worldometer, 2024. https://www.worldometers .info/world-population/world-population-by-year/.

Articles and Books

Abstract of Colonel Herries's Instructions for Volunteer Corps of Cavalry, Adapted to the Use of the Volunteer and Militia Cavalry of the United States. Philadelphia: Anthony Finley, 1811.

Acken, J. Gregory, ed. *Service with the Signal Corps: The Civil War Memoir of Captain Louis R. Fortescue.* Knoxville: University of Tennessee Press, 2015.

[Adams, Francis Colburn]. *A Trooper's Adventures in the War for the Union.* New York: Hurst, [1864].

Allen, Stanton P. *Down in Dixie: Life in a Cavalry Regiment in the War Days from the Wilderness to Appomattox.* Boston: D. Lothrop, 1893.

Allen, Theodore F. "In Pursuit of John Morgan." In *Sketches of War History, 1861–1865: Papers Prepared for the Commandery of the State of Ohio, Military Order of the Loyal Legion of the United States,* 5:223–42. Wilmington, NC: Broadfoot, 1992.

Arkle, J. A. "Old 'Squeezer.'" *National Tribune,* May 24, 1888.

Athearn, Robert G., ed. "The Civil War Diary of John Wilson Phillips." *Virginia Magazine of History and Biography* 62, no. 1 (January 1954): 95–123.

Atkins, Smith D. "With Sherman's Cavalry." In *Military Essays and Recollections: Papers Read before the Commandery of the State of Illinois, Military Order of the Loyal Legion of the United States,* 2:383–98. Chicago: A. C. McClurg, 1894.

Avery, P. O. *History of the Fourth Illinois Cavalry Regiment.* Humboldt, NE: Enterprise, 1903.

Badsey, Stephen. "The Boer War (1899–1902) and British Cavalry Doctrine: A Re-Evaluation." *Journal of Military History* 71, no. 1 (January 2007): 75–97.

Bahde, Thomas, ed. *The Story of My Campaign: The Civil War Memoir of Captain Francis T. Moore, Second Illinois Cavalry.* DeKalb: Northern Illinois University Press, 2011.

Barringer, Rufus. "Ninth Regiment." In *Histories of the Several Regiments and Battalions from North Carolina in the Great War, 1861–'65,* edited by Walter Clark, 1:416–43. Raleigh, NC: E. M. Uzzell, 1901.

Barron, S. B. *The Lone Star Defenders: A Chronicle of the Third Texas Cavalry, Ross' Brigade.* New York: Neale, 1908.

[Bartlett, Napier]. *A Soldier's Story of the War: Including the Marches and Battles of the Washington Artillery, and Other Louisiana Troops.* New Orleans: Clark and Hofeline, 1874.

Barton, John V. "The Procurement of Horses." *Civil War Times Illustrated* 6, no. 8 (December 1967): 16–24.

Beach, W[illiam] H. *The First New York (Lincoln) Cavalry from April 9, 1861 to July 7, 1865.* Milwaukee: Burdick and Allen, 1902.

———. "Some Reminiscences of the First New York (Lincoln) Cavalry." In *War Papers Read before the Commandery of the State of Wisconsin, Military Order of the Loyal Legion of the United States,* 2:276–302. Milwaukee: Burdick, Armitage, and Allen, 1896.

Beale, G. W. *A Lieutenant of Cavalry in Lee's Army.* Boston: Gorham, 1918.

Beale, R. L. T. *History of the Ninth Virginia Cavalry, in the War between the States.* Richmond, VA: B. F. Johnson, 1899.

Beard, Dan W. "With Forrest in West Tennessee." *Southern Historical Society Papers* 37 (1910): 304–8.

Bearss, Edwin C. "Grierson's Winter Raid on the Mobile and Ohio Railroad." *Military Affairs* 24, no. 1 (Spring 1960): 20–37.

Bennett, L. G., and William M. Haigh. *History of the Thirty-Sixth Regiment Illinois Volunteers during the War of the Rebellion.* Aurora, IL: Knickerbocker and Hodder, 1876.

Bergeron, Arthur W., Jr. *Guide to Louisiana Confederate Military Units, 1861–1865.* Baton Rouge: Louisiana State University Press, 1989.

Berkenes, Robert E., ed. *Private William Boddy's Civil War Journal.* Altoona, IA: TiffCor, 1996.

Billings, John D. *Hardtack and Coffee; or, The Unwritten Story of Army Life.* Boston: George M. Smith, 1887.

Birkhimer, William E. *Historical Sketch of the Organization, Administration, Matériel, and Tactics of the Artillery, United States Army.* Washington, DC: Thomas McGill, 1884.

Black, Jeremy. *Cavalry: A Global History.* Philadelphia: Pen & Sword, 2023.

Blackburn, J. K. P. "Reminiscences of the Terry Rangers." Pts. 1 and 2. *Southwestern Historical Quarterly* 22, no. 1 (July 1918): 38–77; 22, no. 2 (October 1918): 143–79.

Blackford, W. W. *War Years with Jeb Stuart.* New York: Charles Scribner's Sons, 1946.

Bliss, George N. "Cavalry Service with General Sheridan, and Life in Libby Prison." In *Personal Narratives of Events in the War of the Rebellion: Being Papers Read before the Rhode Island Soldiers and Sailors Historical Society,* 4:197–295. Wilmington, NC: Broadfoot, 1993.

———. "The First Rhode Island Cavalry at Middleburg, Va., June 17 and 18, 1863." In *Personal Narratives of Events in the War of the Rebellion: Being Papers Read before the Rhode Island Soldiers and Sailors Historical Society,* 6:129–79. Wilmington, NC: Broadfoot, 1993.

———. "How I Lost My Sabre in War and Found It in Peace." In *Personal Narratives of Events in the War of the Rebellion: Being Papers Read Before the Rhode Island Soldiers and Sailors Historical Society,* 9:51–133. Wilmington, NC: Broadfoot, 1993.

———. "Reminiscences of Service in the First Rhode Island Cavalry." In *Personal Narratives of Events in the War of the Rebellion: Being Papers Read before the Rhode Island Soldiers and Sailors Historical Society,* 1:55–82. Wilmington, NC: Broadfoot, 1993.

Bonin, John A. "Challenged Competency: U.S. Cavalry before, during, and after the U.S. Civil War." In *Drawdown: The American Way of Postwar,* edited by Jason W. Warren, 109–36. New York: New York University Press, 2016.

Boring, B. F. "Some Reasons Why the Cavalry and Infantry Did Not Fraternize." *National Tribune,* March 8, 1894.

Boudrye, Louis N. *Historic Records of the Fifth New York Cavalry, First Ira Harris Guard.* Albany, NY: S. R. Gray, 1865.

Bouldin, E. E. "The Last Charge at Appomattox." *Southern Historical Society Papers* 28 (1900): 250–24.

Bouvé, Edward L. "The Battle at High Bridge." In *Civil War Papers Read before the Commandery of the State of Massachusetts, Military Order of the Loyal Legion of the United States,* 2:403–12. Wilmington, NC: Broadfoot, 1993.

Bowen, J. R. *Regimental History of the First New York Dragoons (Originally the*

130th N.Y. Vols. Infantry) during Three Years of Active Service in the Great Civil War. N.p., 1900.

Boynton, Edward C. History of West Point, and Its Military Importance during the American Revolution and the Origin and Progress of the United States Military Academy. New York: D. Van Nostrand, 1864.

Brackett, Albert G. "The Cavalry Bureau." National Tribune, January 26, 1888.

————. History of the United States Cavalry, from the Formation of the Federal Government to the 1st of June, 1863. New York: Harper and Brothers, 1865.

A Brief History of the Fourth Pennsylvania Veteran Cavalry. Pittsburgh: Ewens and Eberle, 1891.

Brinton, John H. Personal Memoirs of John H. Brinton, Major and Surgeon, U.S.V., 1861–1865. New York: Neale, 1914.

Brooke-Rawle, William. "Gregg's Cavalry in the Gettysburg Campaign." In Military Essays and Recollections of the Pennsylvania Commandery, Military Order of the Loyal Legion of the United States, 2:143–79. Wilmington, NC: Broadfoot, 1995.

————. The Right Flank at Gettysburg: An Account of the Operations of General Gregg's Cavalry Command, Showing Their Importance Bearing upon the Results of the Battle. Philadelphia: Allen, Lane, and Scott, 1878.

Brown, Kent Masterson, ed. One of Morgan's Men: Memoirs of Lieutenant John M. Porter of the Ninth Kentucky Cavalry. Lexington: University Press of Kentucky, 2011.

Brown, Shepherd Spencer Neville, Sr., ed. War Years, C.S.A., 12th Mississippi Regiment, Major S. H. Giles, Q.M., Original Letters, 1860–1865. Hillsboro, TX: Hill College Press, 1998.

Bruce, John L. "Lances in the Union Army." National Tribune, April 29, 1886.

Calkin, Homer L., [ed.]. "Elk Horn to Vicksburg." Civil War History 2, no. 1 (March 1956): 7–43.

Calvert, Henry Murray. Reminiscences of a Boy in Blue, 1862–1865. New York: G. P. Putnam's Sons, 1920.

Cannon, J. P. Inside of Rebeldom: The Daily Life of a Private in the Confederate Army. Washington, DC: National Tribune, 1900.

Capron, Albert Banfield. "Stoneman Raid." In Military Essays and Recollections: Papers Read before the Commandery of the State of Illinois, Military Order of the Loyal Legion of the United States, 4:404–15. Chicago: Cozzens and Beaton, 1907.

Carmony, Donald F., ed. "Jacob W. Bartmess Civil War Letters." [Pt. 1.] Indiana Magazine of History 54, no. 1 (March 1956): 49–74.

Carpenter, Louis H. "Sheridan's Expedition around Richmond, May 9–25, 1864." Journal of the United States Cavalry Association 1 (November 1888): 300–324.

Carter, W. H. *From Yorktown to Santiago with the Sixth U.S. Cavalry.* Baltimore: Lord Baltimore, 1900.

Carter, W. R. *History of the First Regiment of Tennessee Volunteer Cavalry in the Great War of the Rebellion, with the Armies of the Ohio and Cumberland, under Generals Morgan, Rosecrans, Thomas, Stanley and Wilson, 1862–1865.* Knoxville: Gaut-Ogden, 1902.

Cavalry Tactics, First Part: School of the Trooper, of the Platoon and of the Squadron, Dismounted. Philadelphia: Lippincott, Grambo, 1855.

Cavalry Tactics, Second Part: School of the Trooper, of the Platoon and of the Squadron, Dismounted. Washington, DC: J. & G. S. Gideon, 1841.

Cavalry Tactics, Third Part: Evolution of a Regiment. Washington, DC: J. & G. S. Gideon, 1841.

Chalaron, J. A. "Battle Echoes from Shiloh." *Southern Historical Society Papers* 21 (1893): 215–24.

"A Chat with Sheridan: The Story of His Raid around Richmond, as Told by Himself." *National Tribune,* May 8, 1884.

Cheek, W. H. "Additional Sketch Ninth Regiment." In *Histories of the Several Regiments and Battalions from North Carolina in the Great War, 1861–'65,* edited by Walter Clark, 1:444–85. Raleigh, NC: E. M. Uzzell, 1901.

Cheney, Newel. *History of the Ninth Regiment, New York Volunteer Cavalry, War of 1861 to 1865.* Jamestown, NY: Martin Merz and Son, 1901.

Clark, James Albert. "The Making of a Volunteer Cavalryman." In *War Papers: Being Papers Read before the Commandery of the District of Columbia, Military Order of the Loyal Legion of the United States,* 3:457–82. Wilmington, NC: Broadfoot, 1993.

Cogley, Thomas S. *History of the Seventh Indiana Cavalry Volunteers.* La Porte, IN: Herald, 1876.

Coles, David J., and Stephen D. Engle, eds. *A Yankee Horseman in the Shenandoah Valley: The Civil War Letters of John H. Black, Twelfth Pennsylvania Cavalry.* Knoxville: University of Tennessee Press, 2012.

Collier, John S., and Bonnie B. Collier, eds. *Yours for the Union: The Civil War Letters of John W. Chase, First Massachusetts Light Artillery.* New York: Fordham University Press, 2004.

Comte de Paris. *History of the Civil War in America.* 4 vols. Philadelphia: Joseph H. Coates, 1875.

Congdon, James A. *Congdon's Cavalry Compendium: Containing Instructions for Non-Commissioned Officers and Privates in the Cavalry Service.* Philadelphia: J. B. Lippincott, 1864.

Connelly, H. C. "Recollections of the War Between the States." [Pts. 1 and 2]. *Journal of the Illinois State Historical Society* 5, no. 4 (January 1913): 458–74; 6, no. 1 (April 1913): 72–111.

Cooke, Jacob B. *The Battle of Kelly's Ford, March 17, 1863.* Soldiers and Sailors

Historical Society of Rhode Island: Personal Narratives, 3rd ser., no. 19. N.p., 1887.

Cooke, Philip St. George. *Cavalry Tactics; or, Regulations for the Instruction, Formations, and Movements of the Cavalry of the Army and Volunteers of the United States.* 2 vols. Washington, DC: Government Printing Office, 1861.

"The Correspondence of Ira Butterfield: A Group of Manuscript Letters in the Possession of the State Historical Society of North Dakota." *North Dakota Historical Quarterly* 3, no. 2 (January 1929): 129–44.

Cox, Jacob D. *Military Reminiscences of the Civil War.* 2 vols. New York: Charles Scribner's Sons, 1900.

Crane, William E. "Bugle Blasts." In *Sketches of War History, 1861–1865: Papers Read before the Ohio Commandery of the Military Order of the Loyal Legion of the United States*, 1:233–51. Wilmington, NC: Broadfoot, 1991.

Crouch, Howard R. *Horse Equipment of the Civil War Era.* N.p.: SCS, 2003.

Crowninshield, Benjamin W. "Cavalry in Virginia during the War of the Rebellion." In *Papers of the Military Historical Society of Massachusetts*, 13:3–31. Wilmington, NC: Broadfoot, 1990.

———. *A History of the First Regiment of Massachusetts Cavalry Volunteers.* Boston: Houghton, Mifflin, 1891.

———. "Sheridan at Winchester." *Atlantic Monthly* 42, no. 254 (December 1878): 683–91.

Curry, W. L. *Four Years in the Saddle: History of the First Regiment Ohio Volunteer Cavalry, War of the Rebellion, 1861–1865.* Columbus, OH: Champlin, 1898.

———. "Raid of the Union Cavalry, Commanded by General Judson Kilpatrick, around the Confederate Army in Atlanta, August, 1864." In *Sketches of War History, 1861–1865: Papers Prepared for the Commandery of the State of Ohio, Military Order of the Loyal Legion of the United States*, 6:252–74. Wilmington, NC: Broadfoot, 1992.

Curtis, Charles A. "A Cavalry Veteran." In *War Papers Read before the Commandery of the State of Wisconsin, Military Order of the Loyal Legion of the United States*, 4:31–50. Milwaukee: Burdick and Allen, 1914.

Cutrer, Thomas W., ed. *Our Trust Is in the God of Battles: The Civil War Letters of Robert Franklin Bunting, Chaplain, Terry's Texas Rangers, C.S.A.* Knoxville: University of Tennessee Press, 2006.

Czarnecki, Jacek. "The Rebirth and Progress of the Polish Military during the Interwar Years." *Journal of Military History* 83, no. 3 (July 2019): 747–68.

Daniel, Larry J. *Cannoneers in Gray: The Field Artillery of the Army of Tennessee, 1861–1865.* Tuscaloosa: University of Alabama Press, 1984.

Davenport, Edward A., ed. *History of the Ninth Regiment Illinois Cavalry Volunteers.* Chicago: Donohue and Henneberry, 1888.

Davis, J. Lucius. *The Trooper's Manual; or, Tactics for Light Dragoons and Mounted Riflemen.* Richmond, VA: A. Morris, 1861.

Davis, William J. "A Winter Raid." *Southern Bivouac* 1 (1885–86): 28–34.

Denison, Frederic. *Sabres and Spurs: The First Rhode Island Cavalry in the Civil War, 1861–1865.* Central Falls, RI: E. L. Freeman, 1876.

De Pardieu. Major. *A Critical Study of German Tactics and of the New German Regulations,* translated by Capt. Charles F. Martin. Fort Leavenworth, KS: US Cavalry Association, 1912.

Deupree, J. G. "The Noxubee Squadron of the First Mississippi Cavalry, C.S.A., 1861–1865." *Publications of the Mississippi Historical Society* 2 (1918): 12–143.

Dickenson, F. S. "The Fifth New York Cavalry in the Valley." *Maine Bugle* 1, no. 2 (April 1894): 147–56.

Dinges, Bruce J., and Shirley A. Leckie, eds. *A Just and Righteous Cause: Benjamin H. Grierson's Civil War Memoir.* Carbondale: Southern Illinois University Press, 2008.

Dixon, Harry S. "Recollections of a Rebel Private." *Sigma Chi* 5, no. 2 (December 1885): 71–77; 5, no. 4 (May 1886): 195–207.

Dodson, W. C. *Campaigns of Wheeler and His Cavalry, 1862–1865.* Atlanta: Hudgins, 1899.

Dornblaser, T. F. *Sabre Strokes of the Pennsylvania Dragoons in the War of 1861–1865, Interspersed with Personal Reminiscences.* Philadelphia: Lutheran Publication Society, 1884.

Dozier, Graham T., ed. *A Gunner in Lee's Army: The Civil War Letters of Thomas Henry Carter.* Chapel Hill: University of North Carolina Press, 2014.

Drews, Robert. *Early Riders: The Beginnings of Mounted Warfare in Asia and Europe.* New York: Routledge, 2004.

Duane, William. *Hand Book for Cavalry: Containing the First Principles of Cavalry Discipline, Founded on Rational Method; Intended to Explain in a Familiar and Practical Manner, the Management and Training of the Horse, and the Instruction, Discipline, and Duties of U.S. Light Dragoons; Conformable to the Established Elementary Discipline of Infantry for the United States' Military Force, and the Latest Improvements in the Modern Art of War.* Philadelphia: By the author, 1814.

Duffy, Christopher. *Austerlitz, 1805.* Hamden, CT: Archon Books, 1977.

———. *Borodino and the War of 1812.* New York: Charles Scribner's Sons, 1973.

———. *The Military Experience in the Age of Reason.* London: Routledge and Kegan Paul, 1987.

Dyer, Alexander Brydie. "Fourth Regiment of Artillery." *Journal of the Military Service Institute of the United States* 11 (1890): 843–67.

Eby, Henry H. *Observations of an Illinois Boy in Battle, Camp and Prisons—1861 to 1865.* N.p., 1910.

Echevarria, Antulio J., II. *After Clausewitz: German Military Thinkers before the Great War.* Lawrence: University Press of Kansas, 2000.

Edmonds, J. R. "The Wastage of Cavalry Horses in the American Civil War, 1861–65." *Cavalry Journal* 4 (1909): 250–51.

Elliott, Colleen Morse, and Louise Armstrong Moxley, eds. *The Tennessee Civil War Veterans Questionnaires.* 5 vols. Easley, SC: Southern Historical Press, 1985.

Emerson, Edward Waldo, [ed.]. *Life and Letters of Charles Russell Lowell.* Columbia: University of South Carolina Press, 2005.

Engerud, H., [ed.]. *The 1864 Diary of Lt. Col. Jefferson K. Scott, 59th Indiana Volunteer Infantry.* Bloomington, IN: Monroe County Historical Society, 1961.

Ewer, James K. *The Third Massachusetts Cavalry in the War for the Union.* Maplewood, MA: William G. J. Perry, 1903.

Ezell, John S., ed. "Excerpts from the Civil War Diary of Lieutenant Charles Alley, Company 'C,' Fifth Iowa Cavalry." *Iowa Journal of History* 49, no. 3 (July 1951): 241–56.

Farlow, Joyce, and Louise Barry, eds. "Vincent B. Osborne's Civil War Experiences." Pts. 1 and 2. *Kansas Historical Quarterly* 20, no. 2 (May 1952): 108–33; 20, no. 3 (August 1952): 187–223.

Farrar, Samuel Clarke. *The Twenty-Second Pennsylvania Cavalry and the Ringgold Battalion, 1861–1865.* Pittsburgh: New Werner, 1911.

Fitzsimmons, Charles. "The Hunter Raid." In *Military Essays and Recollections: Papers Read before the Commandery of the State of Illinois, Military Order of the Loyal Legion of the United States,* 4:392–403. Chicago: Cozzens and Beaton, 1907.

Ford, Charles W. "Charge of the First Maine Cavalry at Brandy Station." In *War Papers Read Before the Commandery of the State of Maine, Military Order of the Loyal Legion of the United States,* 2:268–89. Wilmington, NC: Broadfoot, 1992.

Ford, Worthington Chauncey, ed. *A Cycle of Adams Letters.* 2 vols. Boston: Houghton Mifflin, 1920.

Foster, Alonzo. *Reminiscences and Record of the 6th New York V. V. Cavalry.* [Brooklyn, NY]: n.p., 1892.

Fowler, Donald Marion. "'Mules Won't Do!': The Troubles of a Downsville Soldier in the Civil War, 1864–1865." *North Louisiana Historical Association Journal* 14 (1983): 61–81.

Frank Leslie's Scenes and Portraits of the Civil War. New York: Frank Leslie, 1894.

Galloway, John M. "Sixty-Third Regiment (Fifth Cavalry)." In *Histories of the Several Regiments and Battalions from North Carolina in the Great War 1861–'65,* edited by Walter Clark, 3:529–43. Goldsboro, NC: Nash Brothers, 1901.

Gardiner, William. "Incidents of Cavalry Experiences during General Pope's Campaign." In *Personal Narratives of Events in the War of the Rebellion: Being Papers Read before the Rhode Island Soldiers and Sailors Historical Society*, 3:419–50. Wilmington, NC: Broadfoot, 1993.

Gassman, Jack. "Thoughts on the Role of Cavalry in Medieval Warfare." *Acta Periodica Duellatorum* 2, no. 1 (2014): 149–77.

Gates, Arnold. "For Want of a Shoe: Burden's Machine." *Civil War Times Illustrated* 20, no. 5 (August 1981): 18–19.

Gause, Isaac. *Four Years with Five Armies: Army of the Frontier, Army of the Potomac, Army of the Missouri, Army of the Ohio, Army of the Shenandoah.* New York: Neale, 1908.

Gerges, Mark T. "Command and Control in the Peninsula: The Role of the British Cavalry, 1808–1814." Ph.D. diss., Florida State University, 2005.

Gerleman, David J. "War Horse! Union Cavalry Mounts, 1861–1865." *North & South* 2, no. 2 (January 1999): 47–50, 57–61.

Gibbons, Alfred Ringgold. *The Recollections of an Old Confederate Soldier.* [Shelbyville, MO: Herald, 1931].

Giles, L. B. *Terry's Texas Rangers.* Austin, TX: Pemberton, 1967.

Gill, John. *Reminiscences of Four Years as a Private Soldier in the Confederate Army, 1861–1865.* Baltimore: Sun, 1904.

Gilmor, Harry. *Four Years in the Saddle.* New York: Harper and Brothers, 1866.

Gilmore, D. M. "Cavalry: Its Use and Value as Illustrated by Reference to the Engagements of Kelly's Ford and Gettysburg." In *Glimpses of the Nation's Struggle, Second Series: A Series of Papers Read before the Minnesota Commandery of the Military Order of the Loyal Legion of the United States, 1887–1889*, 38–51. St. Paul, MN: St. Paul Book and Stationery, 1890.

Gilpin, Alec R. *The War of 1812 in the Old Northwest.* East Lansing: Michigan State University Press, 2012.

Glatthaar, Joseph T. *Soldiering in the Army of Northern Virginia: A Statistical Portrait of the Troops Who Served under Robert E. Lee.* Chapel Hill: University of North Carolina Press, 2011.

Gleason, Bruce P. "U.S. Mounted Bands and Cavalry Field Musicians in the Union Army during the Civil War—Background, Duties, and Training." *Journal of Historical Research in Music Education* 27, no. 2 (April 2006): 102–19.

Gracey, S. L. *Annals of the Sixth Pennsylvania Cavalry.* N.p.: E. H. Butler, 1868.

Graham, W. A. "Nineteenth Regiment (Second Cavalry)." In *Histories of the Several Regiments and Battalions from North Carolina in the Great War 1861–'65*, edited by Walter Clark, 4:79–98. Goldsboro, NC: Nash Brothers, 1901.

Grant, Ulysses S. *Personal Memoirs.* 2 vols. New York: Charles L. Webster, 1886.

Gray, Alonzo. *Cavalry Tactics as Illustrated by the War of the Rebellion, Together with Many Interesting Facts Important for Cavalry to Know.* Pt. 1. Fort Leavenworth, KS: US Cavalry Association, 1910.

Greene, Ann Norton. *Horses at Work: Harnessing Power in Industrial America.*
Cambridge, MA: Harvard University Press, 2008.

Greene, Albert Robinson. "Campaigning in the Army of the Frontier." *Collections of the Kansas State Historical Society* 14 (1915–18): 283–310.

Greene, F. V. *The Russian Army and Its Campaigns in Turkey in 1877–1878.*
New York: D. Appleton, 1879.

Gregg, D[avid] M. "The Second Cavalry Division of the Army of the Potomac in the Gettysburg Campaign." In *Military Essays and Recollections of the Pennsylvania Commandery, Military Order of the Loyal Legion of the United States,* 2:115–28. Wilmington, NC: Broadfoot 1995.

———. "The Union Cavalry at Gettysburg." In *The Annals of the War Written by Leading Participants North and South, Originally Published in the* Philadelphia Weekly Times, 372–79. Dayton, OH: Morningside, 1988.

Griffin, Richard N., ed. *Three Years a Soldier: The Diary and Newspaper Correspondence of Private George Perkins, Sixth New York Independent Battery, 1861–1864.* Knoxville: University of Tennessee Press, 2006.

Guild, George B. *A Brief Narrative of the Fourth Tennessee Cavalry Regiment, Wheeler's Corps, Army of Tennessee.* Nashville, 1913.

Haig, Douglas. *Cavalry Studies: Strategical and Tactical.* London: Hugh Rees, 1907.

Halleck, H. Wager. *Elements of Military Art and Science.* New York: D. Appleton, 1862.

Hamilton, William Douglas. *Recollections of a Cavalryman of the Civil War after Fifty Years, 1861–1865.* Columbus, OH: F. J. Heer, 1915.

Hamilton-Williams, David. *Waterloo: New Perspectives.* London: Arms and Armour, 1993.

Hard, Abner. *History of the Eighth Cavalry Regiment, Illinois Volunteers, during the Great Rebellion.* Aurora, IL, 1868.

Harris, Moses. "The Union Cavalry." In *War Papers Read before the Commandery of the State of Wisconsin, Military Order of the Loyal Legion of the United States,* 1:340–73. Milwaukee: Burdick, Armitage, and Allen, 1891.

Harrison, William H. "Personal Experiences of a Cavalry Officer, 1861–66." In *Military Essays and Recollections of the Pennsylvania Commandery, Military Order of the Loyal Legion of the United States,* 1:225–54. Wilmington, NC: Broadfoot, 1995.

Hastings, S. H. "The Cavalry Service, and Recollections of the Late War." *Magazine of Western History* 11, no. 3 (January 1890): 259–66.

Havelock, Henry M. *Three Main Military Questions of the Day.* London: Longmans, Green, 1867.

Heermance, W. L. "The Cavalry at Chancellorsville, May, 1865 [*sic*, 1863]." In *Personal Recollections of the War of the Rebellion: Addresses Delivered before the Commandery of the State of New York, Military Order of the Loyal Legion of the United States,* 2nd ser., 223–30. New York: G. P. Putnam's Sons, 1897.

Hess, Earl J. "The Animal-Human Relationship in War: Cavalry Horses and Their Riders in the American Civil War." *Animal History* 1, no. 1 (March 2025): 71–90. https://doi.org/10.1525/ah.2024.2244950.

———. *Civil War Field Artillery: Promise and Performance on the Battlefield.* Baton Rouge: Louisiana State University Press, 2022.

———. *Civil War Infantry Tactics: Training, Combat, and Small-Unit Effectiveness.* Baton Rouge: Louisiana State University Press, 2015.

———. *Civil War Logistics: A Study of Military Transportation.* Baton Rouge: Louisiana State University Press, 2017.

———. *Civil War Supply and Strategy: Feeding Men and Moving Armies.* Baton Rouge: Louisiana State University Press, 2020.

———. *The Rifle Musket in Civil War Combat: Reality and Myth.* Lawrence: University Press of Kansas, 2008.

Hill, Joshua B. "Forty-First Regiment (Third Cavalry)." In *Histories of the Several Regiments and Battalions from North Carolina in the Great War, 1861–'65,* edited by Walter Clark, 2:767–87. Goldsboro, NC: Nash Brothers, 1901.

History and Roster of the Seventh Pa. Cavalry Veteran Volunteers, 1861–1865. Miners' Journal, 1904.

"A History of Company B, 40th Alabama Infantry, C.S.A., from the Diary of J. H. Curry of Pickens County." *Alabama Historical Quarterly* 17, no. 3 (Fall 1955): 159–222.

History of the Eighteenth Regiment of Cavalry Pennsylvania Volunteers (163d Regiment of the Line), 1862–1865. New York: Wynkoop, Hallenbeck, Crawford, 1909.

History of the Eleventh Pennsylvania Volunteer Cavalry, Together with a Complete Roster of the Regiment and Regimental Officers. Philadelphia: Franklin, 1902.

History of the Fifth Massachusetts Battery. Boston: Luther E. Cowles, 1902.

History of the Service of the Third Ohio Veteran Volunteer Cavalry in the War for the Preservation of the Union from 1861–1865. Columbus, OH: Stoneman, 1910.

History of the Sixth New York Cavalry (Second Ira Harris Guard) Second Brigade—First Division—Cavalry Corps, Army of the Potomac, 1861–1865. Worcester, MA: Blanchard, 1908.

Hitchcock, W. H. "Recollections of a Participant in the Charge." *Century Magazine* 30, no. 5 (September 1885): 779.

Holt, E. J. "Additional Sketch Seventy-Fifth Regiment (Fifth Reserves)." In *Histories of the Several Regiments and Battalions from North Carolina in the Great War 1861–'65,* edited by Walter Clark, 4:91–98. Goldsboro, NC: Nash Brothers, 1901.

Hood, J. B. *Advance and Retreat: Personal Experiences in the United States and Confederate States Armies.* Philadelphia: Burk and M'Fetridge, 1880.

Hosea, Lewis M. "The Campaign of Selma." In *Sketches of War History, 1861–1865: Papers Read before the Ohio Commandery of the Military Order of the Loyal Legion of the United States, 1883-1886*, 1:77–106. Wilmington, NC: Broadfoot, 1991.

Houlding, J. A. *Fit for Service: The Training of the British Army, 1715-1795*. Oxford, Eng.: Clarendon, 1981.

Hsieh, Wayne Wei-Siang. "'Lucky Inspiration': Philip Sheridan's Uncertain Road to Triumph with the Cavalry of the Army of the Potomac." In *Petersburg to Appomattox: The End of the War in Virginia*, edited by Caroline E. Janney, 110–37. Chapel Hill: University of North Carolina Press, 2018.

Hubbard, John Milton. *Notes of a Private*. St. Louis: Nixon-Jones, 1911.

Humphreys, Charles A. *Field, Camp, Hospital and Prison in the Civil War, 1863-1865*. Boston: George H. Ellis, 1918.

"Inspection of Cavalry Horses." *Army and Navy Journal* (February 20, 1864): 404–5.

Isham, Asa B. "The Cavalry of the Army of the Potomac." In *Sketches of War History, 1861–1865: Papers Prepared for the Commandery of the State of Ohio, Military Order of the Loyal Legion of the United States*, 5:301–27. Wilmington, NC: Broadfoot, 1992.

Jennings, Robert. *The Horse and His Diseases*. Philadelphia: John E. Potter, 1860.

Johnson, R. W. *A Soldier's Reminiscences in Peace and War*. Philadelphia: J. B. Lippincott, 1886.

Jomini, Baron de. *The Art of War*. Philadelphia: J. B. Lippincott, 1862.

Jones, James P., ed. "'Your Left Arm': James H. Wilson's Letters to Adam Badeau." *Civil War History* 12, no. 3 (September 1966): 230–45.

Jones, Spencer. "Scouting for Soldiers: Reconnaissance and the British Cavalry, 1899–1914." *War in History* 18, pt. 4 (2011): 495–513.

Jordan, Brian Matthew. "Has He Not Been in the Service of His Country?" In *Animal Histories of the Civil War Era*, edited by Earl J. Hess, 211–27. Baton Rouge: Louisiana State University Press, 2022.

Kaplan, Lawrence M., ed. *The Artillery Service in the War of the Rebellion, 1861-65*. Yardley, PA: Westholme, 2011.

Kempster, Walter. "The Early Days of Our Cavalry, in the Army of the Potomac." In *War Papers: Being Papers Read before the Commandery of the State of Wisconsin, Military Order of the Loyal Legion of the United States*, 3:60–89. Wilmington, NC: Broadfoot, 1993.

Kennedy, John T., and W. F. Parker. "Seventy-Fifth Regiment, (Seventh Cavalry)." In *Histories of the Several Regiments and Battalions from North Carolina in the Great War 1861-'65*, edited by Walter Clark, 4:71–90. Goldsboro: Nash Brothers, 1901.

Kidd, James H. *The Michigan Cavalry Brigade in the Wilderness*. Detroit: Winn and Hammond, 1889.

———. "The Michigan Cavalry Brigade in the Wilderness." In *War Papers: Being Papers Read before the Commandery of the State of Michigan, Military Order of the Loyal Legion of the United States*, 1:225–39. Wilmington, NC: Broadfoot, 1993.

———. *Riding with Custer: Recollections of a Cavalryman in the Civil War.* Lincoln: University of Nebraska Press, 1997.

Kirk, Charles H., ed. *History of the Fifteenth Pennsylvania Volunteer Cavalry, which Was Recruited and Known as the Anderson Cavalry in the Rebellion of 1861–1865.* Philadelphia, 1906.

Kniffin, Gilbert C. "The Cavalry of the Army of the Cumberland in 1863." In *War Papers: Being Papers Read before the Commandery of the District of Columbia, Military Order of the Loyal Legion of the United States*, 1:419–31. Wilmington, NC: Broadfoot, 1993.

———. "General Capron's Narrative of Stoneman's Raid South of Atlanta." In *War Papers: Being Papers Read before the Commandery of the District of Columbia, Military Order of the Loyal Legion of the United States*, 2:99–135. Wilmington, NC: Broadfoot, 1993.

———. "Streight's Raid through Tennessee and Northern Georgia in 1863." In *War Papers: Being Papers Read before the Commandery of the District of Columbia, Military Order of the Loyal Legion of the United States*, 4:195–202. Wilmington, NC: Broadfoot, 1993.

Knight, John. *War at Saber Point: Banastre Tarleton and the British Legion.* Yardley, PA: Westholme, 2020.

Kohl, Rhonda M. *The Prairie Boys Go to War: The Fifth Illinois Cavalry, 1861–1865.* Carbondale: Southern Illinois University Press, 2013.

Kraft, Clayton N., Peter H. Pennekamp, Ute Becker, Mei Young, Oliver Diedrich, Christian Lüring, and Makus von Falkenhausen. "Magnetic Resonance Imaging Findings of the Lumbar Spine in Elite Horseback Riders." *American Journal of Sports Medicine* 37 (2009): 2205–13.

Ladd, David L., and Audrey J. Ladd, eds. *The Bachelder Papers: Gettysburg in Their Own Words.* 3 vols. Dayton, OH: Morningside, 1994–95.

Lancer's Manual, Containing the Complete Exercise of the Lance, Mounted and Unmounted, Compiled from the Latest Works on Cavalry Tactics. New Orleans: Thomas Griswold, 1861.

Lees, William B. "When the Shooting Stopped, the War Began." In *Look to the Earth: Historical Archaeology and the American Civil War*, edited by Clarence R. Geier Jr. and Susan E. Winter, 39–59. Knoxville: University of Tennessee Press, 1994.

Lemmon, J. S. "The 5th Iowa Cav, and Its Brilliant Charge at Sugar Creek, Tenn." *National Tribune*, August 6, 1885.

"Letters of a Civil War Surgeon." *Indiana Magazine of History* 27, no. 2 (June 1931): 132–63.

Lewis, Charles E. *War Sketches* [London: Simmons and Botten, 1897].

Lieven, Dominic. "Mobilizing Russian Horsepower in 1812." *History: The Journal of the Historical Association* 96, no. 2 (April 2011): 152–66.

Lloyd, Harlan Page. "The Battle of Waynesboro." In *Sketches of War History, 1861–1865: Papers Prepared for the Ohio Commandery of the Military Order of the Loyal Legion of the United States, 1890–1896,* 4:194–213. Wilmington, NC: Broadfoot, 1991.

Longacre, Edward G. *A Soldier to the Last: Maj. Gen. Joseph Wheeler in Blue and Gray.* Washington, DC: Potomac Books, 2007.

Lord, Francis A. "Army and Navy Textbooks and Manuals Used by the North during the Civil War, Part II." *Military Collector and Historian* 9 (1957): 95–102.

Lynn, John A. *The Bayonets of the Republic: Motivation and Tactics in the Army of Revolutionary France, 1791–94.* Urbana: University of Illinois Press, 1984.

———. *Giant of the Grand Siècle: The French Army, 1610–1715.* New York: Cambridge University Press, 1997.

Maass, John R. *Defending a New Nation, 1783–1811.* Washington, DC: Center of Military History, 2013.

Mahan, D. H. *An Elementary Treatise on Advanced-Guard, Out-Post, and Detachment Service of Troops, and the Manner of Posting and Handling Them in Presence of an Enemy.* New Orleans: Bloomfield and Steel, 1861.

Main, Ed. M. *The Story of the Marches, Battles and Incidents of the Third United States Colored Cavalry: A Fighting Regiment in the War of the Rebellion, 1861–5.* Louisville, KY: Globe, 1908.

Maness, Donald C., and H. Jason Combs, eds. *Do They Miss Me at Home? The Civil War Letters of William McKnight, Seventh Ohio Volunteer Cavalry.* Athens: Ohio University Press, 2010.

Maury, Dabney Herndon. *Skirmish Drill for Mounted Troops.* Richmond, VA: Ritchie and Dunnavant, 1861.

Maxwell, Jerry. *The Perfect Lion: The Life and Death of Confederate Artillerist John Pelham.* Tuscaloosa: University of Alabama Press, 2011.

Mayo, N. S. "Glanders and Farcy." *Journal of the United States Cavalry Association* 13 (October 1902): 193–94.

Mays, Thomas D., ed. *Let Us Meet in Heaven: The Civil War Letters of James Michael Barr, 5th South Carolina Cavalry.* Abilene, TX: McWhiney Foundation, 2001.

McCain, Warren. *A Soldier's Diary; or, The History of Company "L," Third Indiana Cavalry.* Indianapolis: William A. Patton, 1885.

McCall, Jeremiah B. *The Cavalry of the Roman Republic.* London: Routledge, 2001.

McClellan, George B. *European Cavalry, including Details of the Organization of the Cavalry Service among the Principal Nations of Europe.* Philadelphia: J. B. Lippincott, 1861.

———. *McClellan's Own Story: The War for the Union, the Soldiers Who Fought*

It, the Civilians Who Directed It, and His Relations to It and to Them. New York: Charles L. Webster, 1887.

———. *Regulations and Instructions for the Field Service of the U.S. Cavalry in Time of War.* Philadelphia: J. B. Lippincott, 1862.

McDonald, William N. *A History of the Laurel Brigade: Originally the Ashby Cavalry of the Army of Northern Virginia and Chew's Battery.* Baltimore: Johns Hopkins University Press, 2002.

McFarland, Sarah E., and Ryan Hediger, eds. *Animals and Agency: An Interdisciplinary Exploration.* Leiden, Neth.: Brill, 2009.

McGreevy, Paul, and Andrew McLean. "Behavioural Problems with the Ridden Horse." In *The Domestic Horse: The Origins, Development and Management of Its Behaviour,* edited by D. S. Mills and S. M. McDonnell, 196–211. Cambridge: Cambridge University Press, 2005.

McKoy, C. E. "Dismounted Cavalry: How They Acted in the Shenandoah Valley." *National Tribune,* April 11, 1889.

McMurry, Richard M., ed. *An Uncompromising Secessionist: The Civil War of George Knox Miller, Eighth (Wade's) Confederate Cavalry.* Tuscaloosa: University of Alabama Press, 2007.

McShane, Clay, and Joel Tarr. *The Horse in the City: Living Machines in the Nineteenth Century.* Baltimore: Johns Hopkins University Press, 2007.

McWhiney, Grady, and Perry D. Jamieson. *Attack and Die: Civil War Military Tactics and the Southern Heritage.* Tuscaloosa: University of Alabama Press, 1982.

Means, Paul B. "Additional Sketch Sixty-Third Regiment (Fifth Cavalry)." In *Histories of the Several Regiments and Battalions from North Carolina in the Great War, 1861–'65,* edited by Walter Clark, 3:545–657. Raleigh, NC: E. M. Uzzell, 1901.

Memoir of Thomas H. Malone: An Autobiography Written for His Children. Nashville: Baird-Ward, 1928.

Meyer, Henry C. *Civil War Experiences under Bayard, Gregg, Kilpatrick, Custer, Raulston, and Newberry, 1861, 1863, 1864.* New York: G. P. Putman's Sons, 1911.

Meyer, William E. "The Sailor on Horseback." In *Personal Narratives of Events in the War of the Rebellion, Being Papers Read before the Rhode Island Soldiers and Sailors Historical Society,* 10:176–245. Wilmington, NC: Broadfoot, 1993.

Mikaberidze, Alexander. *The Battle of Borodino: Napoleon against Kutuzov.* Barnsley, Eng.: Pen & Sword, 2007.

Mitchell, Adele H., ed. *The Letters of Major General James E. B. Stuart.* Stuart-Mosby Historical Society, 1990.

Mitchell, Charles D. "Field Notes of the Selma Campaign." In *Sketches of War History, 1861–1865: Papers Prepared for the Commandery of the State of Ohio,*

Military Order of the Loyal Legion of the United States, 1903–1908, 6:174–94. Wilmington, NC: Broadfoot, 1992.

———. "The Sanders Raid into East Tennessee, June, 1863." In *Sketches of War History, 1861–1865: Papers Read for the Commandery of the State of Ohio, Military Order of the Loyal Legion of the United States*, 6:238–51. Wilmington, NC: Broadfoot, 1992.

M'Minn, W. P. "Service with Van Dorn's Cavalry." *Confederate Veteran* 27 (1919): 384–86.

Morey, A. L. "Torpedoes at Yorktown—Rebel Lances." *National Tribune*, August 27, 1885.

Morgan, Speer, [ed.]. "For Our Beloved Country: The Diary of a Bugler." *Missouri Review* 12, no. 3 (1989): 35–142.

Morrison, James L., Jr. "Educating the Civil War Generals: West Point, 1833–1861." *Military Affairs* 38, no. 3 (October 1974): 108–11.

Morton, John Watson. *The Artillery of Nathan Bedford Forrest's Cavalry*. Nashville: M. E. Church, South, 1909.

Mosby, John S. *Mosby's War Reminiscences, Stuart's Cavalry Campaigns*. New York: Pageant, 1958.

Mosgrove, George Dallas. *Kentucky Cavaliers in Dixie: Reminiscences of a Confederate Cavalryman*. Jackson, TN: McCowat-Mercer, 1957.

Moyer, H. P. *History of the Seventeenth Regiment Pennsylvania Volunteer Cavalry; or, One Hundred and Sixty-Second in the Line of Pennsylvania Volunteer Regiments, War to Suppress the Rebellion, 1861–1865*. Lebanon, PA: Sowers, [1911].

Muir, Rory. *Salamanca, 1812*. New Haven, CT: Yale University Press, 2001.

———. *Tactics and the Experience of Battle in the Age of Napoleon*. New Haven, CT: Yale University Press, 1998.

Munford, Thomas T. "A Confederate Cavalry Officer's Views on 'American Practice and Foreign Theory.'" *Journal of the United States Cavalry Association* 4 (January 1891): 197–203.

Murphy, Douglas A. *Two Armies on the Rio Grande: The First Campaign of the US-Mexican War*. College Station: Texas A&M University Press, 2015.

Nanzig, Thomas P., ed. *The Civil War Memoirs of a Virginia Cavalryman, Lt. Robert T. Hubard, Jr.* Tuscaloosa: University of Alabama Press, 2007.

Napoleon's Maxims of War. Richmond, VA: West and Johnston, 1862.

Nelson, Paul David. "General Charles Scott, the Kentucky Mounted Volunteers, and the Northwest Indian Wars, 1784–1794." *Journal of the Early Republic* 6, no. 3 (1986): 219–51.

Nevins, Allan, ed. *A Diary of Battle: The Personal Journals of Colonel Charles S. Wainwright, 1861–1865*. New York: Harcourt, Brace and World, 1962.

Newcomer, C. Armour. *Cole's Cavalry; or, Three Years in the Saddle in the Shenandoah Valley*. Baltimore: Cushing, 1895.

Newhall, Fred C. "With Sheridan in Lee's Last Campaign." *Maine Bugle* 1, no. 3 (July 1894): 201–13.

Ninety-Second Illinois Volunteers. Freeport, IL: Journal Steam, 1875.

Nolan, L. E. *Cavalry: Its History and Tactics*. 3rd ed. London: Bosworth and Harrison, 1860.

Norris, Basil. "Lancers in the Rebel Army." *National Tribune*, October 15, 1885.

Norton, Chauncey S. *"The Red Neck Ties"; or, History of the Fifteenth New York Volunteer Cavalry*. Ithaca, NY: Journal, 1891.

Norton, Henry. *Deeds of Daring; or, History of the Eighth N.Y. Volunteer Cavalry*. Norwich, NY: Chenango Telegraph, 1889.

Nosworthy, Brent. *The Bloody Crucible of Courage: Fighting Methods and Combat Experience of the Civil War*. New York: Carroll and Graf, 2003.

———. *With Musket, Cannon, and Sword: Battle Tactics of Napoleon and His Enemies*. New York: Sarpedon, 1996.

Nott, Charles C. *Sketches of the War: A Series of Letters to the North Moore Street School of New York*. Rev. and enlarged ed. New York: William Abbott, 1911.

O'Brien, Thomas M., and Oliver Diefendorf, [eds.]. *General Orders of the War Department, Embracing the Years 1861, 1862, & 1863*. 2 vols. New York: Derby and Miller, 1864.

O'Connor, Maureen P. "The Vision of Soldiers: Britain, France, Germany and the United States Observe the Russo-Turkish War." *War in History* 4, no. 3 (1997): 264–95.

Opie, John N. *A Rebel Cavalryman with Lee, Stuart, and Jackson*. Chicago: W. B. Conkey, 1899.

Ordronaux, John. *Hints on Health in Armies, for the Use of Volunteer Officers*. 2nd ed. New York: D. Van Nostrand, 1863.

Osborn, Hartwell. "Sherman's Carolina Campaign." *Western Reserve University Bulletin* 15, no. 8 (November 1912): 101–19.

Owsley, Douglas W., Karin S. Bruwelheide, Larry W. Cartmell Sr., Laurie E. Burgess, Shelly J. Foote, Skye M. Chang, and Nick Fielder. "The Man in the Iron Coffin: An Interdisciplinary Effort to Name the Past." *Historical Archaeology* 40, No. 3 (2006): 89–108.

Patten, George. *Cavalry Drill and Sabre Exercise: Compiled Agreeably to the Latest Regulations of the War Department from Standard Military Authority*. Richmond, VA: West and Johnston, 1862.

Peck, R. H. *Reminiscences of a Confederate Soldier of Co. C, 2nd Va. Cavalry*. N.p., n.d.

Perry, Bliss. *Life and Letters of Henry Lee Higginson*. Boston: Atlantic Monthly Press, 1921.

Phelps, Byron. "The Cavalry: The Improvement Made in This Service during the War." *National Tribune*, April 3, 1890.

Phillips, Gervase. "'Of Nimble Service': Technology, Equestrianism, and the

Cavalry Arm of Early Modern Western European Armies." *War & Society* 20, no. 2 (October 2002): 1–21.

———. "Scapegoat Arm: Twentieth-Century Cavalry in Anglophone Historiography." *Journal of Military History* 71, no. 1 (January 2007): 37–74.

———. "'Who Shall Say That the Days of Cavalry Are Over?': The Revival of the Mounted Arm in Europe, 1853–1914." *War in History* 18, no. 1 (2011): 5–32.

———. "Writing Horses into American Civil War History." *War in History* 20, no. 2 (2013): 160–81.

Pickerill, W. N. *History of the Third Indiana Cavalry*. Indianapolis: Aetna, 1906.

Pierce, Lyman B. *History of the Second Iowa Cavalry*. Burlington, IA: Hawk-Eye Steam Book and Job Printing, 1865.

Pooley-Ebert, Andria. "Species Agency: A Comparative Study of Horse-Human Relationships in Chicago and Rural Illinois." In *The Historical Animal*, edited by Susan Nance, 148–65. Syracuse, NY: Syracuse University Press, 2015.

Poulter, Keith. "The Cavalry Bureau." *North & South* 2, no. 2 (January 1999): 70–71.

Powell, David A. *Failure in the Saddle: Nathan Bedford Forrest, Joseph Wheeler, and the Confederate Cavalry in the Chickamauga Campaign*. New York: Savas Beatie, 2010.

Powell, William H. "The Sinking Creek Valley Raid." In *War Papers and Personal Reminiscences, 1861–1865: Read before the Commandery of the State of Missouri, Military Order of the Loyal Legion of the United States*, 1:191–203. Wilmington, NC: Broadfoot, 1992.

Pratt, Harry E. "Civil War Letters of Winthrop S. G. Allen." *Journal of the Illinois State Historical Society* 24, no. 3 (October 1931): 553–77.

Preston, N[oble] D. "The Cavalry Raid to Richmond, May 1864." In *Military Essays and Recollections of the Pennsylvania Commandery, Military Order of the Loyal Legion of the United States*, 1:497–523. Wilmington, NC: Broadfoot, 1995.

———. *History of the Tenth Regiment of Cavalry, New York State Volunteers, August, 1861, to August, 1865*. New York: D. Appleton, 1892.

Prezelski, Tom. "Lives of the Californio Lancers: The First Battalion of Native California Cavalry, 1863–1866." *Journal of Arizona History* 40, no. 1 (Spring 1999): 29–52.

Pyne, Henry R. *The History of the First New Jersey Cavalry, (Sixteenth Regiment, New Jersey Volunteers)*. Trenton, NJ: J. A. Beecher, 1871.

Quarterman, F. J. "Defending the Cavalryman." *Confederate Veteran* 30 (1922): 170.

Quimby, Robert S. *The Background of Napoleonic Warfare: The Theory of Military Tactics in Eighteenth-Century France*. New York: Columbia University Press, 1957.

Rafuse, Ethan S. "Culture and Cavalry, Discourse and Reality: Some Observations on the War in the East." *North and South* 10 (January 2008): 72–86.

Ramsdell, Charles W. "General Robert E. Lee's Horse Supply, 1862–1865." *American Historical Review* 35, no. 4 (July 1930): 758–77.

Rankin, R. C. "A Brave Band: Services of the 4th Independent Ohio Cav." *National Tribune*, September 27, 1894.

Rea, John P. "Four Weeks with Long's Cavalry in East Tennessee." In *Glimpses of the Nation's Struggle, Fifth Series: Papers Read before the Minnesota Commandery of the Military Order of the Loyal Legion of the United States, 1897–1902*, 17–44. St. Paul: Review, 1903.

———. "Kilpatrick's Raid around Atlanta." In *Glimpses of the Nation's Struggle, Fifth Series: Papers Read before the Minnesota Commandery of the Military Order of the Loyal Legion of the United States, 1897–1902*, 152–74. St. Paul: Review, 1903.

Reader, Frank S. *History of the Fifth West Virginia Cavalry, Formerly the Second Virginia Infantry, and of Battery G, First West Va. Light Artillery.* New Brighton, PA: Daily News, 1890.

Redfield, H. V. "Characteristics of the Armies." In *Annals of the War Written by Leading Participants North and South Originally Published in the* Philadelphia Weekly Times, 357–71. Edison, NY: Blue & Gray, 1996.

Rein, Christopher M. *The Second Colorado Cavalry: A Civil War Regiment on the Great Plains.* Norman: University of Oklahoma Press, 2020.

Reminiscences of the South Carolina Confederate Cavalry including "Some Reminiscences of a Confederate Soldier," by Edwin Calhoun, and "Reminiscences of the Sixties," by Charles Crosland. Columbia: University of South Carolina Press, 2009.

Revised Regulations for the Army of the United States, 1861. Philadelphia: J. G. L. Brown, 1861.

Ringwalt, Samuel. "The Horse—from Practical Experience in the Army." In *Report of the Commissioner of Agriculture for the Year 1866*, 321–34. Washington, DC: Government Printing Office, 1867.

Roberts, William P. "Additional Sketch Nineteenth Regiment (Second Cavalry)." In *Histories of the Several Regiments and Battalions from North Carolina in the Great War 1861-'65*, edited by Walter Clark, 4:99–109. Goldsboro, NC: Nash Brothers, 1901.

Robinson, Gavin. "Equine Battering Rams?: A Reassessment of Cavalry Charges in the English Civil Wars." *Journal of Military History* 75, no. 3 (July 2011): 719–31.

———. "Horse Supply and the Development of the New Model Army, 1642–1646." *War in History* 15, no. 2 (2008): 121–40.

Robinson, George I. *"With Kilpatrick around Atlanta:" A Paper Read before the Wisconsin Commandery, M.O.L.L.U.S., December 1st, 1886.* Milwaukee: Burdick, Armitage, and Allen, 1888.

Rockwell, Alphonso D. "With Sheridan's Cavalry." In *Personal Recollections of the War of the Rebellion: Addresses Delivered before the Commandery of the State of New York, Military Order of the Loyal Legion of the United States*, 3rd ser, 228–39. Wilmington, NC: Broadfoot, 1992.

Rodenbough, Theophilus F. "Cavalry War Lessons." *Journal of the United States Cavalry Association* 2, no. 5 (June 1889): 103–23.

———. *From Everglade to Cañon with the Second Dragoons (Second United States Cavalry)*. New York: D. Van Nostrand, 1875.

Roemer, J. *Cavalry: Its History, Management, and Uses in War*. New York: D. Van Nostrand, 1863.

Rowell, John W. *Yankee Cavalrymen: Through the Civil War with the Ninth Pennsylvania Cavalry*. Knoxville: University of Tennessee Press, 1971.

Royall, William L. *Some Reminiscences*. New York: Neale, 1909.

Ryan, Harriet Fitts, [ed.]. "The Letters of Harden Perkins Cochrane, 1862–1864 (Part V)." *Alabama Review* 8, no. 4 (October 1955): 277–90.

Schlotterbeck, John T., Wesley W. Wilson, Midori Kawane, and Harold A. Klingensmith, eds. *James Riley Weaver's Civil War: The Diary of a Union Cavalry Officer and Prisoner of War, 1863–1865*. Kent, OH: Kent State University Press, 2019.

Scott, Douglas D., and P. Willey. "Little Bighorn: Human Remains from the Custer National Cemetery." In *In Remembrance: Archaeology and Death*, edited by David A. Poirier and Nicholas F. Bellanton, 155–71. Westport, CT: Bergin and Garvey, 1997.

Scott, Douglas D., P. Willey, and Melissa A. Connor. *They Died with Custer: Soldiers' Bones from the Battle of the Little Bighorn*. Norman: University of Oklahoma Press, 1998.

Scott, H. L. *Military Dictionary*. New York: D. Van Nostrand, 1861.

Scott, John. "The Black Horse Cavalry." In *The Annals of the War, Written by Leading Participants North and South*, 590–613. Philadelphia: Times, 1879.

Scott, Samuel W., and Samuel P. Angel. *History of the Thirteenth Regiment Tennessee Volunteer Cavalry, U.S.A.* Blountville, TN: Tony Marion, 1973.

Scott, Shelly R. "The Racehorse as Protagonist: Agency, Independence, and Improvisation." In *Animals and Agency: An Interdisciplinary Exploration*, edited by Sarah E. McFarland and Ryan Hediger, 45–65. Leiden, Neth.: Brill, 2009.

Scott, William Forse. "The Last Fight for Missouri." In *Personal Recollections of the War of the Rebellion: Addresses Delivered before the Commandery of the State of New York, Military Order of the Loyal Legion of the United States*, 3rd ser., 292–328. Wilmington, NC: Broadfoot, 1992.

———. *The Story of a Cavalry Regiment: The Career of the Fourth Iowa Veteran Volunteers From Kansas to Georgia, 1861–1865*. New York: G. P. Putnam's Sons, 1894.

Sears, Matthew S., and Carolyn Willekes. "Alexander's Cavalry Charge at

Chaeronea, 338 BCE." *Journal of Military History* 80, no. 4 (October 2016): 1017–35.

Shaw, W. P. "Fifty-Ninth Regiment (Fourth Cavalry)." In *Histories of the Several Regiments and Battalions from North Carolina in the Great War 1861–'65,* edited by Walter Clark, 3:455–72. Goldsboro, NC: Nash Brothers, 1901.

Sheridan, P. H. *Personal Memoirs.* 2 vols. New York: Charles L. Webster, 1888.

Showalter, Dennis. *The Wars of Frederick the Great.* London: Longman, 1996.

Sidnell, Philip. *Warhorse: Cavalry in Ancient Warfare.* London: Hambledon Continuum, 2006.

Simon, John Y., ed. *The Papers of Ulysses S. Grant.* 32 vols. Carbondale: Southern Illinois University Press, 1967–2009.

Simpson, Brooks D., and Jean V. Berlin, eds. *Sherman's Civil War: Selected Correspondence of William T. Sherman, 1860–1865.* Chapel Hill: University of North Carolina Press, 1999.

Sipes, William B. *The Seventh Pennsylvania Veteran Volunteer Cavalry, Its Record, Reminiscences, and Roster with an Appendix.* Pottsville, PA: Miners Journal, [1905].

Smith, William Sooy. "The Mississippi Raid." In *Military Essays and Recollections: Papers Read before the Commandery of the State of Illinois, Military Order of the Loyal Legion of the United States,* 4:379–91. Chicago: Cozzens and Beaton, 1907.

Spring, Matthew H. *With Zeal and with Bayonets Only: The British Army on Campaign in North America, 1775–1783.* Norman: University of Oklahoma Press, 2008.

Stanley, David S. *Personal Memoirs of Major-General D. S. Stanley, U.S.A.* Cambridge, MA: Harvard University Press, 1917.

Starr, Stephen Z. "Cold Steel: The Saber and the Union Cavalry." *Civil War History* 11, no. 2 (June 1965): 142–59.

———. *Jennison's Jayhawkers: A Civil War Cavalry Regiment and Its Commander.* Baton Rouge: Louisiana State University Press, 1973.

———. "The Wilson Raid, June, 1864: A Trooper's Reminiscences." *Civil War History* 21, no. 3 (September 1975): 218–41.

Stiles, Robert. *Four Years under Marse Robert.* New York: Neale, 1903.

Stonebraker, Joseph R. *A Rebel of '61.* New York: Wynkoop, Hallenbeck, Crawford, 1899.

Summers, Festus P., ed. *A Borderland Confederate.* Pittsburgh: University of Pittsburgh Press, 1962.

Supplement to the Official Records of the Union and Confederate Armies. 100 vols. Wilmington, NC: Broadfoot, 1995–99.

Surby, R. W. *Grierson's Raids, and Hatch's Sixty-Four Days March, with Biographical Sketches, also the Life and Adventures of Chickasaw, the Scout.* Chicago: Rounds and James, 1865.

Sutton, J. J. *History of the Second Regiment West Virginia Cavalry Volunteers during the War of the Rebellion.* Portsmouth, OH, 1892.

Swart, Sandra. *Riding High: Horses, Humans, and History in South Africa.* Johannesburg, SA: Wits University Press, 2010.

Tarrant, E. *The Wild Riders of the First Kentucky Cavalry: A History of the Regiment, in the Great War of the Rebellion, 1861–1865.* Louisville, KY: R. H. Carothers, 1894.

Taylor, A. H. "Bayonets and Sabers." *National Tribune,* January 7, 1886.

Taylor, Gray Nelson, ed. *Saddle and Saber: Civil War Letters of Corporal Nelson Taylor, Ninth New York State Volunteer Cavalry.* Bowne, MD: Heritage Books, 1993.

Taylor, Richard. *Destruction and Reconstruction: Personal Experiences of the Late War.* New York: D. Appleton, 1883.

[Tenney, Frances Andrews]. *War Diary of Luman Harris Tenney, 1861–1865.* Cleveland, OH: Evangelical Publishing House, 1914.

Thatcher, Marshall P. *A Hundred Battles in the West, St. Louis to Atlanta, 1861–65.* Detroit: L. F. Kilroy, 1884.

Thomas, Hampton S. *Some Personal Reminiscences of Service in the Cavalry of the Army of the Potomac.* Philadelphia: L. R. Hamersly, 1889.

Tobie, Edward P. *History of the First Maine Cavalry, 1861–1865.* Boston: Emery and Hughes, 1887.

———. "Personal Recollections of General Sheridan." In *Personal Narratives of Events in the War of the Rebellion: Being Papers Read before the Rhode Island Soldiers and Sailors Historical Society,* 6:183–218. Wilmington, NC: Broadfoot, 1993.

———. "Service of the Cavalry in the Army of the Potomac." In *Personal Narratives of Events in the War of the Rebellion: Being Papers Read before the Rhode Island Soldiers and Sailors Historical Society,* 3:121–72. Wilmington, NC: Broadfoot, 1993.

Treichel, Charles. "Major Zagonyi's Horse-Guard." In *Personal Recollections of the War of the Rebellion: Addresses Delivered before the Commandery of the State of New York, Military Order of the Loyal Legion of the United States,* 3rd ser., 240–46. Wilmington, NC: Broadfoot, 1992.

Trout, Robert J., ed. *Memoirs of the Stuart Horse Artillery Battalion: Moorman's and Hart's Batteries.* [Vol. 1.] Knoxville: University of Tennessee Press, 2008.

Trowbridge, Luther S. *The Stoneman Raid of 1865.* [Michigan MOLLUS] War Papers 7. [Detroit]: Ostler, 1888.

Turchin, John B. "Bayonet and Saber: Their Value as Weapons in the Warfare of the Present Day." Pt. 2. *National Tribune,* April 15, 1886.

Upton, Emory. *The Military Policy of the United States.* Washington, DC: Government Printing Office, 1912.

Vale, Joseph G. *Minty and the Cavalry: A History of Cavalry Campaigns in the Western Armies.* Harrisburg, PA: Edwin K. Meyers, 1886.

Vance, J. W., ed. *Report of the Adjutant General of the State of Illinois.* 8 vols. Springfield: H. W. Rokker, 1886.

Vincent, Thomas M'Curdy. "The Greatest of Military Nations: The Military Power of the United States as Shown during the War of the Rebellion." Pt. 2. *National Tribune*, May 7, 1903.

Wall, Edward. "Raids in Southeastern Virginia Fifty Year Ago." *Proceedings of the New Jersey Historical Society* 3, no. 1 (1918): 65–82.

Waran, Natalie K., and Rachel Casey. "Horse Training." In *The Domestic Horse: The Origins, Development and Management of its Behaviour*, edited by D. S. Mills and S. M. McDonnell, 184–95. Cambridge, Eng.: Cambridge University Press, 2005.

Waring, George E. *Whip and Spur.* New York: Doubleday, Page, 1904.

"War Letters of Charles P. Bowditch." *Proceedings of the Massachusetts Historical Society* 57 (May 1924): 414–95.

Warner, Ezra J. *Generals in Blue: Lives of the Union Commanders.* Baton Rouge: Louisiana State University Press, 1964.

The War of the Rebellion: A Compilation of the Official Records of the Union and Confederate Armies. 70 vols. in 128 pts. Washington, DC: Government Printing Office, 1880–1901.

Wawro, Geoffrey. *The Franco-Prussian War: The German Conquest of France in 1870–1871.* New York: Cambridge University Press, 2003.

Weigley, Russell F. *The Age of Battles: The Quest for Decisive Warfare from Breitenfeld to Waterloo.* Bloomington: Indiana University Press, 2004.

Welcher, Frank J. *The Union Army, 1861–1865, Organization and Operations.* Vol. 1, *The Eastern Theater.* Bloomington: Indiana University Press, 1989.

Wentz, R. K., and N. T. De Grummond. "Life on Horseback: Palaeopathology of Two Scythian Skeletons from Alexandropol, Ukraine." *International Journal of Osteoarchaeology* 19 (2009): 107–15.

West, Granville C. "McCook's Raid in the Rear of Atlanta and Hood's Army, August, 1864." In *War Papers: Being Papers Read before the Commandery of the District of Columbia, Military Order of the Loyal Legion of the United States,* 2:31–54. Wilmington, NC: Broadfoot, 1993.

Wheeler, Joseph. *Revised System of Cavalry Tactics for the Use of the Cavalry and Mounted Infantry, C.S.A.* Mobile: S. H. Goetzel, 1863.

White, Julius. "The First Sabre Charge of the War." In *Military Essays and Recollections: Papers Read before the Commandery of the State of Illinois, Military Order of the Loyal Legion of the United States,* 3:25–35. Chicago: Dial, 1899.

Whiting, F. S. "Diary and Personal Recollections." In *War Sketches and Incidents as Related by Companions of the Iowa Commandery, Military Order of the Loyal Legion of the United States,* 1:89–104. Wilmington, NC: Broadfoot, 1994.

Whittaker, Frederick. *Volunteer Cavalry: The Lessons of the Decade by a Volunteer Cavalryman*. New York: By the author, 1871.

Wiggins, Sarah Woolfolk, ed. *The Journals of Josiah Gorgas, 1857–1878*. Tuscaloosa: University of Alabama Press, 1995.

Wiley, Kenneth, ed. *Norfolk Blues: The Civil War Diary of the Norfolk Light Artillery Blues*. Shippensburg, PA: Burd Street, 1997.

[Williams, John A. B.]. *Leaves from a Trooper's Diary*. Philadelphia: By the author, 1869.

Williams, Robert W., Jr., and Ralph A. Wooster, eds. "With Terry's Texas Rangers: The Letters of Dunbar Affleck." *Civil War History* 9, no. 3 (September 1963): 299–319.

———, eds. "With Wharton's Cavalry in Arkansas: The Civil War Letters of Private Isaac Dunbar Affleck." *Arkansas Historical Quarterly* 21, no. 3 (Autumn 1962): 247–68.

Wilson, George S. "Wilder's Brigade of Mounted Infantry in the Tullahoma-Chickamauga Campaigns." In *War Talks in Kansas: A Series of Papers Read before the Kansas Commandery of the Military Order of the Loyal Legion of the United States*, 46–76. Kansas City, MO: Franklin Hudson, 1906.

Wilson, James H. "The Cavalry of the Army of the Potomac." In *Papers of the Military Historical Society of Massachusetts*, 13:35–88. Wilmington, NC: Broadfoot, 1990.

———. *The Life of Charles A. Dana*. New York: Harper and Brothers, 1907.

———. *Under the Old Flag*. 2 vols. New York: D. Appleton, 1912.

Wittenberg, Eric J. *Little Phil: A Reassessment of the Civil War Leadership of Gen. Philip H. Sheridan*. Washington, DC: Brassey's, 2002.

———, ed. *One of Custer's Wolverines: The Civil War Letters of Brevet Brigadier General James H. Kidd, 6th Michigan Cavalry*. Kent, OH: Kent State University Press, 2000.

———, ed. *"We Have It Damn Hard Out Here": The Civil War Letters of Sergeant Thomas W. Smith, 6th Pennsylvania Cavalry*. Kent, OH: Kent State University Press, 1999.

———, ed. *With Sheridan in the Final Campaign against Lee, by Lt. Col. Frederick C. Newhall, Sixth Pennsylvania Cavalry*. Baton Rouge: Louisiana State University Press, 2002.

Woodward, S. L. "Grierson's Raid, April 17th to May 2d, 1863." *Journal of the United States Cavalry Association* 14 (April 1904): 685–710.

Wright, John C. *Memoirs of Colonel John C. Wright*. Pine Bluff, AR: Rare Book, 1982.

Yeary, Mamie, comp. *Reminiscences of the Boys in Gray, 1861–1865*. Dallas, TX: Smith-Lamar, 1912.

Zemtsov, Vladimir. "The Battle of Borodino: The Fall of the *Grand Redoute*." *Journal of Slavic Military Studies* 13, no. 1 (2000): 90–112.

INDEX

independent action by, 9–10, 30, 70, 335, 339; inspections in, 313, 325–327, 388n33; inter-service rivalry, 313–314; losses of, 16, 270, 324–325, 333–334, 315; melees, 19–20, 128, 137, 142–144, 148, 158; mobility of, 119–123, 282–283, 314–315, 354; mounted chases, 144, 147–148, 158; mounted militia, 32–33, 68–69, 72; mounting cavalry, 216–236; night marches, 121–122; number of units, 230, 313, 333, 334; organization of, 14, 17; outpost duty, 70, 113–117, 336, 338; picket duty, 70, 113–117, 121, 247, 295, 336, 338; personal combat, 128–148, 370n29; proportion of cavalry to infantry and artillery, 14, 17–18, 20–21, 34, 44; scouting, 10, 25, 117–118, 165, 336, 337, 339, 341; screening, 10, 336; self-mounting by, 217–228, 234, 327, 349; skirmishing by, 18, 64, 101–103, 151, 152, 342; specialization of, 14–15, 18–19, 24–25, 28–29, 33–34; stream crossings by, 123–126; supporting infantry, 16–18, 22, 103–107; trot, 122; veterinarians, 25–26, 47, 216, 259; videttes, 114–116, 117, 336; war footing of, 26; weather and, 123, 199–200, 256–257, 272–273; see also raids, tactics, and training

Cavalry compared to infantry and artillery, 56–59, 64, 71–72, 75, 77, 79, 88, 92–94, 100, 108–113, 117, 119, 130, 137, 149, 151, 153, 185, 214, 266, 269–270, 272, 283–284, 287, 314, 320, 323–324, 331, 348, 388n22

Cavalrymen, 266–286; boots of, 15–16, 271; casualties of, 131, 137–138, 140–141, 144–148, 157–158, 181, 192–193; headgear of, 271–272; number of, 316; officers, 284, 326–329; pants of, 272; plundering by, 283–284, 315; preference for cavalry service, 267; sleeping in the saddle, 275–276; uniforms of, 23; transfer to and from cavalry service, 221, 230, 233–234

Cedar Creek, battle of, 90–91, 255, 290, 298

Cedar Mountain, battle of, 97, 105, 255

Central Railroad, 178

Chalmers, James R., 156, 179–180, 267

Chambliss, John R., Jr., 158, 211, 218, 259

Champion, Sidney S., 286

Chancellorsville, battle of, 80, 257, 293

Chantilly, battle of, 130

Chattanooga, battle of, 302

Cheek, W.H., 132

Cheney, Newel, 92, 203

Chickamauga, battle of, 251, 302

Choumee, Martin, 264

Clark, James Albert, 46, 80, 113–114, 189, 271, 285, 329, 332

Clark, Henry T., 328–329

Cleburne, Patrick R., 315

Cochrane, Harden Perkins, 157, 282

Cold Harbor, battle of, 85, 131, 152, 204

Colt's Manufacturing Company, 197

Columbus, Georgia, battle of, 310–311, 331

Confederate states units: 8th Cavalry, 79, 96, 118, 147, 156, 194, 219, 273, 282, 329

Congdon, James A., 48–49, 67, 244, 246

Connelly, Henry C., 124, 175

Cooke, Jacob B., 126, 130

Cooke, Philip St. George, 53–55, 58, 61, 63–64, 68, 70–71, 74, 83–84, 86, 101, 104, 129, 307, 351

Cooksey, E. M., 332

Coon, Datus E., 92

Cooper, Samuel, 327

Corinth, battle of, 103

Corydon, Indiana, 174

Cossacks, 24–25

Covert, Thomas M., 227–228, 273

Cox, Jacob D., 182

Cram, George C., 134

Crimean War, 66

Crosland, Charles, 156, 274

Crouch, Howard, 211

King, John H., 104
Klein, Robert, 94
Knipe, Joseph, 306
Kraft, Clayton N., 279

Laffeldt, Battle of, 15
La Grange, Oscar H., 101, 102, 106, 192, 319
Lane, Henry C., 140
Langhorne, J. Kent, 218
Larned, Benjamin F., 35
Lee, Robert E., 220, 261, 291
Lee, Stephen D., 78, 120, 267, 315
Lefaucheux pistol, 195
Legion of the United States, 111
Legions, 111–113, 367n26
Lemmon, J. S., 192
Lewis, Joseph H., 44, 108
Liberal Wars, 83
Lilly, Eli, 110
Lincoln, Abraham, 69, 112, 291, 294
Little Bighorn, battle of, 280–281
Lomax, Lunsford L., 151
London Armoury Company, 194
Long, Eli, 90, 94, 310
Longacre, Edward G., 3
Louis XIV, 13
Louisiana units: 4th Cavalry, 264
Lowell, Charles Russell, 139, 255, 314
Lyford, Stephen Carr, 320

Macon and Western Railroad, 178
Mahan, Dennis Hart, 82, 113, 132
Maine units: 1st Cavalry, 72, 75, 84, 91, 122, 144, 154, 162, 232, 233, 277, 325
Malloy, George A., 218
Malone, Thomas H., 145–146
Mann, William D., 309
March to the Sea, 205
Marengo, Battle of, 18
Marshall, John G., 282
Marshall, Thomas, 167
Maryland campaign, 232, 260, 291
Maryland units (C.S.): 1st Cavalry, 145
Maryland units (U.S.): Purnell Legion, 112; 1st Cavalry, 124, 156, 248, 283, 291, 332

Mason, Isaac Newton, 280
Massachusetts units: 1st Cavalry, 32, 37–38, 43, 46, 48, 73, 75, 96, 115, 120–121, 147, 188, 193, 226, 232, 240, 242, 247, 251, 252, 259, 266, 271, 277, 285, 329; 2nd Cavalry, 120, 125, 159, 205, 227, 261, 268, 278; 3rd Cavalry, 43; 4th Cavalry, 43, 129; 5th Battery, 331; 5th Cavalry, 86; 41st Infantry, 43
Matthews, Amasa E., 144
Mattox, William B., 264
Maury, Dabney Herndon, 67
Mayo, Nelson S., 261, 262
Means, Paul B., 96
McAlister, Robert Milton, 273
McClellan, George B., 23–25, 66, 71, 82, 88, 90–91, 96, 120, 124, 189, 206, 207, 209, 210, 216, 266, 290, 291, 342, 350, 360n33
McClellan saddle, 209–212
McCook, Alexander McD., 45
McCook, Edward M., 103–104, 177–178
McCook-Stoneman Raid, 96, 132, 155, 177–178, 201, 222
McCrillis, Lafayette, 205
McDonald, William N., 110
McGee, William, 137
McKoy, C. E., 233
McNeil, Quincy, 138
Meade, George G., 233, 295, 296
Medieval cavalry, 13
Medina, Benjamin F., 138
Meigs, Montgomery, 181, 229–230, 232, 299, 303
Merrill, James H., 201, 205
Merritt, Wesley, 91, 96, 158, 290, 297
Mexican War, 28, 130, 185, 196
Meyer, Henry C., 147, 275–276
Meyer, William E., 191, 246–247
Michigan units: 1st Cavalry, 131, 151; 2nd Cavalry, 294; 4th Cavalry, 256–257; 5th Cavalry, 88, 151, 155, 180, 324; 6th Cavalry, 84, 130, 145, 151, 226, 246, 281; 7th Cavalry, 135, 151; 9th Cavalry, 232; 10th Cavalry, 96
Middleburg, battle of, 293, 324

Surby, Richard W., 165–166
Surcingle, 308

Tactics, 12, 14–17, 29–30, 50–80, 81–100, 150, 342; columns, 51, 55–57, 61–63, 87–94, 96, 97, 153, 342, 365n18, 366n27; combined arms, 9, 12, 17, 19, 22, 30, 106–107, 111–113, 127, 297–298, 313, 331–332; echelon, 64, 92–93; flank, moving by the, 58; flankers, 121, 366n27; formations, 2, 50–81, 87, 94–99, 342; fours, movement by, 45, 54, 57, 63, 74, 79, 94–96; intervals, 56, 74; lines, 55–56, 61–63, 87–89, 91–94, 97, 366n27; maneuvers, 2, 50–81, 87, 94–99; manuals and handbooks, 15, 50–80, 84, 99, 100, 351; oblique, 52–53, 58, 68, 96–97; platoons, 54–57, 59–60, 63, 65, 74, 88; ranks, 65, 67–68, 82–87, 153, 307–308, 342; squadrons, 14, 38–39, 88, 96; wheel, 52–53, 57–58, 74, 80, 90, 92–93, 96, 98
Taylor, Nelson, 233
Taylor, Richard, 30
Tebbs Bend, battle of, 174
Tennessee units (C.S.): 1st Cavalry, 280; 4th Cavalry, 158, 314; 7th Cavalry, 124, 283; 9th Cavalry, 124; 26th Cavalry Battalion, 182, 200
Tennessee units (U.S.): 1st Cavalry, 110, 199, 239, 243, 246, 362n29; 2nd East Tennessee Mounted Infantry, 154; 4th Infantry, 362n29
Tenney, Luman Harris, 72, 263
Texas units: 3rd Cavalry, 95, 131, 218; 5th Cavalry, 206; 6th Cavalry, 332; 8th Cavalry, 78, 103, 183, 186, 194, 219, 254, 322
Thames, Battle of the, 28
Third Winchester, battle of, 90, 92, 96, 255, 297, 331
Thomas, George H., 45, 304, 312
Thomas, Julius E., 246
Thompson, Osborn D., 147
Tidball, John C., 109

Tilton, George, 275
Tobie, Edward P., 84, 154, 325
Tod, David, 41
Tom's Brook, battle of, 144, 290, 298
Torbert, Alfred T. A., 297–299
Training, 2, 16, 17, 23, 50–80, 84, 86–87, 190, 191, 193, 307; time to make a cavalryman, 97, 99, 314
Trevilian Station, battle of, 258, 282
Trout, Robert J., 110
Trowbridge, Luther S., 95
Tupelo campaign, 115, 156, 324
Turchin, John B., 133

Ulm campaign, 20
United States Military Academy, 29
United States units: Battery A, 2nd Artillery, 109; 1st Cavalry, 34, 191, 338; 2nd Cavalry, 34, 72, 137, 217; 3rd Cavalry, 34, 253; 3rd Colored Cavalry, 269; 4th Cavalry, 34, 89, 202; 5th Cavalry, 34, 103–105, 133, 255; 6th Cavalry, 34, 110, 134, 143; 7th Cavalry, 280–281; 14th Cavalry, 260, 342; 1st Dragoons, 34; 2nd Dragoons, 28, 34, 54; Regiment of Mounted Rifles, 28, 67–68, 82, 107–108
Upperville, battle of, 134, 251, 293, 324
Upton, Emory, 85, 87, 132, 306
Uxbridge, Duke of, 21

Vale, Joseph G., 136
Valverde, battle of, 206
Van Buskirk, Matthew, 95
Van Dorn, Earl, 120, 138, 170–172, 301, 302, 350
Van Dorn–Forrest Raid, 170–172
Vane, Frank, 239
Vermont units: 1st Cavalry, 138, 151
Vicksburg campaign, 164–166, 179–180, 320
Vincent, Thomas M., 333
Virginia units (C.S.): 1st Cavalry, 69, 218, 243, 289, 321; 2nd Cavalry, 135, 218, 293; 3rd Cavalry, 96, 223; 4th Cavalry,

Virginia units (C.S.) (*continued*)
33, 139, 140; 5th Cavalry, 138; 6th Cavalry, 121, 126, 147, 138, 250; 7th Cavalry, 167; 8th Cavalry, 211; 8th Infantry, 104; 9th Cavalry, 96, 199; 10th Cavalry, 67; 12th Cavalry, 218, 221, 282; 13th Cavalry, 219; 18th Cavalry, 86, 134, 219, 325
Virginia units (U.S.): 1st Cavalry, 118, 286; 3rd Infantry, 118; 10th Cavalry, 195; 10th Infantry, 118

Wagram, Battle of, 20
Wainwright, Charles, 181, 316
Wall, Edward, 162, 251, 252, 265
War of 1812, 27
War of the Spanish Succession, 17
Warner, Elias, 186
Warren, E. Willard, 227
Washburn, Francis, 134
Washington, George, 27
Waterloo, Battle of, 21
Watkins, Louis D., 232, 255
Watts, James W., 293
Way, William B., 232
Waynesboro, Georgia, battle of, 83, 138, 331
Waynesboro, Virginia, battle of, 125, 135
Weapons, 50, 136–142, 150–152, 185–208, 214–215, 326, 340–342, 345, 353; Ballard carbines, 201, 205; Bowie knife, 195; breech-loaders, 198, 200–202, 205, 340; Burnside carbines, 202–203, 205; carbines, 103, 105, 137, 150–152, 198–205, 215, 316, 320, 326, 342; Colt's Army and Navy revolvers, 186, 187, 194–197; Colt's revolving rifles, 201–202, 205; edged weapons, 11–14, 16, 18; firing distance of, 205; Gallager carbines, 201; gunpowder weapons, 13–14, 28; Hall carbines, 187, 200; horse pistols, 187, 193, 196, 200; infantry small arms, 150–151; lances, 18–19, 206–208; Maynard carbines, 326; Merrill carbines, 201; Mississippi

rifles, 187, 199; musketoons, 185, 198–200; Pettengill pistols, 196; pistols, 14, 137, 158, 185, 192–198, 214, 215, 316, 320, 326, 342–343; repeaters, 198, 200, 203–204, 215, 319–320, 340; rifle muskets, 4–5, 31, 67, 105; Sharps carbines, 186, 187, 201, 202, 204, 205, 207, 326; Sharps and Hankins carbines, 203; shotguns, 187; Smith carbines, 200–201, 203, 205; Spencer repeaters, 86, 96, 151, 190, 202–205, 295, 306, 308, 326; specialization in use of, 136, 185; Starr revolvers, 188, 196, 200; see also sabers
Weaver, James Riley, 227
Weber, Peter, 130–131
Weed, Theodore H., 152, 204
Weldon Railroad, 177
Weller, William F., 265
Wells, Edward Laight, 243, 247
Wellington, Duke of, 19, 82
West, Granville C., 201
West Point and Montgomery Railroad, 168–169
West Virginia units: 5th Cavalry, 40, 117–118
Western and Atlantic Railroad, 172, 174
Wetschky, Charles, 291
Wharton, John A., 194, 301
Wharton, W. D., 218, 220, 263
Wheeler, Joseph, 3, 68, 70, 79, 86–87, 93, 116–118, 158, 162, 163, 183, 184, 218, 244, 246, 301, 302, 325–327, 329, 331, 335–337, 342
Wheeler-Roddey Raid, 102, 123, 183–184
Whitehead, R. S., 273
Whiting, Charles J., 104
Whittaker, Frederick, 46, 76, 115–116, 149, 160, 190, 197, 202, 204, 205, 208, 211, 224, 248, 257, 261, 270, 271, 274, 318–319
Wilder, John T., 108, 163, 203, 302
Williams, Robert, 285
Wilson's Creek, battle of, 95
Wilson, George W., 302

Wilson, James H., 85–86, 175–177, 190, 203, 287, 295, 303, 305–312, 317, 331, 349, 350, 355

Wilson, William L., 282

Wilson's Raid, 85–86, 92, 132, 154, 310–311

Wilson-Kautz Raid, 175–177, 183, 203

Winslow, Edward F., 92, 320, 324

Wisconsin units: 1st Cavalry, 102, 192; 10th Battery, 109

Wiswell, James H., 202

Wittenberg, Eric, 3–4

World War I, 342, 344–345, 357

World War II, 345

Wright, John C., 267, 333

Wright, John T., 118

Yellow Tavern, battle of, 129, 134, 181, 297–297

Young, Pierce M. B., 286

Young, Samuel, 233

Xenophon, 11